DOMESTIC TRANQUILITY

DOMESTIC TRANQUILITY

A Brief Against Feminism

F. CAROLYN GRAGLIA

SPENCE PUBLISHING COMPANY · DALLAS
1998

*This book is dedicated
to my husband, Lino,
the foundation of it.*

Published in the United States by
Spence Publishing Company
501 Elm Street, Suite 450
Dallas, Texas 75202

Library of Congress Cataloging-in-Publication Data

Graglia, F. Carolyn, 1929-
    Domestic tranquility : a brief against feminism / F. Carolyn Graglia
    p. cm.
    Includes bibliographical references and index.
    ISBN 0-9653208-6-3
    1. Anti-feminism.   2. Feminism.   3. Sex role   I. Title.
HQ1150.G73   1998
305.42—dc21   97-36521

Printed in the United States of America

Contents

v

Acknowledgments

I AM DEEPLY GRATEFUL to my husband, Lino A. Graglia, for everything he has done to make this book possible. His always insightful comments on my manuscript throughout the many stages of its development have been invaluable, and I particularly appreciate his toleration of my saying that which he may disagree with or may think could remain unsaid. Without his unfailing devotion, support, and commitment throughout the forty-three years of our marriage—from the early years when I was a career woman, before this was so fashionable, to the years when I was a housewife, after the housewife had become a pariah—I could never have written this book. Nor would I have become the woman who wrote it without the contributions of our three daughters, Donna, Carol, and Laura. I am most grateful to them for the privilege of sharing in the glorious adventure of their growing up, for the boundless happiness they gave me, and for all they have taught me.

Many thanks to my editor, Mitchell Muncy, for his assistance and suggestions and especially for his patient encouragement to take a fresh look at my old certitudes. I am also very grateful to Stephen Presser for his extensive critique of a portion of the manuscript. Among the many people who have encouraged me in this endeavor, I particularly want to thank William Kristol of *The Weekly Standard*; Gary McDowell of the Institute of United States Studies, University of London; and Eugene Meyer and Leonard Leo of the Federalist Society for Law & Public Policy Studies. They graciously provided me with a forum in which to speak. The responses I received, and especially my contacts with the students in The Federalist Society, showed me that there is an audience for my message.

To my daughter Laura I must give a special thanks. As a student of literature and a teacher of English, she shared with me many insights into the human condition. She introduced me to some new literature and reminded me of some that I had long since forgotten. It was out of our extensive conversations over many years that some of my views evolved, which is not to say that she embraces the results of that evolution.

And finally I want to acknowledge my debt to the women of Hospice Austin with whom I have been associated. This book has been completed while I am closely involved in the lingering death of my mother, a woman whose complete dedication to pursuing what she perceived to be the truth was probably the most powerful influence in my life. In helping me to cope with the wholly unfamiliar experience of intimate association with dying, Reverend Liz Decker, Cheryl Frederick, Nancy Knight, and Laura Thomas have made the seemingly intolerable bearable and taught me more than I ever thought I would be willing to learn at this stage in my life.

Introduction

ﾧINCE THE LATE 1960s, feminists have very successfully waged war against the traditional family, in which husbands are the principal breadwinners and wives are primarily homemakers. This war's immediate purpose has been to undermine the homemaker's position within both her family and society in order to drive her into the work force. Its long-term goal is to create a society in which women behave as much like men as possible, devoting as much time and energy to the pursuit of a career as men do, so that women will eventually hold equal political and economic power with men. This book examines feminism's successful onslaught against the traditional family, considers the possible ramifications of that success, and defends a woman's choice to be a homemaker.

Feminists have used a variety of methods to achieve their goal. They have promoted a sexual revolution that encouraged women to mimic male sexual promiscuity. They have supported the enactment of no-fault divorce laws that have undermined housewives' social and economic security. And they obtained the application of affirmative action requirements to women as a class, gaining educational and job preferences for women and undermining the ability of men who are victimized by this discrimination to function as family breadwinners.

A crucial weapon in feminism's arsenal has been the status degradation of the housewife's role. From the journalistic attacks of Betty Friedan and Gloria Steinem to Jessie Bernard's sociological writings, all branches of feminism are united in the conviction that a woman can find identity and fulfillment only in a career. The housewife, feminists agree, was properly characterized by Simone de Beauvoir and Betty Friedan as a "parasite," a being something less than human, living her life without using her adult capabilities or intelligence, and lacking any real purpose in devoting herself to children, husband, and home.

Operating on the twin assumptions that equality means sameness (that is, men and women cannot be equals unless they do the same things) and that most differences between the sexes are culturally imposed, contemporary feminism has undertaken its own cultural impositions. Revealing their totalitarian belief that they know best how others should live and their totalitarian willingness to force others to conform to their dogma, feminists have sought to modify our social institutions in order to create an androgynous society in which male and female roles are as identical as possible. The results of the feminist juggernaut now engulf us. By almost all indicia of well-being, the institution of the American family has become significantly less healthy than it was thirty years ago.

Certainly, feminism is not alone responsible for our families' sufferings. As Charles Murray details in *Losing Ground*,[1] President Lyndon Johnson's Great Society programs, for example, have often hurt families, particularly black families, and these programs were supported by a large constituency beyond the women's movement. What distinguishes the women's movement, however, is the fact that, despite the pro-family motives it sometimes ascribes to itself, it has actively sought the traditional family's destruction. In its avowed aims and the programs it promotes, the movement has adopted Kate Millett's goal, set forth in her *Sexual Politics*, in which she endorses Friedrich Engels's conclusion that "the family, as that term is presently understood, must go"; "a kind fate," she remarks, in "view of the institution's history."[2] This goal has never changed: feminists view traditional nuclear families as inconsistent with feminism's commitment to women's independence and sexual freedom.[3]

Emerging as a revitalized movement in the 1960s, feminism reflected women's social discontent, which had arisen in response to the decline of the male breadwinner ethic and to the perception—heralded in Philip Wylie's 1940s castigation of the evil "mom"[4]—that Western society does not value highly the roles of wife and mother. Women's dissatisfactions, nevertheless, have often been aggravated rather than alleviated by the feminist reaction. To mitigate their discontent, feminists argued, women should pattern their lives after men's, engaging in casual sexual intercourse on the same terms as sexually predatory males and making the same career commitments as men. In pursuit of these objectives, feminists have fought unceasingly for the ready availability of legal abortion and consistently derogated both motherhood and the worth of full-time homemakers. Feminism's sexual teachings have been less consistent, ranging from its early and enthusiastic embrace of the sexual revolution to a significant backlash against female sexual promiscuity, which has led some feminists to urge women to abandon heterosexual sexual intercourse altogether.

Contemporary feminism has been remarkably successful in bringing about the institutionalization in our society of the two beliefs underlying its offensive: denial of the social worth of traditional homemakers and rejection of traditional sexual morality. The consequences have been pernicious and enduring. General societal assent to these beliefs has profoundly distorted men's perceptions of their relationships with and obligations to women, women's perceptions of their own needs, and the way in which women make decisions about their lives.

TRADITIONAL HOMEMAKING DEVALUED

The first prong of contemporary feminism's offensive has been to convince society that a woman's full-time commitment to cultivating her marriage and rearing her children is an unworthy endeavor. Women, assert feminists, should treat marriage and children as relatively independent appendages to their life of full-time involvement in the workplace. To live what feminists assure her is the only life worthy of respect, a woman must devote the vast bulk of her time and energy to market production, at the expense of marriage and children. Children, she is told, are better cared for by surrogates, and marriage, as these feminists perceive it, neither deserves nor requires much attention; indeed, the very idea of a woman's "cultivating" her marriage seems ludicrous. Thus spurred on by the women's movement, many women have sought to become male clones.

But some feminists have appeared to modify the feminist message; voices—supposedly of moderation—have argued that women really are different from men. In this they are surely right: there are fundamental differences between the average man and woman, and it is appropriate to take account of these differences when making decisions both in our individual lives and with respect to social issues. Yet the new feminist voices have not conceded that acknowledged differences between the sexes are grounds for reexamining women's flight from home into workplace. Instead, these new voices have argued only that these differences require modification of the terms under which women undertake to reconstruct their lives in accordance with the blueprint designed by so-called early radicals. The edifice erected by radical feminism is to remain intact, subject only to some redecorating. The foundation of this edifice is still the destruction of the traditional family. Feminism has acquiesced in women's desire to bear children (an activity some of the early radicals discouraged). But it continues steadfast in its assumption that, after some period of maternity leave, daily care of those children is properly the domain of institutions and paid employees. The yearnings manifested in women's palpable desire for children should largely be sated, the new voices tell us, by the act of serving as a birth canal and then spending so-called quality time with the child before and after a full day's work.

Any mother, in this view, may happily consign to surrogates most of the remaining aspects of her role, assured that doing so will impose no hardship or loss on either mother or child. To those women whose natures make them less suited to striving in the workplace than concentrating on husband, children, and home, this feminist diktat denies the happiness and contentment they could have found within the domestic arena. In the world formed by contemporary feminism, these women will have status and respect only if they force themselves to take up roles in the workplace they suspect are not most deserving of their attention. Relegated to the periphery of their lives are the home and personal relationships with husband and children that they sense merit their central concern.

Inherent in the feminist argument is an extraordinary contradiction. Feminists deny, on the one hand, that the dimension of female sexuality which engenders women's yearning for children can also make it appropriate and satisfying for a woman to devote herself to domestic endeavors and provide her children's full-time care. On the other hand, they plead the fact of sexual difference to justify campaigns to modify workplaces in order to correct the effects of male influence and alleged biases. Only after such modifications, claim feminists, can women's nurturing attributes and other female qualities be adequately expressed in and truly influence the workplace. Manifestations of these female qualities, feminists argue, should and can occur in the workplace once it has been modified to blunt the substantial impact of male aggression and competitiveness and take account of women's special requirements.

Having launched its movement claiming the right of women—a right allegedly denied them previously—to enter the workplace on an *equal* basis with men, feminism then escalated its demands by arguing that female differences require numerous changes in the workplace. Women, in this view, are insufficiently feminine to find satisfaction in rearing their own children but too feminine to compete on an equal basis with men. Thus, having taken women out of their homes and settled them in the workplace, feminists have sought to reconstruct workplaces to create "feminist playpens" that are conducive to female qualities of sensitivity, caring, and empathy. Through this exercise in self-contradiction, contemporary feminism has endeavored to remove the woman from her home and role of providing daily care to her children—the quintessential place and activity for most effectively expressing her feminine, nurturing attributes.

The qualities that are the most likely to make women good mothers are thus redeployed away from their children and into workplaces that must be restructured to accomodate them. The irony is twofold. Children—the ones who could benefit most from the attentions of those mothers who do possess these womanly qualities—are deprived of those attentions and left only with the hope of finding adequate replacement for their loss. Moreover, the occupations in which these qualities are now to find expression either do not require them for optimal job performance (often they are not conducive to professional success) or were long ago recognized as women's occupations—as in the field of nursing, for example—in which nurturing abilities do enhance job performance.

TRADITIONAL SEXUAL MORALITY TRADUCED

The second prong of contemporary feminism's offensive has been to encourage women to ape male sexual patterns and engage in promiscuous sexual intercourse as freely as men. Initially, feminists were among the most dedicated supporters of the sexual revolution, viewing female participation in casual sexual activity as an unmistakable declaration of female equality with males. The women in our society who acted upon the teachings of feminist sexual revolutionaries have suffered greatly. They are victims of the highest abortion rate in the Western world. More than one in five Americans is now infected with a viral sexually transmitted disease which at best can be controlled but not cured and is often chronic. Sexually transmitted diseases, both viral and bacterial, disproportionately affect women because, showing fewer symptoms, they often go untreated for a longer time. These diseases also lead to pelvic infections that cause infertility in 100,000 to 150,000 women each year.[5]

The sexual revolution feminists have promoted rests on an assumption that an act of sexual intercourse involves nothing but a pleasurable physical sensation, possessing no symbolic meaning and no moral dimension. This is an understanding of sexuality that bears more than a slight resemblance to sex as depicted in pornography: physical sexual acts without emotional involvement. In addition to the physical harm caused by increased sexual promiscuity, the denial that sexual intercourse has symbolic importance within a framework of moral accountability corrupts the nature of the sex act. Such denial necessarily makes sexual intercourse a trivial event, compromising the act's ability to fulfill its most important function after procreation. This function is to bridge the gap between males and females who often seem separated by so many differences, both biological and emotional, that they feel scarcely capable of understanding or communicating with each other.

Because of the urgency of sexual desire, especially in the male, it is through sexual contact that men and women can most easily come together. Defining the nature of sexual intercourse in terms informed by its procreative potentialities makes the act a spiritually meaningful event of overwhelming importance. A sexual encounter so defined is imbued with the significance conferred by its connection with a promise of immortality through procreation, whether that connection is a present possibility, a remembrance of children already borne, or simply an acknowledgment of the reality and truth of the promise. Such a sex act can serve as the physical meeting ground on which, by accepting and affirming each other through their bodies' physical unity, men and women can begin to construct an enduring emotional unity. The sexual encounter cannot perform its function when it is viewed as a trivial event of moral indifference with no purpose or meaning other than producing a physical sensation through the friction of bodily parts.

The feminist sexual perspective deprives the sex act of the spiritual meaningfulness that can make it the binding force upon which man and woman can construct a lasting marital relationship. The morally indifferent sexuality championed by the sexual revolution substitutes the sex without emotions that characterizes pornography for the sex of a committed, loving relationship that satisfies women's longing for romance and connection. But this is not the only damage to relationships between men and women that follows from feminism's determination to promote an androgynous society by convincing men and women that they are virtually fungible. Sexual equivalency, feminists believe, requires that women not only engage in casual sexual intercourse as freely as men, but also that women mimic male behavior by becoming equally assertive in initiating sexual encounters and in their activity throughout the encounter. With this sexual prescription, feminists mock the essence of conjugal sexuality that is at the foundation of traditional marriage.

MARRIAGE AS A WOMAN'S CAREER DISCREDITED

Even academic feminists who are considered "moderates" endorse doctrines most inimical to the homemaker. Thus, Professor Elizabeth Fox-Genovese, regarded as a moderate in Women's Studies, tells us that marriage can no longer be a viable career for women. But if marriage cannot be a woman's career, then despite feminist avowals of favoring choice in this matter, homemaking cannot be a woman's goal, and surrogate child-rearing must be her child's destiny. Contrary to feminist claims, society's barriers are not strung tightly to inhibit women's career choices. Because of feminism's very successful efforts, society encourages women to pursue careers, while stigmatizing and preventing their devotion to child-rearing and domesticity.

It was precisely upon the conclusion that marriage cannot be a viable career for women that *Time* magazine rested its Fall 1990 special issue on "Women: The Road Ahead," a survey of contemporary women's lives. While noting that the "cozy, limited roles of the past are still clearly remembered, sometimes fondly," during the past thirty years "all that was orthodox has become negotiable." One thing negotiated away has been the economic security of the homemaker, and *Time* advised young women that "the job of full-time homemaker may be the riskiest profession to choose" because "the advent of no-fault and equitable-distribution divorce laws" reflect, in the words of one judge, the fact that "[s]ociety no longer believes that a husband should support his wife."[6]

No-fault divorce laws did not, however, result from an edict of the gods or some force of nature, but from sustained political efforts, particularly by the feminist movement. As a cornerstone of their drive to make women exchange home for workplace, and thereby secure their independence from men, the availability of no-fault divorce (like the availability of abortion) was sacrosanct to the movement. *Time* shed crocodile tears for displaced homemakers, for it made clear that women must canter down the road ahead with the spur of no-fault divorce urging them into the workplace. Of all *Time*'s recommendations for ameliorating women's lot, divorce reform—the most crying need in our country today—was not among them. Whatever hardships may be endured by women who would resist a divorce, *Time*'s allegiance, like that of most feminists, is clearly to the divorce-seekers who, it was pleased to note, will not be hindered in their pursuit of self-realization by the barriers to divorce that their own mothers had faced.[7]

These barriers to divorce which had impeded their own parents, however, had usually benefited these young women by helping to preserve their parents' marriage. A five-year study of children in divorcing families disclosed that "the overwhelming majority preferred the unhappy marriage to the divorce," and many of them, "despite the unhappiness of their parents, were in fact relatively happy and considered their situation neither better nor worse than that of other families around them."[8] A follow-up study after ten years demonstrated that children experienced the trauma of their parents' divorce as more serious and long-lasting than any researchers had anticipated.[9] *Time* so readily acquiesced in the disadvantaging of homemakers and the disruption of children's lives because the feminist ideological parameters within which it operates have excluded marriage as a *proper* career choice. Removing the obstacles to making it a *viable* choice would, therefore, be an undesirable subversion of feminist goals.

That *Time* would have women trot forward on life's journey constrained by the blinders of feminist ideology is evident from its failure to question any feminist notion, no matter how silly, or to explore solutions incompatible with the ideology's script. One of the silliest notions *Time* left unexamined was that young women want "good careers, good marriages and two or three kids, and they don't want the children to be raised by strangers." The supposed realism of this expectation lay in the new woman's attitude that "I don't want to work 70 hours a week, but I want to be vice president, and *you* have to change." But even if thirty hours were cut from that seventy-hour workweek, the new woman would still be working the normal full-time week, her children would still be raised by surrogates, and the norm would continue to be the feminist version of child-rearing that *Time* itself described unflatteringly as "less a preoccupation than an improvisation."[10]

The illusion that a woman can achieve career success without sacrificing the daily personal care of her children—and except among the very wealthy, most of her leisure as well—went unquestioned by *Time*. It did note, however, the dissatisfaction expressed by Eastern European and Russian women who had experienced as a matter of government policy the same liberation from home and children that our feminists have undertaken to bestow upon Western women. In what *Time* described as "a curious reversal of Western feminism's emphasis on careers for women," the new female leaders of Eastern Europe would like "to reverse the communist diktat that all women have to work." Women have "dreamed," said the Polish Minister of Culture and Arts, "of reaching the point where we have the choice to stay home" that communism had taken away.[11] But blinded by its feminist bias, *Time* could only find it "curious" that women would choose to stay at home; apparently beyond the pale of respectability was any argument that it would serve Western women's interest to retain the choice that contemporary feminism— filling in the West the role of communism in the East—has sought to deny them.

Nor was its feminist bias shaken by the attitudes of Japanese women, most of whom, *Time* noted, reject "equality" with men, choosing to cease work after the birth of a first child and later resuming a part-time career or pursuing hobbies or community work. The picture painted was that of the 1950s American suburban housewife reviled by Betty Friedan, except that the American has enjoyed a higher standard of living (particularly a much larger home) than has the Japanese. In Japan, *Time* observed, being "a housewife is nothing to be ashamed of." Dishonoring the housewife's role was a goal, it might have added, that Japanese feminists can, in time, accomplish if they emulate their American counterparts.

Japanese wives have broad responsibilities, commented *Time*, because most husbands leave their salaries and children entirely in wives' hands; freed from drudgery by modern appliances, house-wives can "pursue their interests in a carefree manner, while men have to worry about supporting their wives and children."[12] Typically, a Japanese wife controls household finances, giving her husband a cash allowance, the size of which, apparently, dissatisfies one-half of the men. Acknowledging that Japanese wives take the leadership in most homes, one husband observed that "[t]hings go best when the husband is swimming in the palm of his wife's hand." A home is well-managed, said one wife, "if you make your men feel that they're in control when they are in front of others, while in reality you're in control."[13]   It seems like a good arrangement to me.

Instead of inquiring whether a similar carefree existence might appeal to some American women, *Time* looked forward to the day when marriage would no longer be a career for Japanese women, as their men took over household and child-rearing chores, enabling wives to join husbands in the workplace. It was noted, however, that a major impediment to this goal, which would have to be corrected, was the fact that Japanese day-care centers usually run for only eight hours a day. Thus, *Time* made clear that its overriding concern was simply promoting the presence of women in the work force. This presence is seen as a good *per se,* without any *pro forma* talk about the economic necessity of a second income and without any question raised as to whether it is in children's interest to spend any amount of time—much less in excess of eight hours a day—in communal care.

IRONIES WITHIN FEMINISM

Feminist success in reshaping social attitudes has been facilitated by our media's eagerness to adopt and propagate the feminist perspective and by feminism's ability to piggyback on the black civil rights movement by portraying women as victims. In acquiring "minority" status, women (who are the sexual majority) secured preferential entitlement to educational and employment opportunities afforded to blacks and other minorities. Feminists have also promoted their goals through a large body of law developed under the rubric of "women's rights," much of it laid down by the

United States Supreme Court in decisions invalidating distinctions on the basis of sex.

Contemporary feminism's remarkable ability to enlist social institutions in its war on the traditional family has entailed two ironies, the first relating to the women spearheading the attack and the second to feminist reliance on the black civil rights movement to obtain preferential treatment for women. As detailed in *The Sisterhood*,[14] the most influential leaders of the women's movement that was revived in the 1960s were Betty Friedan, Kate Millett, Germaine Greer, and Gloria Steinem. Including the international movement, Simone de Beauvoir was a fifth. Of these five women, only Betty Friedan had both married and borne children. But she was unhappy with her marriage and life in the suburban home, which she compared to a "comfortable concentration camp" in which the housewife performs "endless, monotonous, unrewarding" work that "does not require adult capabilities" and causes "a slow death of mind and spirit." She felt "like a freak, absolutely alone" and afraid to face her "real feelings about the husband and children you were presumably living for."[15]

Denying that contemporary women could "live through their bodies" and derive satisfaction from child-bearing as the "pinnacle of human achievement" that it was on Margaret Mead's South Sea Islands, Friedan recommended the path of women who remained in the workplace by "juggling their pregnancies" and relying on nurses and housekeepers. Characterizing her marriage as one based not "on love but on dependent hate," Friedan concluded that she could no longer continue "leading other women out of the wilderness while holding on to a marriage that destroyed my self-respect."[16] And so the self-proclaimed Moses from the New York suburbs obtained her divorce.

While Betty Friedan had tasted a life devoted to marriage and motherhood and pronounced it foul, the remaining four women were unacquainted with the experience. Kate Millett and Simone de Beauvoir, both bisexuals, agreed that women were prevented from becoming free human beings by the myths revering maternity and the expectations that women should personally care for their children. Gloria Steinem declared that she deliberately chose childlessness because "I either gave birth to someone else" or "I gave birth to myself."[17]   Germaine Greer, who was the best known of the feminist sexual revolutionaries and wrote the very popular *The Female Eunuch*, was childless and argued that marriage was outmoded. Greer indicated a certain distaste for the female body, opining with respect to menstruation that women "would rather do without it."[18] Later, as a revisionist and to the regret of other feminists, she attacked sexual permissiveness and lauded motherhood and fertility. Her preference for abstinence, anal intercourse, and *coitus interruptus* over other contraceptive methods, however, suggested a lingering distaste for the womb as well as for phallic potency.[19]

Although she never married or shared living quarters with him, Simone de Beauvoir maintained a life-long liaison with Jean-Paul Sartre. Their relationship was based on sexual freedom for both, and as one commentator has described it, "her role was not unlike that of a eunuch in charge of a harem," inspecting the women who wished to have affairs with Sartre and "disposing of past sexual partners of his who became troublesome in their continued affection for him."[20]   Simone de Beauvoir's life was a blueprint for the woman "liberated" through radical feminism: a bisexual[21] who was neither wife nor birth mother, but an aborted woman, a fact she disclosed in an advertisement by women who had obtained illegal abortions.[22]

Reflecting the female's hypergamous impulse, de Beauvoir allied herself with a man she considered her intellectual superior. Upon meeting Sartre as a university student, she recognized that he "had a deeper and wider knowledge of everything," "a true superiority over me." She recalled "the calm and yet almost frenzied passion with which he was preparing for the books he was going to write." In comparison, her "frantic determination seemed weak and timid" and her "feverish obsessions," "lukewarm." Their early discussions, she said, were "the first time in my life that I had felt intellectually inferior to anyone else": "Day after day, and all day long I set myself up against Sartre, and in our discussions I was simply not in his class"; "he soon demolished" my theories and in "the end I had to admit I was beaten."[23] De Beauvoir's evident excitement at being bested by this superior man is familiar to women (it was not entirely with regret that I realized my future husband might beat me in an argument). This excitement can serve women well. But while losing to a superior man may enhance a woman's sexual as well as intellectual satisfaction, whatever intellectual pleasure a heterosexual man may derive from being bested by a superior woman, he is unlikely to find the experience sexually affirmative.

Eschewing marriage and childbirth, de Beauvoir undertook to live a life of the intellect on the basis of presumed equality with a man she believed to be superior and who achieved greater fame. When compared to "great men," she said, the woman of achievement "seems mediocre,"[24] a view echoing Beatrice Webb's assertion that women lacked "that fullness of intellectual life which distinguishes the really able man."[25] According to Paul Johnson, Sartre's superiority was more apparent than real: de Beauvoir was "in a strictly academic sense, abler." She almost beat Sartre for first in the philosophy degree, the examiners thinking her "the better philosopher." Johnson thinks her "in many respects a finer" writer, her novel, *Les Mandarins*, being "far better than any of Sartre's."[26]

It has been the norm for women to ally themselves with men who achieve greater market success than they. David M. Buss has established the biological basis for our attraction to the powerful, superior men best able to protect and care for us while we bear children.[27] Her affinity for a superior man well serves a woman who enjoys the many rewards afforded by marriage and child-bearing. But it must surely bring discontent to the woman who confines her life to seeking achievement in the workplace as the equal of that superior man. Not only was de Beauvoir unmarried and childless, but "there are few worse cases," says Johnson, "of a man exploiting a woman": she "became Sartre's slave from almost their first meeting and remained such for all her adult life until he died"; yet, although she was his "mistress, surrogate wife, cook and manager, female bodyguard and nurse," she never held "legal or financial status in his life." Their sexual relationship, moreover, ended in the mid-1940s as she became a "sexually-retired, pseudo-wife," while he pursued innumerable affairs with ever younger mistresses, one of whom, in his ultimate humiliation of de Beauvoir, he legally adopted so that she was his sole heir and literary executor.[28]

In *The Coming of Age*, de Beauvoir attested to the bitterness of life's fruits, describing old age as "life's parody" and "a degradation or even a denial of what has been." "What," she repined, "is the point of having worked so hard if one finds that all is labour lost" and "if one no longer sets the least value upon what has been accomplished?" Those old people who do not "give up the struggle" but stubbornly persevere, continued her lament, "often become caricatures of themselves."[29] Only with great difficulty, one must think, can it be otherwise for those who forgo the bearing of children that can fill our lives with the richest meaning, enabling us to greet old age with equanimity and the expectation that we too will "come proud, open-eyed and laughing to the tomb."[30] To trade the rewards of child-bearing for an aborted fetus and production of intellectual constructs—however great their merit—seems, to some of us, an unsatisfactory exchange.

Upon this exchange—in theory, if not fact—were grounded the lives of all, save one, who spearheaded the contemporary feminist movement. Their qualifications to speak for women as a class are rarely questioned, however, nor are they viewed simply as representing the interests of lesbians and other women who forgo marriage and reproduction. The one exception, Betty Friedan, had concluded that a life devoted largely to marital and maternal responsibilities could never be satisfying. It was these jaundiced abdicants from traditional femininity who led the assault on the traditional wife and mother, the kind of woman only one had ever been, and none would choose to be. Their aim was to make this woman's domestic role untenable; their method was to revile, disdain, and calumniate her. Which leads us to the second irony of their offensive.

Feminism's ability to piggyback upon the black civil rights movement has greatly facilitated women's acquisition of educational, job, and other market preferences. Yet, the principal weapon feminists have employed to devalue the housewife's status has been an attack based on stereotypical analysis, arrant bigotry, and undisguised contempt, all the antithesis of respect for the worth and integrity of each individual that was the wellspring of our civil rights movement. To see this clearly, one need only substitute the word "African-American," "Jew," or "Hispanic" for the word "housewife" in the statements of Betty Friedan and her sisters in the movement. These feminists (who surely thought themselves good people and committed to liberal values) would recoil from characterizing any other group in society in the degrading terms they have routinely applied to the housewife.

FEMINISM'S FALSIFICATION OF REALITY

Contemporary feminism is the creation of women who rejected the traditional family and traditional femininity, who were career-oriented, and who either rejected motherhood altogether, or believed it should play a very subordinate role in a woman's life. The ideology they developed is based on misrepresentation of the facts—feminism's falsification of reality. Feminist success has depended on convincing both men and women that a woman's devotion to home and children is a sacrifice, a virtually worthless pursuit which affords no opportunity to use the energies and intelligence of even an average woman.

A crucial step towards inculcating this attitude has been to foster the belief that mothers previously stayed at home to rear their children only because they had no alternative. The allegation that women have been discriminatorily denied jobs has been, of course, the predicate for giving women job preferences within the legal framework of affirmative action remedies. But this allegation also has been essential to the task of convincing younger generations of women that, if older generations had been permitted to do so, they themselves would have pursued careers rather than staying at home to rear their children.

The major complaint of working mothers is usually not workplace discrimination in the ordinary sense, but their exhaustion, lack of leisure time, and the discrepancy between their own image of what being a good mother entails and the reality of their lives. One feminist response has been to demand alteration of workplace requirements to accommodate child-rearing responsibilities. In addition to these palliative measures, feminists have also undertaken to alter the traditional image of a good mother. They began by creating the myth that the decision of women of an earlier generation to decline participation in the workplace did not arise from their own vision of motherhood; rather, they stayed at home with their children only because they had been denied any opportunity to enter or succeed in the workplace. To feminists, who were certain they themselves would never willingly stay at home to rear children, this myth was believable and accorded with the view of sociologist Jessie Bernard that a woman who said she enjoyed being a home-maker had to be somewhat mentally disturbed.

Feminist myth-making meant that women of my generation who had willingly exchanged market production for child-rearing found ourselves represented as victims in analyses designed to document the denial of career opportunities to women. Workplace discrimination in fact played no part in the decisions many of us made to cease working outside the home. We were impelled to stay with our children by the strong emotional pull they exercised on us and because we thought our presence in the home was the single best guarantee of their well-being. A life caring for them at home, we often discovered, was good for us as well. We were confident, moreover, that society respected us and believed us to be engaged in a valuable activity—not acting as sacrificial victims—when we functioned as full-time homemakers.

It is this confidence that contemporary feminism has destroyed by successfully propagating the idea that homemakers' activities are largely valueless, convincing younger generations of men and women that society disdains a woman's domestic role. Yet feminism has been less successful in expunging women's own image of a good mother and relieving working mothers of their ambivalence and feelings of guilt about leaving their children. While workplace modifications can help accommodate working mothers, they offer, at best, mild palliatives for those mothers who do yearn to be with their children and for those children who never find an adequate replacement for lost maternal care.

Workplace modifications can usually only compensate slightly for what is often a mother's nearly insupportable burden of dual responsibility. Instituting these changes serves a very important function, nevertheless, by helping assuage mothers' guilt. The message conveyed through these changes is that society is willing to impose the cost upon taxpayers and consumers because it believes a mother *should* work outside the home and that her presence at home would be of little value to either mother or child. Reinforcing this message is the fact that costs of workplace modifications benefiting working mothers will be disproportionately borne by one-income families which must pay for, while not sharing in, these benefits.

Like all special interest groups, feminists seek subsidies for themselves. Their economic interests and professional advancement have been greatly enhanced by claims of past societal discrimination against women, including the claim of being forced to assume a sacrificial role as homemaker.

My own experience differs sharply from the tales feminists tell. I was a practicing lawyer in the 1950s. From the time in junior high school when I decided to become a lawyer until I ceased working in order to raise a family, I always received unstinting encouragement and support. It was scarcely possible that someone from the working class, living on the edge of poverty with a divorced mother, could have succeeded otherwise. My entire college and law school educations were funded by scholarships and my employment. Teachers and counselors in high school and college energetically assisted in my efforts to secure these scholarships and other aid, without ever questioning the suitability of my aspirations for a woman. Not once in all the sessions where we discussed my educational options and planned how I would pay for them was this issue ever raised.

Contrary to the received opinion that society consistently discouraged women's market activity, I found social acquaintances were extremely supportive, while employers and many colleagues generously encouraged my pusuit of a career. At the same time, those of my female friends in the 1950s who were traditional housewives little resembled the stereotype, so effectively popularized by Betty Friedan, of intellectually shallow, bored, underachieving child-wives. Nor do I believe the stereotype accurately applied to me when I, too, became a homemaker.

Attending law school and practicing law during a period when feminists would have us believe women were systematically discriminated against, I was treated as well as, and I sometimes thought even better than, the men with whom I was competing. But feminists tell a very different story. Justice Ruth Bader Ginsburg, for example, upon her nomination to the United States Supreme Court, reiterated the feminist mythology. Paying homage to her mother, Justice Ginsburg expressed the hope that she herself would be all her mother "would have been had she lived in an age when women could aspire and achieve." Reflected in these words are the feminist assumptions that women can "achieve" only through market production and that failure to achieve within the workplace cannot have been a willing choice. Cannot Justice Ginsburg conceive that her mother may not have wanted to sacrifice the time at home with her child that would have been required to gain what that child has achieved?

The nominee also attested to the discrimination she faced when, having graduated from Columbia University Law School (on the Law Review and tied for first in her class), "not a law firm in the entire city of New York bid for my employment as a lawyer." It was reported—surely inaccurately—that she had to take a job as a legal secretary.[31] The phrasing of her remarkable statement raises the question whether, resume in hand, she had actually sought a job with every law firm in New York City or simply waited to receive "bids."

When I graduated from the same law school several years before Justice Ginsburg (also on the Law Review, but not first in my class) and began my job search, I received an offer from a major Wall Street law firm. As I recall, most of the fourteen women in my class sought and obtained legal positions,[32] although only two of us were on the Law Review and none was first in the class. It is true that the other woman on the Law Review (who was Jewish) did not share my good fortune of receiving an offer from any of the major Wall Street law firms, which did discriminate at that time against Jews and other ethnics. My future husband, for example, who graduated with me—also on the Law Review and with a virtually identical record but without the advantage of being a "Pennington"— was among the many men who could claim they were so discriminated against. Many Jewish graduates during that period, including women, took jobs with what were known as the midtown Jewish law firms, and it seems hardly possible that this avenue was foreclosed to a woman who had graduated first in her class. If her complaint is that she received no offers from major Wall Street firms, my own experience and that of my classmates would indicate the controlling variable was not her sex. It is, of course, more beneficial to plead sex, rather than ethnic, discrimination. Reparation for the latter still leaves her in competition with all the men who share her ethnicity.

Similarly, Barbara Aronstein Black, at the time Dean of Columbia Law School, discussed what it was like for her and other women to go to law school when they did not think they could get jobs or have a career: "We all knew that once we attempted to move into practice (but of course I never did), we would meet active discrimination. That was perfectly clear, and we were pretty angry about it."[33] But we did *not* all know this; it was *not* perfectly clear. The then-Barbara Aronstein graduated from Columbia Law School the year after I did. I never was part of such discussions and never doubted that I could obtain a good legal job and pursue a career for as long as I wanted. Like most of my classmates, male and female, I set out with my resume and obtained a job. Those women, who, like Barbara Aronstein Black, were Jewish or members of other ethnic groups, did know—just as similarly situated men knew— that for them the job search would be harder and that they were unlikely to receive offers from major Wall Street law firms. The distinction then usually made—but certainly not always—was between white, Anglo-Saxon Protestants and ethnics, not between men and women.[34] Now that it has become fashionable to plead one's victimization at every opportunity, what I find most interesting is that my classmates who were disadvantaged because of their ethnicity rarely did seem angry, but only determined to overcome whatever obstacles they faced.

Feminist Susan Brownmiller entered Cornell University as a freshman the year after I had finished my undergraduate work there and gone on to law school. In a letter to the *Cornell Alumni News* of April 1973, Brownmiller wrote that when she entered Cornell in 1952, "I had secret hopes of going to Law School. Two years later I abandoned that goal as a rather unseemly ambition for a woman." She does not say who made her believe this ambition was unseemly—perhaps it was her family. I doubt it was any of the faculty or administrators with whom I dealt at Cornell. After my first year, I was given a job that enabled me to earn my room and board without working so many hours that I would be unable to maintain the grades required for my full-tuition scholarship; this job was given only to students whose ambition was thought serious and seemly. The Registrar at Cornell Law School took my aspirations very seriously. My only doubt about those aspirations was that it might be foolish for one as poor as I to continue her education. The Registrar always encouraged me to pursue my ambitions, and he helped me to choose the law schools where I should apply and then to decide between Harvard, Yale, Columbia, and Cornell. That these law schools accepted me and offered me scholarships and other aid belies the claim that being a lawyer was considered un- seemly for a woman.

My own career pursuits elicited a vastly more tolerant reaction four decades ago than is now evoked by a decision to devote oneself to being a full-time mother and housewife, a choice that, in recent years, has usually been depicted as a waste of time and talent. What were once considered valuable and respected activities—raising children, attending to a husband's needs, and managing a household—the present society created by contemporary feminism views as benighted and beyond rational justification. No woman with a brain in her head, feminists have largely convinced society, could possibly be happy devoting herself to what they portray as worthless, even degrading, activities. No woman, as Justice Ginsburg implied, would *willingly* live a life of such limited achievement.

Feminists have inaccurately depicted women's past lives both in home and workplace and falsely claimed that the intensive devotion of a woman at home cannot significantly benefit her marriage and children. But feminists are accurate when they deny that all women should be expected to become mothers. The denial seems superfluous, however, since it has rarely been asserted that motherhood must be every woman's destiny. Monasteries and nunneries, for example, have been among the social institutions recognizing that reproduction is not expected of everyone. Clearly, some women are not suited to motherhood and some mothers prefer delegating child-rearing to others in order to pursue a career or other interests. The insidiousness of the women's movement is that, while claiming—and being perceived by society—to speak for all women, it has represented only these two groups.

THE AWAKENED BRÜNNHILDE

The woman who wishes to rear her children within a traditional marriage, to whom contemporary feminism has been an implacable enemy, I call the "awakened Brünnhilde." Best-known from Richard Wagner's *The Ring of the Nibelung*, Brünnhilde is a warrior maiden who was transformed by her love for the hero Siegfried. The Brünnhilde I seek to defend is a woman who finds that the satisfactions of full-time commitment to being a wife and mother outweigh the rewards of pursuing a career. This realization is part of what I call her awakened femininity.

But Brünnhilde's choice, according to societal consensus, is a sacrifice. It is viewed as a sacrifice because society has acquiesced in feminism's depiction of the homemaker's role as worthless, boring, unrewarding, unfulfilling, and incapable of using a woman's talents. Even those who support this choice as being in children's best interest will speak of it as a sacrifice. For women like me, however, the sacrifice lies in precisely the opposite choice. It would have been a virtually unendurable sacrifice for me to have left my children with anyone (including my husband who, while possessing many virtues, was ill-suited to a mother's role) in order to remain in the workplace.

I have been happy in every period of my adult life: attending college and law school, practicing law, staying at home to raise a family, and creating a new life once my family responsibilities had largely ended. Yet those many years I spent as a mother at home from the birth of my first child until the last left for college were the best, the ones I would be least willing to have forgone. Feminists recount endless tales of women's oppression throughout the ages, but one of the greatest injustices to women is feminists' own success in convincing society to treat as a sacrifice what for some women can be the most rewarding occupation of their lives.

By undermining the status and security of awakened Brünnhildes, contemporary feminism has inflicted undeserved injury upon many good women. And society itself has been weakened by its curtailing of women's domestic role, which contributes substantially—possibly more than any other single activity—to societal health and stability. All indicia of familial well-being demonstrate that our society was a significantly better place for families in the decade before the feminist revival—when the primary concerns of most mothers were their husbands, their children, and their home. Those of us who concluded that our marriages and families would thrive better if we devoted ourselves to home and children rather than to market production find our belief validated by studies showing that "when women can support themselves, there is a lesser degree of bonding between husband and wife and more relaxed sexual mores" and that "the higher the relative degree of power attributed by respondents to the male partner, the lower the rate of marital dissolution."[35] These findings are consistent with the long-known fact that the women "with high incomes and/or graduate degrees have the highest divorce rate—a rate far higher than successful men."[36]

Our belief is also confirmed by several findings of a recently concluded long-term study of married couples: (1) husbands "who do more household tasks are less satisfied with the way the tasks are distributed," and this division of tasks "is associated with declines in their love for their wives"; (2) the "more fathers in dual-earner marriages are involved with child care, the more negativity in the marriage," and those fathers "who report more negative interaction tend to be less satisfied with the division of child care tasks and also tend to be less in love with their wives"; and (3) the extent to which husbands who are the sole breadwinners are involved in child care is unrelated to the amount of negativity toward their wives, and "the more single-earner fathers are in love with their wives, the more (rather than less) involved they are in child care and leisure activities alone with their children."[37]

That mothers provide daily care for their children is in the interest of those men who would resist the feminist effort to refashion them into mother-substitutes, a role for which men are usually not well-suited. It is in the interest of those children who would have both a father and a mother, each filling different roles, and who would be spared the day care and surrogate mothering that can be a source of misery and are likely to be inferior to care at home from a competent and contented mother. And it is in the interest of those women who could find a motherhood that is unencumbered by marketplace commitments to be an incomparable joy.

Admittedly, life at home with their children cannot be a joy—either incomparable or ordinary—for women who regard that life as a sacrifice. It is not my purpose to convince these women otherwise. Such persuasion, my own experience has taught me, is more likely to spring from their own physical and emotional experience than from discussion. It is the experiences in her marital relationship, together with the experiences of pregnancy and childbirth—forces more subtle than intellectual reasoning—that will usually awaken a woman's response to her children and then mold the dimensions of that response.

I use the term "awakened femininity" to describe Brünnhilde's response to her sexual experiences and to her children. The purpose of the feminist endeavor was to discourage a response like Brünnhilde's and encourage what I call women's "spiritual virginity." This is the term I use to describe a response that permits a woman to resist the emotional pull exerted by her child so that she can continue her life as a market producer after childbirth. At the same time as feminists promoted the sexual revolution that mocked women's premarital sexual virginity and marital chastity, they vilified and disadvantaged those women who refused to adopt a feminist "spiritual virginity," but chose, instead, to become homemakers and child-rearers.

Clearly, some women do experience full-time child-rearing as a joy, not a sacrifice, even when their initial decision to stay at home is prompted by the altruistic motive that this will be best for their children. That these women should find life at home to be enjoyable and rewarding is, I contend, at least reasonable. It is, therefore, scarcely debatable that society should support, not undermine, their lives at home. In the interests of such women, their families, and society, we should begin to restore the level playing field that the women's movement has destroyed.

We must recognize that proposals with an initial appeal can often have detrimental effects on traditional families and must therefore be resisted by those who want to support such families. The proposed equal rights amendment, for example, would have forbidden denial of "equality of rights under the law ... on account of sex." It was intended to make sex distinctions identical to distinctions on the basis of race so that men and women—like blacks and whites—would have to be treated alike for all purposes. The amendment was intended, like many of the judicial decisions reached under the Fourteenth Amendment's equal protection clause, to promote the feminist goal of an androgynous society. It would forbid, among other things, the existence of publicly run schools, classes, or athletic activities for one sex only and require drafting of women for military service, including combat. Feminists sought the amendment to signify that our nation endorsed the aim of the National Organization for Women to disfavor the traditional family with a breadwinner husband and homemaker wife. Like no-fault divorce laws, the amendment was designed to force women to abandon their traditional roles and refashion themselves after the feminist role models who promoted it.

Similarly, government-funded child care programs must inevitably harm traditional families. The greatest financial need in our society exists in households with children. It is not this financial need, however, which leads the women's movement to endorse government-funded child care, but its firm belief that a woman's proper place is in the work force, rather than in the home caring for her children. Financial hardships of families with children could be alleviated by increasing the federal income tax exemption for dependents or providing family allowances (through tax credits or some other method) that would benefit *all* families with children, including those in which the mother stays at home. Such reforms would lighten the financial burden of one-wage-earner families and permit some women to leave the work force.

But any outcome that enables women to exchange market activities for life at home is disfavored by the women's movement. It consistently argues, instead, for government-funded institutional child care that would require expenditures rivaling social security and medicare. The lure of subsidized child care, together with the resulting tax burden imposed on all families, would serve feminist goals by encouraging women to continue working and enticing women into the work force who prefer caring for their children at home. Through the legislation they seek, feminists demonstrate their preference for a government policy that disfavors families where the mother remains at home with her children by taxing these families in order to pay for child care, as well as other benefits, for families in which the mother works outside the home. Acting upon their belief that women should do market work rather than care for their children, feminists advocate discriminatory methods designed to deprive women of a real choice and push them into living in accordance with the feminist ideology.

IN *Nineteen Eighty-Four*, George Orwell describes an old man in a pub who, having survived revolution and purges, is one of the "last links that now exist with the vanished world of capitalism." When told by the barman that there are no pints of beer, the old man responds that "a pint's the 'alf of a quart, and there's four quarts to the gallon," to which the barman replies that he'd never heard of them: "liter and half liter—that's all we serve."[38] All that is now served by the reigning cultural elite are views like feminist Karen DeCrow's: "[N]o man should allow himself to support his wife— no matter how much she favors the idea, no matter how many centuries this domestic pattern has existed, no matter how logical the economics of the arrangement may appear, no matter how good it makes him feel. . . . [I]t will diminish and destroy affection and respect. . . . [L]ove can flourish between adults only when everyone pays his or her own way." [39]

Contained within DeCrow's brief statement is the entire feminist ideology. Andrea Dworkin had earlier stated it even more briefly, asserting that "to have what men have one must be what men are." [40] This ideology dictates that marriage should not be an institution in which a man and a woman assume different, complementary roles, but a relationship like that of roommates, each fully and independently committed to market production—something resembling a homosexual relationship, yet between heterosexuals. DeCrow assumes that only a paycheck can fulfill a woman's half of the marital bargain. To Brünnhilde, however, the arrangement DeCrow proposes, in which the woman (who for all purposes could just as well be another man) must pay her own way, has two fatal flaws: first, the arrangement requires child-rearing by surrogates; second, it discards the different, complementary roles that she believes are most likely to produce a stable marriage, enlivened by satisfying sexuality. DeCrow's market-oriented roommates, who are little more than clones of each other, are the least likely to satisfy what Roger Scruton identified—Brünnhilde believes accurately—as the foundation of heterosexual sexual excitement: "the energy released when man and woman come together is proportional to the distance which divides them when they are apart." [41]

That this feminist ideology is now substantially institutionalized in our society is evidenced by the wide acceptance of Justice Ginsburg's assumption that what can properly be considered achievement occurs only within the marketplace. A woman who seeks an alternative achievement within the domestic arena is dismissively described by Ginsburg—in words reflecting the same ideological assumptions as those of DeCrow and Dworkin—as being "reduced to dependency on a man." [42] It is beyond the ken of these feminists to perceive the homemaker—in the way I have always viewed myself—not as being "reduced," but as happily being spared the market work which would have required an unbearably constricted maternal role.

Feminism's ideological victory has been a significant factor in producing the conditions cited by public school administrators when recommending full-day public school education for very young children because government institutions must take responsibility for children at ever younger ages. One administrator, for example, stated at a public hearing that children are no longer being reared by their families since the family "as we once knew it, has been destroyed." The family, he said, "is gone" and so "we are going to have to do something else": "You can forget the family part."[43] But not all those mothers whose employment has contributed to creating this situation celebrate it as the social advance it is to feminists. Some of these mothers, instead, acknowledge a strong yearning to be at home with their children and guilt because of the choices they have made.[44]

If this maternal yearning is ever to influence behavior, it must be powerful enough to overcome the feminist triumph that has entrenched within our society views of elite opinion-makers like those expressed by Justice Ginsburg and Karen DeCrow. The traditional family that the women's movement targeted as its enemy is, like the pints and quarts of *Nineteen Eighty-Four*, on its way to extinction. While not yet dead and gone, as the school administrator claimed, it will be unless those who believe in the value of this family structure attempt to reverse feminism's victory. Such an attempt will not succeed until society begins again to respect and support—rather than disfavor, patronize, and demean—the woman who undertakes a traditional role and the man who makes it possible for her to do so.

I

Women's Divine Discontent

The recurrent problem of civilization is to define the male role satisfactorily enough . . . so that the male may in the course of his life reach a solid sense of irreversible achievement, of which his childhood knowledge of the satisfactions of child-bearing have given him a glimpse. In the case of women, it is only necessary that they be permitted by the given social arrangements to fulfil their biological role, to attain this sense of irreversible achievement. If women are to be restless and questing, even in the face of child-bearing, they must be made so through education. . . . Each culture—in its own way—has developed forms that will make men satisfied in their constructive activities without distorting their sure sense of their masculinity. Fewer cultures have yet found ways in which to give women a divine discontent that will demand other satisfactions than those of child-bearing.

Margaret Mead[1]

The main waft of the current . . . pours over us all the mighty
river, butterscotch on top, and underneath, sewage. Boating about
on it is the child wife, the infantile personality, the woman who
cannot reason logically, the bridge fiend, the golf fiend, the mother
of all the atrocities we call "spoiled children," the middle-aged,
hair-faced clubwoman who destroys everything she touches, the
murderess, the habitual divorcee, the weeper, the weak sister, the
rubbery sex experimentist, the quarreler, the woman forever
displeased, the nagger, the female miser, and so on and so on and
so on, to the outermost lengths of the puerile, rusting, raging crea-
ture we know as mom and sis—unrealists, all—flops in the impossi-
ble attempt to become Cinderellas, shrill ones, pushing for more
yardage in the material world, demanding only that the men,
obviously no Princes, at least make up in some small way by acting
like Santa Claus who has become, also, an Americanized archetype.

Philip Wylie [2]

I FIRST READ THESE WORDS of Philip Wylie over forty-five
years ago when, a college senior, I was preparing to enter law
school. Even allowing for Wylie's hyperbole, his words seemed
to me far removed from reality, as would many feminist writings
two decades later. Reading Wylie did not make me thankful that
pursuit of a professional career would prevent me from ever resembling the women he describes. Rather, I was angered by his
degrading caricature of the mothers and housewives I had known
all my life to be, on the whole, good women seeking to do their
best for husbands and children.

Two perceptions with which I had emerged from my youth
were that women were usually better persons than men and that it
would be highly risky ever to place my welfare in the hands of a
man. These perceptions derived from my experiences growing up
during the Great Depression and living in straitened financial
circumstances with my divorced mother. My parents separated

when I was two years old, and I never saw my father from the time I was seven, although we lived in the same city. The neighborhood in which I lived with my mother was an ethnic mix of mainly lower-middle-class and working-class Irish and Germans. I knew no parents who had attended college; many—including all my maternal relatives except my mother—had not graduated from high school. My keenest perception was that women's and children's lives would have been much improved if men consumed less alcohol and allocated more money to their families' support.

It was my good fortune, nonetheless, to fall in love with books which enabled me to invent a very rich fantasy life peopled by strong, reliable, and desirable men. I cherished many literary portrayals of men who fit the fantasy: Laura Ingalls Wilder's Pa in *The Little House* books; Ernest Hemingway's Lieutenant Frederic Henry in *A Farewell to Arms* and Robert Jordan in *For Whom the Bell Tolls*; Leo Tolstoy's Prince Andrey and Pierre in *War and Peace* and Levin in *Anna Karenina.* Nevertheless, prudence seemed to dictate that I be prepared for the likelihood that, in real life, I would never find a trustworthy man.

Because I anticipated having to provide for myself, greatly enjoyed studying, was academically successful, and would be able to obtain scholarships for my education, I determined to become a lawyer. Buoyed by encouragement and assistance, I achieved my goal without ever experiencing the discouragement and discrimination feminists would have us believe have always been women's lot. Nor did I ever share with feminists their scorn and contempt for the housewife, although I never thought it likely that I would become one myself. While I read Philip Wylie with a sense of outrage, contemporary feminists have echoed his sentiments.

Although calling themselves "feminists," the movement's advocates have consistently sought to relegate to an ever more diminished status what has always been considered the most essentially feminine part of woman's nature—her child-bearing ability and close nurturing ties to her children. Instead of defending women against truly misogynistic attacks like Philip Wylie's, contemporary feminists have turned reality on its head and attacked as misogynists commentators like George Gilder, one of the most valiant and loyal defenders of femininity. Ratifying Wylie's vituperations against the homemaker, feminists have scorned the domestic role and exhorted other women to join them in forsaking it as unworthy of their talents.

The assault on the worth of a traditional female role has succeeded in degrading it to the most inferior status it has ever had in our society. Feminists have undertaken their unrestrained attack because they declined to resolve their own disaffection simply by entering the marketplace on an individual basis, as some women, including myself, have always chosen to do. They have sought instead to form a kind of female trade union by convincing other women to join them in the marketplace. Recruiting other women has facilitated the acquisition of sufficient political power to gain educational and job preferences for women and has provided a greater number of female co-workers to help insulate women from the direct competition with males that some women fear. Nevertheless, the main reason feminists recruit women to the workplace is the belief that equal political and economic power for women will never be achieved without the virtual demise of the homemaker.

Feminists vowed that they would try to become as much like men as possible. They would be sexually available on male terms without commitment. They would abort their babies, or if they gave birth, they would place their children in surrogates' care and continue to work outside the home at "meaningful" jobs so that someday, if they tried very hard, they might possibly be as interesting and worthy as men. The women's movement could have been orchestrated by the editors of *Playboy*: readily available sex for men without marriage; if married, a working wife to unburden the male from responsibility for supporting the household; readily available abortion to eliminate unwanted children; and devaluation of maternal commitment to child-nurturing so that mothers would remain in the workplace, ensuring that women would never become dependent upon their husbands.

Bourgeois Family Values vs. the Market

How did contemporary feminism come to adopt these goals? Why did women so readily reject the value of their traditional family roles and concede the superiority of roles that males play in the marketplace? What instilled in women Margaret Mead's "divine discontent" that led them willingly to embrace and act upon the anti-feminine message that care of children and home are inferior occupations? Feminism did not always disdain domesticity and the child-nurturing dimension of femininity. As Christopher Lasch noted, feminists in the 1930s had allied with Freudian revisionists to give women "a more positive conception of femininity," glorifying the vagina, the womb, and motherhood while attacking the conventional belief that menstruation was a "curse" and that women were not fully capable of sexual pleasure.[3]

In the nineteenth century, Lasch observed, it was often feminists who had led the "forces of organized virtue" to stamp out drunkenness and debauchery, gradually subduing the older "patterns of male conviviality" and domesticating males to "bourgeois hearth and home." An important element in this campaign to "feminize society" by substituting "domestic enjoyments for the rough and brutal camaraderie of males" was the "glorification of the child and of maternal influence on the child's development." This conflict between the feminine and masculine spheres was often reflected in women's efforts to combat the "competitive, work-oriented values of their husbands": "Men valued achievement; women, happiness and well-being."[4]

Treating domestic life as an emotional refuge from the world of work rested on a separation of private and public life that developed with the bourgeois nuclear family. Lasch described this as a family where "glorification of privacy in turn reflected the devaluation of work," which was viewed simply as a means to an end—as a "way of achieving satisfactions or consolations outside work."[5] The Victorian home, as Gertrude Himmelfarb puts it, became "a haven not only from the pressures of the marketplace but from the temptations of sin and corruption."[6] The attitude that market activity within the public arena is not the ultimate good reflected what Brigitte and Peter Berger have identified as a fundamental bourgeois belief that the "'little things' in life, the ordinary and seemingly unimportant details of everyday events, matter as much as the 'great things.'"[7]

It is the critical significance of these simple, commonplace events comprising our daily routines that Jane Austen celebrates in her writings of delicate precision and Leo Tolstoy portrays in his monumental novels. In *War and Peace*, Tolstoy captures in Natasha the essence of the woman who finds satisfaction in attending to the particularities of her family's daily activities by preserving routines and discharging the obligations they impose. Indeed, it was at the figure of Natasha that Simone de Beauvoir in 1949 fired the first salvo of feminism's current war against the housewife, when she ridiculed the "supreme self-abasement" of Natasha's "passionate and tyrannical devotion to her family."[8]

Women who cherish as an ideal Tolstoy's portrayal of the domestic bliss that Natasha finally achieved—perceiving that bliss as self-fulfilling, not abasing—stand athwart the course of feminism's advance. Society can choose to honor this ideal, to grant significance to the ordinary details of everyday life, and to respect, rather than disdain, a woman's devotion to her family's daily routine. If it does, then this woman can easily derive more satisfaction from baking a loaf of bread with her child than from writing the legal briefs that feminism would celebrate as the only genuine achievements. Such a woman might well describe the purpose of her daily life in the way Mark Helprin described the paintings of Edward Schmidt: this artist's purpose, said Helprin, is not "to reinvent the universe, but rather, like Raphael, and Caravaggio, and Sargent, and a thousand others before, to attend to it."[9]

Contemporary feminism would have women devote themselves to reinventing the universe—as Hillary Rodham Clinton urges them to "remold society." But devotion to grandiose schemes within the public arena necessarily requires relinquishing to others the cultivation of one's own garden. The essence of the traditional woman is her preference for attending to the welfare of her own small universe, hoping to create therein a simple canvas of quotidian beauty. If T. S. Eliot's J. Alfred Prufrock thinks his life diminished because it is measured out with coffee spoons, the traditional woman cherishes the daily ceremonies in which she arranges these spoons. Henry James speaks for her when he begins *The Portrait of a Lady* by observing that "there are few hours in life more agreeable than the hour dedicated to the ceremony known as afternoon tea."[10]

Traditional bourgeois family life was also shaped by the belief that parents should be primarily responsible for their children's education. Because the bourgeoisie distrusted the influence of both servants and tutors, parents were the adults with whom children spent most of their time. Children were the center of attention in the bourgeois household and were closely supervised by their parents, who were the only ones thought to be "properly aware of the unique characteristics and individual needs of their children."[11] Thus, children were socialized in the course of participating with their parents in the myriad activities of daily living. The Center for Studies of Suicide Prevention has advised parents to spend "one-on-one time" with a child every day, demonstrating how far children have fallen from the cherished position they once occupied in the traditional bourgeois family.

In the struggle between masculine work-oriented values and feminine domestic values, the feminine lost. The "Angel in the House"—that Victorian-era wife who, as Robert Wright puts it, "could tame the animal in a man and rescue his spirit from the deadening world of work"[12]—was evicted. Heeding Virginia Woolf's admonition to "kill" the angel in the house, those who now call themselves feminists have assured these angels that, far from deadening, the world of market work is vastly superior to the "almost pathetic ordinariness" of their lives.[13] This ideal of "The Angel in the House" had been created as the foundation for withdrawing women (who were seen as morally superior) "from the exhaustion, the contamination, the vulgarity of mill-work and professional work."[14]   But it has succumbed to the feminist ideal of sexual equivalence.

The new feminists warn the domestic angel that she must sacrifice her role as child-nurturer and her home as the primary locus of child-rearing to the goal of achieving status—as defined in male terms. The traditional bourgeois family, the new feminists assert, has no value; it is, in fact, the source of women's oppression. Market production is the ultimate good, far surpassing what feminists invariably describe as the dull and dreary task of maintaining a home and caring for children. Contemporary feminism has taught us to substitute marketplace for familial activities. Work has become an end in itself and has, in large part, taken the place of women's families.

Regardless of the concern otherwise expressed for their well-being, children know that inherent in this shift of their mothers' attention to the workplace is a decreased valuation of the time devoted to them. When a mother who chooses to do market work says that she is very particular about the nanny she hires because her baby is the most precious thing in her life, she puts a distinct gloss on the word "precious." Her costly oriental rug, which is valuable, pleasing to sight and touch, and completes the furnishing of her home, might also be called "precious," but it does not take up much of her time. Neither does her baby, for it is her job to which she has chosen to devote the bulk of her personal attention. This dramatic shift in mothers' exertions away from the daily routine of their home is the most critical change wrought by the feminist revolution and one its apologists seek to deny. It is not the case—

as they would have us believe—that women have continued their domestic endeavors within the home, particularly tending to their children, even as they have "expanded their horizons" outside the home. Whatever the arrangements for surrogate care, the relationship which exists between the mother who is at home all day and her child no longer exists when that mother enters the workplace.

The attempt to rationalize this change—even to make it appear for the better—spawned that most ironic phrase "quality time" to describe those moments a working mother spends with her child. It is as if the phrasemakers thought a mother fresh from her day in the marketplace would infuse those moments with a vim, vigor, and verve that would readily surpass the anemic exertions to be expected from the type of woman who chooses to stay at home. In child care there is no quality without quantity. Most mothers who have competently provided the full-time daily care of their children know that spokesmen for the "helping professions" who employ the jargon of "quality time" (now blessedly in waning use) are either blinded by their commitment to feminist ideology or have no grasp of the depth of the interactions that can occur with one's children during the course of an ordinary day at home.

To understand how the women's movement so readily achieved its goal of vastly reducing the number of full-time homemakers, it is necessary to identify the seeds from which women's discontent grew and which blossomed into the women's movement. One factor, the increasing feminization of males, is doubly significant. It contributed to women's disenchantment with a traditional female role—a role that most women cannot find satisfying without the support and encouragement of a masculine man—and it helped dispose large numbers of men to endorse feminist goals. Ten percent more men than women supported the women's movement in 1972,[15] and more men than women supported the Equal Rights Amendment in 1978.[16] The alacrity with which so many men acceded to feminist demands, no matter how illogical or outrageous, evidenced an emasculation which itself contributed to the discontent fueling the movement.

A sea change had occurred in men who only two decades before had taken pride in their ability to provide for wife and children. With scarcely a whimper, many males accepted the new androgyny and capitulated to the very feminist demands which have impaired their earning ability. Then, they too encouraged their wives to leave children hostage to the vagaries of surrogate care and pursue the economic opportunities which would spare husbands from assuming the now apparently overwhelming role of breadwinner.

THE MARKETPLACE CULTURE

Writing in 1948, Margaret Mead described American society as one that over-rewarded male positions. Female envy of the male role, she stated, reflects both an overvaluation of the public aspects of men's achievements and a devaluation of "the sensuous creative significance of the female role of wife and mother"; when the home is undervalued "women will cease to enjoy being women, and men will neither envy nor value the female role."[17] It is not necessary to pinpoint when the devaluation occurred to understand that contemporary feminists correctly perceived that our society valued male achievements in the marketplace more highly than female contributions as wife and mother. Feminists reacted, unfortunately, by agreeing that this relative valuation was correct. Conceding the inferiority of the traditional female roles of wife and mother, feminists exhorted women to enter the marketplace in search of the status society conferred on males.

What explains the devaluation of the female role that Mead described in 1948? One explanation, according to Amaury de Riencourt, is the classical Greek overestimation of male mental creativity and underestimation of female life-creating activity. It was this attitude, he claimed, that induced ancient Roman women to ape men and disdain child-bearing. Our Western culture, rooted in this Greek culture, similarly tends to value a "masculine power of mental creation" more highly than "female physiological gestation." The result is Western woman's perception that her distinctive role of motherhood is "crassly undervalued by a Western man who has fallen in love with his own cerebration." This overvaluing of "cerebral creation" and undervaluing of "physiological maternal creativity," argued de Riencourt, leads Western man to see woman "as a defective, incomplete, lower-grade male who lacks something" and, in turn, makes women want to become pseudo-males.[18]

Feminism, in de Riencourt's view, will only take hold in societies that are "aggressively masculine, such as the Jewish one," and the rebellion always stresses "the greater value" of man's work.[19] Whether or not the phrase "aggressively masculine" describes Jewish men in the United States today, it is the case that Jewish women have been disproportionately represented in the women's liberation movement.[20] Jewish women, as Jay P. Lefkowitz has noted, are among the most highly educated members of our society as well as "the most urban, wealthy, and secular," the Jewish woman being a typical "member of the yuppie-careerist class." They have "not only been prominent in the feminist movement but also among its leading beneficiaries."[21] Michael Lerner, editor of *Tikkun* magazine, has described Jewish women as being among the "greatest beneficiaries" of affirmative action.[22]

Certainly, Jewish women's educational qualifications well positioned them to benefit from feminist success in securing preferential treatment for women. But their commitment to our feminist revival may well have been dictated less by the prospect of economic advancement than by their particular vulnerability to the trait of Western man that de Riencourt deemed crucial in explaining feminism: overvaluing mental and undervaluing maternal creativity. In my own associations with professional men, many of whom were Jewish, I have observed a tendency to disdain a woman's domestic endeavors and to condition their respect upon her market accomplishments. This may explain why many of the very men whose valiant efforts in defending maligned individuals I often gratefully witnessed over the years have routinely acquiesced in the feminist disparagement of those women who choose domesticity over career.

Helena Lopata found that many of the homemakers whom she surveyed believed themselves to be "the power behind the throne"; the more highly-educated women, in particular, felt that they participated, if only vicariously, in their husband's job, its problems, and social relations. The exception was Jewish women who would largely "disclaim their own significance in this area of the mate's life" and "are much more definite than any other group in stating that *no wife* should influence her husband's job."[23] Stanley Rothman and S. Robert Lichter have analyzed the inability of the Jewish female, unlike women in other cultures, to satisfy her desire for power through identification with a husband. One solution has been to seek careers that "enabled them to create their own power."[24]

Bruno Bettelheim speculated that it was the traditional Jewish "rejection of femininity" and "glorification of masculine pursuits" that influenced the first kibbutzniks "to view man's work as preferable to woman's, including the work of rearing children." This reaction logically follows, he said, from the fact that "few religions have been as rejecting of womanhood as the Jewish one," viewing as it does "her very femininity as a curse" and requiring "men to thank God each day that He has not created them female."[25]

A combination of the Jewish man's low valuation of a traditional female role and high valuation of wives who achieve in the workplace, together with the wife's inability to derive self-affirmation from identifying with her husband, would seem reason enough for Jewish women to champion a feminist cause. The plight of the Jewish woman, whose assumption of a traditional female role is burdened by hostile religious and cultural traditions, entitles her to sympathy. But this plight also renders disaffected Jewish feminists unsuitable as mediators of women's roles to other women who are not burdened by such hostile traditions. Some of us have never experienced such sustained hostility to our femininity. We have, instead, been shaped by cultural and religious traditions that glorify the feminine, and we have found that it is our femininity that affords us the greatest satisfactions in our lives.

At the announcement of her nomination to the Supreme Court of the United States, Justice Ruth Bader Ginsburg opined that her mother had not lived in an age when "daughters are cherished as much as sons."[26] How vastly different from my own must the culture have been that produced a woman who could make such a shocking statement. How could we have grown up in the same part of the same country at about the same time? That daughters had not been cherished as much as sons is a belief which nothing in my own background could have ever led me to hold. It was in daughters, I always thought, that sobriety, competence, and reliability were more likely to reside. Are these qualities not cherished?

Perhaps it is precisely because boys are often perceived to lack these qualities that they are believed to need more overt encouragement than girls. In Betty Smith's *A Tree Grows in Brooklyn*, it is out of a cultural background similar to my own that Francie's mother speaks when she explains why she gives more encouragement to Francie's brother: "Neeley needs more encouragement. You can go on with what you have inside you, like I can. But he needs so much from outside." And when one child has to stay out of high school to work for a year, her mother chooses Francie, although Neeley wants to drop out: "'Because if I don't make him, he'll never go back,' said mama, 'where you, Francie, will fight and manage to get back somehow.'"[27]

Francie's mother's explanation made perfect sense to me when I read Betty Smith's book in high school—such perfect sense, in fact, that I have remembered it for fifty years and seen its truth confirmed many times throughout those years. It is this cultural disparity that may explain the incredulity I experience at the bitter recriminations of contemporary feminists who seem blessed with the best educational and material resources and yet think of themselves as oppressed victims and expect society to favor them to compensate for their alleged victimhood. One can speculate that the continuing and somewhat morbid dissatisfaction of these women, despite their evident success in the marketplace, indicates that market achievement is unlikely to affirm femininity and that pursuit of status as a virtual male clone negates one's distinctive worth as female.

Western men's tendency to overrate their market accomplishments now prevails almost wholly unchecked by feminine counterbalance. Society has largely acquiesced in feminism's championing of this male view and is overtly hostile to any defense of traditional femininity. Feminine counterbalance does not lie, as some would argue, in the efforts of "difference" feminists (so-called Gilliganism[28]) to reconstruct workplaces and reevaluate scholarship to reflect a distinctive female voice. The goal of difference feminists is not to affirm the worth of domesticity and child-rearing activities, but rather to domesticate, as it were, the workplace. Having relegated home and children to surrogates' care, they attempt to create a surrogate domestic haven for themselves within the marketplace—what I call the "feminist playpen." In her cogent criticism of the effort, for example, to reconceptualize art courses in order to " 'go beyond' the great public works of art, such as cathedrals, to look at what women have done," Christina Hoff Sommers concludes that "the loveliest quilt is plainly inferior to the canvases of Titian and Rembrandt."[29] But if difference feminism were ever to go beyond the feminist playpen and affirm the value of domesticity, then I would say—and I wonder if Sommers might agree—that in the sense of what counts most in life quiltmaking can indeed trump Titian.

It is now considered fatuous to question the view of male professionals that the ideal wife should be a clone of themselves and their workplace colleagues, clones who may also be expected to produce offspring without genuinely interfering with their market work. A woman who would assume only the roles of wife and mother is seen as inherently uninteresting and undesirable. Exemplifying this attitude is the explanation a law school classmate once gave for divorcing his first wife (a college graduate who was a traditional homemaker): she could not discuss the First Amendment with him and her lawyer replacement could. (Since the replacement was also replaced, one wonders if her insights into First Amendment jurisprudence proved to be hopelessly uninspired.) This friend's statement reflected today's attitude that the only important and interesting aspects of life occur in the workplace. Such view is a dramatic change from attitudes prevailing just forty years ago when the home and its activities were at least as important as the workplace. Social conversations then were supposed to be concerned with subjects other than one's work. It was once thought the mark of a very limited intellect if one's conversation turned more than briefly to workplace affairs; even in the most intellectual milieu a wife who was fairly well-read and apprised of current events could be a completely satisfactory companion and conversationalist.

Satirizing this attitudinal change reflected in our friend's explanation, my husband and I have speculated about "personals" in the classified seeking "a mate who can discuss the First, Fourth, and Fifth Amendments—not interested in the Second." But this attitude has led to tragedy, not farce. The fact that so many in our society— especially trend-setting intellectuals—have narrowed their interests to the world of work seriously inhibits family formation and maintenance of a satisfying family life. For a man to tell his wife that in order to interest him she must *act* as he does means she must perform market, at the expense of domestic, activities. This preoccupation with the public world of the workplace requires devoting herself to what a traditional woman views as the most peripheral and ephemeral aspects of life and shunting aside the private world of family relations once considered the stabilizing center of mankind's deepest concerns.

Although my husband and I both practiced law (and participated in First Amendment obscenity litigation, probably as interesting as any), our dinner conversation scarcely depended on our having both devoted ourselves to that work. When a man has worked all day on any intellectual activity—and frequently, as many lawyers do, nights and weekends as well—does he really want to devote his leisure conversation to detailed analyses of that same topic? Even if he does, why should it be necessary that his companion also participate in such activities in order to discuss them intelligently? Only those who have for too long taken themselves and their market activities too seriously could possibly think so. We once thought— and maintained more stable marriages when this was the case— that current events or what the children or the dog or the cat did that day were matters more at the center of life.

Another of our friends has written of arguing with his first wife about the validity of traditional sex roles, an argument he rarely won because he "could never find an adequate answer to her question: 'How would you like to change places with me?'"[30] For those firmly committed to a feminist ideology that posits the inferiority of women's traditional role, there is no adequate answer to the question. But not all women are so committed. For them, the question can be answered. Many men have been unable to do so because they have accepted the feminist ideology. It is these men who made possible the great success of the women's movement. Men will continue to relinquish the field to feminism until they learn a response that will affirm the value of women who perform a traditional role. If men fail, they leave women no choice but to travel a feminist path to seek affirmation of their worth. This path, a man should understand, is extremely demanding and can leave very little of the woman for him or their children.

THE EXPERT CULTURE

The simmering discontent aroused by Western society's bias for male achievement was compounded by women's increasing dissatisfaction with the roles of mother and housewife. As sociologists have observed, a person is affected not so much by a particular situation as by how that situation is defined.[31] The housewife's role became less attractive the more it was analyzed by sociologists. My own experience has convinced me the role plays out a lot better than it reads in the script. The Bergers have described how the rational analysis of science and technology was applied to make the family "an object of scientific quantification and experiment," so that family members began to feel like "participants in an engineering enterprise." The most intimate human relationships lost their naturalness and spontaneity as they came to be viewed as "other-directed mechanisms": "good home," "healthy sexuality," "good marriage," "good relationship"—the "goodness" in each case "being determined by the allegedly scientific standards proclaimed and administered by the experts."[32]

In subjecting the family to scientific analysis, these experts analogized a wife's roles to jobs in the workplace. But the homemaker has a nebulous job description and lacks specific qualifications or training. When "professional" standards of achievement are set for such a job, one can easily doubt both the job's desirability and one's own ability to do it well. Helena Lopata has described the housewife's role as lacking the basic criteria of a job: no organized social circle sets qualifications, tests for competence, or dismisses for incompetence. Nor is there a set pay scale for the job of housewife; in the ordinary sense, there is no pay at all. The role never receives a high social prestige, a homemaker being "typically portrayed as someone who needs little intelligence, since the duties are routine and narrow in scope." As society has assigned increasing importance to education and has given prestige to work proportional to the education it requires, the housewife's role—perceived as requiring no education at all—has become even less prestigious.[33]

Lopata's interviews with housewives, on the other hand, disclosed that respect for the knowledge required of them increased in proportion to the respondent's level of education; many of them regretted the lack of specific training for the homemaking role. Lopata concluded that working women, many of whom were not deeply concerned with the housewife's role and performed it minimally, believed the role required no special skills; but those who were "performing the role of housewife in a complex and creatively competent manner see it as requiring many different areas of knowledge."[34] This conclusion accords with my own experience that the familiar metaphor of peeling an onion best describes the housewife's role, for it is only when one undertakes the task that one can appreciate its magnitude.

Because of its indeterminacy, the housewife's role very likely requires more self-motivation than any other. A homemaker has maximum freedom to define the scope of her duties and obtain whatever knowledge she believes their performance requires; hence her dilemma. Sociologists had established that much is expected of the housewife; surely, it is she who must actualize for her family all those "goods" being analyzed and quantified. Yet she is never told exactly what she is expected to do or how she should go about doing it. In the 1950s and 1960s the fact that upwardly mobile suburbanites had often abandoned their ethnic subcultures exacerbated the difficulty of assuming this burden of freedom, for the older generation that had traditionally helped the housewife was much underutilized.[35]

These difficulties were particularly acute for women who were also mothers. Their role had received the most attention from psychiatrists, psychologists, and social workers of the "helping professions," who made it abundantly clear that the likelihood of successfully performing this role was slim indeed. These "helping professions" attributed the psychological problems then plaguing society (insignificant in comparison with today) to the family's failure to secure each child's healthy psychological development. That task, said these practitioners, required child-rearing by professionals trained in the requisite psychological skills, a view that seriously undermined the ordinary mother's confidence in her own ability to do the job properly.

Such were the attitudes, says Christopher Lasch, that caused psychiatrists from the 1940s on to see themselves as doctors to a sick society in which the "training of children is making a thousand neurotics for every one that psychiatrists can hope to help with psychotherapy." Educators and psychiatrists believed they must "assume the burdens of parenthood, so wretchedly performed by most parents." This perception of near universal parental failure underlay the sociological theory that modeled the family on a doctor-patient relationship and postulated an identity "between illness and the status of the child in the family." It was this therapeutic view of the family that brought "domestic life under the growing domination of outside experts." The proliferation of their often conflicting advice, which itself varied with changes in psychiatric fashions, greatly eroded parents' confidence.[36] The better educated the woman the more likely she was to be aware of and disturbed by these trends. The woman who had performed successfully in school and work, where she knew the goals and how to achieve them, was especially struck by how very poorly marked is the path to success in motherhood in our society.

Any suggestion that women were frightened away from child-rearing by the awesome responsibility it entailed must now seem fatuous to a society that has largely accepted the feminist view that child-rearing—even of the youngest infants—is a task that requires few skills, presents no challenges, and can be safely left to the impersonal care of a day care center. It seems counterintuitive today to say that trends of the 1940s and 1950s aroused women's dissatisfaction with a traditional role precisely because that role seemed complicated, even overwhelming. The life of today's two-career family is predicated on precisely the opposite view that, being inherently uninteresting, undemanding, and unnecessary, the homemaker role is easily jettisoned.

The analyses of Lasch and Lopata are, nonetheless, completely accurate. When, over forty-five years ago, my female college classmates and I discussed the attractions of graduate school, we were, of course, making freer choices than women now make. Unlike today, when all the cultural expectations are that women will pursue market careers, society was not pushing us to obtain more education, nor did it think us inferior for failing to do so. The very last thought on our minds would have been that failure to acquire further education and pursue careers would ever diminish our desirability as wives. In this we were wrong, as events demonstrated, and many of our contemporaries paid a very heavy price for this lack of foresight when—with the blessing of no-fault divorce laws—they were often supplanted by their husbands' younger colleagues.

Our discussions left no doubt that most of us who were preparing for graduate school were apprehensive about the prospect of being housewives and mothers. Market production seemed much simpler and safer: we knew what would be expected of us and believed we could do it well. Far from picturing housewifery and motherhood as dull and undemanding, we suspected they required social skills we did not possess. We were confident, on the other hand, that our academic skills promised success in the workplace. While that workplace beckoned as a ready-made niche of structured security, the home repulsed as a vast expanse of emptiness we felt inadequate to fill. Constructing an edifice of domesticity seemed to require capabilities that we did not naturally possess and our education had not provided.

Somewhere beyond remoteness was the prospect of motherhood, an event we could contemplate only in a far distant future when we had somehow acquired the necessary psychological background and training. Probably, our own psychoanalysis would be best, but at a minimum, extensive counseling was a prerequisite; the alternative would be psychological disaster for our children. In short, like the very conscientious students we were, we had absorbed everything the helping professions were preaching about our inadequacy for a job that all viewed as important and demanding. The workplace offered us a structured haven from an indeterminate future in a role for which we felt hopelessly ill-equipped. Fortunately maturity, experience, and a good man can cast a new light on perceived inadequacies.

In our case, as with many women, intrusion by experts had undermined whatever intuitive confidence and capability our femininity might have given us. It is for this reason, Geoffrey Gorer said, that the American mother "can never have the easy, almost unconscious, self-assurance of the mother of more patterned societies, who is following ways she knows unquestioningly to be right."[37] This truth became apparent to me when, one month after I stopped practicing law, my first child was born. I may well have been the most educated woman on the maternity floor at that time, but no one could have felt less confident. Still believing the answer to all problems was more knowledge, I consulted with the head of pediatric nursing, complaining that, despite classes in child care, I lacked adequate information to deal with this increasingly frightening responsibility. Offering what I came to appreciate as the best possible advice, she assured me that I had more than enough information. My baby, she advised, would let me know what she needed— I had only to relax, be receptive, and respond to the cues I received from her.

That it may be difficult to follow this advice, when one has been accustomed to a job that requires a high level of aggression for success, does not diminish its validity. It does indicate, however, that much reeducation may be necessary before women, who have learned to rely for their success on knowledge, technique, and the processing of information, can be confident and competent mothers. Even the mother who has learned "home remedies" from her kin within a patterned subculture can be intimidated by the conviction of experts in the helping professions that their own views are "scientifically superior" to those of ignorant laymen. The confidence of a mother who accepts the experts' authority, Lasch noted, is further undermined by the fact that she is accepting "measurement of her child's development against a normative standard to which it rarely conforms."[38]

Helena Lopata documented the increasing difficulty of learning child-rearing procedures once families abandoned traditional formulas and sought knowledge from medical and psychologcial experts. Compounding this difficulty was the fact that the mother bore almost the entire responsibility for child-rearing without support from the extended kinship group that formerly had lived with or near her. This responsibility seemed heavier because of the discontinuity between child care and the training increasingly larger numbers of women were receiving in school and work that taught them to be task-oriented, organize work in blocks of time, and measure achievement by a finished product.[39] By contrast, the salient characteristic of a mother's role, my own experience taught me, should be cheerful responsiveness to constant interruptions—the antithesis of organizing anything in blocks of time. And because I saw my goal as a mother to be simply the contentment and well-being of my household, the product is never finished.

Many respondents in Lopata's interviews complained of having to make very important decisions as mothers while feeling incompetent to do so: a mother would frequently express "self-doubt over her ability to function effectively in the dimensions opened up by the knowledge explosion." Mothers were especially disturbed by the feeling of "being pulled in all directions by all members of the family," so that they must constantly make choices between family members as to whose is the most important need. Just as they had recognized the vast scope of the housewife's role, the better-educated women also experienced the problems of motherhood the most keenly; the least-educated woman was the most likely to say there are no problems because "you know what you have to do and go on and do it." Mothers with a college education were the most concerned about the emotional responsibilities of child-rearing, particularly their own responsibility for successfully managing complicated family conflicts. They were the women who most appreciated the "great potential in the role of mother" and stressed its "creative and influential aspects."[40]

It was, in the phrase of sociologist Talcott Parsons, the "profes-sionalization of parenthood" that made parents distrust their own child-rearing abilities and competence to deal with family prob-lems and to accept that their capabilities were inferior to those of experts in the professional child-rearing establishment.[41] These professionals, Rita Kramer observed, not only set the standards for performance of a parental role but also argued that since par-ents are "rank amateurs," they should "be replaced by professional parents . . . by children's caretakers prepared professionally for the arts and science of children's socialization."[42] The logical culmi-nation of this theory, Lasch concluded, was the "supersession of the family and the assignment of child rearing to trained experts," more suited to the task than the "amateurs and dilettantes" who were the parents.[43]

Through these ideas, the helping professions not only under-mined the confidence of "amateur" parents but also encouraged and justified the surrogate child-rearing that is a precondition of mothers' entry into the work force. They emphasized how crucially important the child-nurturing role is and how injurious the effects of improper child-rearing are to children's psychological adjustment. But the ironic result has been that their teachings encourage the relinquishing of that crucial nurturing role by the very individuals who would logically be the most devoted to their children's welfare.

Assuming that it matters very much what happens in a child's daily life, there is no cogent basis for favoring surrogate care. None but a limited number of the very best child care establishments (or the very best nannies) do, in fact, provide care which even remotely resembles care by professionals educated in the latest child-rearing techniques. But even if this were not the case, the happiness and well-being of infants and young children depend very little on any specific knowledge or technique employed by a caregiver. They depend far more on responsiveness to need as undivided as pos-sible and on a continuing, loving interaction with a person to whom *this* child is uniquely precious. In the eyes of such a person, what this child does is happening for the first time. And this child knows that what he does is incomparably important *because* this person thinks it so. Those of us who reject surrogate care for our children doubt that such response to our child is likely to come from any worker in a day care center or from an average nanny. It is a response that cannot be taught; and rarely can it be bought.

THE ANDROGYNOUS CULTURE

All great revolutionary movements, de Riencourt contends, "are triggered by earthquaking shifts in women's feelings" which occur in response not to ideology, but to "specific, concrete grievances" that overcome women's natural conservatism and lead them to seek a fundamental change in their lives.[44] One such grievance was the waning of masculinity that our society had witnessed for at least several decades before the 1960s. It is surely not contentment and sexual fulfillment that the disaffected, often distraught, woman exhibits when vehemently proclaiming her grievances against men. She might sometimes be described, on the contrary, as having—in words Ernest Hemingway applied to the opposite sex—the air of a dog in heat.[45] Ironically, as the Bergers note, feminist wrath was turned upon what had become, by the late 1950s, the "father figure of diminished and comic status."[46] But that diminished status was itself a factor in evoking the wrath. Commenting on the "inexplicable rage among contemporary women," Michael Novak queries whether it does not stem from the fact that men are not masculine enough. The capitulation of so many men before feminist rhetoric, moreover, must "only increase the rage, by proving its unconscious point."[47]

Men, according to Dr. Harold Voth, have abdicated their leadership position in the family as, with each generation, they "have tended to become progressively less responsible and more passive, retiring—even effeminate—and women more domineering and aggressive and masculinized."[48] Writing in 1948, Margaret Mead had perceived this trend, describing the "little girls and boys of kindergarten age," facing each other "with the same stance, the same gleam in their eyes, the same readiness to fight or to avoid fighting." Although boys and girls were being raised more and more alike, the little girl appeared to have been given "greater resources than her brother," for her relationships to her father are "less exacting and more immediately rewarding" than are her brother's to his mother. As a result, a girl emerging from childhood is more sure of herself than is a boy. In other cultures, "the mother who bows her head before the lordly maleness of her four-year-old son encourages his assurance as a male," but in our culture, the mother's role is one of "demandingness towards husband and son." Thus, girls see their fathers and later their husbands as requiring "a lot of working on"—"no victory is a final one, but must be re-enacted the next day"—while boys see their mothers and later their wives as the source of "assurance that they are good."[49]

These attitudes described by Margaret Mead reflect what I have recognized in myself as a common female characteristic, one which George Eliot had long since memorialized in *Middlemarch*, published in 1872. In that book, Mary Garth explains her love for Fred Vincy by saying she "should never like scolding any one else so well; and that is a point to be thought of in a husband," for "husbands are an inferior class of men, who require keeping in order." And when Fred protests that his rival is "ten times worthier of you than I," Mary replies that "to be sure he was"; "for that reason he could do better without me."[50]

Changes in the American family's power structure were documented in Lopata's interviews in the mid-1960s, which disclosed women's widespread perception that men had lost power in the family. Men were frequently described as having been "king," "czar," "lord and master," or "ruler" three generations ago; now, said respondents, they were on an equal footing with their wives. While most women appeared satisfied with men's loss of power, some voiced hostility towards men's perceived status as "emasculated," "inse-cure," and "deteriorated."[51]

One striking manifestation of these changes was an increased sharing by men in "home-maintaining functions." Interviews with suburban women (very few of whom worked outside the home) disclosed, for example, that 41 percent of husbands helped their wives with cooking and cleaning up after meals, 39 percent assisted with household cleaning tasks, 34 percent with laundry and other forms of clothing care, and 64 percent with shopping; 66 percent of husbands with young children assisted with care of their children.[52] Betty Friedan had already commented in 1963 on the suburban husband's "meek willingness to wax the floor and wash the dishes when he comes home tired on the 6:55."[53]

It is significant—and probably a source of resentment on men's part—that so many husbands were performing household tasks even though their wives were not employed outside the home. My husband and I divided domestic chores equally when I was in the work force, at least as equally as an unfussy Italian male can divide chores with an Irish female from a culture that proclaimed clean-liness to be next to Godliness. (This particular drawback to shar-ing domestic chores was addressed by a Chinese woman whose husband was responsible for shopping and washing clothes: "But nothing seems to get clean when he does it because he doesn't wash thoroughly."[54]) Once I left the work force, however, I would have thought it unreasonable (except in emergencies) to expect my husband to perform routine household tasks, other than play with the children. Nor did we regard his playing with the children as a chore. It was an enjoyable part of his daily routine, which it easily can be at the end of a workday when one has no other household responsibilities.

With respect to financial matters, Lopata's interviews disclosed that in 37 percent of the families finances were handled jointly, in another 37 percent they were handled by the husband, and in 21 percent by the wife. Among suburban respondents, however, 41 percent of the wives and 27 percent of the husbands took complete responsibility for financial matters, the remainder handling them together.[55] Wives' substantial participation in financial matters is also significant. I always managed the finances in our family but never realized how common this was in suburban households. One of the accepted feminist myths is that a traditional wife had very little control over, and was usually kept in ignorance of, her family's financial affairs—a criticism obviously wide of the mark.

Is it the case, then, that Philip Wylie had it right in *Generation of Vipers*? Probably partly right. He did identify some real problems, but unfairly attributed most of the blame to women. Wylie coined the word "momism" to describe a domineering and emasculating mother of the modern middle-class family. But when women became more aggressive, more masculine, they were often filling a void left by the waning masculinity of men. Wylie's "mom" evolved, as Lasch noted, in response to a father who was "weak and acquiescent at home."[56] Society's dilemma was captured in Wylie's observation that the "mealy look of men today is the result of momism and so is the pinched and baffled fury in the eyes of womankind."[57] Yet, how much mealier the men, and angrier the women, in the years after he wrote those words.

This widening chasm between men and women fostered a deterioration in family relationships that culminated in our 1960s youth rebellion with its rejection of traditional values, a rebellion possible only after a widespread decay of patriarchal authority. A prescient Wylie had seen this decay manifested in "mom's" premature yet successful encouragement of her son to defy his father's authority. The son's triumph further emasculated the father and—because the son was too young for independence and had achieved it only through an unholy alliance with his mother—the son as well. Thus, said Wylie in his pungent prose, "mom has thrust her oar into the very guts of man."[58]

Our youth rebellion was indeed a feminist triumph, constituting as it did the most far-reaching acceptance of androgyny and devaluation of masculinity our society had ever witnessed. It was also a triumph of femininity or feminization which, as James Nuechterlein has observed, is very different from a feminist ideology that rejects most attributes of the "feminine."[59] What matters above all to the traditional, feminine woman are her children and her motherhood: the woman nursing her baby knows—in a way a man can never know—that she is the center of the universe. She feels in her bones the truth of Steven Goldberg's insight that "ultimately she is the one who matters": "The central role will forever belong to women; they set the rhythm of things. Women everywhere are aware that sublimation is an ignorance of the center. . . . Nature has bestowed on women the biological abilities and bio-psychological propensities that enable the species to sustain itself. Men must forever stand at the periphery, questing after the surrogate powers, creativity, and meaning that nature has not seen fit to make innate functions of *their* biology."[60]

It is this feminine narcissism that the philosopher Oswald Spengler described when he said woman "experiences the Man and the Sons only in relation to herself and her ordained role."[61] A woman's single-minded narcissism (that will usually include the man she loves within the ambit of her self-satisfaction) enables her to face childbirth and motherhood, well serving the woman (and thus society) in performing her biological role. Society is disserved, however, when women are permitted by weak men to convince a generation of young men to embrace a feminine narcissism. Yet this is what our effete males allowed to happen from the late 1960s into the 1970s, when women in revolt fostered what came to be called the generation gap of the youth rebellion.

Feminist revolutionaries illustrated de Riencourt's observation that the woman who becomes sufficiently "frustrated by her unsatisfactory relationship with the other sex" "will invariably attempt to rouse her children against their father."[62] Our disastrous experience in Vietnam evidenced feminization triumphant, when the sons who had been roused against their fathers—even against the concept of masculinity itself—embraced a feminine pacifism. Denouncing what she called "an obscene, immoral war like the one in Vietnam," Betty Friedan accurately characterized the actions of war protesters (including her own son) at the 1968 Democratic National Convention in Chicago as "defying the masculine mystique as we had defied the feminine one."[63]

Pervasive feminine pacifism and narcissism at that time undermined the virtues of patriotism, loyalty, courage, and decisiveness and led to our sending men to fight a war under conditions that made victory impossible. Under the derisive onslaught of contemporary feminism, femininity had been deflected away from domestic endeavors within the home and had taken hold in the public arena. One result was, in Nuechterlein's words, that a "war gone terribly wrong aroused protest not only against itself but against virtually any expression of American power."[64] This feminizing of our public life has increased, not diminished, producing an America that Christopher Caldwell has described as "less and less congenial to men"[65] — and I would add, to those women who do not think feminized males suit either their own or society's needs.

In *The New People: Desexualization in American Life*, Charles Winick skillfully analyzes the process of male feminization and female masculinization that, by the end of the 1960s, had produced a society in which a significant number of boys and girls and men and women were fast becoming androgynous.[66] Winick documents the unprecedented neutering of our society through a detailed examination of music and dancing, fiction, painting, the theater, men's and women's clothing, the phenomenal increase in the use of beauty products by men, our manner of speaking, the names given to children, recreational activities, and the manner of consummating sexual relations.

Winick observes one example of this process in the change from ballroom dancing to the rock and roll dancing in the discotheques of the 1960s. Ballroom dancing reinforces masculinity: the dance is predicated on physical contact between the partners with the male assuming a dominant position as "leader" in a sequence of steps; other men comprise a stag line from which a man may "cut in" on a dancing couple, choosing the woman he would, in turn, lead through the dance. Little imagination is required to understand—and those raised in an era of ballroom dancing knew—that this dance was symbolic of the sex act in which the man also is the leader.

By contrast, partners in the discotheque do not touch "but each shimmies around the axis of his own body." Dancing which had once been a symbol of "man-woman interaction"—with a "definite leader and follower, as in the traditional courtship type of dance"—was replaced by the rock and roll dance. This new style with its "autistic, self-absorbed actors" is symbolic of the identical, hard-edged, and independent participants who seemed to be communing only with themselves on the dance floor.[67] Again, it requires little imagination to perceive the sexual symbolism of a dance that replaced complementary interaction with solitary, individualized display.

We have experienced the changes documented by Winick as part of our daily lives and have usually accepted them as natural evolutions of style and taste. That some of the practices have seemed novel, somewhat daring, or even perverse has often generated an excitement that facilitated their adoption. Only several decades ago, for example, the beauty shop was a female domain where women—who usually wanted to be at their best when seen by men—underwent refurbishment safe from male scrutiny. But in the span of a few years, the beauty shop evolved into a place where a woman might sit like a drowned rat having her hair cut, colored, and permed, while next to her men were having their hair cut, colored, and blow-dried. Women could hardly help thinking that those blow-dried, perfumed, bejeweled men were more like us than we were.

All of the developments Winick analyzes tend towards androgyny. While androgyny advances the feminist cause, it is for the traditional person the ultimate perversion. Because of its essential elimination of what is singularly masculine or feminine, an ideology of androgyny is an attack on the biological constitution of society, a muting of the excitement created by that sexual distinctiveness and complementarity most conducive to satisfying heterosexuality. The widespread desexualization of our lives through a proliferation of androgynous styles has created fallow soil for growth of contemporary feminism. Societal acceptance of androgyny has validated feminist efforts to trivialize sexual differences. When androgyny becomes fashionable, women will become diffident about, even somewhat ashamed of, the sexual differentiation announced by their reproductive capability. Striving to become more like men, they will eschew the distinctively feminine satisfactions inherent in being female.

The Emasculated Culture

Philip Wylie concluded that woman was the problem, but he never entirely gave up on her. While his sympathies were always with the male, he launched his vicious, impassioned attack so that women would improve their performance as wives and mothers, not abandon these roles altogether. Another kind of male appeared, however, who was a much more formidable enemy of the woman who wished to be a wife and mother. Like the homosexual, he wants an alliance with neither. It may seem harsh to characterize as unfavorable to women men who do not want to marry and raise children, but the description is justified because they decrease the pool of men available to women who seek husbands.

Some of these men are, of course, members of a celibate priesthood, operating within an institutional framework that views the forsaking of marriage and family as a necessary sacrifice; at the same time, it always stresses the marital family's overarching value to that institution and society. Other such men, however, shun the responsibilities of marriage and family without institutional justification. Their idiosyncratic behavior poses a minimal threat so long as they are a small minority of the population which maintains a low profile. When their numbers increase, however, or they commend their behavior as appropriate, even socially desirable, then all who acknowledge the primacy of family life—particularly women who desire a husband and children—must recognize and deal with the challenge these men represent.

In *The Hearts of Men: American Dreams and the Flight From Commitment*, feminist Barbara Ehrenreich cogently analyzes the societal impact of males who have eschewed a role as supporter of wife and family and withdrawn from the marriage market.[68] Describing the "breadwinner ethic" of the 1950s that encouraged men to marry, become reliable jobholders, and support their wives and children, she accurately observes that this ethic was reinforced by a societal perception that one doing otherwise was "less than a man." By the end of the 1970s, however, this ethic was so eroded that the "man who postpones marriage even into middle age, who avoids women who are likely to become financial dependents, who is dedicated to his own pleasures, is likely to be found not suspiciously deviant, but 'healthy.' "[69]

Erosion of the breadwinner ethic, Ehrenreich argues, began well before revival of, rather than in reaction to, the feminist movement. In this she is certainly correct. The male retreat from commitment to marriage and family that she describes so well must be counted as one of the primary causes of the female discontent that revived the feminist movement. Yet, from the perspective of women who hoped to benefit from a breadwinner ethic, feminists completely misdirected their response. Not only did their rhetoric accelerate male retreat, as the two revolts fed upon each other, but feminists themselves rejected the breadwinner ethic, echoing every complaint the male rebels lodged against what both camps depicted as "parasitical" housewives. When the stallions champed at the bit—a habit of stallions that should not defeat women's attempt to domesticate them—feminists removed the bit from their mouths, opened the barn door, and told them to go about their business, an outcome acceptable only to women with little long-term interest in stallions.

One explanation for the male rebellion was white-collar males' dissatisfaction with their lives of "other-directed" conformity described in David Reisman's *The Lonely Crowd* in 1950.[70] Eight years before, Philip Wylie had already deplored the male's pitiful imprisonment within an increasingly centralized and bureaucratized society, attributing creation of that society to the evil "mom." Mom, he said, invented bureaucracies because they emasculate by crushing initiative and rewarding conformity: "mom is organization-minded," having found that organizations "are intimidating to all men."[71]

Ridiculing the "nonsensical notion of honoring and rewarding women for nothing more than being female," Wylie berated men for heaping cash at women's feet, thereby giving them control of "most of our fixed wealth" and "an inordinate power." In order to support a "huge class of idle, middle-aged women," he lamented, "a great nation of brave and dreaming men" have had to abandon their dreams and "take a stockroom job in the hairpin factory." Then, having set out on the "road to hell" that this job portended, the luckless man is blindfolded by the pretty girl "so he would not see that she was turning from a butterfly into a caterpillar." Telling the man that "although caterpillars ate every damned leaf in sight, they were moms, hence sacred," "she snitched his checkbook." "Thus," Wylie concluded, "the women of America raped the men," indenturing them to degrading labor in order to satisfy mom's ever-increasing demands for more consumer goods.[72]

Almost three decades later, feminists responded to the rejection of women proclaimed in Wylie's powerful prose by, in turn, rejecting female dependence upon men. Feminists declined the alternative of defending a dependence that requires women to accept what to some of us seems the exhilarating challenge of domesticating these stallions and helping them come to appreciate the rewards—and there surely can be many—of toiling in the hairpin factory for us and our children.

Wylie issued his manifesto against mom in 1942, challenging men to "face the dynasty of the dames at once, deprive them of our pocketbooks when they waste the substance in them, and take back our dreams which, without the perfidious materialism of mom, were shaping up a new and braver world."[73]   Eleven years later, men publicly accepted Wylie's challenge when the first issue of *Playboy* magazine was published with a nude Marilyn Monroe as its centerfold. The passage of years demonstrated how fitting was this choice: she was everything both male rebels and feminists expected of the new woman, liberated at last from what feminists depicted as the stifling cocoon spun by the oppressive patriarchy.

Liberated Monroe surely was. Pursuing a successful career until she died a suicide at age 36, she depended on no breadwinner. Not requiring the sexual revolution to unfetter her from any vestiges of constricting morality, she was the paradigmatic sexually liberated woman. Diana Trilling described her as sleeping her way to her early opportunities and, once famous, continuing to be "compliant" in numberless sexual encounters with men and "on occasion" another woman. Finally, she was no mom for, to her great sadness, Monroe was unable to give birth (one of her suicide attempts followed a miscarriage); this failure, one might speculate, could have been related to the fact that "she had had a dozen or more abortions."[74]

Our society now chooses to protect and celebrate the independence from men that these abortions represent. But for some of us the plight of a woman whose body is violated in this fashion—while never once experiencing the joy of giving birth—is as great a degradation of womanhood as any society has ever accomplished. Whatever derelictions Wylie's sometimes foolish moms were guilty of, women could not have deserved this fate. It was and is the lot of many because only the ready availability of abortion affords what both feminists and the male rebels value most highly: the complete freedom of sex without responsibility, which guarantees that the female objects of men's sexual attentions will remain independent.

Playboy trumpeted the message that to be free a man had to be single. The sexual revolution it zealously promoted with feminism's able assistance guaranteed that plenty of sex was available, nonetheless, and at a much lower cost than marriage. While *Playboy* depicted men as fools for working to support wives and children, it never disparaged sex or work as such. As Ehrenreich so aptly puts it, *Playboy* "loved women—large-breasted, long-legged young women, anyway—and hated wives." And work was justified simply to satisfy men's own consumer interests in acquiring the stereos, sports cars, toiletries, and designer clothes heavily advertised in the magazine. A man, Ehrenreich observes, "could display his status or simply flaunt his earnings without possessing either a house or a wife." As protection against the charge of homosexuality, which had always been the "ultimate sanction against male rebellion," the Playmate was there to prove that "a playboy didn't have to be a husband to be a man."[75]

The great irony was that the institution which took up the gauntlet thrown down by Wylie to challenge "the perfidious materialism of mom" and take back men's dreams of a "new and braver world" espoused only a dream of consumerism writ large. It offered a hedonistic vision of conspicuous consumption by single men that was surely neither new nor brave but only more selfish than the acquisitiveness of Wylie's mom on behalf of her family.

The "Beats," popularized in Jack Kerouac's *On the Road*,[76] and the mimicking "beatniks" continued the male revolt against family life through a rebellion that extended to the world of work and the consumer consumption work supported. Our media accorded these new rebels a visibility that further popularized men who, in Ehrenreich's words, "refused to undertake the support of women and seemed to get away with it."[77] They also got away with something else equally inimical to women's interests: their obvious attachment to each other and to the male adventures that they found much more interesting than female companionship. While the playboy avowed that he enjoyed sex with women a great deal—and rejected only the responsibility of wives and children—the Beat had women but made clear that he neither needed nor enjoyed them much at all. It was but a short step from the Beat's indifference to women to the homosexual's complete rejection of them. This rejection became increasingly less stigmatized partly because of the missionary work the Beats had performed in conditioning society to view women and the responsibilities they created as uninteresting, unrewarding, and unnecessary.

Further undermining the breadwinner ethic were the medical facts that, by 1970, women's life expectancy of 75 years was eight years longer than men's, and men were three times more likely to die prematurely from heart disease. These results, Ehrenreich notes, were frequently attributed to the stress of men's breadwinning responsibilities that could, according to one commentator, "make many men feel tense and anxious at all times." In contrast, the job of homemaker allowed the woman to "relax and let some things go," "find time for interesting hobbies," and "vary her activities." Men, it was suggested, should lower their career goals and "regress to a more feminine, dependent state," while wives should decrease the pressure on their men by lowering their own material expectations. Blame was soon assigned, however, to the institution of the one-income family. Marya Mannes, for example, indicted the "millions of women [who] still claim that they find total fulfillment as homemakers" even though "the price of their fulfillment is the death by continuous strain of the men who provided it."[78]

Various forms of pop psychology such as the Human Potential Movement provided a final apologia for the retreating male. Rejecting society's right to set standards of deviancy, conformity, or maturity, these faddish movements freed people—in that 1970s cliche—to "do their own thing" by seeking self-fulfillment according to their own unique growth pattern.[79] This quest culminated in the androgynous males of Charles Reich's *The Greening of America*[80] who exemplified the hippie counterculture's abandonment of any standards of masculinity. Reich found the practice of law offensive because the "atmosphere in the firm was so often full of tension, overconcern, and uncomfortable pressure," and lawyers—who exhibited "anxiety" and "a total absorption in their work"—were "fiercely competitive," "tough-minded," and "hard-nosed." Marriage was out of the question because it meant "staying permanently in my present job" and "children" and "spending all of my time with one person" and "being 'adult'," which meant "no more hope of excitement, no more fun."[81] Dedicated to a hedonistic satisfaction of all appetites, the counterculture Reich promoted rejected middle-class, professional goals of "status, promotion, institutional approval, and a correct image for the outside world." Members of Reich's new generation would abandon the "aggressive, disciplined, competitive pursuit of definite goals" and recover their true self, their new consciousness, based on "a non-material set of values."[82]

Those women who were propelled into that same competitive marketplace which had so offended Charles Reich can easily be seen to have filled a void created by the retreating males. This retreat had been manifested in the decision by playboys, Beats, and hippies to reject the value of women's traditional role and of men's contributions that make the role viable. But without those contributions, one must wonder, what do men think will define their masculinity? If the woman's traditional role is expendable, then, as increases in the number of well-educated, never-married mothers indicate, so also is the man expendable for all purposes other than sperm donor; a relative handful can, of course, perform that function.[83] When men who no longer value the traditional role of either sex abandon women to fend for themselves in the marketplace, they teach these women to cease valuing men.

THE CONSUMER CULTURE

Writing at the height of feminist activism, economist Richard Easterlin argued that factors such as declining birth rates and increases in rates of crime, youth suicides, illegitimacy, divorce, and the number of working mothers were all a function of large generation size. These factors should markedly decrease, he said, as the baby bust generation, coming of age in the 1990s, entered an improved labor market for young adults. While recognizing that this was a minority view, he claimed that there would also be an increase in both earlier marriage and the birth rate and a decline in the number of younger women working outside the home, accompanied by an increase in work outside the home for older women.[84] Analyses of the United States Bureau of Labor Statistics have confirmed some of Easterlin's predictions.[85]

The Importance of Relative Income

Those born into a "baby boom" generation (the description for a period of high national birth rate, the most recent being 1945-60) face greater job competition throughout their lives, and it is from the concomitant economic distress, Easterlin argued, that most other unfortunate social phenomena flow. The claim that young women curtailed child-bearing and entered the job market for economic, not ideological, reasons is supported by several analyses. On the basis of numerous surveys, Easterlin concluded that traditional sex-role attitudes still predominated, with a man being judged on whether he was a "good provider" and a woman on whether she was a "good mother"; the man was generally seen as being a full-time worker throughout his life, while the woman was expected to drop out of the labor force to raise several children at home. Women were seen as holding traditionally female jobs and, despite the declining birth rate, there was great tolerance for large families and intolerance for a one-child family or childlessness. In a national survey of high school seniors in 1977, seven out of ten rated as not acceptable the situation in which both parents of preschool children work full time, over one-half of the remainder gave this situation the second lowest rating, and four out of five gave the two highest ratings to the traditional arrangement in which the husband works full time and the wife does not work.[86]

Helena Lopata had reached similar conclusions on the basis of her surveys, conducted six years earlier, which showed that no matter what roles the surveyed women played outside the home—either in the job market or in community affairs—they restricted the roles women are "supposed to play" to the family institution. An overwhelming majority of those surveyed felt that "every woman should be married, that she should have children, and that none but family roles should be of even secondary importance to her before, during, or after the time that she is intensely involved in these relations by virtue of the life cycle." The only exceptions to this view were expressed by highly-educated and affluent women.[87] While the ideal still retained vitality, its actualization was thwarted, said Easterlin, due to perceived economic necessity, not the triumph of feminist ideology.

Appraisal of economic need is always a function of expectations. While young people appraise their earning potential on the basis of conditions in the labor market, they base their material aspirations on the pattern set in the family environment in which they grew up. When the birth rate dropped to a new low in 1976 (14.7 per 1000), young people were entering a job market crowded with other baby boomers, while carrying with them material aspirations based on the past income of their parents who had been competing in a baby-bust job market. Although earnings have been increasing since 1957, they have been exceeded by the upward trend in aspirations; as a result, relative income—the ratio between earnings and aspirations—has steadily declined. In 1957 a young man's prospective income could alone support 73 percent of a couple's aspired standard of living, while in 1978 it could support only 54 percent of that standard. This decline in relative income, Easterlin argued, caused an increased entry of young women into the work force, the postponing of marriages, declining birth rates, and failure to legitimate conceptions out of wedlock.[88]

The theory that a decline in relative income largely explains young women's increased entrance into the workplace is buttressed by the inadequacy of alternative explanations. Most women were not attracted by career opportunities from which they were previously barred. Women workers remained concentrated mainly in 20 of the 480 job categories listed by the United States Department of Labor; these jobs were always regarded as typically female, either clerical or resembling activities done within the home, frequently of a "nurturant" nature (teaching, social work, nursing, waitressing, and hairdressing). Nor were women attracted by higher wages. In 1977 full-time, year-round women workers earned 58.5 percent as much as men, slightly below the long-term average.

Neither was women's increased work force participation a response to growing demand in those fields in which female employees are concentrated. There were greater opportunities in those fields in the 1950s, when there were unprecedented demands for female workers in the seriously understaffed fields of nursing and teaching, and yet young women could not be lured out of their homes and into these occupations. And finally, the explanation was not women's increased educational attainments. In 1977 women in their late twenties had 0.7 years more education than their counterparts in 1960, but in 1960 women had 2.2 years more education than their counterparts in 1940; women in 1960 nevertheless largely declined to enter the job market. Moreover, in the 1940s and 1950s young women had more years of education than young men; by 1977, when the rate of female participation in the work force had greatly increased, young men had a slight educational advantage.[89]

Easterlin did not believe feminist ideology had caused young women to seek employment. He did think, however, that their employment caused them to support the women's movement because people favor ideological viewpoints consistent with their behavior, and a woman does not want to believe her employment harms her marriage or her children. He concluded, nevertheless, that (except among highly-educated persons) feminism will not have sufficiently undermined societal acceptance of traditional sex roles to prevent baby boom conditions sometime in the 1990s, when increased relative income would permit substantial female withdrawal from the work-place.[90] Relevant to Easterlin's prediction is the 10-percent decline that has occurred in the rate of approval given traditional sex roles by high school students surveyed ten years after the study he cited. Nevertheless, 52 percent of the surveyed students still found unacceptable the full-time employment of both parents of pre-school children.[91]

The Myth Of Economic Necessity

Whether or not Easterlin's predictions eventually prove accurate, his analysis underestimated how much contemporary feminism has influenced women's decisions. Although economic factors deter-mine one-half of the relative income equation, attitudes and value judgments account for the other half. The women's movement profoundly affected the attitudes and value judgments on which baby boomers relied when weighing their material aspirations against the importance of family life. Their own backgrounds, against which they gauged their aspirations, after all, had included not only a certain standard of living but also an upbringing which rarely involved working mothers and surrogate child care.

The decision baby boomers made to approximate their parents' standard of living by putting mothers in the workplace and children in day care involved a value judgment that economic advancement justifies sacrificing the personal home care their own parents had given them. This choice was encouraged by, and became fashionable because of, feminist teaching that career achievement was of greater value to a mother and her society than child-nurturing and that the material benefits children received outweighed the worth of a mother's personal care. If, as feminists insisted, the status and satisfaction afforded by market activity already justified women's choice to leave their children, then surely economic advancement—which would benefit the children as well—provided even greater justification. Thus, the aspiration side of the relative income equation reflected what Jennifer Roback Morse has criticized as the feminist choice of "'Having it All' as our slogan and equality of income as our goal." In so choosing, she continues, "we embraced a shallow materialism and a mindless egalitarianism."[92]

When the mother in a two-parent family chooses to work, economic *necessity* (as opposed to *advantage*) is more likely to be the rationalization than the explanation for her decision. Feminism's effort to bring about the demise of the full-time housewife required diminishing the guilt felt by working mothers. Thus began the constant effort to depict a two-income family as economically *necessary* when in most instances one income would provide the basic necessities of life—food, housing, and clothing. That the best-educated and highest-paid women are the ones who return to work the soonest after birth of a child makes clear that something other than economic necessity has impelled women to abandon child care in favor of the workplace.[93]

Yet, even when there is no question of economic necessity remotely involved in discussions of two-career families, feminists will pretend that somehow there is, invariably treating this self-imposed need for surrogate child care as a societal problem that calls for a governmental solution. Typical was the use made of Zoë Baird's withdrawal of her nomination as United States Attorney General when it was disclosed that she employed illegal aliens as household help and was delinquent in paying the required taxes. Her affluence apparently made her plight an even more compelling illustration of the great difficulty two-career families experience in their search for "affordable, quality child care"—another paradoxical slogan of our era.[94]

For Erica Jong, the controversy illustrated how our society had failed those women who "wanted careers and children": "child care is a 24-hour job," she lamented on the op-ed page of the *New York Times*, "and there are almost no Americans who want that job." She seemed resentful that some women—apparently unaware that they were cut out for the job—were unwilling to do for the children of others what those others did not themselves choose to do. "We live in a culture," she complained, "that loves babies in theory, not practice"—a sentiment, one might think, less appropriately applied to those who are apparently reluctant to be paid providers of child care than to the mothers seeking that care. Observing that "legal child care is virtually unfindable," she demanded that society devise some way to provide "legal nannies."[95] Would she suggest, perhaps, that we require less educated women to care for the children of the credentialed elite or require those with highly developed nurturing attributes to care for the children of women with lesser maternal endowments?

It is, of course, not the case that legal child care is virtually unobtainable. As a spokesman for one New York City employment agency stated: "If they want legal, they can get it, but it costs"; in the New York area, the going rate for a legal nanny is close to $400 a week. According to one commentator, Zoë Baird and her husband, with an annual income of $600,000, hired their illegal couple for $1000 a month, plus room and board.[96] Thus, $500 a month, plus room and board, is apparently what they were willing to pay for the "affordable, quality child care" feminists claim is due to any woman who wants children and a career. And the difficulties Zoë Baird experienced in finding such child care is deemed illustrative of a societal problem in desperate need of a solution.[97] Do we really think it justifiable that women who choose to work should have their child care subsidized by appropriating the earnings of one-income families with mothers who may be less educated and affluent, but who also have a different vision of motherhood?

Reliance on economic necessity as the explanation for using surrogate child care was noted by Bruno Bettelheim in his study of the Israeli kibbutz movement. Although the kibbutzniks justified communal child-rearing on the grounds that it was required by economic necessity, in fact it was "historically and factually incorrect" that "economic need demanded that women, like men, work in the field." Observing that women of the kibbutz "felt deeply guilty about the radical rejection of their mothers' readiness to make sacrifices for children," Bettelheim concluded that these women wished to believe they had been forced by circumstances to submit to such an outcome and that "the kibbutzniks' purpose in claiming necessity is to quiet their guilt about refusing to personally care for their own children."[98]

Similarly, the employment of most married women in our country is not dictated by economic *need* in any ordinary sense of the term; rather, that employment has secured their families' relative affluence. As economist William R. Allen has noted, families supported by sole-earner husbands between 1967 and 1987 had a median income from 92 to 99 percent of the median income for all families, while the median income of two-earner families greatly exceeded that of all families. These women were not forced into the workplace to stay on par with the average family; their choice to work secured relative affluence by pushing their families' earnings far above the average. That this is so is further indicated by the facts that entrance of mothers into the work force increased at the same time that their husbands' real earnings increased and that there is no systematic relationship between the unemployment rates of married men and changes in the rate at which married women enter the work force.[99]

If women are being forced to work by economic necessity, there should be more working women with husbands in the lower income brackets and fewer working who have more affluent husbands. But the opposite is the case. In 1988 only 42 percent of women with husbands whose income fell below the median worked, as opposed to 71 percent of those whose husbands earned more than the median.[100] Aside from the additional expenditures necessitated by the wife's employment (food away from home, child care, women's apparel, and gas and oil), families with full-time working wives spend much more than one-earner families on mortgage or rental costs.[101] By the end of the 1980s, homes had become very accessible, the annual after-tax carrying costs of a median-price home taking 22.5 percent of the median family's income, as opposed to 36.3 percent of that income in 1980.[102] The monetary function of a wife's employment became, in large part, the acquisition of above-average housing.

That relative affluence, not economic necessity, is what is weighed against home care of one's child was conceded by one father whose own income could have carried the costs of the family home. His wife, nonetheless, had returned to work seven weeks after giving birth, and their three-year-old son spent ten and one-half hours a day in a day care center. It was "to protect our lifestyle" that his wife worked: "Families of the past," he said, "were less material-minded. The way today's society is, in order to buy that microwave, that VCR, the two cars, two incomes are necessary."[103]

In the *Time* magazine survey of "Women: The Road Ahead," discussed earlier, two reasons were offered why American women should turn away from what *Time* described as the Japanese house-wife's relatively "carefree existence" and choose a destiny that, after long experience, women "liberated" by communist systems have pronounced seriously flawed. The first reason was our no-fault divorce laws and the second that the "earning power of young families fell steadily during the '80s, so that two incomes are a necessity, not a luxury."[104] *Time* itself subsequently contradicted the second reason, when it noted that "the largest category of families with young children" consists of the homemaker mother and breadwinner father.[105] For these families, obviously, two incomes are a dispensable luxury.

Unlike single mothers, who usually are forced into the workplace by economic need, married mothers who work are usually making a free choice. In many cases, their choice has produced relative affluence for their families and greatly increased the disparity in wealth between sole-earner families and those of the two-income professional class that is becoming our new aristocracy. Noting the large gap that had grown between rich and poor by 1986, the *Wall Street Journal* stated that among married couples, "the working woman is lifting millions of families out of the middle class"; the result was a "growing overclass of well-educated, two-income families." Economists expected, moreover, that there would be "a steady increase in families with two highly paid wage-earners because the number of women professionals and managers is skyrocketing" and "high-income men and women increasingly tend to marry each other, a trend that widens the gap between rich and poor."[106] This expectation has been realized: the expanding income disparity between rich and poor is "one of the direct consequences of the increasing prevalence of married women in high-paying jobs in the labor force."[107] As Richard J. Herrnstein and Charles Murray have observed, our "cognitive elite is getting richer" and "is increasingly likely to intermarry."[108]

Further rebutting the claim of economic necessity are two statistics. Until the second salary in a two-earner family rises above the $60,000 range, only 20 percent of the second paycheck will remain after paying taxes and work-related expenses.[109] At the same time, studies of managerial and professional men have shown that traditional fathers had received 20-percent higher raises than had men with working wives and that "all else being equal, those whose wives were at home with the children had earned 25 percent more than those whose wives held jobs of their own."[110] Yet, feminist apologists ranging from *Time* magazine to Elizabeth Fox-Genovese will always plead "economic necessity" to foreclose any discussion of why women choose to forego the Japanese housewife's "carefree existence." Why they do so is plain: for divorce insurance; because they believe society respects career women more than housewives; to increase their standard of living; and because, on balance, many of them prefer careers to domesticity. "Most mothers who work outside the home," notes sociologist Pepper Schwartz, "say that they work for more than economic reasons" and "would work even if they did not need the money," a conclusion that has been confirmed by the recent research of Arlie Russell Hochschild.[111]

This plea of economic necessity, moreover, played no part whatsoever in feminism's initial assault on the housewife; she was told to enter the workplace to secure self-fulfillment and independence from male domination and oppression. Little thought was given to children. Viewed as impediments to the movement's goals, they were largely absent from the lives of most early activists. Only when "liberated" women continued to bear children did demands for government-subsidized child care and market interferences to benefit working mothers enter the feminist agenda and the plea of "economic necessity" become a crucial part of the movement's strategy. The proposition that working mothers should be subsidized is surely more compelling when economic necessity forces them into the workplace than when they willingly enter to achieve self-fulfillment and independence from men.

And when the perils of haphazard child-rearing become more evident, reliance on a plea of economic necessity becomes an increasingly attractive strategy. *Time* indeed painted a grim picture, describing children as being raised in ways that little resemble their parents' youth. "Home," said *Time*, "has been left an impoverished place, little more than a dormitory, a spot for a shower and a change of clothes. And as mothers have increasingly departed for the office or factory, children's isolation from the adult world has accelerated dramatically." *Time*'s rhetorical inquiry, "How will these marginalized kids turn out?,"[112] exposes the irony that mothers' entry into the workplace to escape the marginalized existence of housewives has resulted in what even feminist apologists see as the marginalization of children.

But apparently no indictments of current child-rearing conditions led *Time* seriously to question the accuracy of feminism's negative depiction of the housewife's role and its assumption that women can find fulfillment only in the marketplace. In oblique recognition that economic *necessity* is not necessarily responsible for women's choosing to work, *Time* posed the issue faced by the working mother as whether she should "stay at home, providing the values, discipline and security her children need, and let her hard-earned job skills go fallow? Or should she take a chance that her kids will be O.K. and pursue a life that brings more personal satisfaction and economic advantages?"[113] *Time* framed the issue in terms that admit of only one outcome, for if women cannot find personal satisfaction in the home—and *Time* had no doubt that they cannot—altruism will not keep many of them there for very long. The solutions *Time* offered to the problem of "marginalized kids," such as parental leave and subsidized child care, reflect the outcome it anticipates and are designed solely to ease the financial burdens on two-income families, compounding even further their economic advantage over the single-earner families that must subsidize these benefits.

In our country today, one income can usually provide something more than an apartment, one used car, and essential food and clothing. But even these basic necessities would produce at least as good a standard of living as most people had in the neighborhood of my youth, when every family had a rented house or apartment, three meals a day, enough clothes to go to work and school, and almost no married mothers worked. In the words of one feminist who rejects the claim of economic necessity, "in what sense does the family 'need' the wife's paycheck?" The husband in the 1980s, she notes, had a salary that, after accounting for inflation, was perhaps four times that of a turn of the century husband, "whose wife did not 'need' to work."[114] As David Gelernter has put it so well, the economic necessity argument makes no sense because "as a nation we used to be a lot poorer, and women used to stay home."[115] Easterlin himself recognized that much of the American population in the 1970s lived as well as the wealthy of colonial times.[116] He should also have recognized the role that contemporary feminism—the most materialistic of social movements—played in justifying attainment of that standard of living as the overarching goal of life to which family interests—particularly the home care of children—should be willingly sacrificed.

Careers As High Fashion

Perhaps Easterlin failed to give feminism's impact its due because he underestimated the great influence exerted in our society by highly educated persons who, as he noted, are most likely to adopt feminism's rejection of traditional sex roles. The Bergers have described how nineteenth-century women of the upper-middle class—where bourgeois family values first took hold—undertook to spread bourgeois civilization throughout society; through their very successful efforts "the bourgeois family and its norms became the standard for *all* classes." Yet today, the anti-family animus is most firmly rooted in that same upper-middle class which, with its control over the "knowledge industry," has evangelized against traditional values. Whatever remains of the bourgeois family ethos is now more likely to be found in the working class. The Bergers have speculated that American society may recover its stability only if working-class immigrants defend the family against our "decadent elite."[117]

A working-class family ethos might possibly overcome the influence of our cutural elite. Norbert Elias has described how models of behavior pass from one social unit to another: this passage moves in all directions between the classes within a society and is among the most important facets of the civilizing process.[118] The passage throughout our society of a traditional family ethos, however, must overcome the formidable obstacle of a contemporary feminism ideologically descended from the nineteenth-century Russian intelligentsia who were defined by their "[c]ontempt for everything bourgeois, especially the family."[119] In its attempt to remold humanity by destroying the traditional family, our women's movement has acted with the hubris of that earlier intelligentsia which believed itself to possess "special powers to understand the world with a unique ability to redeem it politically."[120]

So long as our upper-class knowledge industry remains committed to a feminist ideology that values and promotes female market production over the bourgeois domesticity it considers worthless, that feminist message will continue to be very successfully propagated. The feminist message exercises enormous influence precisely because it reflects the authoritative view of today's most educated sophisticates, sometimes identified as the "new class." As Gertrude Himmelfarb has observed, this "new class"—"now firmly established in the media, the academy, the professions, and the government"—has legitimated "the values of the underclass and illegitimated those of the working class, who are still committed to bourgeois values and the Puritan ethic."[121]

Upper-class behavior is especially influential in our society because we do not see ourselves as class-bound, but believe upward mobility is commendable and attainable. Perceiving upper-class behavior as correct and status-conferring, the upwardly mobile will adopt this behavior if it is within their financial and cultural capacity. When upper-class women for whom financial need is clearly not an operative factor take employment outside the home, they send a very powerful message to the rest of society as to how the upper classes view the status of housewives. Jane Mansbridge concluded that "the decision of most college-educated women to pursue careers other than homemaking" caused homemakers to suffer a tremendous loss in social prestige, resulting in "status degradation" of their role. "Full-time homemaking," she stated, "lost status primarily because high-status women abandoned it." Thus, while only 37 percent of all wives were employed outside the home in 1962, by 1978 this proportion had risen to 58 percent. In both years, 34 percent of the women whose husbands had only a grade school education were employed; the percentage of employed women whose husbands had attended college, however, increased from 38 percent in 1962 to 65 percent in 1978.[122]

By their actions, high-status women have not only proclaimed that homemaking was an unworthy endeavor but also—and even more important—have served as extremely powerful role models in leaving their infants and young children in surrogate care. High-status women have, of course, always been financially able to free themselves from domestic chores and child care. So long as they were not employed outside the home, however, it could be assumed they were still spending a great deal of time with their children and closely supervising their domestic employees. This assumption cannot be made once these mothers enter the work force and place their children in institutional care or leave them all day with caretakers whom the mothers are no longer at home to supervise.

Since it is generally presumed that the upper class—with its superior wealth and education—has access to the best information and wants and can obtain the very best for its children, the decision of upper-class women to organize their lives in this fashion has made a very persuasive statement to the rest of society. The example of upper-class women is always a significant factor in setting child-rearing trends, and their example is followed as they embrace bottle feeding or breast feeding, demand feeding or strict scheduling, the acceptability of pacifiers, thumb-sucking, or neither, and early, late, or very minimal toilet training. The entry of these women into the work force has been a clear manifestation of their view on the worth of child-rearing activity. By substituting the strict demands of market production for the flexible scheduling of domestic and community activities, these women have announced their willingness to forgo any substantial personal commitment to the daily care of their children.

Through this choice that was wholly unrelated to economic need, high-status women have rejected—and have been perceived by society to reject—the value of those child-rearing activities which their choice has precluded. Thus, these high-status women have made it fashionable to remove infants and young children from their mothers' direct care or supervision for most of the day. Because the choice's fashionableness does not derive from economic conditions, more than a change in those conditions will be required to strip the choice of its fashionableness. A portent that such a change may be occurring appears in what the *Wall Street Journal* has described as those "pockets of middle-and upper-middle-class America" where "the stay-at-home mom is fast becoming the newest status symbol of the conscientious 1990s."[123]

THE MEDIA CULTURE

Among the factors present in the 1960s that enabled feminist ideology to triumph so easily was the dominating influence of an expansive popular media. A large part of the population perceives as more or less accurate most of the information they receive from the communications and entertainment industry. The substantially uniform biases of these industries shape our perceptions and judgments, and remarkably homogeneous opinion-making results. The uniform backgrounds and views (largely left of center) of those who staff newspapers, magazines, and television news have been documented in *The Media Elite*, which concludes that these staffers "are united in rejecting social conservatism and traditional norms," while tending "to perceive elements of social controversies in terms that correspond to their own attitudes."[124]

It is scarcely possible to overestimate the effect of the substitution of this opinion-making monolith for the diverse sources from which society's views were once fashioned.[125] Earlier popular forms of communication—books, periodicals, letters, and interactions between individuals who had been shaped by a variety of influences—were largely replaced by passive reception of virtually identical messages delivered by television, movies, and popular music.[126] Televisions throughout the country, for example, were turned at the same time to the very popular program *M*A*S*H*, and by and large, our youth accepted its viewpoints as correct. *M*A*S*H* effectively promoted pacifism, disparaged authority, glamorized the sexually predatory male, and depicted casual sexual intercourse as common and acceptable.

Those who have raised families since the 1970s know the great influence wielded by popular music, movies, and television. Parents who sought to impart views at odds with popular culture have often found that this attempt causes great conflict with their children. Youth have readily embraced the media's messages of disdain for social traditions and parental authority without questioning their truth or the media's impartiality. But how could youth resist? Some parents have sanctioned the popular media's teachings, and many who have not have been too uncertain of their own beliefs or lacked the willpower to fortify their children against the siren songs surrounding them. In *The Thanatos Syndrome*, Walker Percy wrote "We've got it wrong about horror. It doesn't come naturally but takes some effort."[127] Many in this older generation were unable or unwilling to teach what horror means.

Parents have failed, in part, because they themselves have embraced the popular media's cultural views. Many, for example, have ratified the ubiquitous message of sexual revolutionaries by themselves adopting sexually promiscuous lifestyles, reinforcing these teachings to their children. Others have been shamed, as it were, into tacitly accepting what they believe to be wrong but have lacked the fortitude to condemn, lest their children think them unsophisticated and old-fashioned. In a reversal of the normal hierarchy, many parents now crave their children's approval, an attitude fostered by feminist ideology. By exhorting women to seek individual self-fulfillment in careers rather than in family roles, feminists have encouraged adult women to minimize their own daily responsibility for their children and view themselves, not as in charge of their children, but on the same level—all striving for achievement as the peers, even competitors, of each other.

Allan Bloom described this older generation's bewilderment when a vastly increased youthful sexual promiscuity upended the traditional hierarchy of sexual knowledge: "Superior sexual experience was always one of the palpable advantages that parents and teachers had over youngsters who were eager to penetrate the mysteries of life. But this is no longer the case, nor do students believe it to be so."[128] Deprived of their status as custodians of sexual experience and shaken by the unremitting attacks on traditional sexual morality from all segments of society, many parents lost confidence in their ability and right to mediate standards of sexual behavior to their children. And just as teachings of the media and academia undermined parents' status as transmitters of sexual values to their children, these same opinion-makers promoted the status degradation of the housewife.

Again, Bloom precisely delineated the problem: "Students today understandably believe that they are the beneficiaries of progress. They have a certain benign contempt for their parents, particularly for their poor mothers, who were sexually inexperienced and had no profession to be taken as seriously as their fathers'."[129] But while youth's contempt for their parents may have been benign, the contempt heaped upon the housewife was not. In a world now dominated by the feminist perspective, it required courage and a strong ego to undertake or continue in that role; that so many declined the endeavor is hardly remarkable.

When Charlotte Perkins Gilman derided the housewife as an economic parasite in 1898, most women probably remained blissfully unaware of her insult. Feminist derision, moreover, was refuted by President Theodore Roosevelt himself, declaring that a wife and mother "is not a parasite on society": "She *is* society. She is the one indispensable component part of society."[130] Extolling the duties of a husband as the breadwinner and a wife as housewife and mother, Roosevelt observed that the man's work is not "as hard or as responsible as the work of a woman who is bringing up a family of small children": "This does not mean inequality of function, but it does mean that normally there must be dissimilarity of function. On the whole, I think the duty of the woman the more important, the more difficult, and the more honorable of the two; on the whole, I respect the woman who does her duty even more than I respect the man who does his."[131]

But when accusations of parasitism were resurrected in the 1960s and hurled against homemakers, there was no refuge from the salvoes. Unless one altogether avoided contemporary books, magazines, newspapers, television, theater, and movies, escape from feminism's assault was impossible.

THESE WERE THE PIVOTAL FORCES operating in the 1960s from which the feminist movement re-emerged and successfully spread its message throughout society. It is not necessary to assess their relative importance or to assume they were the only operative factors to be confident that, without the convergence of at least these strands of discontent and the cooperation of the media, this feminist message would have been appreciably muted, and our society would have reacted less favorably to it. The organized women's movement, the academic knowledge industry, and the popular media all quickly subscribed to Wylie's depiction of the homemaker as a parasitical child-wife boating about on the sewage of her misspent life.

Soon our society was daily ratifying Wylie's portrayal—though by then few had ever heard of Wylie. The objective was to reeducate those women who still experienced a sense of irreversible achievement with the fulfillment of their biological role and still found satisfaction in lives that were predicated on financial dependence upon men. It was through this reeducation that society would further intensify the discontent, and thereby make women restless and questing enough to abandon their domestic role.

2

Status Degradation Achieved

Women can never hold half the economically and politically powerful positions in the country if a greater proportion of women than men withdraw from competition for those positions. More important, if even 10 percent of American women remain full-time homemakers, this will reinforce traditional views of what women ought to do and encourage other women to become full-time homemakers at least while their children are very young. . . . If women disproportionately take time off from their careers to have children, or if they work less hard than men at their careers while their children are young, this will put them at a competitive disadvantage vis-à-vis men, particularly men whose wives do all the homemaking and child care. . . . This means that no matter how any individual feminist might feel about child care and housework, the movement as a whole had reasons to discourage full-time homemaking.

Jane J. Mansbridge [1]

ONTEMPORARY FEMINISM has predicated its war against the homemaker on a rejection of traditional marriage. A single issue that distinguishes supporters from opponents of feminism is the ideal relationship between husband and wife. From the feminist perspective, they should live together much like roommates of the same sex. Such roommates may, of course, also have a sexual relationship. (The influence of lesbians in the contemporary feminist movement leads it to consider as appropriate sexual contact between both opposite and same-sex roommates.) In either relationship, the roommates should maintain their economic independence by pursuing equally fulfilling professional careers, while sharing a home and equally dividing expenses and household chores. Without feminist prodding, the early years of my own marriage, when I was in the work force, fit this model.

Childbirth, in the feminist view, should be followed by a maternity leave short enough to permit resumption of the mother's career without any competitive disadvantage. The care of children becomes another household chore—feminists always refer to child-rearing as a "burden," as if akin to mopping the floor—any part of which that is not performed by surrogates the roommate-parents will share equally. The unisex word "parenting" was coined to describe these child-caring activities. The roommates' sexes are irrelevant: feminists believe society should not distinguish between a unit of man, woman, and child and one of two women (or men) and a child born to a marriage of one of them, or adopted, or conceived by one of the women either naturally or through artificial insemination.

Allan Bloom observes that "a man and a woman have a work to do together that is far different from that found in the marketplace, and of a far greater importance."[2] A feminist might accept Bloom's statement if this work does not interfere with the woman's career, so that whatever cannot be delegated to third parties is divided equally with the man. But the anti-feminist woman who yearns to do that work together with her husband knows that the feminist vision would not evoke her yearning. For her, marriage is not a relationship of independent individuals who share living quarters while working towards separate, equally important lifetime career goals. Rather, it is a complementary relationship binding man and woman into a single marital unit: he provides the financial support while she assumes responsibility for the care and well-being which make the unit thrive. His career *must* be more important than her own. Only his employment can free her from the workplace to rear their children at home, and his job satisfaction will help him achieve the self-affirmation she gains with childbirth and thus content him in his life with her.[3]

Women's responses to a 1962 Gallup poll reflected this anti-feminist perspective: most wanted to marry, have four children, and work outside the home only until birth of a child. These women probably worked for several years, often to finance the education—and thus the future job success—of their husbands and to accumulate a down payment on a house. Most thought they were working to increase the fortunes of their marital unit, not to further their own careers. And when she ceased working, the wife viewed her husband's income as dedicated to their marital unit and, therefore, equally hers. She prospered with her husband and rejoiced in his job success. These wives believed they contributed to this job success and would have agreed with James M. Barrie's sentiment: "Every man who is high up loves to think he has done it all himself; and the wife smiles, and lets it go at that. It's only our joke. Every woman knows that."[4] They *could* smile and let it go at that because society respected them, and it is what "every woman knows" that counts most with women.

In the eyes of these women, their husbands' jobs were important because they supported the family. It was, of course, fortunate if the man could also enjoy what he did all day, but market production was not considered the glamorous activity that feminists have led us to imagine. A husband's job was valuable largely because it made possible the marital home as a "haven," to use Christopher Lasch's word, where his wife could rear their children and he could return each evening for sustenance and renewal. Home, not work, was what counted most; without the wife and children at home to work for, work was somewhat pointless. Most pointless would have seemed the choice to have both parents devote themselves to the market, while others care for their children and home. And as stage manager and central actor in this marital haven, a wife was her husband's equal; her status respected and secure.

But to dispel the discontent we have just examined, feminists urged women to abandon their traditional roles and pursue careers with the same dedication as men. The sexual revolution advanced this goal by convincing women to adopt male sexual patterns and reject the way of life which the 1962 Gallup poll had shown that most women seek. As Jane Mansbridge explains in the epigraph to this chapter, however, feminism's goal required that virtually *all* women enter the work force. To ensure this outcome, the movement set out to destroy the traditional wife's sense of self-worth and undermine her security by institutionalizing feminism's perspective on marriage. Katherine Kersten attested to the success of this endeavor when she recounted how, after deciding to stay home with her children, she felt unable to describe herself as a "home-maker" or believe she "was an equal partner in the family although I was no longer contributing financially."[5] Her feelings are shared by many of the respondents to a recent survey of women who have left the work force to raise their children. "Lack of extra income was seen as a major disadvantage by only a few respondents," the survey disclosed, while "the disadvantage of not being in the work force most frequently mentioned by respondents was lack of respect from society in general." "I get tired of people ranking mother-hood so low," stated one woman: "We need credibility for making our families a priority and caring for our own children."[6]

While sometimes discontented—a common condition of man-kind—we housewives in the early 1960s never doubted that management of our homes and care of our children made us equal partners in our marriage. It was feminism's triumph to convince society that only a wage-earning woman, preferably a professional, was a worthy and equal marriage partner. Because of this triumph, Professor Elizabeth Fox-Genovese can confidently warn women that "[f]ew men these days would want a wife who could not contribute to the family income and share the anxieties of having to do so."[7] The success of the feminist effort to inculcate this message is indicated by a study which showed that in 1968 only 28 percent of white women ages fourteen through twenty-four said they planned to be working at age thirty-five, but when they reached thirty-five, more than 70 percent of them were in fact working.[8]

DESTRUCTION OF THE WOMEN'S PACT

The women's movement presents itself, and is usually perceived, as an alliance to advance women's economic interests. In this view, women constitute a homogeneous class sharing interests distinct from those of men. Yet female job preferences and other market interferences favoring women disadvantage not only men but also those women who have established a marriage with the disadvantaged men. Women who would like to depend upon men—not the men themselves—are feminism's primary enemy. The salient characteristic of contemporary feminism—distinguishing it from an earlier social feminism—is that it belittles and seeks to undermine a woman's traditional role as wife and mother, thereby repudiating an understanding or pact that women at one time sought to maintain with each other.

This pact recognized that women generally fall into three groups: women in the first group are unable or unwilling to marry, or are overwhelmingly afraid of childbirth, and will devote their lives to a career (many of these women once entered religious orders); a second group will marry and often bear children but, like an earlier aristocracy or elite of the entertainment industry, will delegate to others maintenance of their household and rearing of their children and pursue careers or other interests; a third group will choose marriage as their primary career, devoting themselves largely to husband, children, and domesticity. Between these women there was, in effect, a pact—part of women's cultural knowledge and an essential component of "what every woman knows"—that they would let each other live peacefully without attacking one another's integrity in following their chosen path.

Women in the third group were quite content that those in the first group did not compete much for men. Homemakers may have lamented what to them were the empty lives of women without husband and children. And they may have believed women in the second group slighted their obligations as wives and mothers (a suspicion fostered by the disproportionately high divorce rates and other familial instabilities that have always characterized this group). But they usually refrained from articulating these feelings and, lest they break the pact, would demur if asked to express them. In turn, women in the first and second groups may have thought themselves intellectually and culturally superior to homemakers, but—keeping faith with the pact—they avoided publicly stating such view and went quietly down their chosen path.

Though sometimes uneasy and strained, the pact had never before been completely shattered as it was in the 1960s by Betty Friedan and a revitalized feminist movement. To women, it does not matter a great deal what a Philip Wylie and other male rebels against the breadwinner ethic think. If men can be coaxed to do what women want—and they surely can if women have the support of society—women who are confident that what they want is right are little disturbed by men's complaints. But women care very much what other women think; it is from each other that we seek approval. Other women's opinions can profoundly affect a woman's confidence. The pact is necessary and its shattering was significant precisely because other women's approval is important to most women—

and to men as well, for as Margaret Mead has told us, men look to mothers, and later to wives, for assurance that they are good.

When feminists broke the pact in the 1960s by openly and loudly proclaiming their disdain of domesticity and contempt for house-wives, women at home were consigned to what was, for many, a perilous state of intolerable isolation from female approbation. Homemakers had two options. Conceding the accuracy of the feminist assessment, they could restructure their lives by abandoning domesticity for market production, or they could defend their choice by articulating a vision of woman's happiness and fulfillment that starkly contrasts with feminist dogma. But to limn her own vision, a housewife must, in turn, break the pact.

Why Domesticity?

In choosing domesticity, she must explain, she rejects the feminist alternatives which offer what she regards as either an unfulfilled life without children or inadequate devotion to the obligations and joys of being a wife and mother. In undertaking her task, a gentle woman (and most housewives, I believe, try to be gentle women) is reluctant to offend and hesitant to appraise other women's choices. But her diffidence must give way before the hostilities initiated by feminists. Choosing not to go gently into that good night of the marketplace, feminists went in rage and viciously warred against the housewife who declined to join them.

To rebut feminist dogma, it is also necessary to appraise the relative merits of male and female roles within a traditional marriage. A wife who is happy with her life as a homemaker must always be appreciative of her husband's workplace efforts, which make this life possible. There can be no doubt that what her husband does all day is of great worth since it supports their family. Whether it is always very interesting, however, or requires great intellectual abilities, while furnishing comparable intellectual rewards, is a matter of some doubt. The inclination of homemakers—also part of "what every woman knows"—was not to articulate such doubts. The women's movement, in essence, called the homemaker's bluff. Painting a picture of the male role's superiority because of the excitement, inherent interest, and intellectual rewards of the workplace, contemporary feminism challenged homemakers to substitute glamorous market production for dull and dreary domesticity.

Answering this challenge, however, requires homemakers to articulate what they would leave unsaid, because to state how one feels about one's role as wife and mother may seem to impugn those who have chosen differently. The woman who chooses to exchange the marketplace for the home does so because to her all market work is fungible and can be done equally well by someone else; what she does at home with her child is unique. In fact, if not in theory, during the time that someone else assumes the mother's role, the mother-child relationship ceases to exist. The surrogate relationship which must replace it will always be different and, unless the mother is greatly deficient in nurturing aptitude, often inferior as well. The world will largely be mediated to the child by the surrogate who performs the mother's role, as child and mother play out their lives in a relationship necessarily truncated by their failure to experience daily life together. The child will enjoy this experience mainly with a surrogate or perhaps not at all; the mother will enjoy it only sporadically. Thus, by entering the work force, a mother chooses a fungible role that any number of people can perform over a unique role that no one else can fill—so that the role ceases to be played, although others undertake some of its duties. Those who choose domesticity think this exchange a bad bargain.

That homemakers did believe their role to be unique was recognized by Betty Friedan in discussing a survey defining the "True Housewife Type" as one who "feels that she is indispensable and that no one else can take over her job"; she has "little, if any, desire for a position outside the home, and if she has one it is through force or circumstances or necessity."[9] Destruction of the housewife's confidence that she *is* in fact engaged in an important and worthwhile enterprise for which she is uniquely qualified was the purpose of Friedan's *The Feminine Mystique*. Society is now imbued with her message: those under the age of thirty-five have rarely heard the housewife depicted in any but demeaning terms.

Women know the implication, for example, of describing a vice-presidential candidate's wife as one who gave up her career to marry and become one of "the rolling-bandage school of Senate wives."[10] Clear to any woman is the intended disdain and the societal consensus that she will be held in low esteem if, like *this* woman (whose own status could be excused as imposed by the oppressive patriarchal mores of her day), she gives up her career for marriage, mother-hood, and the feminist *bête noire* of volunteer work. The strength of this consensus was reflected in the words of a participant in a women's studies course in 1980, who declared it was no longer possible to enjoy staying at home because "you don't have dignity if you stay home"—if "you don't work you have the image of a leftover."[11]

It is this consensus that underlay the explanation of the president of Wellesley College for some students' outrage at the selection of Barbara Bush as commencement speaker. Their objection that the president's wife did not represent the career women their college sought to educate was, said Wellesley's president, "largely a generational thing" since Mrs. Bush had pursued the normal course for women of her era when few other opportunities were available.[12] Again, the message was clear: while Mrs. Bush can be excused for her non-achievement, young women will not be.

This same consensus explains the critical reaction of a baffled American media when Masako Owada gave up her career in the Japanese foreign ministry to marry the Japanese crown prince.[13] Our media's uniform depiction of Owada's choice as evidence of her victimization clearly demonstrates that its consistent reliance on economic necessity as a justification for married mothers' employment is merely a pretense to support the only choice feminists sanction, whatever economic realities might be. It is simply unthinkable to our cultural elite either that Owada's choice is anything but a sacrifice or that some women can happily exchange market production for marriage and motherhood—even without a prince.

Feminism's Vulnerable Quarry

Feminism's campaign to convince the housewife of her degraded status has been facilitated not only by the monolithic media and no-fault divorce laws but also by the vulnerability of its quarry. The personal characteristics that dispose a woman to contentment in a homemaking role are usually incompatible with the aggressive combating of hostile feminist attacks. A homemaker's cardinal attributes are her role as peacemaker within her family and her satisfaction in being valued for herself, rather than for what she accomplishes. She is appreciated for being, not doing. If she does her job well, her endeavors are usually not obvious to those who benefit from her efforts. Jean-Paul Sartre expressed this essential truth in describing the woman who, while being "a good mother and a good wife, passed nonetheless in her husband's eyes, in the eyes of the people of Rouen, even in her own, for a useless marvel—a housewife's work is scarcely noticed since it consists of restoring."[14]

A successful homemaker will compromise and negotiate to create to the best of her ability a smooth-running household in which all family members feel assured that their needs and desires are respected and will be satisfied consistent with the competing claims of others within the household. Someone who is good at fulfilling this task will usually not have aspirations of her own which *significantly* compete with the requirements and interests of other family members. Her primary source of self-satisfaction—the essence of her own aspirations—will be satisfying others' desires as the organizer and harmonizer of her family's well-being.

Because the defining characteristic of any woman who fills this role happily is a well-developed nurturing aptitude, her position within the household entails no element of self-sacrifice. On the contrary, her domestic role provides the most direct and appropriate outlet for a quality that must otherwise be sublimated into surrogate and therefore less satisfying activities. This woman is usually fortified by pride in being the stage manager of her family's drama and by the affection of family members which she enjoys without guilt. She is, nevertheless, usually unprepared to withstand a feminist assault that belittles her seemingly self-effacing role and condemns her failure to engage in market production like her husband.

Feminism's war against the housewife has pitted the best educated, most sophisticated, most aggressive, and most masculinized portion of the female population against women who generally possess less education and less worldly experience, who are more likely to be docile than aggressive, feminine than masculine. Phyllis Schlafly is rare in combining appreciation for the importance and pleasures of a homemaking role with the intellectual resources, sense of mission, and requisite combativeness to face the unremitting hostility directed against a defender of traditional women. An average homemaker not only has had no forum in which to speak, but never imagined she would be called upon to defend her *raison d'être*. Until recently, society had led her to expect that repelling vicious attacks upon her worth was more the responsibility of men than women.

Except for a few brave souls, however, men have declined to defend the housewife—for many reasons. Some men have felt a quasi-chivalrous reluctance to counter an offensive waged by women. Wherever feminist dogma is firmly entrenched—in academia, the media, and government bureaucracies—one often pays a very high price for opposing it. The early confluence of feminism and the sexual revolution led many men to favor quite readily a cause they correctly perceived as assuring them sexual access to an increasing number of women. The feminist message has also been congenial to those men who have welcomed the relief from the role of sole breadwinner that their wives' market production has provided.

In any event—despite meager resources and paucity of societal support—women who share the anti-feminist perspective should defend the homemaker. Housewives, not men, were the prey in feminism's sights when Kate Millett decreed in 1969 that the family must go. Feminists do not speak for traditional women. Men cannot know this, however, unless we tell them how we feel about them, our children, and our role in the home. Men must understand that our feelings towards them and our children are derided by feminists and have earned us their enmity. Whether or not this understanding garners men's support, traditional women must defend ourselves because the feminist offensive is, most essentially, a breach of solidarity with us, a disavowal of the obligation to honor the Women's Pact that women in the movement owed to us.

THE HOUSEWIFE AS PARIAH

As a backdrop for analyzing the writings that made the housewife a pariah, I suggest an analogy that, while it may seem shocking, is, I believe, also enlightening. The feminist attack on the housewife is structured rhetorically in a way that resembles pornography. I am not calling the attack "obscene" in the sense that this word is often used simply to denounce what one does not like. I am saying that the way feminists attack the woman they disdain, the housewife, follows the style of pornographic writing. Further, the feminist insistence that the housewife constrict her marital and maternal relationships to enable her to devote herself fully to market production is analogous to the constricting of emotional ties that is the essence of pornographic sex. That is, feminists want the traditional woman to redefine her marriage and her motherhood in the same constricted way that the pornographer defines the sexual experience.

Andrea Dworkin's *Intercourse*, a powerful work of critical importance to feminism, well illustrates the accuracy of this analogy. Dworkin has asserted her determination to destroy the pornography industry and joined Professor Catharine MacKinnon and others in efforts to obtain anti-pornography legislation that would include as pornographic "the graphic sexually explicit subordination of women, whether in pictures or words," including presentation of women as "degraded or tortured or filthy, bruised or bleeding, or in postures of servility or submission."[15] If such legislation were enacted, it would not be frivolous to suggest the possibility of applying it against *Intercourse*—a telling argument, I believe, against the merits of their proposed legislation. It is ironic that a movement which attacks pornography as being degrading to women itself has mounted the most vicious attack of all for the precise purpose of degrading the traditional woman.

The Pornographic Structure of Intercourse

Intercourse contains the elements common to pornography, as they have been outlined by Steven Marcus in *The Other Victorians*. Why did Dworkin choose to elaborate her sexual analysis in *Intercourse* so as to resemble pornographic writing as much as it does? She may have thought—correctly, I believe—that pornography, because of its shockingly dramatic effect, is naturally suited to expressing her aversion to the female heterosexual sexual experience.

A typical pornographic work, Marcus explains, has no distinct beginning, middle, or end. Once begun in some fashion, the work "goes on and on and ends nowhere." Pornography displays a compulsion "to repeat endlessly," a process described by "again, again, again, and more, more, more." There is no fulfillment of aroused expectations because fulfillment implies "completion, gratification, an end; and it is an end, a conclusion of any kind, that pornography most resists."[16]

True to a pornographic structure, *Intercourse* could as logically begin with its ending, end with its beginning, or begin with the middle. It is one seamless diatribe against men's sexual usage of women; then, the tirade abruptly stops, as if the author wearied of describing men's brutality and women's degradation. Dworkin's introductory depiction of Gustave Mahler's and Leo Tolstoy's use and abuse of their wives in intercourse could equally well be her ending. And she could have as logically begun with her concluding condemnation of circumcision and incestuous rape. Male circumcision, she asserts, (the "genital is wounded, mutilated, so that it will stay clean as it immerses itself obsessively in dirt") and female circumcision both demonstrate "a hate of male over female" that leads the male to wound the genitals of both sexes out of his anger that they make him penetrate the vagina of dirt and death. Her denunciation of incestuous rape (men "slice us up the middle, leaving us in parts on the bed"[17]) evokes an image of sadistic pornography that could appropriately fit anywhere in the text. The book arouses no expectations of fulfillment. Its purpose, like pornography's, is arousal itself—arousal, in *Intercourse*, of antipathy towards men and sexual intercourse.

Pornography, Marcus further explains, "vainly tries to reach what language cannot directly express but can only point toward, the primary processes of energy upon which our whole subsequent mental life is built." For this reason, pornography is "the repository of the forbidden, tabooed words," those primitive words that are "minimally verbal" and "present themselves to us as acts; they remain extremely close to those unconscious impulses in which they took their origin and that they continue to express."[18] Dworkin's obsessive repetition of her tabooed primitive word of choice mimics pornographic writing which is characterized by what Marcus describes as "the obsessive frequency or the lunatic virtuosity" with which this particular word has been used in some segments of society.[19] The word perfectly suits Dworkin's purpose, since its use is usually intended to degrade the act the word denotes.

By incessantly repeating the tabooed word and asserting the fact of men's brutal, debasing, and violent sexual usage of women, Dworkin seeks to create scenes in which the sex act appears horribly degrading to women. She also attempts to fashion this same kind of scene through her persistent theme of woman as dirt, employing a metaphor common in Victorian pornography which, Marcus explains, modeled the "genital organization . . . upon the earlier anal system," so that "the woman's body, particularly her genitals, becomes a toilet."[20] The theme of woman as toilet pervades some of Dworkin's sexual scenes. The "vagina of the woman," she notes, "is not phenomenologically distinct from the mucous membrane of the rectum"; viewing the woman as "excremental" thus "legitimates . . . the brutal domination through sexual subjugation of a worthless, essentially scatological thing." And so the man "immerses himself—for love, for sex, for children" in her secretions, as the woman is filled with "loathing in the form of semen driven into her to dirty her or make her more dirty or make her dirty by him."[21]

Dworkin assumes that applying the toilet metaphor to the woman's role in sexual intercourse, like denoting the sex act with the tabooed word, degrades the act through distasteful associations. But why should this be so? In one of the best of his many profound insights, Roger Scruton argues that Yeats had no cause to regret that "love has pitched his mansion/In the house of excrement." Love chose the best residence. It is, says Scruton, our observation of how our sexual parts perform their other "vital and regularly exercised function"—a function that lies "beyond the reach of our intentions"—that "prepares us for the drama of the sexual act" in which we must be overcome by our sexual parts. Our excretory transactions teach us that the body eventually triumphs over the will.[22] This is the lesson we must learn before we fully understand the sex act which is, most essentially, an event our will can forestall but not actualize. The metaphor that teaches so crucial a lesson cannot be a bad or distasteful one.

Just as the toilet metaphor fails, on analysis, to serve Dworkin's purpose, so too—although she wields it skillfully—is the device of constant repetition ultimately ineffective. In pornography, what

Marcus calls the "compulsion to repeat," "this repetition without a real termination,"[23] is employed to achieve sexual arousal (usually of the male) through repetitive descriptions of the sexual organs and their deployment. It is for the exact opposite purpose that Dworkin employs the pornographic tool of repeatedly describing sexual activity: to create a visceral aversion to, rather than arousal for, the sex act. Like pornography, her highly graphic writing relies for its effect not on sustained logical argument, but on the evocation of an emotional response to the tableaux she constructs. Our reactions to her tableaux must, therefore, necessarily draw upon our own experiences.

For this reason, Dworkin probably can succeed in arousing aversion to sexual intercourse only in those women whose own experiences have already disposed them to such aversion. Her words and scenes are incapable of arousing aversion in the woman who experiences delight, not loathing, at the "semen driven into her" in sexual intercourse—the woman whom experience has taught that no part of her is dirty, that the analogy with dirt does not appropriately characterize either semen or her sexual parts. And for some women (but probably not for men) Dworkin's scenes can sometimes fulfill the role of true pornography which, as Marcus tells us, "proves itself upon our pulses, and elsewhere."[24]

The third component of pornography Marcus identifies is a lack of concern with the "relations of human beings among themselves," since pornography is interested not "in persons but in organs." "Emotions are an embarrassment to it, and motives are distractions"; what pornography offers is "sex without the emotions."[25] This is, of course, also the only heterosexual sex that Dworkin's analysis countenances. If the woman submits to intercourse, she should, admonishes Dworkin, survive penetration with her being "intact,"[26] the self of her mind, her emotions, remaining as it was before—untransformed, possibly even untouched, by the sexual encounter. Dworkin's book is titled with precision; its topic is sexual intercourse—and nothing more. In pornography, "the woman herself is an organ" and there is "the final absence of almost all emotions except the aggressive ones."[27]   And so it is on Dworkin's pages. When dealing with heterosexual sex, the only emotions expressed in her writing are men's consuming contempt for women and women's fear of men and aversion to the sex act.

The sex Dworkin portrays is that of the typical pornographic fantasy described by Marcus in which "other human beings are only objects whose sole function is to satisfy our needs"; the man need only be "aggressive, importunate, masterful enough, and the animal" is his. That the women who are objects of his lust "should have feelings is clearly an inconvenience," for then what "had been pastime to [the man] was going to be misery to her."[28] Antipathy to emotional ties is the *sine qua non* of pornographic fantasy because the man's ceaseless quest for satisfaction of sexual lust can only be impeded by emotional ties.

I use the phrase "spiritual virgin" to describe the woman who, as Dworkin exhorts her to do, survives penetration with her being intact, unchanged by the experience. Just as the sexual pursuit in a pornographic fantasy requires freedom from emotional ties, so the freedom of the spiritual virgin requires her detachment from binding ties. She must avoid being encompassed by connections with husband and offspring, a bonding that will deflect her energies away from the public arena and towards what feminist Carolyn Heilbrun denigrated as the traditional woman's "lifetime of marginality," devoting herself to "fulfilling the needs of others."[29] If a woman allows herself to be so encompassed, her being will not remain intact after penetration, and thus her integrity as a market producer with aspirations of her own will be compromised.

But since freedom from the constraints of binding emotions is precisely what makes sex pornographic, the price some women will pay for the freedom of spiritual virginity is to experience sex as pornographic, the way Dworkin describes it in *Intercourse*. It is not surprising that submission to sexual experiences that are so perceived would evoke the frenzied hatred and despair exhibited on nearly every page of her book. This hatred and despair is proof that—however well their own versions of spiritual virginity may serve some women—there are others who experience it as painfully dysfunctional.

Those women who are ill-served by spiritual virginity might ask themselves what changes in attitude and situation would enable them to perceive the sexual experience as non-pornographic. They might find it in their interest to know that the sexual experience can bring delight and contentment to the woman who permits herself to be subsumed by the bonding connections of marriage and motherhood. This is the woman I call the "awakened Brünnhilde," a woman who is transformed by the sexual experiences in her life (especially childbirth) and resists feminism's demand that her commitment to market production continue unchanged by motherhood. It is this woman that contemporary feminists have targeted as their enemy. Just as Dworkin repeatedly describes sexual activity in brutal terms in order to create aversion to the sex act, so feminists have repeatedly bombarded society with their denunciation of the housewife in order to create aversion to her role.

Charlotte Perkins Gilman's Parasitic Housewife

Today's prevailing feminist perspective repudiates the very different perspective articulated by Catherine Beecher in the mid-nineteenth century. Allan Carlson has described how Beecher promoted women's status as the socializing force for transforming bourgeois families into havens of domesticity, separate from the competitive, industrialized marketplace. At the end of the nineteenth century, feminist Charlotte Perkins Gilman derided Beecher's vision of separate spheres.[30] "We are the only animal species," went Gilman's rebuke, "in which the female depends on the male for food" and "the sex-relation is also an economic relation": "With us an entire sex lives in a relation of economic dependence upon the other sex."

Assailing unemployed women in the home with the reproach that no "economic product" is given by them "in exchange for what they consume," Gilman denounced them as "parasitic creatures" which constitute "an enormous class of non-productive consumers,— a class which is half the world, and mother of the other half."[31]

These housewives, said Gilman, comprise an "endless array of 'horse-leech's daughters, crying, Give! Give!'" This "parasite mate devouring even when she should most feed" possesses "the aspirations of an affectionate guinea pig."[32] Such a worthless creature could not long continue, of course, and Gilman predicted the homemaker's demise. Domestic tasks, she argued, would be better performed in the public sphere because they required skills that most women are unable to develop proficiently. Children should be cared for by profit-making businesses organized on an industrial model, while food should be prepared and distributed by industries that provide efficient feeding outside the home. Thus emancipated from all domesticity, women could fully devote themselves to market production.[33]

Those who view Gilman's vision as a dystopia must, nonetheless, acknowledge the prescience of a woman who, a century ago, accurately predicted the daily lives of today's women who, early in the morning, leave their babies in some child care establishment and after collecting them at day's end, dine on the products of our industrialized, efficient fast food industry. Gilman's goal of equal female representation in the work force was furthered by an alliance between the National Woman's Party and the National Association of Manufacturers to support an Equal Rights Amendment and oppose all legislation protecting women and children, including minimum wage laws, regulation of the hours and times women could work, and laws limiting some dangerous occupations to adult males. Their alliance, however, was opposed by those, including "social feminists," who wanted husbands to support their wives and families without wives' enduring "the drudgery of a cotton mill." Denouncing mothers' employment as the cause of neglected children and dissolute husbands, these opponents chose as their weapon payment of a "family wage" to male heads-of-household.[34]

Led by Secretary of Labor Frances Perkins and Mary Anderson of the Women's Bureau, the "social feminists" of the New Deal opposed business and the National Woman's Party by seeking to strengthen protective laws regulating employment of women and children. The family wage they sought would spare mothers from working and children from the day care that social feminists rejected as "a general custom" and saw as simply a temporary solution in emergencies. If "the provider for the family got sufficient wages," said Mary Anderson, "married women would not be obliged to go to work to supplement an inadequate income for their families." This strategy was so successful that in 1960 a family wage was paid by an estimated 65 percent of all employers and by more than 80 percent of major industrial companies.[35] William Tucker suggests a revival of this mechanism that had assured a breadwinner's salary so that it would be unnecessary "for a working man to farm out his wife and children to feed and clothe all of them." It was this wage, he notes, that produced the 1950s "golden age of the family, in which marriage was a remarkably stable institution and the country had a broad and deep middle class." As a variant on the principle of one breadwinner per family, Tucker suggests that the breadwinner could be either husband or wife.[36]

Yet by 1970, the ideology of Charlotte Perkins Gilman reigned, while social feminism had virtually disappeared. Among the most well known of its few champions was Phyllis Schlafly. This courageous woman—one of the very few who defended the homemaker—organized defeat of the Equal Rights Amendment against a greater force of supporters than has probably been amassed in favor of any social issue. One might even think that her remarkable organizing ability, perseverance, and courage in the face of overwhelming opposition and scorn from the supposedly enlightened and correct-thinking members of the media and academia would make her a feminist heroine.

Simone de Beauvoir's Housewife: "A Parasite Sucking out the Living Strength of Another Organism"

Simone de Beauvoir's *The Second Sex*, which became the intellectual touchstone of contemporary feminism, was published in France in 1949 as an attack on what the 1962 Gallup Poll later documented as women's "matrimonial strategy." Through education and social custom, she argues, patriarchal mores have steered girls towards a life in which they would rely on men's financial support in marriage, while boys have been programmed for a free and independent life of market production. Thus are women relegated to being the secondary sex, prevented from living as independent beings. That women—or some of them, at least—might enjoy the life secured for them by the market work of their financial providers and that not all men may think themselves free and independent are attitudes de Beauvoir does not countenance.

It is crucial to de Beauvoir to show that no "maternal instinct" exists. She writes of women who find their babies "burdensome": "Even nursing affords such a woman no pleasure; on the contrary, she is apprehensive of ruining her bosom; she resents feeling her nipples cracked, the glands painful; suckling the baby hurts; the infant seems to her to be sucking out her strength, her life, her happiness. It inflicts a harsh slavery upon her and it is no longer a part of her: it seems a tyrant; she feels hostile to this little stranger, this individual who menaces her flesh, her freedom, her whole ego."[37]

It is in an eloquent passage such as this that de Beauvoir seems most certainly to be speaking from her heart. She also quotes from a story by Katherine Mansfield about the feelings of a new mother towards her husband and children: "Her whole time was spent in rescuing [her husband], and restoring him, and calming him down, and listening to his story. And what was left of her time was spent in the dread of having children. . . . It was all very well to say that it was the common lot of women to bear children. It wasn't true. She, for one, could prove that wrong. She was broken, made weak, her courage was gone, through childbearing. And what made it doubly hard to bear was, she did not love her children. It was useless pretending."[38]

Having established with examples like these that "no maternal 'instinct' exists," de Beauvoir then tells us that the great danger threatening the infant in our culture is the fact that its mother "is almost always a discontented woman: sexually she is frigid or unsatisfied; socially she feels herself inferior to man; she has no independent grasp on the world or on the future. She will seek to compensate for all these frustrations through her child."[39] "The worst of it all," writes de Beauvoir, is that the housewife's "labor does not even tend toward the creation of anything durable." Denouncing "woman's work within the home" as "not directly useful to society," de Beauvoir argues that because her work "produces nothing," the housewife "is subordinate, secondary, parasitic."[40]

Nor is it in man's interest, de Beauvoir continues, that "woman is supported by him like a parasite." It is, she says, "precisely because marriage makes women into 'praying mantises,' 'leeches,' 'poisonous' creatures" that marriage must be transformed so that the man "will free himself in freeing her . . . in giving her something to *do* in the world." "It is for their common welfare," concludes de Beauvoir, "that the situation must be altered by prohibiting marriage as a 'career' for woman."[41] The answer, of course, will be to send her into the marketplace, for in the home, she cannot "establish her existence": "she lacks the means requisite for self-affirmation as an individual; and in consequence her individuality is not given recognition." Society must, however, take steps to facilitate her market work. "In a properly organized society," she admonishes, "children would be largely taken in charge by the community." That "no effort has been made to provide for the care, protection, and education of children outside the home" is, she laments, "a matter of negligence on the part of society."[42]

Despite the sorrowful condition in which the housewife finds herself, de Beauvoir perceives that she could be a roadblock to the quest for liberation by the independent woman. Particularly harmful, de Beauvoir warns, is the threat women who remain at home pose to the well-being of women in the workplace: "What is extremely demoralizing for the woman who aims at self-sufficiency is the existence of other women of like social status, having at the start the same situation and the same opportunities, who live as parasites." It is unfair, complains de Beauvoir, that men who started out equally reached about the same level, but "women of like situation may, through man's mediation, come to have very different fortunes." Women at home can, by their example, sap a working woman's ambition, for a "comfortably married or supported friend is a temptation in the way of one who is intending to make her own success."[43]

The woman at home is the enemy to be combated, in de Beauvoir's analysis, because her example may entice others to follow her path. Such example could prevent a student, who is already concerned that she must "get everything by my own brain," from "unreservedly applying herself to her studies and her career." And so with complete candor, de Beauvoir tells us why the need is so great to neutralize the threat by depicting this comfortably married woman at home—whose example the aspiring careerist might find too tempting—as "clinging" and "dead weight," living like "a parasite sucking out the living strength of another organism."[44]

Feminism's totalitarian impulse, which will be discussed later, is clearly evident throughout *The Second Sex*. De Beauvoir knows how women should lead their lives, and she is willing to force them to be free. There is no talk of choice here, but of "prohibiting marriage as a 'career' for woman" and of the "properly organized society" taking charge of the children. All the ideas advanced by contemporary feminism can be found in *The Second Sex*. Betty Friedan adopted them, expressed them in a more accessible way, and drastically changed the American family.

The Feminine Mystique

Betty Friedan's *The Feminine Mystique* is an impassioned expression of overwhelming antipathy for the life of a suburban housewife. Although her own discontent pervades the unsparing criticism—I cannot recall one favorable comment about the housewife's lot—Friedan does not simply recount her own reaction to the experience, but like de Beauvoir, rejects domesticity as unsuitable for anyone. While the impetus for her attack is her own acute dissatisfaction, its object is the housewife's role *per se*. Painting with a wide brush, her stroke never touches herself. Her denigration of her fellow housewives apparently sets her apart from the women with whom at one time she regrettably shared suburbia—whom she terms childlike underachievers whose daily lives never call for the exercise of adult capabilities.

In trying to understand the vast chasm that separates Friedan's from my own reaction to living in the suburbs of New York City, I must reject the obvious explanation that she is much more intelligent or better educated than I. When I moved to the suburbs, I had already been a practicing lawyer, indicating I was at least in the same ballpark with her. The disparity in our reactions, I believe, stems in part from our different backgrounds; she came from a Jewish, and I from a working class Irish-German, cultural tradition. Having completed my education and worked at my career before becoming a housewife, I also had the exposure to marketplace reality which can diminish the glamorous appeal that "what men do all day" has for those unfamiliar with the experience.

The very different cultural traditions that shaped middle class Jewish women in our urban metropolitan areas and Irish-German working-class women make it much easier, I believe, for me to maintain a sense of self worth as I perform domestic chores. Quite simply, I have never felt that I lose dignity and status by doing my own housework, something I have always done (just as my husband has always done the yard work), except when in the work force and for a period after the birth of each child. Friends of my adulthood have often found my attitude towards housework rather quaint. This explained the surprise that a young playmate of one of my daughters expressed one day (stated, however, with a candor that would have shocked her very liberal parents): why, she asked, was I mopping the kitchen floor; she didn't think white women did that.

One friend, who was suffering mightily trying to combine motherhood and career, confided to me that she would like to stay home with her child as I did, but then she would, like me, have to do her own housework, and her family would think her husband a failure. When their relatives arrived as immigrants, she explained, the first step towards upward mobility was to have a "girl" do the housework, even if that meant economizing on everything else. To live as I did would announce her family's downward mobility. In the very different cultures that shaped my husband and me, however, downward mobility was more likely to be announced when a mother worked in the marketplace, while others cared for her children.

Doing one's own housework has many advantages. It is very good exercise and I find it less boring than working out on the stair-climbing and rowing machines, the treadmills and exercise bicycles that have become status symbols for the professional class. It is among the many money-saving options that enable mothers to rear their children at home. And it has the inestimable benefit that one's children will not acquire the notion—common among those raised in today's fashionable aristocracy of two-income professionals—that conduct of their families' daily lives requires a lower-class minority infrastructure.

During my early years as a housewife in the 1960s, the servant problem caused great concern in the New York area. If the previously plentiful source of cheap servants—often young black girls brought up from the South—had not dried up, the women's movement might never have gotten off the ground. The workplace might never have seemed so attractive if cheap servants had remained available. Nor is it frivolous to suggest that, in part, the movement was an effort to substitute husbands for the scarce servants. As sociologist Jessie Bernard observed, the "departure of the servants" from the home that began a century ago had an impact that was "almost traumatic and with an effect on marriage not even yet fully assessed" since it threw "the entire burden of housekeeping and child care on wives."[45]

The fact that I undertook a housewife's role as a secure, mature woman also helps explain the different responses Friedan and I had to Simone de Beauvoir's *The Second Sex*, as well as my own reaction to Friedan's book. When she first read *The Second Sex* in the early 1950s, Friedan tells us she was "writing 'housewife' on the census blanks, still in the unanalyzed embrace of the feminine mystique." She found the book so depressing that she "felt like going back to bed—after I had made the children's breakfast in the suburban morning—and pulling the covers up over my head."[46] I first read *The Second Sex* in 1954, after I began to practice law. Nothing in this book seemed to speak to any aspect of my life, nor did I think it spoke to any aspect of de Beauvoir's life since she was a successful writer, exactly what she had set out to be. Neither de Beauvoir nor I, as yet, had been swayed by her bugbear, the myth of maternity, nor had we been obstructed in pursuing our careers. *The Second Sex* spoke to Friedan because she apparently felt herself manipulated into being a housewife and cooking breakfast for her children in the suburban morning, something she had never, or no longer, wanted to do.

Although like most feminists, de Beauvoir constantly bemoaned the plight of being a woman, her market success indicated that her career was little disadvantaged by her sex. As for me, assistance— not discrimination—and encouragement—not obstruction—had always been my happy lot. Never in my life was I made to feel inferior because I was a female. In 1941—a time when de Beauvoir tells us girls' ambitions were not taken seriously—I was in the seventh grade and had to choose between an academic program or a commercial one that would lead to clerical work; I chose the academic. I lived with my divorced mother; we were working-class and relied on credit from the grocer (upward mobility would later begin with paying cash in supermarkets). Knowing this, my teacher asked what I wanted to be if I attended college; fearfully, I replied "a lawyer." My fear stemmed not from the fact that I was female, but from the fact that I aspired to rise above my class. To my relief, my teacher expressed no surprise and said merely my mother was too poor to help me much, so I must study hard to win scholarships.

From then on, I was consistently supported in my academic and career endeavors. Teachers and counselors—many of them men—put great effort into helping me obtain the scholarships and jobs that would fund college and law school. One college scholarship came from my city's all-male Firemen's Association. And although I had a scholarship from the Cornell Women's Club, I still lacked $100 for my first year; the Men's Club gave it to me. Throughout those years until I left my law firm to raise a family, I found college, law school, and workplaces to be congenial environments, where I always felt welcome and was treated with respect.

Having left the practice of law and become a suburban wife and mother of three children, I first read Friedan's book in 1965. I was stunned both by her egregious disparagement of everything I was and by her inability, even though a graduate of Smith College, to see the great possibilities for exercising imagination and initiative in a life that I found afforded me virtually unlimited freedom—the greatest freedom I had ever known—to create a design for living for myself and family and direct its performance. In *All Things Considered*, G. K. Chesterton captured my perception of this freedom when he contrasted the true savage—a slave who is always talking about what he must do—with the true civilized man—a free man who is always talking about what he may do. "The average woman," said Chesterton in 1908, "is at the head of something with which she can do as she likes; the average man has to obey orders and do nothing else."[47] I felt that I had indeed exchanged the life of a savage for that of a true civilized woman. Compared to life in the marketplace—quintessentially, a life bounded by "must do" when others demand—a housewife's life, I always thought, has few musts (breakfast, dinner, and sex as her husband desires); for the rest, she can choose to do what she wishes, when she wishes.

It was clear to me then and remains so today that neither I, nor my husband (even though he has largely been the sole supporter of our family), nor our children would have fared nearly as well as we have if I had followed Friedan's script and turned my children over to a nanny so that I could slave away in a law practice. Legal work sometimes provides an intellectual challenge akin to a good crossword puzzle, with the advantage that doing the puzzles well can bring handsome financial rewards. But at worst—and worst probably occurs with some frequency in most professions—it resembles alphabetizing the Manhattan phone book. To have convinced myself that market production was more gratifying than caring for my children, attending to the needs of my husband, and managing my home would have required me either to deceive myself about what I really did in the workplace or to value a job for its monetary rewards.

That not all women flourish in the marketplace is evidenced by a female attorney's description of her life, which appears in an article about a group commuting in a van to Washington, D.C. It is an eighty mile round trip; in winter, they leave home in the dark and return in the dark; they see each other more than they see their spouses. What sounds to me like a trip from hell, however, is the highlight of the day for this woman. Her companions are "an alternate family"; her "hectic job leaves scant time for socializing at work"; she is "so weary" at night that she often will just "collapse in front of the TV set." Watching the morning traffic grind to a halt, she observed: "This is the most exciting part of my day." "After this we all go sit in our little offices and wait patiently to get back in the van."[48] Ah, what joyful liberation from domesticity! In all my years as a mother at home, not one day was so uninteresting that I would have looked forward to that van ride.

The Mystique's *Indictment*

Now that it has become fashionable to plead the economic necessity of two incomes in order to avoid discussing the relative merits of market production and domesticity, one easily forgets that Friedan spoke not of monetary reward, but only of intellectual challenge and fulfillment. The problem she addressed was neither economic need nor denial of educational and workplace opportunities to women. It was simply women's preference for domesticity: although "more American women than ever before were going to college," fewer went on to "distinguish themselves in a career or profession than those in the classes graduated before World War II." Even the most able college women, she lamented, "showed no signs of wanting to be anything more than suburban housewives and mothers."[49] Re-reading Friedan's book today, one is struck by the refreshing honesty with which she referred to the myriad opportunities these women were blithely forgoing.

When Friedan was writing in the early 1960s, the black civil rights movement had not yet developed the affirmative action law which feminists would later use to claim preferential treatment for women on the grounds that they had suffered the same discrimination as blacks. Alleged victimhood not yet being profitable, Friedan candidly acknowledges—what was clearly the fact—that college-educated women were eschewing careers and devoting ourselves to our families because this was what we wanted to do, not because we suffered discrimination. Writing at the same time, Jessie Bernard had concluded that the number of women academics declined in the 1940s and 1950s because women found other investments of time and emotion more rewarding and fewer were seeking these jobs, not because women were being denied positions they sought.[50] In 1898, Charlotte Perkins Gilman had similarly conceded that the mistreatment of professional women "is largely past." "The gates are nearly all open," she said, and the "main struggle now is with the distorted nature of the creature herself."[51]

It was this struggle to convince the "creature" of her "distorted nature" that Friedan took up. Why, Friedan queried in 1963, don't more women pursue careers now that "all professions are finally open to women in America," with the "removal of all the legal, political, economic, and educational barriers that once kept woman from being man's equal." Why, she asks, "despite the opportunities open to all women now," do "so few have any purpose in life other than to be a wife and mother?"[52] These women, she concludes, are "victims of a mistaken choice," prevented from "growing up" but, instead, subjected to "continued *infantilizing*" so that they live in "a state inferior to their full capabilities."[53] And they do so, not in response to discriminatory denial of career opportunities, but under the sway of the "feminine mystique," Friedan's term for the wholly fanciful and unjustifiable notion that making a career of being a wife and mother is a worthy undertaking in which a woman can rightly take pride and find contentment.

Since the problem she identifies was not discrimination but a housewife's perception of herself as a woman of achievement, Friedan attacks this perception. She contrasts the housewife with a woman who has "a real function," who has "a commitment that will utilize her abilities and will be of some importance to society and herself"; the housewife's lot is one of "emptiness, idleness, boredom, alcoholism, drug addiction, disintegration to fat, disease, and despair after forty, when [her] sexual function has been filled."[54] Not only did Friedan summarily reject the conviction of many women that their domestic role does have a real function, which uses considerable ability and is greatly important to themselves and society, but her description of housewives' health was entirely fatuous. Those allegedly disease-ridden women that she maligned had very low rates of alcoholism and drug addiction, while their life expectancy was significantly longer than their husbands'. One must also query whether Friedan did not mean to say that woman's reproductive—not her sexual—function has been filled by the age of forty. If a woman's sexual function ended at such an early age, her discontent would be understandable.

Women "leading the traditional feminine life of housewife and mother," says Friedan, neither "used their education" nor had "interests beyond home, children, family, or their own beauty." They are the products of a culture that "does not expect human maturity from its women"; the result is "waste of a human self," as the housewife stays home "to live by sex alone, trading in her individuality for security."[55] Always contrasting what women do at home with "truly creative goals in the outside world," Friedan describes housewives as failing to "grow up," as "mindless and thing-hungry" and "not people." They are trapped "in trivial domestic routine" and "meaningless busywork" within the community that "does not challenge their intelligence." Refusing to "take the time from my family," this woman devotes herself to the "trivia of housewifery," and by declining "to pursue a professional career, evades a serious commitment through which she might finally realize herself."[56]

Indicting the housewife as "afraid to face the test of real work in the world," and wasting her "creative energy, rather than using it for some larger purpose in society," Friedan describes housework as "peculiarly suited to the capacities of feeble-minded girls"; it "can hardly use the abilities of a woman of average or normal human intelligence." Because a "woman's work—housework—cannot give her status," she must "acquire her status vicariously through her husband's work," and so "becomes a parasite." Echoing Charlotte Perkins Gilman and Simone de Beauvoir, Friedan levels the charge of parasitism against the woman in the home, castigating her for "that passive, weak, grasping dependence known as 'femininity.'"[57]

The life housewives lead, Friedan contends, "arrests their development at an infantile level, short of personal identity, with an inevitably weak core of self." They will "suffer increasingly severe pathology, both physiological and emotional," and their children also suffer because the "greater the infantilization of the mother, the less likely the child will be able to achieve human selfhood in the real world"; the mothers "with infantile selves will have even more infantile children." Society, she concludes, must recognize "the emptiness of the housewife role" and cease "encouraging girls to evade their own growth by vicarious living, by non-commitment," while women must abandon "their weakness, their passive childlike dependency and immaturity."[58]

In her most outrageous falsification of reality, Friedan argues that being a housewife "can create a sense of emptiness, non-existence, nothingness, in women," making it "almost impossible for a woman of adult intelligence to retain a sense of human identity": those women who "adjust" as housewives "are in as much danger as the millions who walked to their own death in the concentration camps." This contention is not as "far-fetched as it sounds," Friedan admonishes the reader, because "the conditions which destroyed the human identity of so many prisoners were not the torture and the brutality, but conditions similar to those which destroy the identity of the American housewife." Concentration camp victims and housewives are alike, she claims, in being "forced to adopt childlike behavior, forced to give up their individuality and merge themselves into an amorphous mass," and in suffering destruction of their "capacity for self-determination, their ability to predict the future and to prepare for it."[59]

Friedan elaborates her analogy by rebuking housewives with her allegation that even the concentration camp victims could have rebelled. The "guns of the ss," she claims, "were not powerful enough to keep all those prisoners subdued," and "the rage of the millions" could, if properly focused, "have knocked down the barbed wire fences and the ss guns" which the prisoners perceived as "even more impregnable than they were."[60] Is there any greater absurdity than to diminish, even trivialize, the horrors of German concentration camps by comparing them with the benignly conventional conditions of amiable civility prevailing in 1950s American suburban homes? Perhaps, Friedan did not know the facts about the camps, or perhaps, she had some idiosyncratic suburban experience, akin to living in such a place. The contention that concentration camp victims could have successfully resisted has been refuted by Hannah Arendt, who stated that the question "of whether the Jews could or should have defended themselves" is "silly and cruel, since it testified to a fatal ignorance of the conditions at the time."[61] Nevertheless, society has not yet refuted Friedan's condemnation of the housewife.

As though the concentration camp analogy has not gone far enough, Friedan dredges up a final degrading comparison to conclude her portrayal of the housewife as something less than a complete human being. The failure of women who have become "adjusted to the housewife's role" to "realize the full possibilities of their existence" can be analyzed, she suggests, on the basis of "insights" derived from the study of "male patients with portions of their brain shot away and schizophrenics who have for other reasons forfeited their ability to relate to the real world." Such patients "have lost the unique mark of the human being: the capacity to transcend the present and ... shape the future." There "is something less than fully human," she advises us, "in those who have never known a commitment to an idea, who have never risked an exploration of the unknown, who have never attempted the kind of creativity of which men and women are potentially capable." And it is in "the name of femininity" that these women thus "evade human growth."[62]

It is profoundly sad that one who bore children could think the experience of raising them was so valueless. For the sake of market production, Friedan would have women abandon what many of us believe is the single greatest opportunity for human growth. When a woman embarks on the conception, birth, and rearing of a child, I suggest that she undertakes the quintessential exploration of the unknown and exercise of creativity. None of what Friedan calls the serious commitments and truly creative goals in the marketplace can, in the eyes of women like me, provide nearly as great an opportunity to transcend the present and shape the future as the domestic commitments entailed in bearing and raising children. Our children embody society's future. Compared to raising them, it is Friedan's goals in the outside world that are trivial.

Friedan's analogy between the housewife and a concentration camp victim is, to say the least, inapt. But another analogy is suggested by Friedan's malignant description of housewives as parasites, analogous to schizophrenics and men missing part of their brains, and less than fully human, without ever knowing a commitment to an idea or attempting creativity. Her use of the pejorative "parasite" to describe the housewife—feminism's pejorative of choice wielded by Simone de Beauvoir fifteen years earlier—recalled to me its use in Hitler's *Mein Kampf*. The word "parasitism" (one I do not recall seeing applied, during the intervening years, to any other group in America) is repeatedly used in that book to describe Jewish people. There is so little difference in some of the phrasing that Hitler's description of the Jew in German society could be substituted for Friedan's and de Beauvoir's description of the housewife.

Hitler writes of "peoples who can sneak their way into the rest of mankind like drones, to make other men work for them" and "under whose parasitism the whole of honest humanity is suffering, today more than ever: the Jews." The "Jewish people," he said, "despite all apparent intellectual qualities, is without any true culture"; the Jew is "always a *parasite* in the body of other peoples" and is "forced to deny his inner nature."[63] Both *Mein Kampf* and *The Feminine Mystique* employ similar rhetoric to isolate and vilify the group each work condemns; both have succeeded, although only one author continues to receive acclaim. That acclaim, however, should spare neither her writing nor contemporary feminism the obloquy merited by such scornful denunciation of other women.

Some of us were very happy in our marriages, although Friedan rejected her own as one of dependent hatred. We were happy cooking breakfast for our husband and children in the suburban morning, although she found this activity deeply depressing. We were happy taking our children to the park, sitting on the benches with each other, watching our children play, and pushing them on the swings. Was it, perhaps, our happiness that made feminists believe we deserved such calumny?

The Mystique's Progeny

Underestimating *The Feminine Mystique*'s impact—and often not knowing what it actually says—commentators sometimes dismiss it as a journalist's work of no more importance than an article in one of the women's magazines for which Friedan wrote. But even if her infamous message has not been subjected to extensive critical analysis, its dissemination was facilitated by the fact that it had been midwifed with the skill of a journalist, whose first goal is to get the reader's attention. The message was clear to the housewives who were her quarry; its clarity was one reason for the creation of the myth of societal, especially male, oppression of women.

It was not possible to savage the housewife so brutally without throwing a life preserver of solace to the debased women boating, in Wylie's metaphor, through the sewage of their misspent lives. Her plight was not freely chosen, feminists told the housewife, for no one would willingly live such a truncated life of intellectual and social stagnation. Surely, chorused the feminist sisterhood, an oppressive male patriarchy imposed this servitude upon women. Though they now live in a limbo of stunted growth and non-achievement—as Justice Ginsburg put it, "reduced to dependency on a man"—with feminist guidance, these victims can be redeemed. Thus they fabricated the fantasy that we housewives are not autonomous adults following a freely chosen path, but childlike victims fitted to Procrustean beds by a patriarchal society.

Just as Friedan candidly admitted that all career opportunities were open to women (although the feminine mystique made women reject them), she was equally candid that her goal was not simply to apprise women of alternatives to homemaking and make them equally available. Friedan's precise complaint was that *despite* their availability, women did not want careers. Nothing more clearly exposes the pretense that feminism's goal was limited merely to allowing women to make free choices than its unremitting disparaging and disadvantaging of the housewife. As one feminist baldly put it when discussing social security, the law should not make it psychologically comfortable to be a housewife because this will impede feminist goals.[64]

Whatever subsequent apologists might argue to mitigate feminism's excesses, status degradation of the housewife has been the purpose of its attack. Far from being the enemy, it was men that feminists admired—at least in the public sphere. The enemy is the housewife who contentedly lives a different life from the male role models feminists seek to emulate. Tracking Friedan's path, the women's movement set out to undermine the self-esteem and contentment of a woman at home and to diminish her worth in men's eyes.

Thus, in an essay describing a society in which feminist goals had been achieved, Gloria Steinem assures men they will reap the advantage of no longer being "encouraged to spend a lifetime living with inferiors; with housekeepers, or dependent creatures who are still children." She includes the disclaimer—which has become *de rigueur* in feminist writing—that "the revolution would not take away the option of being a housewife" for the "woman who prefers to be her husband's housekeeper and/or hostess." This reassurance is surely faint, however, following on the description of housewives as "inferiors," "dependent creatures who are still children," and "parasites."[65] Steinem's essay echoes Helen Gurley Brown's earlier paean to the single career woman's superiority over the married housewife: "Economically she is a dream. She is not a parasite, a dependent, a scrounger, a sponger, or a bum. She is a giver, not a taker, a winner and not a loser."[66]

Most of the writing on women and the family after *The Feminine Mystique* has been based on this perception of the housewife's inferiority. The very popular 1972 book *Open Marriage: A New Life Style For Couples*, by Nena and George O'Neill, is a typical rejection of the "closed marriage" of two people "fused into a single entity—a couple" (an anti-feminist perspective of marriage) and advocacy for "open marriage"—"a relationship of peers" that is "based on the equal freedom and identity of both partners." A housewife cannot be a peer with an equal identity, of course, because only a career provides identity. The "woman's world" of the home, write the O'Neills, is "less interesting than the one outside" and gives women an "inferior status" which cannot be "compensated for by the high status associated with motherhood" since "the importance of motherhood has been inflated out of all proportion." Child care, the "longest and most laborious aspect of motherhood," must become a "shared responsibility" so that motherhood can be "disentangled from the wife's role."[67]

In words that became the mantra to justify husbands' sloughing off aging wives, the O'Neills tell us that without a career the wife "fails to 'keep up' with her husband" and "he simply outgrows her." His work provides "far greater challenges and wider opportunities for growth than are available to his wife," whose "horizons are inevitably limited by her relegation to domestic duties" which "programs her for mediocrity and dulls her brain." Women who enliven their domesticity with community and cultural activities are admonished, moreover, that they cannot achieve growth and equality "by dabbling—whether in painting classes, lecture-going, the local drama group." Such "dilettantism" does not make "sufficient demands to bring about real growth," and "only if you are materially rewarded" for what you do "is it going to be taken seriously by others." A woman must choose "active productivity" in the workplace from which motherhood, if undertaken at all, can "only be a temporary detour."[68]

Although few today have heard of *Open Marriage*, the book cannot be dismissed as inconsequential "pop-sociology." It embodies the feminist ideology that was perpetuated—virtually without dissent—in subsequent discussions about the family and that is the basis on which so many women now play out their lives. This ideology's premise that only paid employment counts means that no matter how dull that employment—doing title searches, for example, or due diligence work, or preparing prospectuses—it provides status and is therefore worthy, and no matter how interesting the housewife's social, cultural, and community activities may be, they constitute mere "dilettantism" that can provide neither growth nor status. Virginia Woolf expresses a similar view in *A Room of One's Own*: "Money dignifies what is frivolous if unpaid for."[69] Georges Seurat's "Sunday Afternoon on the Island of La Grande Jatte"—now a crown jewel of the Chicago Art Institute—and many of Vincent Van Gogh's works—which eventually set record prices at auction—went unsold in their lifetimes. Would Woolf have said these paintings were frivolous until the market established their worth? I think not. No more frivolous are a mother's efforts to create masterpieces of daily living for her family, although the market sets no price on them.

Feminist ideology proliferated through literature like *The Future of the Family*, edited by Louise Kapp Howe, a compilation of writings attacking the sex-role models of "male-breadwinner" and "female-homemaker." The husband's role as economic provider must be abolished, claims one sociologist in this collection, while another contributor, Olof Palme—the Swedish Prime Minister who wanted all women at work and all children in day care—proudly acknowledges his society's "ridicule" of traditional marriage.[70] The intent of all these one-sided analyses to indoctrinate is illustrated by a 1976 cover story in *U. S. News & World Report*, entitled "Liberated Women: How They're Changing American Life." In the cover's foreground is a smiling woman, striding forward, briefcase in hand. In the background are the backs of two much smaller figures who are walking away, a man and child holding hands; the child's head is slightly bowed, and although the man's shoulders appear to be squared, he seems a frailer man than she is a woman.

Although her skirt ends above her knees, the woman has a somewhat neutered appearance; it seems more appropriate for her to carry a briefcase than caress a child. She appears to be a strong, happy, confident woman—without doubts or maternal yearnings—striding away from a saddened child and a rather slight man, both trying to make the best of it. According to the article, all is as it should be. A social revolution, we are told, has transformed traditional roles, nearly half of all mothers are working outside the home, and 70 percent of all women say they favor this lifestyle. Joan Huber, professor of sociology and active in the women's movement, claims it has "become normative for married women with children to work and for men to love to have their wives work" because they have "double incomes." Expecting the wife to work "makes her independent of her husband," which Huber concedes will cause a continuing increase in the divorce rate and decline in fertility: working couples "can have a really smashing life" and males, particularly the better educated, realized "that children were economic liabilities."[71]

There are, Huber tells us, "no data to make us believe that men are naturally breadwinners and women are naturally nurturant." Faced with the fact that in all societies men have been primarily breadwinners and women the nurturers of children, she adopts feminism's ideologically correct view that such outcomes result solely from cultural conditioning without any biological promptings. Nonetheless, she doubts it will be easy to make men assume a nurturing role. In what she terms our "kind of slave society," Huber asserts that if she were a man, she would "think twice about changing a world where I had a nice, soft, warm creature trained to treat me with tender loving care, to change my baby's diaper, to watch the kid lest it be creamed by a fire truck, and to do all the things that aren't so much fun while I went off and had a zesty life in the world of work."[72]

A reader might have thought something could be said in favor of being a soft, warm creature giving tender, loving care to a husband, diapering a baby, and watching over children; a woman like myself might have experienced such a life and found it satisfying—even more fun than market production. But in the supposed counterpoint presented by Urie Bronfenbrenner, readers of *U.S. News* find no hint that such sentiments are even within the realm of socially acceptable possibility. This expert on children and the family assents to feminism's goal to put women in the workplace, with the caveat that workplaces must no longer reflect the "values of a power-oriented male society" that make it difficult to "function as a parent."[73]

Yet children, Bronfenbrenner is certain, are adversely affected when both parents work: they are not properly socialized through interaction with adults and "are not getting what they need." He rejects the solution of substantial reliance on day care, which accords with his writings deploring the neglect and isolation of children caused by delegation of child care to specialists with the increase in working mothers:[74] the "most humane and economic method known for bringing up human beings is the family." Nevertheless, while opining that he does not care which parent stays home with the child, he says nothing affirmative about life at home as a child-rearer, nor does he question pervasive criticisms of that life. He simply recommends flexibility in working hours and part-time employment. And lest anyone believe he thinks women are any more likely than men to want to stay home with their children, he specifically notes that part-time employment need not "mean that women would go back into the home to look after the children themselves," but instead we will find "both parents doing different things with their children."[75]

Further, Bronfenbrenner endorses a Swedish law requiring each parent to take one-half of the parental leave allowed to care for a sick child so that, as he put it, the mother can not take it all. (No doubt he would also approve the recent Norwegian law forbidding the father to transfer his parental leave to the mother.[76]) It is not clear whether Sweden forbids choice in this matter in order to stamp out a latent patriarchal belief that mothers are more appropriate attendants of sick children or a latent yearning of the mother, herself, to care for her child—feelings that would have had to survive many years of socialist and feminist indoctrination.

Bronfenbrenner's failure to express any approbation of a woman in the role of homemaker reflects what the Bergers have identified as the consensus of the helping professions that "only paid work is to be considered as supplying status."[77] Such is the brutally stated view of the renowned sociologist of the family Jessie Bernard, who believes traditional marriage confers substantially greater benefits of health and emotional well-being upon the husband than the wife.[78] A woman who marries, she observes—quoting Congreve— will "dwindle into a wife": traditional marriage lowers the woman's status by confining her to an "individual, separate, isolated, privatized household," where she performs unpaid "menial labor." The "housewife is a nobody," Bernard tells us in *The Future of Marriage*, and housework "is a dead-end job" in which she "cannot grow." Because of its "nonspecialized and detailed nature," housework "may actually have a deteriorating effect on her mind," thus "rendering her incapable of prolonged concentration on any single task" so that she "comes to seem dumb as well as dull." "[B]eing a housewife makes women sick," Bernard contends, and the "paradox" of so many housewives claiming to be happy can only be explained by a "socialization process" that "deforms" them; to be happy in a traditional marriage, "a woman must be slightly ill mentally."[79]

Declaring it ludicrous that men and women play "separate roles," Bernard challenges women to cease being "dependent," "docile," "domestically inclined," and "feminine" and instead develop "lifelong work histories." She welcomes the pressures exerted by no-fault divorce laws to force women to abandon homemaking: the "very deprivation of assured support as long as they live may be one of the best things that could happen to women" since it "would demand the achievement of autonomy" through their lifelong commitment to the workplace. Women must treat childbearing as "a transitory occupation which, once over, frees them for a major, serious, adult commitment." Only a career can guarantee the autonomy that prevents "parasitism in marriage."[80]

The social scientist's unexamined intuition of the housewife's inferiority is implicit in Mary Jo Bane's *Here To Stay: American Families in the Twentieth Century*, a book that seeks to demonstrate the "persisting centrality of family commitments" in American life.[81] In a work extensively documented with demographic data, Bane simply accepts as given that housework is "a wretched job." This statement appears, moreover, only one page after she cites surveys showing that, of the women surveyed, 41.5 percent of those employed full time, 42.7 percent of those employed part time, and 46.4 percent of the housewives said that they were "very happy"; of the husbands surveyed, 38.6 percent with full-time working wives, 44.9 percent with part-time working wives, and 50 percent married to house-wives said they were "very happy."[82] One must query how doing "a wretched job" can leave so many women "very happy" and how so many husbands can, in turn, be "very happy" married to women doing a wretched job.

Presuming the wretchedness of housework and believing that sexual equality requires sexual fungibility, Bane concludes that women will always be inferior until we create a society in which women are no more likely than men to care for children. Doubting the feasibility of universal day care, Bane prefers family child allowances and a feminist fantasy world of sexual fungibility. In this world where "men and women are distributed randomly through jobs, there should be as many marriages in which the wife makes more than the husband as those in which the husband makes more than the wife." Just as there are many women who "now prefer the job of child care to the other jobs they might hold," men "might express the same preference, if their own jobs were not interesting and if their wives' earnings could support the family."[83]

Despite her contempt for the homemaker, Jessie Bernard also assumes that many men have an aptitude for the role "and would prefer it to what they are doing." Since Bernard's discussion of the "marriage gradient" shows that women usually marry men at least slightly superior to them in education and occupation,[84] one wonders how she can assume that within many marital units the husband would perceive himself as the more appropriate candidate for the homemaking, child-rearing role. Bane herself admits that this circumstance is not known to have obtained anywhere: "All societies that have been studied by anthropologists and historians allocate the care of young children to women."[85] And all modern socialist states have relied on institutional child care, not househusbands, to keep women in the work force.

Perhaps it is because many contemporary feminists are women who never felt themselves to be sexually affirmed by motherhood that they deny George Gilder's insight that there "is no way that early nurture of children will be sexually affirmative for males" in the way it can be for a female.[86] The fearful price that many children have paid for society's efforts to socialize men to do what nature never fitted them for is demonstrated by a report of The United States Advisory Board on Child Abuse and Neglect, which concludes that violence against young children has reached public health crisis proportions: "Abuse and neglect in the home is a leading cause of death for young children in this country," the vast majority of abused and neglected children being under four years old. "Most physical abuse fatalities," the report notes, "are caused by enraged or extremely stressed fathers and other male caretakers."[87]

Conceding that little progress had been made toward converting husbands into child-rearing homemakers, Bane notes that women employed full time "spend an average of 4.8 hours per day on household work, while their husbands spend 1.6 hours per day." This 1.6 hours was, interestingly, the same amount of time spent by husbands with non-working wives.[88] Working women have continued to assume a vastly disproportionate share of domestic tasks.[89] And as Richard Vigilante has noted, to make their schedules tolerable, mothers have cut back significantly on time with their children, a reduction for which fathers don't compensate, since husbands of working mothers spend less time with their children than husbands of full-time housewives.[90] One is tempted to conclude that married men have a finite tolerance for domesticity, unrelated to the reality of their wives' workplace commitments. Confirming this was a joint study of households in a Soviet and American city which showed that in both cities the time spent on household work was about 25 hours a week for women and 11 hours for men. Yet, only 55 percent of the American women were in the labor force, versus 81 percent of the Russian women.[91]

Although Bane rejects day care subsidies because they "prefer women who want to work over women who want to care for their own children,"[92] her failure to acknowledge the force of maternal yearnings led her to believe that no more women than men would choose a homemaking role. And contrary to all our experience as to the kind of men to whom women are attracted, she envisions a world in which one-half of the women will marry men of an economic and intellectual stature so much less than their own that the men will choose to stay home and rear the children—and the women will be content with this outcome. As David Buss has shown, the evidence is clear that American women "value economic resources in mates substantially more than men do"—"roughly twice as much": "Women across all continents, all political systems (including socialism and communism), all racial groups, all religious groups, and all systems of mating" place 100 percent "more value than men on good financial prospects."[93] Despite this strong proof of what it is women want from men and the harsh lessons of contemporary familial decay, feminists still cherish Bane's fantasy and plead its viability as an alternative to institutional child care.

Betty Friedan's 1981 book, *The Second Stage,* in no way retracts the stereotypes of *The Feminine Mystique,* although Friedan acknowledges that she "resorted to a rather extreme metaphor" in comparing the suburban home to a concentration camp.[94] *The Second Stage* argues for the restructuring of our institutions on a basis of real sexual equality and seeks to dissociate what Friedan calls "mainstream" feminism from the "anti-man, anti-family, bra-burning image of 'women's lib.'" Experience had demonstrated—what one might think should have never been in doubt—that it would not be easy to remold men into nurturing mothers and competent housewives. The reluctance of men to be recruited in women's endeavor to juggle pregnancies, children, household chores, and a full-time career demands basic structural changes within society, Friedan claims. Not only must there be a "new sharing of roles by women and men" but also "new kinds of housing and neighborhoods" combining "private space and shared communal spaces and services that are needed."[95]

Sweden—the feminist paradise—provides a model: private apartments with a "small kitchenette" were combined with "a common kitchen and dining room where all could take their meals—or pick them up after work to eat in their own apartments." This "service housing" includes "a common child-care center, a nursery for babies, and an after-school program," while residents "share cleaning and gardening and laundry services, instead of each doing it separately." Characteristic of utopian communalism, coercion lurks in the background, and Friedan notes that Swedish feminists are "trying to get such services required by law in new buildings, and even provided in some form in existing neighborhoods."[96] This Swedish scheme resembles the cooperative housing envisioned by Charlotte Perkins Gilman at the turn of the century. Gilman did not want even small kitchenettes in private units, however, proposing that apartments and clustered suburban homes be "kitchenless" and connected to central dining rooms and day nurseries.[97] Perhaps she feared that a kitchen, offering as it would the possibility of preparing a meal to be shared by members of a single family sitting around their own table, would arouse within the working woman a dangerous longing for domesticity and a more nurturing role within her own family.

Because Friedan seeks in *The Second Stage* to distance herself from radical feminism, she is often considered a moderate. In his

Preface to *Men and Marriage*, George Gilder refers to the serious setbacks suffered by radical feminism, noting that even Friedan had embraced the nuclear family that she once denounced as "a cradle of evil."[98] Brigitte Berger groups her with "liberal feminists" who constitute a "pro-family feminist camp focusing on issues of day care, paid maternity/paternity leaves, the comparable worth of traditional female categories of work."[99] But the family which these liberal feminists favor is very different from the traditional family which Friedan earlier had condemned, and the vision of communal living which she divines in *The Second Stage* is more a kibbutz than a nuclear family.

Friedan's attack on radical feminism, nevertheless, has created an aura of moderation about her original assault on the housewife, an assault as radical as the most outrageous claims of later so-called radicals. By contrasting her own lack of moderation with something ostensibly worse, Friedan stakes a distance between herself and what she terms the "most ludicrous fulminations of radical feminists": men portrayed as "the oppressor" by Kate Millett, as driven by "metaphysical cannibalism" by Ti-Grace Atkinson, and as a "natural predator" by Susan Brownmiller; and Shulamith Firestone's characterizations of the fetus as a "parasite" and of pregnancy as "the temporary deformation of the body for the sake of the species."[100] But one must wonder how Friedan would spell out a meaningful distinction between the radicals' chimera of male oppression and her own creation, the oppressive feminine mystique, or between Firestone's and her own use of the pejorative "parasite."

In fact, no meaningful distinction can be drawn. What Friedan says about the accomplishments and worth of the woman in the home is as intemperate and loathsome as the radicals' "most ludicrous fulminations." It is no more radical to castigate men as oppressors and to renounce childbearing than to denounce the homemaker as a parasite, less than fully human, living without using adult capabilities, lacking a real function, and resembling schizophrenics and men with part of their brain shot away. If this calumny is moderate, such "moderation" seems to support Ayn Rand's view: "There are two sides to every issue: one side is right and the other is wrong, but the middle is always evil."[101] So-called moderation surely is evil if, like the attempt to cast Friedan as moderate, it requires portraying egregious extremism as prudent restraint, arrogant contempt as benevolent concern, and revolutionary destruction as benign reform.

TRIUMPH OF THE FEMINIST PERSPECTIVE

The feminist perspective now governs most public discourse on marriage and family. Although some voices, usually of social or religious conservatives, endorse an anti-feminist perspective, they are dismissed by most of the communications and knowledge industry as a strident minority of intellectually suspect malcontents.[102] Today's public discourse usually assumes that the feminist perspective reflects the interests and desires of virtually all women and is the only worthy perspective on "women's issues." The National Organization for Women (NOW), the Fund for the Feminist Majority, and other feminist groups always present themselves as representatives of women voters in general, warning legislatures and political parties that rejection of their demands demonstrates contempt for women's needs.[103]

But these groups speak only for women who adopt the feminist perspective and support the demand in NOW's call for "a different concept of marriage, an equitable sharing of the responsibilities of home and children and of the economic burdens of their support."[104] Homemakers comprise only a small part of its membership, yet NOW is never challenged when it presumes to speak for women who reject its founding principles because they do not want to entrust their children and their domestic role to surrogates.

One commentator was baffled at the absence of female presidential and vice presidential candidates, even though more women than men are registered voters. With that kind of voting strength, she queried, why do so few women hold elective offices. Perhaps, she speculated, more day care will do it. She recounted her attempts to explain the women's movement to her first husband, only to have him inquire: "Honey, where are my clean socks?"—a response that apparently fatally compromised his fitness as a mate. Some of us have goals different from men's; we are content to provide clean socks for our husbands and are even grateful for each day we can do so. Our needs are well satisfied in a relationship where that is part of our job description. His insensitivity to feminist teachings would not lead us to reject a man who, as she described her husband, was "of otherwise noble character."[105]

The Lure of Subsidization

Like the neutering of our society analyzed by Charles Winick, the feminist perspective is so firmly embedded in our thinking as to be scarcely noticed or questioned. It daily provides the standards by which the media analyze issues related to women. Whenever, for example, the topic is women in the work force, more is always considered better; women's status is always perceived to be best wherever the greatest number work outside the home. Even when other facets of their lives are criticized, such as the fact that they perform the bulk of domestic chores, women's employment is always viewed as a good. It is one of the major factors, together with a low birth rate and a large allocation of societal resources to day care, on which a high status is assigned the women of a country. Our opinionmaking cultural elite unquestioningly assume that women fare best who have the fewest children, work outside the home as nearly as possible on the same terms and for the same number of years as men, and play a marital role as similar as possible to the male's.

If this feminist perspective were not pervasive, our federal tax laws would not provide a tax credit for the cost of surrogate child care, a policy that discriminates against one-income families which rear their children at home and favors two-income families which pay others to care for their children. Our tax laws reflect an institutional commitment to feminism by encouraging surrogate care and discouraging the one-income marital relationship. Family allowances and an increased tax exemption for dependents would benefit *all* families with children. If adjusted for inflation and real growth in income since 1948, the dependency exemption would have been $8,652 in 1993 instead of $2,350.[106] Feminists, however, consistently endorse policies that disfavor families where the mother stays home with her children by taxing and otherwise economically burdening them to provide child care and other benefits for working women.

Except when a representative of a social or religious conservative viewpoint is speaking (a view usually dismissed as "ultra-right-wing"), it is assumed to be in the interests of all women that society expend resources to provide maternity leaves and surrogate child care. An illustration of this pervasive bias is a featured article on child care in the premier issue of the magazine *World Monitor*, which betrays no awareness that there could be two legitimate sides on the issue of government- and employer-funded child care.

Referring to American progress in providing day care facilities, the author leaves no doubt that institutional child care is never anything other than "progress" and that such progress cannot adversely affect the interests of some women. The author recommends the Swedish restructuring of the traditional family relationship: 85 percent of women with pre-school children work outside the home in Sweden; twelve-month parental leave with full pay and an additional six-month leave at 70-percent pay are provided; after-school programs function full-time during vacations, with provisions for sick children; "[m]ost imaginative," she observes, are programs that place children in sibling groups, thus "mixing ages as naturally occurs in families."[107] She raised no questions about the government's use of its taxing and regulatory power to replace—while trying to mimic—what "naturally occurs in families."

Comprehensive child care and parental leave programs necessitate taxes and other economic costs that, as Swedish experience demonstrates, make it very difficult for mothers to remain at home. By endorsing the Swedish model, the author was recommending that the number of American pre-school children with working mothers increase almost 30 percent to the Swedish rate of 85 percent.[108] Without addressing the desirability of this change, she proposed that our society allocate resources to replace maternal home care with institutional care for most children. She thus adopted Simone de Beauvoir's premise that society should be organized to prevent women from choosing to raise their children at home because society works best when children are raised in institutional facilities while their mothers work in the marketplace.

But such resource allocation is not in the interests of any woman who rears her children at home rather than taking advantage of these workplace benefits. And while she has no use for these benefits herself, the costs of conferring them upon other women will be borne by her family through increased taxes, the increased cost of goods produced by enterprises providing the benefits, and the decreased profitability of these enterprises. The costs of providing these benefits, for example, might otherwise be allocated to increase wages, thus benefiting *all* employees, including breadwinners in one-income families. Yet, it is relatively taboo, as Richard Vigilante has noted, to raise the question of the extent to which government policies pushing women into the work force are "responsible for the decline of male wages."[109]

Similarly, all affirmative action programs that benefit women (including contract set-asides for female-owned businesses), whether in federal and state governments, private businesses, or educational institutions, are in place only because society has accepted and daily implements the feminist perspective. Feminism's phenomenal success in making the alleged past oppression of women an incontrovertible fact is demonstrated by the institution of this vast affirmative action bureaucracy that assumes any statistical disparity in outcomes for men and women results from discrimination against women—not from women's choice—and must be "remedied." Until equality of outcome has been achieved, it is largely assumed—without inquiry into whether discrimination has actually occurred—that equality of opportunity has been denied.[110] Implementation of initiatives for the preferential treatment of women is a continuing source of injury to any woman who adopts the anti-feminist perspective and has formed, or hopes some day to form, a family with a breadwinner husband.

The Bludgeon of Deprivation

The feminist perspective was further entrenched in our society when all of our state legislatures—the great majority of legislators are men—cooperated with feminists to enact no-fault divorce laws. No-fault unequivocally reinforced feminism's aspersion of the homemaker by seriously compromising her ability to resist her husband's quest for divorce, while denying adequate recognition of her contributions to the marital household. These contributions had entitled her, if divorced and not the party at fault, to future financial security commensurate with her marital economic status. Instead, she now receives a comparatively short period of what is sometimes called "rehabilitative alimony,"[111] a term that insults all who have competently performed a housewife's role. *Rehabilitation* has always described a criminal's reformation and therapy after trauma. Today it denotes the financial support given a divorced housewife during the brief transitional period allotted her to prepare for supporting herself after what our society now characterizes as her years misspent as a housewife from which, like a delinquent, she must be rehabilitated.

Enactment of no-fault divorce laws unambiguously warned women to adopt the feminist perspective and replace homemaking with a full-time career. The "present legal system," concluded Lenore

Weitzman, "makes it clear that instead of expecting to be supported, a woman is now expected to become self-sufficient."[112]   As Professor Mary Ann Glendon has observed, through our divorce laws society tells mothers it is unsafe to devote oneself to raising children.[113] Thus, as always, feminist ideology converged with the interests of men who would avoid the responsibility for women that traditional marriage entails.   Contending that "if a woman isn't working in a career, that's her choice and responsibility," such men are well served by no-fault's guarantee that she will bear the brunt of suffering for bad choices.   As one court put it, "a marriage license is not a ticket to a perpetual pension,"[114] but that is precisely what it must be to give a housewife security.   In denying that security, society has rejected traditional marriage.

Because of women's rational fear that they might become comparatively destitute if they were divorced, our no-fault divorce laws exerted tremendous pressure on women to decline the housewife's role.   The Equal Rights Amendment (ERA) would have served the same goal.   By the end of the campaign for enactment, the amendment's only real purpose was to compound further the pressures to drive all women into the work force.   As Jane Mansbridge has noted, decisions of the United States Supreme Court had, by 1982, already changed almost all the laws the ERA was designed to change. The amendment's major legal effect would have been to subject women to the draft and combat service and invalidate certain laws that benefited women; supporters could point to little else they claimed was discriminatory.[115]   But what the amendment had come to represent—and the reason its enactment seemed crucial to the women's movement—was a societal affirmation of the feminist perspective.

In the eyes of both supporters and opponents, passage of the ERA was seen as a repudiation of what Jane Mansbridge has called the "symbolic force" of the "contract between the sexes" that if the woman does the housework and raises the children, the man was obligated to support her.[116]   Barbara Ehrenreich states the issue with honesty and clarity: "What was at stake in the battle over the ERA was the *legitimacy* of women's claim on men's incomes"; the force of feminism, Ehrenreich concedes, was to "allow men to think they have no natural obligation to support women."[117]   Mary Jo Bane anticipated that the ERA would encourage reexamination of marital roles to "stimulate questioning and perhaps change behavior," thereby fostering families where wives are no more likely than husbands to take time from the workplace to rear children.[118]

Contemporary feminism sought the ERA to make a societal declaration that—as divorce courts throughout the nation were already demonstrating—women *have no legitimate claim* on their husbands' earnings and to warn women that they would adopt an anti-feminist perspective and become homemakers at their peril and without institutional support from society. The ERA was to be the final nail in the coffin where feminists hoped to inter the role of homemaker. Assuming the mantle of social feminism, Phyllis Schlafly opposed the amendment to prevent further institutionalization of a feminist perspective that was already discouraging and disheartening women who might be tempted to undertake the much-maligned homemaking role. Although the ERA failed of enactment, the wide acceptance of its message that women *should* have no claim to men's support helped justify preferential treatment of women. Such treatment will always militate against a homemaking role both because the granting of preferences is seen as a societal statement that women are expected to do market work, and because preferences for some women always injure others for whom the disfavored men might serve as family breadwinners.

Stereotype Becomes Cultural Truth

The bulk of writing about women in the past three decades has, in Helena Lopata's words, adopted the "stereotype" of *The Feminine Mystique* "which evaluates work for money as the only worthy effort." Lopata's own studies of housewives disclosed a picture of "increasingly competent and creative" women who have built a "many-faceted life" out of the housewife's role. Yet the prevailing stereotype assumes the "impossibility of creativity in the role," portraying its tasks as "unrewarding, lacking in mental stimulation, and unconnected with mental ability"; women performing the role are depicted as "basically passive, unimaginative, uninterested in events outside their walls, chained to routine tasks, and unable to understand the work their husbands and children perform away from the home." The stereotype is so committed to the view that only a paid career can furnish intellectual identity, observes Lopata, that it dismisses all of the housewife's non-remunerative activities—"such as community participation, artistic effort, educational or child-oriented actions"— as "not challenging to anyone with intelligence."[119]

This stereotypical portrait limned by Friedan and most of the popular and scholarly literature dealing with women is now incorporated as a truth within the fabric of our society. Acquiescence in the housewife's degraded status is part of our cultural knowledge. As Allan Bloom observed, the "woman who now wanted to be a woman in the old sense" would have "to brave the hostile public opinion."[120] Perhaps there is no more telling proof of feminism's success in dishonoring the housewife than the assent given to this feminist teaching by those who otherwise reject its dogma or, at least, recognize its harmful impact on family life.

Thus, when Allan Bloom addressed the argument that women "had a right to cultivate their higher talents instead of being household drudges," he said this view reflected "the view that the bourgeois professions indeed offered an opportunity to fulfill the human potential, while family and particularly the woman's work involved in it were merely in the realm of necessity, limited and limiting" so that "the household was not spiritually fulfilling for women." In this, he allowed, "the feminist case is very strong indeed."[121] Professor Bloom was surely courageous, and so the reader is left to wonder whether he declined to rebut the strong case because he lacked interest, or thought it irrefutable.

In *Children Without Childhood*, Marie Winn sets forth one of the best and most moving descriptions of the great disparity between a good home life and the isolation and neglect of many children with working mothers. She, nonetheless, echoes the harshest feminist appraisals of mothers at home, calling them "childlike," "protected from the realities of life," and "treated as little pets." Winn assumes that women play a subordinate role in the traditional family, being "submissive," "child-wives," "sequestered in almost haremlike seclusion" in a "male-dominated arrangement" in which women are "treated more like children than adults."[122] And thus she validates devaluation of the female role that was designed to fill the very void in children's lives that she had so masterfully depicted.

Amaury De Riencourt deplores feminist denigration of the maternal role, towards which he was almost reverential. But even he alludes to how the rebellious youth who fostered the generation gap of the late 1960s identified "with the feeling of emptiness and uselessness of their largely idle, status-symbolizing mothers."[123] Sociologist David Popenoe argues that "family organization is based on very real, biological differences between men and women," that parental androgyny is neither "what children need" nor is it "a good basis for a stable, lasting marriage," and that "limited infant-parent contacts and non-parental childrearing" carry "considerable risk." At the same time, he also makes today's *pro forma* disclaimer that "it is neither possible nor desirable to return to the traditional nuclear family."[124] But why not? What other family has so successfully devoted itself to rearing children in stable homes?

Even Gertrude Himmelfarb asserts that no one proposes that men and women retreat to their "separate spheres." Immediately after disclaiming support for a revival of such traditionalism, Himmelfarb notes how the decline of the Victorian ethos correlates with the vast increases in those "two powerful indexes of social pathology, illegitimacy and crime." Today's illegitimacy ratio, she states, is "unprecedented, so far as we know, in American history going back to colonial times, and in English history from Tudor times." This explosive increase in illegitimacy began only after 1960. What force, we should ask, had emerged so powerful that it wrought a calamity which, as Himmelfarb observes, some of the most disruptive experiences in our times—including two world wars and the most serious depression in modern times—had never produced.[125] Was the force, perhaps, feminism's successful assault on the traditional nuclear family in which fathers were primarily breadwinners and mothers the child-rearers? If so, why should we withhold support from those who would restore the primacy of separate and distinct sexual roles within the family?

Himmelfarb has documented that this remedy would hardly be draconian. Analyzing Elizabeth Roberts's *A Woman's Place*, which is based on extensive interviews of working-class women about their own and their mothers' lives, Himmelfarb is struck by the "contentment expressed by the women with their roles as wives and mothers—not mere acquiescence but a sense of satisfaction and fulfillment." Roberts has found that, contrary to her own expectation, her research refuted feminist history and did not bear out theories of patriarchy or male oppression of women: "Most of the women she interviewed did not feel that they or their mothers had been exploited by men, at least not by their own men." None "craved to break out of their separate sphere" or "sought the freedom to work outside the home." Those who worked out of necessity "would much have preferred not to have to do so." Furthermore, as Himmelfarb notes, the entire concept of "separate spheres" was "more didactic than descriptive." While middle-class women did not work for pay, "a large number did do serious, regular, *unpaid* work outside the home" in the areas of "philanthropy, social work, social reform, education, local government," areas that were not peripheral to, but at the heart of, Victorian concerns.[126] This kind of activity—which is entirely consistent with child-rearing responsibilities—is, of course, precisely what contemporary feminism has dismissed as worthless "dilettantism."

To say that the feminist perspective has triumphed is not to deny that some within our society are fighting to preserve the traditional family and restore respect to women at home.[127] Among others, Midge Decter, Allan Carlson, Nicholas Davidson, George Gilder, Steven Goldberg, and Michael Levin have opposed the feminist perspective. And self-identified feminists like Christina Hoff Sommers are now scathingly attacking the unscholarly and anti-intellectual developments within academic feminism.[128] But Sommers affirms what she views as Friedan's good "liberal" feminism and denounces only what she identifies as the recent excesses. To include among "the classically liberal feminists," whom she praises, the woman who, more than any other, made the housewife a pariah, indicates that feminism's betrayal of women, which Sommers deplores, does not include its betrayal of traditional women.[129]

Although they are willing to publicize the internecine battles within the feminist movement, publishers have been reluctant to disseminate views that support women at home. Such views not only arouse feminists' wrath but also are largely rejected by the knowledge industry and by both the liberal and conservative cultural elite as being idiosyncratic and somewhat intellectually disreputable.[130] There are, on the other hand, a plethora of books devoted to questioning the merits of traditional families with the mother-at-home and supporting the family with two working parents.[131] Since the feminist perspective is represented to encompass the interests of all women—or at least all women who count—those who adopt an anti-feminist perspective are generally perceived as anti-woman. Hence, Patricia Ireland, President of the National Organization for Women, can assert—with assurance and rare contradiction—that members of the "religious right" (who are among the staunchest defenders of traditional women) "typically don't have the best interests of women at heart."[132] This view, moreover, is not confined to the members of NOW but has significant support among the newly powerful conservatives of the so-called Counter Counterculture. Largely concerned with economic issues, this new conservative elite is wary of both "anti-feminist traditionalism" and the "religious right."[133]

That the stereotype of the housewife has become a mainstream cultural truth explains how the academic feminists of "Women's Studies" can view Professor Elizabeth Fox-Genovese as unacceptably moderate, even though she affirms the stereotype.[134] Concluding that the societal changes reflected in contemporary feminism "will not be reversed," Fox-Genovese admonishes young women to reject dependence on men for support and protection: they must dismiss celebration of "women's maternal roles and instincts" as "nostalgia for a world that has gone beyond resurrection." Nor is this to be regretted, she maintains, since women who found "their sense of self-worth and self-respect in their roles as wives and mothers" were only making the best of their situation in the absence of any alternatives.[135] Whatever her disagreements with the radicals, she is in their camp on this most crucial issue.

Although in *Feminism Is not the Story of My Life*, Fox-Genovese now acknowledges that many women attach great importance to child-rearing and suffer guilt because of their absence from home, she retracts nothing that she had said in *Feminism Without Illusions*. Recognition of women's yearnings to mother their children, she believes, calls for maternity leaves (up to a year is considered ideal), followed by return to a job that permits one to be home for an illness or other "emergency"—as if the most important and rewarding part of child-rearing activity after age one occurs during sickness or emergencies.[136] There is no doubt that for some women this amount of child-rearing activity is adequate, or more than adequate. But any woman who might be considering marriage, motherhood, and domesticity as her primary career cannot look to Fox-Geno-vese for support. She tells us that "women owe Friedan an incal-culable debt for *The Feminine Mystique*," the very book that calls the housewife a parasite, a being less than human, who lives without using adult capabilities or intelligence and who lacks any real function. And why do women owe this incalculable debt? It is because *The Feminine Mystique* showed us that "domesticity was not a satisfactory story of an intelligent woman's life."[137]

The title of her book notwithstanding, feminism is indeed the story of Fox-Genovese's life, the only story she advocates for women. Warning again that the changes wrought by feminism are irreversible, she argues that women must reject reliance on men for support and protection and remain independent, because full-time domesticity should not be the story of their lives.[138] She delights in the role reversal that is the essence of contemporary feminism, noting that her husband will have dinner on the table when she comes home, and telling us that she earns more than he.[139] In *Feminism Without Illusions*, she discusses the rewards of her feminist awakening, recalling her sense of achievement in gaining mastery over her very large male dog and her exhilaration at unsettling her husband by asserting to the dog that she was "boss of all the bosses" within the household. Observing that her husband "has lost a good deal in the way of service since the early days of our marriage," she states that he is more likely to do the cooking than she and has "especially lost the right to be the one who is busier, who faces the greater demands from the outside world."[140] But mastering a man in this way seems, to some women, an adolescent thrill. We have not sought the economic independence she values so highly, because we believe that this independence extracts too high a price.

Fox-Genovese's concession to the force of maternal yearnings is to declare "what a pity it would be to have women throw away the possibility of enjoying their children for a few years, before returning to work."[141] She never refers to mothers staying home with their children without including some modifier like "for a few years" or "at least for a while." I would have found her "few years" a pitiful token of what might have been a full and rich life at home throughout the many years it takes to raise a family well. Only the dependence on our husbands that Fox-Genovese so decisively rejects can afford women those many precious years rearing our children at home. And that dependence, some of us discover, can also afford us a great emotional and sexual satisfaction that can continue long after those children are gone.

When I was a co-panelist with Fox-Genovese on this topic, she opined that one might think someone like me would have wanted to pay back to society for my education by returning to work.[142] It is beyond her ken that women like me believe we have made the greatest possible contribution to society by personally raising our children in stable families. If she had chosen to validate our feelings—even though she does not share them—her book would have championed reform of no-fault divorce laws; instead, like the feminist she is, she relies on the existence of those laws to persuade women that they must shun dependence on men. Whereas reform of no-fault divorce laws should head the agenda of anyone who would support traditional women, Fox-Genovese merely observes that these laws, "beginning in 1970, might have warned those who cared to pay attention"; those who did not pay attention "learned the hard way that marriage is no longer a reliable career."[143]

And if she chose to validate the aspirations of traditional women, she would also stop avoiding any discussion about the merits of domesticity versus market work. Instead, she relies on the ploy that economic necessity requires almost all women to work, an unsupported claim she steadfastly asserts, although it is untrue for all upper-class and most middle-class women in two-parent families. As one commentator has recently observed, a "greater percentage of families classifed as poor in this country own color televisions, vcrs, microwaves, dishwashers and dryers, than do *all* families in a number of other industrialized countries, including Belgium, Denmark, France, Germany, Great Britain, Italy, the Netherlands, Spain, Sweden, and Switzerland." This indicates that when two parents decide that they both will work, "they are choosing to sustain a certain standard of living rather than one of them remaining at home with the children."[144]

IT IS NOW CONSIDERED excessively polemical—indeed in poor taste—to question feminism's stereotypical portrait of the housewife by examining, as I have done, the words used to paint the portrait. Young women, the cultural elite assure them, must accept the feminist stereotype and not analyze its origins or question its accuracy. De Beauvoir, Friedan, Millett, Steinem, and the rest were, in feminist eyes, like the storm troopers of the movement; they did what had to be done to bring down the edifice of the traditional family. But what they said that enabled them to bring it down should now be dismissed as the rhetoric of ancient history. Do not examine this rhetoric, the elite tell young women, but blindly join the brave new world of working mothers and surrogate child-rearing that the rhetoric helped feminists to create.

It is because society has accepted this stereotype of the housewife as a cultural truth that Professor Carolyn Heilbrun can go virtually unchallenged when she asserts that the woman who devotes herself to domesticity lacks "selfhood," since she fails to act "in the public domain" and exists, instead, as a "female impersonator," simply "fulfilling the needs of others."[145] How can anyone familiar with the real world of demanding market production (possibly, some academics really are not) ever believe a worker in the marketplace does anything *except* fulfill the needs of others? What did I do as a practicing attorney except fulfill clients' needs?—they were surely not my own needs. It was during those years in the marketplace, before I had borne my children, that I sometimes did feel like a female impersonator.

Why, one must wonder, are feminists convinced that fulfilling the market demands of strangers is so much worthier an endeavor than attending to the needs of one's own family? Is it really too late to challenge this conviction? A challenge seems necessary because a life that requires the constriction of marital and maternal relationships in favor of a materialist pursuit of career achievement bears a remarkable resemblance to the pornographer's world of sex without emotions. This is the sexual world that the feminist revolution also embraced.

3

The Groined Archway

Men will always be of the opinion that the one serious thing in life is sexual enjoyment. Woman, for all the members of my sex, is a groined archway opening on the infinite. That may not be a very elevated attitude, but it is fundamental to the male.

Gustave Flaubert [1]

Of all the riddles of a married life, said my father . . . there is not one that has more intricacies in it than this—that from the very moment the mistress of the house is brought to bed, every female in it, from my lady's gentlewoman down to the cinder-wench, becomes an inch taller for it; and give themselves more airs upon that single inch, than all the other inches put together.

I think rather, replied my uncle Toby, that 'tis we who sink an inch lower. If I meet but a woman with child, I do it. 'Tis a heavy tax upon that half of our fellow-creatures, brother Shandy, said my uncle Toby.

Laurence Sterne [2]

*H*OW SHOULD WOMEN HAVE RESPONDED four decades ago
to the conditions provoking their discontent? The general
grievance that society undervalued a woman's status as
wife and mother was hardly new, for an apprehension of being
underappreciated often gnaws at men and women alike. New were
the increased public attention devoted to women's alleged deficiencies and the fact that many men not only failed to appreciate
her but were also rejecting the breadwinner ethic by declining to
marry and support her. Chapter 2 discussed the response the revitalized women's movement chose—a further devaluation of the
housewife's role to drive women into the marketplace. There was
another response that could have alleviated women's discontent,
but the movement not only rejected this response, but promoted
an ideology that was its diametric opposite.

The rejected response would have relied on the two attitudes
expressed by Flaubert and Sterne. These are attitudes sufficiently
widespread that they provide the framework within which most
men and women play out their relationships with each other and
resolve the resulting conflicts. Although accurately appraising the
majority's view, Flaubert certainly did not speak for all members
of his sex—nor apparently for himself at all times, since he also
engaged in homosexual affairs.[3] Neither do all women delight in
their fertility, nor do all men feel in awe of this capacity or acknowledge its cardinal significance. Nevertheless, the pervasiveness of
these attitudes makes man's sexual need of woman, together with
the acknowledgment by both of the overarching value of woman's
fertility, the best foundation for a stable society in which most
individuals can lead satisfying lives.

In *Sexual Suicide* and its revision, *Men and Marriage*, George
Gilder describes with keen insight how woman uses man's sexual
need to bind him to her and their offspring, socializing him to
work and provide for them; thereby is created the "sexual constitution"
of society. Gilder may be the writer feminists most despise. A

feminist reviewer's description of *Men and Marriage* as "profoundly misogynist"[4] reflects this antipathy. Gilder defends a family structure predicated on loving, procreative sexuality in a monogamous marriage with a dependable man, who happily assumes the obligation of supporting his family so that his wife can enjoy all the delights motherhood has to offer, without the burden of working outside the home. Characterizing as "woman-hating" Gilder's cogent advocacy makes very clear that feminism is no friend of any woman who would choose this family structure. Such a woman is the kind feminists have set out to eliminate.

Contemporary feminism has consistently derided efforts like Gilder's to validate the worthiness of this traditional woman, whom I call the awakened Brünnhilde. An apt rebuke to this now triumphant feminism can be taken from Disraeli's comment at the end of his first speech in Parliament when, as his voice was drowned out by derisive shouting, he rejoined: "I will sit down now, but the time will come when you will hear me."[5] Disraeli was heard eventually, and so too may those who, like Gilder, support traditional women someday be heard. He does not address the interests of lesbians, but if heterosexual women begin to listen, many will find that he mediates to them a paradigm of practicable relations between men and women that not only is more realistic for them than what feminists offer, but also is erotic and can provide the best guidelines for a fulfilling life.

Although the sources of their discontent were complicated and mutually reinforcing, women would have alleviated that discontent if they had resisted the emasculating forces in our society and encouraged the growth of mature masculinity. Instead, feminists undertook to deprecate masculinity more viciously than ever, while at the same time joining the sexual revolution and according men sex on male terms. This gift of easy sex impairs the long-term interests of both men and women by catering to the male's adolescent pursuit of sex without responsibility. Because it guaranteed men success in this pursuit, the sexual revolution further undermined the breadwinner ethic by inhibiting development of the mature masculinity which fosters the willingness to assume reponsibility for a wife and family.

Granted that achieving societal change can be a lengthy and difficult process, a woman can, nonetheless, readily alter her own behavior. It is easy enough to value and acknowledge what Margaret Mead referred to as "the lordly maleness" of husband and son; no single action is better designed to thwart their emasculation. Both Philip Wylie and *Playboy* perceived that suburban housewives could have the best game in town—as some of us privileged to enjoy that role well know. But many of these fortunate women had come to take their good fortune for granted, ignoring Margaret Mead's insight that boys look to their mothers, and men to their wives, for "assurance that they are good."

Neglecting to acknowledge the importance of their good fortune's provider, women had become unmindful of William Butler Yeats's admonition: "No man has ever lived that had enough of children's gratitude or woman's love."[6] Satisfying this male need comes easily to those women who possess, in turn, what George Eliot described so well in *Middlemarch* as "the ardent woman's need to rule beneficently by making the joy of another soul."[7] In short, a man usually derives greater satisfaction from being loved and a woman from giving love. In this difference, as well as many others, men and women—contrary to feminist teaching—are quite different animals and can complement each other very well.

To ameliorate the problems caused by society's overvaluation of male marketplace activities and women's dissatisfactions with a traditional female role, masculinity must be reinforced. Only a man secure in his masculinity will place a high value on the traditional female role and exert himself to make the role viable. The fiber of effete, attenuated, androgynous males must be shored up so that they can happily marry, reproduce, and assume responsibility for supporting a family. A man secure in his masculinity will not usually believe himself suited to the female role, but he will respect the woman who assumes it and take pride in providing for her and their children. Such a man will afford his wife the security and affirmation that enable her to deal with the troubling aspects of her role and perform it with satisfaction.

In Midge Decter's beautiful expression, a woman needs a husband "who will agree to keep her safe while she brings forth her gifts and who by accepting these gifts will not only provide the measure of their value, and so of hers, but will help her to her own sense of having contributed fully to the human estate."[8] Many mature heterosexual women can find the implications of this statement, like many of Gilder's observations, to be erotic and to describe what they would consider an ideal relationship.

To the contemporary feminist, however, this relationship is not ideal but undesirable and oppressive, because it makes women dependent on men. She does not want men to value a woman simply for being wife and mother, nor does she want the traditional female role to be more satisfying. A man's valuation of the gifts she might bring forth within the marital home is trivial, even ludicrous, compared to the value she places on societal acclaim of her marketplace achievement. The male who fits within the feminist mold—*the male that all feminist social and political endeavors are designed to form*—is the androgynous male who happily performs aspects of the traditional female role and shuns a sole breadwinner role that would enable his wife to devote herself to home and child-nurturing.

Traditional marriage is flawed, however, by the fact that it is a particularly risky relationship for the woman. In the long run, as Gilder argues, men's ability to become mature, productive, and full participants in the life cycle depends on women's willingness to socialize them and bear their children. But we play out our daily lives in the short run; there, the man's dependency is not so evident, while the traditional woman is fatally dependent upon one man. The marketplace usually affords various options for achievement so that, if dissatisfied, one can move about within his present workplace or seek another job. Within a traditional marriage, on the other hand, a woman is stuck with the valuation that one man places on the gifts she brings forth. Her life, as Euripides's Medea lamented, "is enviable" if "our husband does not struggle under the marriage yoke." However, "if a man grows tired of the company at home, he can go out, and find a cure for tediousness," while "wives are forced to look to one man only."[9]

As true today as in the classical Greece where a betrayed Medea deplored her fate, woman's one-sided economic dependency is the most serious flaw in her traditional role. It constitutes a risk that was once—and could again be—ameliorated by divorce laws that, unlike our present no-fault laws, are designed to protect home-makers and their children. With the disingenuity that pervades their arguments, contemporary feminists now indict no-fault divorce laws for causing women's insecurity within marriage, citing the risk of divorce as the reason women must abandon their tradition-al role in favor of career pursuits. Yet, enactment of these very laws was probably the single most important tool the women's movement employed to destroy the viability of woman's traditional role by eroding the institutional supports that had insulated women from the hazards of their marital economic dependency.

Erosion of the institutional supports protecting homemakers from the risks of divorce was crucial to achieving feminism's primary goal of convincing women that their traditional role is oppressive and inferior. And so trusting young women were told by Professor Elizabeth Fox-Genovese, speaking as an authority on "women's studies," that the "most dramatic change in the lives of young women—although many have no wish to recognize it—is that mar-riage is not a viable career." Marriage, she says, "no longer serves as a surrogate career," for "[t]oday, no law . . . can force a man to support a woman."[10] But, of course, our laws could do so if we wished.

Until our society capitulated to feminism's quest to make a career serve as woman's surrogate life, we fairly successfully compelled financially able men to support the women to whom they were legally obligated. We fail to do so today only because society acquiesced in teachings like Fox-Genovese's that women's traditional role as "bearers and rearers of children and helpmeets to men" is not properly viewed as involving "work that draws upon their talents and enhances their self-respect."[11] It is precisely because feminists believe this above all else that they have endorsed no-fault divorce. Although, like Fox-Genovese, feminists will plead that economic realities preclude women's return to their traditional role, their antipathy for domesticity is what precludes them from supporting that return, whatever the economic realities might be.

Fox-Genovese has taught "women's studies," the cottage industry of academic feminism dedicated to instilling in women a conscious-ness of their oppressed status and convincing them that only market production will use their talents and enhance their self-respect.[12] Those young women, who, Fox-Genovese tells us, do not want to accept her teaching that marriage is no longer a viable career, already suspect that the economic independence which feminists value so highly comes at a fearful price. To construct her life in accordance with this feminist teaching ill serves any young woman who yearns for satisfactions beyond the marketplace, but whose heart is grip-ped by a chilling dread at the thought of leaving her child to go earn the paycheck that feminists assure her is today's only path to self-respect.

If society would challenge contemporary feminism by restor-ing institutional supports for homemakers, traditional marriage would not be seriously threatened by western man's tendency to overvalue male achievements, so long as a man acknowledges the appropriateness of his wife's path and happily assumes responsi-bility for her. He must recognize that in those aspects of her life involving her reproductiveness, she is indeed stepping to the mu-sic of a different drummer. This acknowledgment comes easily to a man secure in his masculinity; only through the blurred vision of an androgynous male are men and women perceived as fungible and a husband's status seen to be enhanced by his wife's achievement in the workplace. De Riencourt and Mead believed that the overvaluation of male achievement is a flaw peculiar to Western man, but probably—while most pronounced in Western society—it occurs everywhere. The benign effect of its presence is reflected in our remarkable technological development and affluence, which are lacking in those societies deemed free of this overvaluation.

The subject of men's evaluation of their own achievements was exhausted when George Eliot observed in *Middlemarch* that: "A man is seldom ashamed of feeling that he cannot love a woman so well when he sees a certain greatness in her: nature having intended greatness for men. But nature has sometimes made sad oversights in carrying out her intention."[13] Virginia Woolf echoed this sentiment in *To the Lighthouse*, when describing Mr. Ramsay's appraisal of the hallowed Mrs. Ramsay: he "exaggerated her ignorance, her simplicity, for he liked to think that she was not clever."[14] Because of the "solid sense of irreversible achievement" that child-bearing affords woman, she can well afford to tolerate the male's tendency to overvalue his own achievements, a tendency that simply reflects his need for comparable satisfaction.

So long as a man will do for her what she wants done, a woman—including she who has received nature's unintended gift of greatness—suffers no injury by acceding to his more urgent need for claiming that attribute. A serious problem arises only when (as has happened with the revived women's movement) a substantial number of women themselves undertake to devalue the traditional roles of wife and mother and, out of envy of the male role, collaborate with men in their overvaluation of male achievements.

In feminist eyes, only a male chauvinist could recommend reinforcement of masculinity as a response to women's discontent. This is heresy to an ideology that, in one of its many falsifications of reality, attributed women's discontent to the strong, patriarchal male. That this figure had become a vanishing species was recognized by Herb Goldberg, a leading figure in the "men's liberation movement." Not women's oppression, he notes, but "the decay and demise of the male" inspired the feminist movement.[15] Yet, invoking a chimera of male oppression that existed only in their fantasies, feminists took up battle against the very concept of masculinity. Let Margaret Mead's native woman bow her head before the lordly maleness of *her* four-year-old son, our liberated woman would squelch the last spark of manhood in her own son, as feminists undertook to spur our effete, attenuated males further down the path to complete androgyny.

In prosecuting their attack on traditional women, feminists undertook to revolutionize our terms of discourse in order daily to exhort society with the message that women *must* change. This overwhelmingly successful revolutionary effort has produced today's variation of Orwellian newspeak. The word "sex"—clearly evocative of an unequivocal demarcation between men and women—has been replaced by the pale and neutral "gender," and the words "man" and "he"—now avoided as if they were worse than obscenities—have been replaced by the neuter "person" and by gramatically confusing, cumbersome, or offensive variants of "he/she" or "she" alone as the pronoun of general reference.

Since it was never even remotely in doubt that when used as a general referent, the male pronoun included females, this change was never designed to prevent confusion. The change has, on the contrary, often created confusion. Its purpose is solely ideological. Making the pronoun of general reference male is, logically—and this is how I always thought of it—a counterbalance to the quint-essential importance conferred on women by their role of child-bearer and nurturer. Males were given the pronoun because child-bearing is what really counts, and only women can do it; men must do other things to justify their existence. Each refusal to use the male pronoun as the general referent is intended as—and is understood by society to be—an assertion that the traditional female role is inferior. By taking back the pronoun, society is de-claring that this child-bearing ability—the one thing women pos-sess and men lack—is of much less value than we once thought.

But of all the reactions to women's discontent, the most revolutionary was women's embrace of the "sexual revolution." Through its endorsement of that revolution, contemporary feminism has successfully persuaded a large number of females to adopt male sexual patterns and thereby abandon the bargaining power of the groined archway. Feminists have encouraged women to reject the double standard of sexual morality which has traditionally tolerated male sexual promiscuousness, while expecting the female to cultivate modesty, sexual reticence, and discretion about whom she permits to enter her inner space. By convincing women to mimic male sexual promiscuity, feminists have taken a giant step towards achieving the goal most crucial to their success: convincing women and society that sexual differences are unimportant. If, as feminists have claimed, men and women are virtually fungible, then women should be no more likely than men to stay home caring for children.

The result of women's dramatic abandonment of their sexual bargaining power that the double standard had assured them has been a decline in marriage rates, an increase in divorce rates, and a surge in the number of women entering the work force. And thus women also have relinquished their role as the civilizers of men, who teach them to become responsible job holders, husbands, and fathers. Instead, women now bestow sexual rewards on men without requiring that they work in the hairpin factory to support women and their children.

FEMINIST ENDORSEMENT OF PROMISCUOUS SEX

An effective response to women's discontent would have been a strategy based on the bedrock truths of man's sexual need of woman and the primacy of a woman's fertility. A woman's ability fully to exercise and enjoy her reproductive capabilities depends on the breadwinner ethic. Without this ethic, she is forced to participate in marketplace activities that require her to curtail and diminish her reproductive accomplishments. To serve the interests of traditional women, therefore, it is necessary to revive the eroded breadwinner ethic, and the primary tool is man's sexual need.

What should women have done when faced with men whose prototypes were the Beat, the Hippie, and the Playboy? Beats should have largely been abandoned as hopeless, for they did not take the delight in women, so well described by Flaubert, that is probably the single best foundation for a successful marriage. The Hippie resembled a Playboy without ambition, but with the sometimes endearing characteristic of reminding a society (which Philip Wylie perceived with some accuracy as ravenously consumerist) that it could easily live on less—an insight congenial to some of us who had experienced the Great Depression.

Playboys and Hippies, both, could have been reclaimed by women determined to uphold Gilder's sexual constitution of society. Most of these men were not seeking access to prostitutes—an ever-present option—but access to women who were as sexually available as prostitutes, and often costing less, while considered socially respectable. The male revolt against the breadwinner ethic could have respectable sex without marriage only if society changed the standards by which female sexual behavior was judged. Contemporary feminism has given the male revolt what it wanted by promoting male sexual patterns as the ideal for women as well.

Why, feminists argued, should women be deprived of the delights offered by a sexual promiscuity that men may enjoy? Because, they reasoned, imposition of discriminatory patriarchal biases forces women to acquiesce in the sexual double standard that values premarital virginity much more highly in a woman than in a man. In the view of many women, acquiescence in this double standard—which feminists attacked for inhibiting women's sexual freedom—always served women's interests by helping them resist male pressure to engage in sexual activity they wished to avoid or postpone. Contemporary feminism taught them otherwise. To establish what feminists perceived as "equality" with men, women were exhorted to become sexual revolutionaries. For many, this pursuit necessitated feigning an interest in sexual activities as casual as those of prostitutes, whose own interest, not surprisingly, is also usually feigned.

The sexual revolution, whereby so-called liberated women mimicked male sexual promiscuity by engaging in casual sexual intercourse without commitment, was a gift these liberated women gave to males. Like many feminist social "contributions," this gift mainly benefited men and particularly harmed those women who wanted to be wives and mothers. In their desperation to be like men, feminists encouraged women to imitate the limited male sexuality of a biological contribution and satisfaction that is confined to a brief copulatory act of ejaculation. Feminists ridiculed the idea that women possess a very different and diffuse sexuality which can provide a widespread biological contribution and satisfaction of virtually limitless dimension. This diffuse sexuality encompasses, in Margaret Mead's words, the woman's "maternal functions as a whole," from conception through pregnancy, birth, and suckling.[16]

It is precisely their innate awareness of the magnitude of the event's unrealized implications that causes many women to find casual sexual encounters to be relatively meaningless experiences affording scant pleasure. The post-coital *tristesse* integral to many women's—but rarely men's—experience of sexual intercourse can also be explained, in part, by the overwhelming significance this event can assume in a woman's life. Only when the event terminates in a fashion that assuages her sense of loss can it be a thoroughly satisfying sexual encounter. Ministering to her *tristesse* is an obligation happily assumed by any competent lover. This consolation, together with satisfaction of the other requirements of her own diffuse sexuality, can be obtained by women who are not diffident about their differences from men. It is a man's reciprocal delight in the gratifications he attains within the groined archway that enables a woman to secure both his acknowledgment of her very different female sexuality and his devotion to helping her obtain to the fullest extent possible the rewards that are promised by that sexuality.

Feminist sexual revolutionaries have grievously disserved women by convincing them to become diffident about their differences and to trade their immense power of the groined archway for the short-term, inconsequential, ultimately unsatisfying, pseudo-male sexuality that the liberated woman has received in return. A fragment of a Greek epic poem from the sixth century B.C. says about the pleasures of the sex act: "Of ten shares the man enjoys one, the woman by enjoying ten satisfies her mind."[17] The consequence of the sexual revolution was to confine women to a male's one share of sexual pleasure.

The sexual revolution and the accompanying creation of a virtually unrestricted abortion right are among the most significant events of the past thirty years. Premarital sexual intercourse very likely occurred in the pre-revolutionary period with greater frequency than was acknowledged, and the incidence of post-revolutionary heterosexual casual sex may well be less than our society's ubiquitous eroticism indicates. Nevertheless, sexual promiscuity has vastly increased, and most important, it has been promoted as the acceptable and respectable ideal for women.

All instruments of communication—television, movies, theater, the music of rock and roll, and contemporary writing, from trash journalism to serious literature—have delivered the virtually unchallenged message that "good girls do." The assumption that sexual intercourse is just as acceptable and *expected* a part of even the most casual dating relationship as a good-night kiss has been institutionalized in our society. The groundwork for the adoption of this new morality had already been laid by spokesmen of the mental health movement and the "helping professions" who, as Christopher Lasch noted, had "positioned themselves in the vanguard of the revolt against old-fashioned middle-class morality."[18] By the early 1970s, with the exception of some religious groups, our society was giving no institutional support whatever to any girl or woman who attempted to uphold an ideal of premarital chastity. This ideal was, on the contrary, treated with scorn as a vestige of discredited Victorian morality.

With respect to sex, the message of *Playboy* magazine and the pornographers became feminism's message, endorsed by many established women's magazines (which were sympathetic to and often staffed by feminists) and by *Ms*, the magazine established to disseminate feminist views. It was certainly not a new message. Women have always been bombarded with it in the course of entreaties to comply with a man's sexual demands: only an insensate vegetable, goes the mantra, would not desire sexual intercourse with him as much as he desires it with her. Now, however, the importunate males were joined, and their arguments buttressed, by organized groups of articulate and well-educated women who claimed to be, and were perceived by society as, speaking for all women.

Instead of justifying women's sexual reluctance and fortifying their resistance to male seduction—the traditional role of female solidarity—feminists depicted this reluctance as proof of women's inequality and argued that females should feel the same undifferentiated lust for males that males feel for females. Once women learned through feminist consciousness-raising that their reluctance to become sexually promiscuous had been inculcated in them solely to benefit the oppressive patriarchy, then said feminists, women would be freed to enjoy casual sex just as much as sexually predatory men do. Responding to the lesson, women, in Midge Decter's words, "undertook the obligations of an impersonal lust they did not feel but only believed in."[19]

While vehemently insisting that women should not be viewed as "sex objects," feminists ironically adopted a model of female sexual behavior in which the woman became nothing but a sex object, the status of prostitutes and women depicted in pornography. Most heterosexual men, I believe, think that one of the most important functions a woman serves is as a sex object. This is a good quality in men that well serves traditional women, for it is what gives us power over men and enables us to demand that we become a great deal to them before we will allow them to use us in sex. There is nothing wrong with being a sex object; it can be very gratifying. The moments when I become the objective of my husband's sexual attentions are the most enjoyable of my life; they surpass by a wide margin those spent as an intellectual object discussing the First Amendment. Except for nursing my babies, I have experienced no pleasure remotely comparable to that of being the sex object of a dependable and loving man who fathered my children and always provided for me and those children.

What is wrong is to be a sex object and nothing more, which is precisely what is involved in the sexual encounters that feminists have promoted. I can imagine nothing more sterile and disheartening for a woman than to become a sex object in a relationship that lacks commitment, stability, and futurity, offering only what Roger Scruton calls "the curious pleasure" kindled by the contact of sexual parts.[20] Falsifying reality yet again, contemporary feminism has compared traditional women like me to prostitutes on the grounds that the sexual activity that affords our pleasure, together with our other household activities, constitutes the purchase price of our support.[21] No such aspersion, said feminists, could be cast upon the woman who supported herself through market production; her sexual pursuits—however casual they might be—proclaimed her equality with the man, since she received no more than he from the sexual transaction. To their distress, many of these women soon realized how valueless was that which they did receive.

Feminism's conviction that women should adopt male sexual patterns follows from its commitment to an ideology that, whenever possible, denies the existence of sexual differences. As always, the movement has taken the position that men and women should behave in the same way and that what males do is better than what females have traditionally done. While dissenters within the movement have argued that real differences do exist between men and women and must be taken into account, they have almost never questioned the superiority of traditional male market activities; nor have they given any support to women who would return to their traditional role.[22]

Women's admitted differences, contend the dissenters, must merely be permitted to shape the way in which they perform market activities. Thus, Felice Schwartz's finding that it cost more to employ women in management than men was the foundation for demanding modifications that would adapt workplaces to the reality of women's differences. In practice, this demand for recognition of their differences has amounted to a reduction in what is required of women in the workplace and the securing of changes in the standards by which women's performance is judged, usually by lowering them.[23] Despite its internal battles, activist feminism has remained committed to the belief that most differences between men and women are culturally imposed by a patriarchal society. Every position taken by the movement has sought to minimize the importance of whatever biological differences between the sexes it must concede do exist.

The crucial biological difference, woman's ability to conceive, is the basis of the double standard of sexual morality. Just as aggressive and undifferentiated lust enables a man to compete most effectively for the woman who will bear his children, so feminine modesty and chastity enable a woman to stand back, in Midge Decter's words, like "a fortress meant for storming,"[24] until she chooses the man she finds most suited to father and provide for her children. Among the strategies developed in response to the two sexes' very different evolutionary psychologies, this sexual double standard has been the single most powerful ally of women seeking to maintain their sexual reticence and secure a husband. As Robert Wright bluntly puts this cultural truth, "if it is harder to drag men to the altar today than it used to be, one reason is that they don't have to stop there on the way to the bedroom."[25]

In order to persuade society—and women in particular—that women are equal to and fungible with men, it was crucial that contemporary feminism seek to destroy this double standard of sexual morality. Convincing women to mimic male sexual patterns would be a significant step towards minimizing the importance of biological differences between the sexes enough to make men and women seem to be virtually indistinguishable.

FEMALE CHASTITY AND THE PRECIOUSNESS OF WOMEN

Female chastity is valued because the woman's inner space generates and then houses our progeny. Attribution of value to feminine chastity protects the male's interest in rearing only those children he has in fact sired. Male esteem for chaste women, however, is largely theoretical: most women's experience has confirmed the likelihood that, in any particular instance, males readily forego the abstract benefits conferred by an ideal of female chastity in order to obtain concrete and immediate sexual satisfaction. Men's motivation for valuing female chastity, moreover, is immaterial to women: they usually do know who has fathered their children and will make the man privy to whatever knowledge on the subject serves their own best interests. Feminists regard the double standard of sexual morality as one of the worst abuses of patriarchal oppression, but it has been largely through women's efforts that an ideal of feminine chastity has been upheld. Only men with a minimal drive for heterosexual sex and women with scant knowledge of men could ever believe that women remained chaste because of male reticence and forbearance.

Women with choices (non-sequestered women) upheld the double standard not simply because it was forced upon them, but because most of them perceived it to function as a protection, not an affliction. Pathetic Hetty Sorrel in George Eliot's *Adam Bede* suffers because she kills her baby, not because she violates the sexual double standard; Arthur Donnithorne refuses to marry her because she is not of his social class and could never be a suitable wife, not because she is unchaste. Yet, even critics of other aspects of feminist ideology subscribe to the myth of contemporary feminism that, prior to the recent sexual revolution, the double standard was an affliction to women. A typical example is Katherine Kersten's belief that "women have benefited significantly from their new-found sexual autonomy" afforded by the sexual revolution.[26]

To credit the sexual revolution with providing previously unavailable sexual opportunities to women is to believe that there has ever been a time in history when relationships between women and heterosexual men were customarily marred by the man's refusal to have sexual intercourse with a willing woman. Such refusal has rarely been women's problem in dealing with heterosexual men. The only result feminists have accomplished by endorsing the sexual revolution has been to deprive women of the societal support they need to *refuse* to engage in casual sexual intercourse in the fashion of sexually predatory males. There is no justification whatever for feminism's claim that its sexual revolution afforded women sexual opportunities previously denied them. That women in my generation lacked opportunities to engage in premarital sexual intercourse is one of the most ludicrous of the feminist falsifications of reality.

Absent a societal custom of having a trained examiner conduct a physical inspection to determine virginity, a woman is not much deterred by any sexual double standard. The memory of few living today in Western society runs back to a time when a woman would be impugned for not shedding blood on her bridal sheets. Certainly, for many years before the sexual revolution, women's athleticism and indulgence in a wide range of premarital sexual activities short of penile vaginal penetration greatly decreased any expectation that blood *would* stain her wedding bed. As a practical matter, certain knowledge of her virginity, like complete confidence in the orgasmic outcome of her sexual encounters, is solely in a woman's domain.[27] If a double standard *could* reliably inhibit women, some African societies might never have adopted such draconian measures as clitoridectomy and infibulation to insure the virginity and marital chastity these societies insist upon.[28]

Justifying Chastity

Women's justification for chastity is that our inner space is infinitely precious because of its child-bearing potentiality: the physical and psychological vulnerability that characterize our submission to sexual intercourse preclude casual participation in that act. It is this feeling of our preciousness that reluctant women have often tried to articulate when parrying male entreaties to engage in sexual intercourse. The man would argue—as feminists argued when telling women they should feel and behave just like men in sexual matters—that since males so very much enjoy thrusting their penises into numerous vaginas, what is wrong with us that we do not want our vaginas to serve as receptacles for numerous penises—or at least for his. Increasingly effective methods of contraception and ready availability of abortion weaken the argument that one fears pregnancy, although rejection of abortion as an option can add some strength to this claim. Yet, we always knew there was another reason for our reluctance. We attempted to express it by saying the act is too special for us to be done casually; it would be so much more important to us than to them. Males, under the sway of a more urgent need than ours (a reality feminists would deny), emphasize the act's physical pleasure and minimize its metaphysical implications.

Chaste Women: Stupid and Uninteresting

Deprecation of female chastity is always grounded in a denial of a symbolic or metaphysical dimension to the sex act. Thus, the theme of Judge Richard A. Posner's *Sex and Reason* is to "propose the concept of *morally indifferent sex*," a concept that treats premarital intercourse as simply "a generally harmless source of pleasure."[29] His objective is not merely to set aside the topic of sex "as charged with moral significance" in order to concentrate on sex "as just another source of regulatory issues." Rather, he questions whether the sex act *has* a moral dimension—whether "a moral conception of sex . . . is vital to civilization" (a proposition he finds unconvincing)—and he seeks to facilitate societal treatment of sex as a topic of moral indifference by dispelling our ignorance about sex and its consequences.[30]

Posner, like feminist sexual revolutionaries, believes women upheld the double standard only because they valued virginity and marital chastity as commodities to be traded for a husband's support within a traditional marriage. In this view, once participation in market production frees women from dependence on men, the commodities of virginity and marital chastity have no further value to a woman. Yet they do. Women like myself can grow up far from sequestered (lying about my age, I obtained my first job at fourteen, working a night shift with working-class men). We can enjoy the best education. We can have a profession that guarantees complete financial independence. And still we recoil from the sexual promiscuity that is so attractive to men.

Financial independence may depreciate the commodity value of women's virginity and marital chastity, but some of us will shun sexual promiscuity nonetheless. We would feel demeaned and degraded by the casual sexual activities that were urged upon us by feminist sexual revolutionaries and artfully justified as harmless sources of pleasure by Posner, the erudite economist and jurist. He tells us that the "traditional female role, in which premarital virginity and marital chastity are so emphasized, is an impediment to women's educational and occupational, as well as their sexual, equality." "For the sake of chastity," says Posner—quoting the thrice-divorced, habitually adulterous, libertine philosopher Bertrand Russell—women "have been kept artificially stupid and therefore uninteresting."[31]

As Paul Johnson has shown, to arouse Bertrand Russell's interest a woman needed little more than to be sexually available and minimally attractive. That Russell would seriously look to women for intellectual stimulation—however unchaste they might be—is belied by the testimony of his second wife that he "did not really believe in the equality of women with men . . . he believed the male intellect to be superior to that of the female." Since he had "no scruples about seducing any woman who fell in his way"—his victims included "chambermaids, governesses, any young and pretty female whisking around the house"[32]—one doubts that women could have been made *more* interesting to him. Nor is it credible that he wanted women relieved of their "artificial stupidity" so that they might develop the resources and confidence to resist his seduction. Russell denigrated chastity not because it made women less interesting—it surely makes younger women, at least, more interesting—but in order to make them more sexually available, without the necessity of engaging in what he regarded as the very burdensome subterfuges his adulterous activities entailed.[33]

Posner offers no other coherent reason for condemning the sexual modesty and reticence integral to traditional femininity. Why *would* premarital virginity and marital chastity impede either a woman's educational or occupational endeavors? It was certainly never my experience that they did. They were, on the contrary, part of a sexual ethos which militated against what could have been distracting and personally harmful interference with academic and career pursuits.

For centuries, of course, the best-educated women—far better educated than most men in their society—were cloistered nuns. To what element in the experience of sexual intercourse, one must wonder, does Posner attribute the quality of furthering women's educational and occupational advancement? Precisely the opposite effect, in my experience, can follow from meaningful marital sexual encounters that may well ease the woman into domesticity rather than propel her into the marketplace. On the other hand, the triviality and exploitative nature of the meaningless promiscuous sexual encounter seriously inhibit such sexual experiences from playing any affirmative role in a woman's life. Women may rightly believe themselves better served by adopting the "rebel virginity"[34] Andrea Dworkin endorses in *Intercourse* than by undertaking the sexual promiscuity Posner defends.

Dworkin's descriptive words, "classy guy"[35]—with all the distrust of men's motivations she intended them to convey—fit both renowned philosopher Russell and esteemed judge Posner when they undertake to instruct women on the desirable dimensions of women's sexual activity. Their instruction mimics the adolescent male in the back seat of a Chevrolet, urging the girl to do it for her own good. But these eminent men invent a classier argument that promiscuous sex is in women's interest because it furthers our educational and occupational advancement, while also doing us the inestimable favor of making them think us less stupid and more interesting. It better serves our interest to dismiss the instruction of classy guys and heed Leo Tolstoy's admonition that "real debauchery lies precisely in freeing oneself from moral relations with a woman with whom you have physical intimacy."[36]

But knowing where real debauchery lies—and many women know very well—and having the courage to say so are two different matters. How can women, who have been consistently derided by feminists for not being as worthy, interesting, and successful as men, defend a chastity that those classy guys—Bertrand Russell, the philosopher, and Richard Posner, the erudite judge—agree contributes to making us stupid and uninteresting? To defend concepts of virginity and chastity invites ridicule from the sophisticated cultural elite of our knowledge class.

The Courage to Say No

Women once confidently controlled the sexual aspects of their dating relationships, setting and enforcing the rules while viewing the male as a suppliant who would be grateful for whatever sexual favors he received (which would usually be something short of vaginal intercourse). Not yet misled by feminist teachings, females knew these *were* favors. Cultural mores entitled us to rebuff sexual advances because no one believed male and female sexuality were the same or that women's craving for casual sexual activity equaled men's. It was understood that whatever casual sexual activity the woman did permit the man would likely be a greater source of pleasure to him than to her.

The woman also knew there was nothing wrong with her for feeling this way; to suggest that her equality with males required that she pretend otherwise would have seemed absurd. No one questioned that men and women differed in their taste for premarital sexual activity: the average man, we knew, was born with lust in his heart for raw sex; the average woman with a yearning for romance and the ability, if given the right circumstances, to cultivate a taste for satisfying her physical lust through sexual intercourse. Casual sexual activity, we also knew, was ill-suited to providing those circumstances.

These convictions were part of our cultural knowledge; they required no corroboration from science. We would have found it interesting—although unnecessary to our certitude—that evolutionary psychology now grounds our convictions in biological facts. The male sexual strategy, which, as Robert Wright describes it, developed in the "environment of evolutionary adaptation," is to compete aggressively for as many female reproductive resources as possible in order to get as many genes as possible into the next generation. The strategy of the female, whose possible offspring will be few and require huge commitments of her time and energy, is to practice sexual reticence so as to be highly selective in choosing the man who will "help her build each gene machine." The result, in the words of geneticist A.J. Bateman, is "an undiscriminating eagerness in the males and a discriminating passivity in the females."[37] Further support for our sexual reticence would also eventually come from Doctor Seymour Fisher's extensive studies of female orgasmic capability. A woman, concluded Fisher, will "probably be more orgasmic with a man when her relationship with him has been formally stabilized (as through marriage)"; she "should be less orgasmic in transient, temporary sexual liaisons."[38]

Having absorbed feminist teachings, however, women became confused and diffident as to their right to control the nature and extent of premarital sexual activity. They feared that less than enthusiastic participation in such activity (which was now usually expected to be vaginal intercourse, not some lesser range of sexual favors) would establish their difference from, and hence their inequality with, men. Today, well-educated professional women, who are embarrassed to defend the unsophisticated concepts of virginity and chastity, are less competent to control men's sexual advances than high school girls were in the 1940s. One result is the invention of concepts like "date rape" and an expansive law of sexual harassment in an attempt to provide the protection for women against seduction that unsophisticated high school girls once felt completely confident in securing for themselves with a graceful—and, we sometimes thought, even elegant—refusal.

Neil Gilbert has analyzed feminist efforts to depict rape as "an act that most educated women do not recognize as such when it has happened to them, and after which almost half of the victims go back for more."[39] These are simply desperate attempts to distort the criminal law in order to reassert some form of female control over ordinary dating relationships. Their new campaign demonstrates how vulnerably bereft of self-confidence women became after feminist sexual revolutionaries convinced society that women share a male proclivity for promiscuous sexual intercourse. Correctly perceiving these efforts as a disavowal of feminism's endorsement of the sexual revolution and of its dogma that women should enjoy casual sexual intercourse as much as men do, Katie Roiphe decrys this admission by some feminists that fundamental sexual differences do exist.[40]

Manipulating the concepts of date rape and sexual harassment in this fashion, as Roiphe correctly argues, subverts feminism's earlier success in convincing society that males and females are inflamed by an identical sexual lust. She chides women with what is, to her, the ideologically repellent fact that men would never gather in groups to whimper and wail about their sexual exploitation by manipulative women whose coercive seduction left the men feeling violated and dirty. Revisionist "rape-crisis feminists" have indeed resurrected what Roiphe calls an "archaic, sexist" paradigm of man's lasciviousness versus woman's relative innocence—man's single-minded advance towards a penile vaginal penetration the woman would avoid if only she had the courage to say no.

It is true that the paradigm is of ancient origin and rests on the recognition of real differences between the sexes (the meaning of sexist), demonstrating that the ancients had better sense than sexual revolutionaries. The paradigm accurately depicts the reality of sexual differences, even though Roiphe and other feminist sexual revolu-tionaries wish the facts were otherwise. Those feminists who are reviving the paradigm are finally accepting reality instead of falsifying it, as Roiphe would have them continue to do. If their predecessors had not given up so much ground to the sexual revolutionaries within their movement, feminists would not now be resorting to such strained, illogical interpretations of the law of rape and sexual harassment in order to secure for women the protection they once were afforded by attributing, in Roiphe's words, a "quasi-religious value to the physical act."[41]

Precisely because they have ceded so much ground to those who advocate sexual promiscuity as an ideal for women, feminists have reduced women to a condition of pathetic vulnerability to male persuasion. The cure, rape-crisis feminists believe, is compulsory programs, like that at Antioch College, which spell out every possible scenario of sex play step by step. At each step, there must be an explicit verbal request by the man for permission to continue and consent by the woman. With such a desensitizing, clinical precision and detail, one wonders how there will ever be enough magic or mystery to make any sexual activity even minimally pleasurable.

The purpose of these programs, say their sponsors, is to "give women the courage and vocabulary to say no to unwanted sex"; within the workshops, girls are "trying on the idea that they could have sex if they wanted and refuse if they did not."[42]

Why is it, rape-crisis feminists should ask themselves, that women were once able, without the benefit of such programs, to conduct satisfactory dating relationships, usually avoid pregnancy until they chose it, then go on to enjoy stable marriages, and raise relatively happy children in what were overwhelmingly two-parent families? The women who accomplished these goals were in firm possession of the "courage and vocabulary to say no to unwanted sex." We did it all the time, being completely comfortable with our right to refuse sex, now an apparently revolutionary idea these college girls are "trying on." It is to the great shame of contemporary feminism that it stripped from women this courage and vocabulary to say no which rape-crisis feminists are now attempting, in such clumsy fashion, to restore to them.

But what does impel a woman to say no? Rape-crisis feminists tell her only that she can say no to what she does not "feel like" doing. This is simply the beginning of the inquiry, not its conclusion. What a woman feels like doing in the sexual arena depends on what meaning sexual activity has for her. Most women "feel like" romance; most "feel like" experiencing pleasing tactile sensations other than penile vaginal penetration; many will trade a more extensive sexual activity than they may "feel like" in order to attain— or with respect to romance, convince themselves they attain—these first two objectives. But how much more? "Feelings" alone are an inadequate guide: they must be fleshed out by an understanding of the nature of the sex act. For a woman, contrary to Posner, sexual intercourse can never be a morally indifferent activity.

A woman who values virginity and marital chastity as something more than commodities to be exchanged for male support believes the act of sexual intercourse has more significance for her than for the man. This feeling that a woman does not want to do it because it would affect her more profoundly than it would a man is very dramatically expressed in Andrea Dworkin's *Intercourse*. Although I reach conclusions very different from Dworkin's, I believe that she forthrightly, graphically, and accurately appraises the nature of sexual intercourse from the woman's point of view, capturing the feelings that can prompt our refusal to engage in this activity.

Dworkin depicts sexual intercourse as a much more momentous experience for a woman than a man, because it is "an act of possession in which . . . a man inhabits a woman, physically covering her and overwhelming her and at the same time penetrating her . . . . By thrusting into her, he takes her over. His thrusting into her is taken to be her capitulation to him as a conqueror; it is a physical surrender of herself to him; he occupies and rules her, expresses his elemental dominance over her . . . ." In intercourse, says Dworkin, a woman "is occupied—physically, internally, in her privacy."[43]

Her description might be considered an outrageous exaggeration (many of Dworkin's critics so characterize it), but I find it a dramatic portrayal—from the woman's, but not necessarily from the man's, perspective—of sexual intercourse at its best. Dworkin describes an overwhelmingly personal, a truly awe-inspiring, event in which a woman should shrink in horror from participating on any basis even remotely casual. One might think that in her lifetime a woman would meet few men that she considers worthy of exercising such power over her. This may explain why women often invest their romantic relationships with a meaning the facts do not support, endeavoring to convince themselves that the man is what he is not and that the woman means much more to him than she truly does.

Quite clearly, the average man who takes advantage of the opportunities for casual sexual intercourse created by the sexual revolution would respond to Dworkin and to me: "I don't want to dominate you, conquer you, or rule over you; I just want to get laid and then leave you." Feminist sexual revolutionaries agreed that women should view sexual intercourse in the same way, as nothing more than getting laid. Because these feminists deny that the sex act has a metaphysical dimension or possesses, in Roiphe's words, a "quasi-religious value," they agree with Posner that the question whether the woman "feels like" getting laid is one of moral indifference. But Dworkin more honestly and courageously acknowledges the disparity between male and female reactions. The woman can experience profound psychic effects from an event which the man defines by physical sensation.

Dworkin is absolutely correct that in intercourse a woman is occupied "physically, internally, in her privacy." At no other time, except when giving birth, is a woman so compromised in her privacy. The fact is that when intercourse works for the woman and she is vaginally orgasmic, the experiences of intercourse and childbirth are very similar. During both events, she usually lies in the same position (while feminists may promote female ascendancy, it is usually more conducive to heightened vaginal orgasmic satisfaction to submissively relax on the bottom). In both events, the woman is physically inhabited by another. And throughout both, she surrenders herself to a force over which she has no control and that for a time will overwhelm her—in one event, with spasms of pleasure and in the other, with contractions of pain.

Others have described intercourse in terms similar to but less emotional and dramatic than Dworkin's. She quotes from the famous (infamous to feminists) marriage manual of Theodore Van De Velde that what both man and woman wish to feel in intercourse "is the essential force of *maleness*, which expresses itself in a sort of violent and absolute *possession* of the woman."[44] George Gilder describes the woman during intercourse as loving the man for his "strength and protectiveness," for his "ability to support and protect her while she bears children—or while she surrenders to orgasmic ecstasy," and for his power "to control her in sexual intercourse."[45]

The male, in Gilder's account, is "initiatory and managerial," "preparing the woman" as he "manages her readiness," while she "loses control," and "completely relaxes," "surrendering as well as she can to climactic abandon."[46] Roger Scruton describes the woman as "interested in her lover's sexual parts because she wishes to be penetrated by *him*, and to feel him feeling pleasure inside her. The penis is the avatar of his presence, and the ground that it crosses in entering her is at once overrun and occupied by the man himself." "At the same time," Scruton continues, "crucial features of his embodiment—such as the thrusting motion of his sexual parts—stand out in the field of her attention, sharply etched and immovable in the enveloping cloud of pleasure."[47]

These are all very good descriptions, and if a mature heterosexual woman were so inclined, they might inspire erotic fantasies. They are also completely accurate. Feminists, however, dislike this talk of men controlling, penetrating, and thrusting, while women relax, lose control, surrender, and are then enveloped in clouds of pleasure. To describe the penis as an "avatar"—an incarnated deity—is anathema to those women who reject "phallocratic sex," propose imagining sexual encounters in which the man is "constrained from bringing the male organ into play,"[48] and suggest a decreasing reliance on thrusting in intercourse and the substitution of a "mutual lying together in pleasure," "with female orgasm providing much of the stimulation necessary for male orgasm."[49] The increasing numbers of women who have become dissatisfied with sexual relationships indicate the women's "clouds of pleasure" were wispy indeed, a result to be expected from the pursuit of casual sex and rejection of the traditional paradigm of female sexuality on which Van De Velde, Gilder, and Scruton based their analyses.

I like and quote Dworkin's description of sexual intercourse because it portrays the experience as very meaningful to the woman, an activity of importance and consequence in which she wagers a lot and can lose a lot. The meaning Dworkin finds in the experience, however, is a very bad one. She counsels rejecting participation in intercourse, viewing it as degrading to women and a stigma of what she believes is their social inferiority. The meaning I derive from the experience is a very good one. I deny, however, that the experience can be coherently included within a casual relationship. This is because I both agree with Dworkin that sexual intercourse is an overwhelming compromise of woman's privacy and also believe that intercourse is inextricably tied, if only psychically, to conception and childbirth.

A woman must choose very wisely the man with whom she has sexual intercourse. She should give such immense power over herself only to a man whom she considers worthy of fathering her children and who is prepared to take responsibility for her and those children—a man who deserves her. If she does choose wisely, however, I would have Dworkin know that a woman can find intercourse and the conception and birth that it portends and continually commemorates to be incomparably gratifying experiences.

But the attribution of any purpose or metaphysical meaning to sexual intercourse other than the physical assuaging of a genital itch is precisely what the women's movement wished to deny. Search for such meaning must necessarily lead to the woman's ability to conceive and give birth and, thus, to the recognition of important biological differences between the sexes. Because the new wave of feminism that emerged in the 1960s has been singlemindedly careerist, all its endeavors have been designed to convince women of their equivalence to, rather than difference from, men.

Women had to be persuaded that they were just like men in their interests, their capabilities, their sexual lust, and their desire for and attachment to children. Towards this end, the movement aligned itself with *Playboy* magazine, the pornographers, and other promoters of the sexual revolution in telling the woman to behave, in Gilder's words, like "a man without a phallus" and to embrace the effort "to dethrone procreative genital intercourse as the normative form of sexual activity."[50]

Feminist Denial of Female Preciousness

So long as society views sexual intercourse as tied, if only symbolically, to procreation and values this connection, it must, in turn, view women as being very different from men and likewise value this difference. Women's preciousness derives from our child-bearing ability: our bodies are precious because they are now, or may someday be, or have once been, or could have been the seed cases of the next generation. Because its primary goal has been to get women out of the home and into the marketplace, contemporary feminism has had to deny—even to treat as ludicrous—any attribution of preciousness to women and their children.

If children are really precious, they must be perceived to deserve a great deal of their mother's active love, attention, and care, which they cannot receive from the careerist mothers envisaged and created by the women's movement. Nor are children precious in the eyes of those who support abortion on demand, a *sine qua non* of achieving the female fungibility with males sought by feminists. Legalized abortion requires the community's acquiescence in a mother's decision to destroy the life within her. But when a human life can lawfully be destroyed simply because the mother so chooses, the preciousness of human lives must be diminished. Those children permitted to live are inevitably rendered less precious by virtue of the fact that their society would have afforded them no protection had their mothers made the choice to destroy them. When there is a virtually unlimited right to abortion, all children live under the pall of the dreadful knowledge that they are alive not because society considers them precious beings deserving of protection, but by the accident of fate that their mothers did not opt for their destruction.[51]

The success of the sexual revolution has depended on divorcing sexual intercourse from all factual or symbolic attachment to procreation; this divorce has required that abortion be both legally available and socially acceptable. As Ehrenreich, Hess, and Jacobs state in *Re-Making Love: The Feminization of Sex*, the feminists' aim, in which these authors completely concur, was to take the "mystery" and "magical meanings" of "eternal love" and "romance" out of sex. For feminists, sex was no longer a "symbolic act to be undertaken for ulterior aims—motherhood, emotional and financial

security, or simply vanity"; it would now have "no ultimate meaning other than pleasure."[52]   What they consider the benefits and
achievements of their sexual revolution would be "rolled back" by
adoption of more restrictive abortion laws that would prevent women
from approaching sex "lightheartedly," an attitude best achieved
the "more decisively sex can be uncoupled from reproduction."[53]

Feminism's pro-abortion stand follows from its commitment
to convincing society that there are no critical differences between
the sexes and to minimizing, whenever possible, the effects of
whatever differences it must concede do exist. Of all social questions,
feminists are probably most united in their support of expansive
abortion rights. Women who seek to participate in feminist causes
as opponents of abortion are given very short shrift by an organized
feminism that largely believes it is "not possible to be a feminist
and anti-abortion."[54]

That some feminists eventually began to repudiate the sexual
revolution does not negate the fact that feminism's initial willing
embrace of that revolution and commitment to making possible
whatever abortions it required necessarily promoted feminist goals—
for two reasons. First, women's participation in casual sexual intercourse furthered the movement's objective of convincing women
to pursue the same career goals as men. Second, by adopting male
sexual patterns and submitting to the abortions this pursuit entailed, women took a large step towards becoming more like men:
women began to lose their sense of feminine preciousness.

Careers and Casual Sex

The sexual revolution encouraged women's career pursuits because
participation in casual sexual activities is inconsistent with the "matrimonial strategy" that had generally impeded women's serious career
commitment. In order to be fungible with men, women must decide
that their primary goal in life is to choose a professional career

(the women's movement has been almost exclusively concerned with professional women), educate themselves toward that end, and then devote the rest of their lives to pursuit of that career. Since the traditional family was correctly seen as the greatest obstacle to this goal, women had to be encouraged to view marriage and family as either unnecessary to their happiness or, at most, peripheral to their marketplace activity. They should, said feminists, be no more anxious to undertake creation of a home and family than men are and devote no more time and energy to these endeavors than men do.

But as Betty Friedan had bitterly lamented, although large numbers of women attended and succeeded in college, their primary goal in the 1950s was to marry and raise a family. Instead of dreaming about finding a cure for cancer or how to put a man on the moon, they dreamed of having a husband, a house in the suburbs, and four children. The 1962 Gallup Poll reflected the attitudes Friedan deplored: of the surveyed women between the ages of 16 and 21, most expected to be married by age 22, have four children, and work outside the home only until birth of a child. These young women also rejected male sexual patterns for themselves and accepted responsibility for setting and enforcing the sexual standards of their dating relationships, attitudes that Ehrenreich et al. accurately characterized as the "matrimonial strategy."[55] Any attempt to substitute long-term career goals for young women's traditional goals of marriage and motherhood had to attack this matrimonial strategy in which most young women were investing most of their emotional energies (a usually successful investment as evidenced by the high marriage and birth rates and low divorce rates prevailing at that time).

Deeply rooted needs of women were reflected in this matrimonial strategy that feminists encouraged them to abandon for pursuit of the now glamorized market activities. Our great literature confirms that women have usually defined happiness and sadness, satisfaction and discontent, achievement and loss in terms of family attachments and, particularly, their romantic relationships with men. This is true of literature created by both sexes. With few exceptions, as Helen Hazen has noted, "all novels of any substance written by women in the nineteenth and early twentieth centuries deal primarily with the love of men and the enchantment of family life."[56]

In almost all of this literature, the woman suffered. Whether she was merely pathetic, like Hetty Sorrel in George Eliot's *Adam Bede*, or achieved the stature of a heroine, like Hester Prynne in Nathaniel Hawthorne's *The Scarlet Letter*, her suffering was caused by a man in whom she had mistakenly placed her faith. Her heroism derived from her ability to endure and, through her endurance, to triumph over his inadequacy and betrayal. This is the same message that has come down to us from ancient Greece where, says Mary R. Lefkowitz, women "attain heroic stature in epic and drama by managing through suffering to understand and to endure."[57] Analyzing literary portrayals of women, Elizabeth Hardwick has described how those depicted as heroines are women who "wronged in one way or another, are given the overwhelming beauty of endurance, the capacity for high or lowly suffering" and "for the radiance of humility, for silence, secrecy, impressive acceptance."[58]

Almost always, the heroic woman is portrayed in terms of her selfless devotion to a man and her children. By contrast, women who defined themselves through the acquisition of power (Shakespeare's Lady Macbeth, for example, and his *King Lear*'s Regan and Goneril) or through adulterous sexual liaisons unleavened by devoted motherhood (Leo Tolstoy's Anna Karenina, for example, and Gustave Flaubert's Emma Bovary) are among the most unrelievedly evil, or the most woefully pathetic, women depicted in literature. Again, this has been so since ancient Greece, where women's primary joy was believed to come from devotion to family and children. "The only women who are seen to express different notions about their primary role in life, or are seen to complain of it," Lefkowitz observes, "are the evil women of epic and tragedy, who bring destruction on their families and on themselves, like Clytemnestra, Deianeira and Medea."[59]

There was in the 1960s no reason to doubt the continuing validity of the assumption that most women defined their interests and achieved their heroism in terms of family relationships. Eventually, academic feminists would revive "neglected" works to contradict this paradigm. Not only had the fact of exceptions never been denied, but additional exceptions further corroborated that the paradigm probably reflected women's nature, not men's oppression. Feminism's task in the 1960s, however, was to deny the truth expressed in Chaucer's tale of the Wife of Bath that what women desire most is to have mastery over their husbands. Pursuit of a career will not fulfill women's romantic longings; even the most highly glamorized market activity cannot be proxy for all possible satisfactions of womanhood.

Any attack on the matrimonial strategy had to offer women something in its place. Contemporary feminism offered them the sexual revolution. Just as women were to pursue careers with the same dedication as men, feminists told them to pursue raw sex as men do; it would, they said, be even better than romance. Men very obviously do not require the lubricant of romance and commitment to enjoy the slippery delights of a depersonalized groined archway. Surely, in their quest for what feminists termed equality with men, women could learn to enjoy the thrusting of a depersonalized penis on the same terms. How contrary to women's nature such learning is should have never been in doubt. Studies have now documented the vastly greater interest men have in casual sex than do women. In one study, all of the women refused a request to have sex with an attractive stranger, while seventy-five percent of the men accepted this proposition.[60]

Women are virtually the sole readers of romance fiction.[61] They invent their own elaborate romantic fantasies that sharply contrast with the very specific, clinically precise, pictorial male sexual fantasy that focuses on "body parts and sexual positions stripped of emotional context." Sex, in the male fantasy, is "sheer lust and physical gratification, devoid of encumbering relationships, emotional elaboration, complicated plot lines." For women, on the other hand, "[e]motions and personality are crucial," the focus is on "feelings as opposed to visual images," and the emphasis is on "tenderness, romance, and personal involvement."[62]   Unless she is selling sex, a woman will usually attempt to intertwine it with romance.   The sex act will somehow be part of a romantic story, whether that story was fashioned long ago and now lives only in the recesses of her memory, or it is still sharply etched in her immediate perceptions.   Nonetheless, feminist sexual revolutionaries told women to forget romance, spread their legs like whores, and enjoy equality with men by experiencing sheer sexual lust unenhanced by the mystery and magic of love.

WOMAN DEFEMINIZED

Feminism's second motive in endorsing the sexual revolution was to make women not only mimic male sexual behavior but also develop attitudes and emotional reactions that are more like men's and less traditionally feminine. This goal required societal acceptance of the sexual revolution's underlying premise that sexual intercourse derives no special importance or moral significance from its connection with procreation. When a society adopts the premise—well-articulated by Richard Posner—that sexual intercourse is simply a morally indifferent, harmless source of pleasure, the society institutionalizes feminism's commitment to male-female fungibility. To view sexual intercourse as a morally relevant act defined by its procreative potentialities must always thwart the goal of sexual fungibility.

Attributing a value to the act of intercourse because of its procreative nature necessarily entails acknowledging the female's unique preciousness as a potential child-bearer and, inevitably, children's preciousness as well. This acknowledgment contemporary feminism must avoid at all costs because the movement has always been profoundly anti-child. Its most basic belief is that only patriarchal oppression would ever lead a woman to leave the workplace and devote herself to what feminists consistently describe as the boring, unstimulating, and unfulfilling occupation of personally caring for one's child. Feminists correctly perceived that a female's devotion to her children is antithetical to the movement's goal that women seek achievement in the workplace equal to men's. Just as men can happily leave their children all day in their wives' care, feminists argued, women must learn just as happily to leave their children in a surrogate's care.

Submission to Surrogate Child-Rearing

If she is to leave her child in order to compete in the workplace equally with men and childless women, the tie that binds a mother to her child—the strong emotional pull that child exerts on her—must be weakened.[63] A mother must steel herself if she is to leave her baby in a crib in a day care center or at home with a caretaker. She must suppress her longing to respond to her baby's cries and to satisfy that yearning for contact with her baby's body that her own body has been groomed to anticipate and desire. She knows, moreover, that her baby's cries will be answered by one with no special feeling of love for the child, but at most only a feeling of obligation to do as well as possible the job for which one is paid.

To leave her baby requires a kind of defeminization of the woman, a constriction of the longing to be with and care for her child that is integral to woman's humanity. It requires her to develop an attitude of remoteness and withdrawal from her baby reminiscent of those mothers who boarded their infants out with wet nurses in sixteenth to nineteenth century Europe.[64] During this period, lack of hygiene and aseptic methods made animal milk unsafe, the very rudimentary nature of the available implements made artificial feeding impracticable, and continual pregnancies could produce a new infant before the weaning of a sibling. A wet nurse might, therefore, have seemed the only acceptable alternative when a mother was unable to nurse her infant.

Use of a wet nurse came to be perceived as a sign of gentility, indicative of upper-class behavior, just as, in our own country, bottle feeding was viewed not very long ago and a mother's pursuit of a professional career is viewed today. This perception very likely contributed to the persistence of a custom which—long before Rousseau pleaded that mothers should nurse their own infants— was condemned by virtually everyone who advised on early child-rearing. Partly in response to this condemnation, the custom was substantially modified, before its demise, by having the wet nurse live in the home with infant and parents. As Rita Kramer notes, an infant at that time had only one chance in four of living past childhood, a fact creating great emotional hazards for the mother who formed loving bonds with her babies. Curtailing the wet nurse practice (a practice which had itself contributed to infant mortality) and a determination by mothers to nurse and care for their own babies created the intimacy between mother and child on which the nuclear bourgeois family was founded.[65]

John Bowlby, the authority on childhood attachment behavior, has stated that "most mothers experience a strong pull to be close to their babies and young children. Whether they submit to the pull or stand out against it depends on a hundred variables, personal, cultural, and economic." The "usual household duties," he observed, compete with infant care but can be quickly dropped and so are "quite consistent with mothering." But a "mother's activities that merely compete for time and energy with her caring for a child," he concluded, "are in a quite different category from behaviour that is inherently incompatible with care."[66]

The decision of many women today to adopt behavior that is "inherently incompatible with care" by leaving their infants and young children in order to work outside the home constitutes a return to what resembles a wet nurse era. This decision evidences a profound alteration in women's attitudes that cannot be explained by the existence of unalterable physical realities similar to the lack of alternative sources of infant nourishment and the devastating infant mortality rates of two hundred years ago. Nor can the change be explained by overriding emergencies requiring participation of mothers in the work force, such as wars or dire economic need.

A mother's desire and ability to provide individual, personal care to her children within the traditional bourgeois family are benefits that both mothers and children derive from the civilizing process. But contemporary feminism, like totalitarian collectivism, champions as "progressive" a return to the communal, impersonal care of a wet nurse era. And feminists warn mothers that in order to avoid the attachment to their babies that encourages women to sacrifice careers for children, mothers must not assume any more child-rearing responsibilities than their husbands do.[67] These feminist teachings seem a reversal of the civilizing process with a loss in the humaneness of which that process has made us more capable.

Jennifer Roback Morse has wisely asked, "When we harden our hearts to place a six week old baby into the care of strangers, who will moderate us?"[68] Some mothers cannot so harden their hearts. I would have felt like the wire monkey mother in Harlow's famous experiment, if I had pumped out breast milk at my office for another to feed to my baby.[69] What can possibly moderate a society that encourages its mothers so to harden their hearts and denigrates those who refuse to do so? The "grief, the listlessness, the obvious and heart-rending despair" of the infant monkeys deprived of maternal care in Harlow's experiment evoked this reaction: "Thank God we only have to do it once to prove the point."[70] The success of contemporary feminism in hardening women's hearts, however, indicates that the monkeys suffered in vain.

A mother who withdraws from personal care of her child must somehow stave off or stifle her natural yearning for proximity and close personal attachment to that child.[71] She must accept curtailment of the mother-child relationship and the resulting disparity between the potentiality and reality of her maternal role. Such an attitudinal change towards motherhood was fostered by the sexual revolution, which very successfully disparaged motherhood, justified abortion, and ridiculed any suggestion that the sex act is a meaningful and important event circumscribed by moral constraints. By denying that the sex act derives any special significance from its procreative potentiality, the sexual revolution trivialized sexual intercourse. And this trivialization fostered women's defeminization as society came to perceive women to be fungible with men and stripped of that aura of preciousness once conferred by their child-bearing capability.

When the prevailing mores teach that sexual intercourse is merely a morally indifferent, mechanical act designed to produce a physical sensation with any number of individuals and without the prerequisites of love and commitment, the act—like inflated currency—loses value. Then, sexual intercourse becomes what one of Allan Bloom's female college students described in *The Closing of the American Mind*: "it's no big deal."[72] And when the sex act becomes degraded in value—when it ceases to be a big deal—society decreases the value it places both on a child as the product of conception in this degraded act and on a woman in her role as mother of the child. Casual sex leads, as it were, to casual motherhood.

Submission to Abortion

Women's defeminization through sexual promiscuity was exacerbated by their submission to abortion. To succeed, the sexual revolution required that abortion be destigmatized and made readily available. Without legalized abortion (with its implicit guarantee that what is legal cannot be terribly wrong) there would have been significantly less participation by women in casual sexual intercourse. Women's frequent use of abortion in our society (at the highest rate in the Western world) has contributed to their defeminization and further weakened the ties between mothers and children. To deny that submission to abortion diminishes women's sense of pre-ciousness—making them more like men—requires denying what actually happens during an abortion.

Despite many criticisms leveled in our society against the management of the birth experience, there can be no doubt that women have often felt exquisitely precious—even with their feet in stirrups—when pushing out a baby. Of all the events in their lives, most women would, I believe, identify childbirth as the activity which most clearly defines womanhood. In this affirmation of her femaleness, a woman least resembles a man. In her submission to abortion, she most resembles a man. Through abortion, women seek to replicate the male sexual experience by freeing themselves from pregnancy and childbearing. However much feminism would minimize the abortion trauma, a feeling of preciousness must surely be the last sensation felt by the woman who submits to having the life within her reamed out, very likely the most dehumanizing ex-perience to which she will ever be subjected. That abortion apologists appreciate the horror of what actually occurs is demonstrated by their avoidance of the word "abortion" and insistence on calling the procedure a "choice," much as genocidal extermination of Jews was described as a "solution."

Abortion not only defeminizes women—de Beauvoir herself said "woman feels it as a sacrifice of her femininity" as the man asks her "to relinquish her triumph as female"[73] —but its unlimited legal availability also diminishes devotion to children. By issuing a blanket authorization to women to choose life or death for their babies, society delivers a pernicious message that the child who is permitted to live has few further claims upon the mother. Society's declaration that a woman has no duty to permit her baby to live undermines any claims upon her time and interest that might be made by the child once born—he is, in a very real sense, quite lucky just to be alive. This conclusion necessarily follows from a dialogue with a fetus that one abortion advocate created to justify its death to the fetus: "What claims do you," asks the advocate, "feel you could have made, with the law's coercion, against your own Mother?" "What sacrifice would you have coerced? What loss of freedom would you have imposed on her? What pain would you have inflicted?"[74]

The fetus might well have replied: "I would make whatever claims are required to enable me to live and flourish." But in that dialogue, it could not. This pro-abortion argument rejects any fetal right by positing that society can properly declare the fetus not entitled to demand of the mother that she make some sacrifice, endure some amount of pain or some loss of freedom—no matter how small—in order to let him live, the condition antecedent to all lesser claims. By this declaration, society teaches its mothers that, once born, the child cannot claim from them any more care and attention than is necessary to prevent the violation of laws against child abuse.

Our society permits a woman to abort her baby for any reason: because she does not wish to be pregnant during the hot summer months, because she wants a child of the opposite sex or wishes to eliminate multiple births, because she is too involved in her work, or because she fears the pain of childbirth or the responsibilities of motherhood. To grant this permission is to adopt what Margaret Mead, in another context, called a "definition of children as joy rather than as duty."[75] Once we have adopted this definition, it governs all relations with our children. In particular, it reinforces the message of contemporary feminism that women's primary concern should be their own needs and self-interest, while care of their children should be primarily the responsibility of society. As the mantra goes, society has the duty to provide affordable, quality child care.

When children are seen primarily as joy rather than duty and most of whatever duty there may be is seen to rest upon society, a woman's response to her children's claims for time and attention depends less on asking what the duty of being a good mother requires than on weighing the pleasure she derives from time devoted to her children against the rewards of competing activities. If the joy of caregiving seems less evident and other pursuits more attractive, society offers the mother no reason why she should not turn the child over to another's care. On the contrary, society's subsidizations of institutional child care encourage that choice. It is a cruel message children learn so young that the source of mother's devotion is not the strength of what George Eliot called "Duty"—"peremptory and absolute"[76]—but the frailty of children's ability to make time spent with them a joyful experience.

Submission to Combat Service

Women's increased sexual promiscuity and the high rates at which they have exercised their unlimited abortion rights have well served feminism's goal of defeminizing women so as to make them androgynous male equivalents. Dramatically illustrating this commitment to promoting fungibility of the sexes, the women's movement rejected changes to the proposed equal rights amendment that would have lessened opposition to the amendment by forbidding military drafting of women or, at least, their service in combat.[77] Since combat service would validate their consistent denial of female preciousness, feminists have always favored placing women in combat. Any significant exposure of women to combat duty would, of course, be suicidal for a society. "Males," as Steven Goldberg so well put it, "are expendable and females are not": "If all but a handful of males were killed while protecting females, the population would be replaced by the next generation; the loss of a large number of females would be disastrous for survival."[78]

Even if only relatively few women could meet the physical requirements of combat service, denying women exemption from that service serves feminism's need to confute any perception of females as soft, yielding, potential mothers. Society must concede, say feminists, that the potentiality of motherhood is no reason for viewing a young woman's remains in a body bag with any more horror than a young man's. But feminists are wrong. If a nation must wage war, a young man's death in combat fulfills his destiny as protector of a society the fundamental purpose of which is to reproduce itself and secure its children's safety and well-being. A young woman's death in combat can never fulfill, but only negate, her destiny as bearer of those children. What a society is fighting for when it sends its citizens to war rests entirely in the body of a young woman with the potentiality of motherhood.

Feminists argue that injuries, sexual assaults of female prisoners of war, and deaths are the price that women should pay in order to benefit from the military career advancement that combat service secures. Although our military sought to hide the fact that female prisoners were sexually assaulted in the Persian Gulf War, after the fact's disclosure, feminists treated rape of female war prisoners as being—apparently, like intercourse for the female sexual revolutionary—"no big deal." One of the sexually assaulted women (who advocates putting women into combat) said the experience "ranks as unpleasant; that's all it ranks."[79] Hitherto, feminists have excoriated our society for the horrors of rape to which women are subjected, often greatly exaggerating the probability of rape's occurrence within the average woman's lifetime and even redefining rape to include seduction.[80] Now, however, because of the overarching importance to their movement of establishing sexual equivalence, feminists are willing to trivialize—to treat as merely unpleasant— the sexual assaults on female war prisoners that are virtually certain to occur.

Contemporary feminism has exhorted women to reject the sexual double standard and mimic males' sexual promiscuity. Feminists have fought successfully for expansive abortion rights and have sought to justify women's submission to abortions that might logically be considered at least as great a violation of women's bodies as the act of rape. And now they trivialize rape by demanding that female soldiers be deliberately exposed to its virtually certain occurrence in the event of their capture. Our society's perception of women is influenced by women's increased sexual promiscuity, the extremely high rate of more than 1.5 million legal abortions performed each year in our country,[81] and feminism's demand that, as the price of female career advancement, women be placed in combat to court injuries, rape, and death.

Some women think this perception is offensive and degrading, but it tars us all, nevertheless, and profoundly affects men's attitude towards and treatment of us. In the eyes of men who have enjoyed women's increased sexual availability, who have sloughed off old wives and acquired young "trophies" under the sanction of no-fault divorce, who encouraged abortions—thus avoiding responsibility for children they have bred—and who will send women into combat, women are not uniquely precious individuals but merely easily disposable sex objects. Contemporary feminism has well taught that lesson to men.

Commenting on United States Air Force prisoner of war survival training designed to desensitize male recruits to witnessing the torture of female prisoners, David Horowitz correctly describes feminists as having "enlisted the military in a program to brainwash men so they won't care what happens to women."[82] But how will a feminine woman who recoils from the combat service that some other kind of women claim as their right reckon with the men who undergo this training? Without the constraints and inhibitions that acknowledgment of female preciousness imposes upon men in their dealings with women, what do feminists think protects women? Society cannot provide each of us with a bodyguard or a battered women's center on every corner.

A male can be made sufficiently effete that he will not make a very good husband, but he will rarely become so effete that, even with her karate and body-building classes, the average woman can protect herself against him. This is the reason why the United States Army felt it necessary to further its goal of male-female fungibility by instituting a six-month program to see whether selected women can, through weightlifting and aerobics, "be brought into the lower range of male strength." Women, said the program's director, are now "almost completely out of the male range": "The strongest female is generally weaker than the weakest male."[83]

It is a man's acknowledgment of female preciousness that gives a feminine woman power over him and makes her equal to him. Divesting her of that preciousness in pursuit of contemporary feminism's version of sexual equivalence has left women pathetic and vulnerable, like raped female prisoners of war and the nursing mothers that our society (in what we can hope will be the nadir of our descent into decadence) sent off to serve in the Persian Gulf War. How many of our men, one must wonder, really want to be part of a society that treats its women in this fashion?

Evidence of some men's willingness to sacrifice women to the goal of sexual fungibility appears from the United States Navy's actions with respect to the death of Lieutenant Kara Hultgreen, the first of two women to qualify as pilots of the F-14A fighter plane.[84] The official Navy report on her fatal crash, when attempting to land on an aircraft carrier, stressed engine malfunction as the cause, but a confidential Navy mishap investigation report attributed the crash to pilot error: Lieutenant Hultgreen had overshot the center line on her carrier approach and lost "situational awareness."[85] The engine stalled because she "mistakenly had jammed on the rudder"; in twenty years of operation of F-14As, "no pilot had ever stalled an engine this way before."[86] Many critics—often anonymous because the Navy will not tolerate criticism of its efforts to put women into combat—have questioned whether Lieutenant Hultgreen, who had initially failed the carrier-landing phase of her training, had the experience and qualifications for her assignment. The question whether Lieutenant Hultgreen was held to a lesser standard of competence because of "political pressure to place females in combat billets as soon as possible," is one that the Navy will apparently not even permit to be publicly discussed.[87] In allocating blame for women who "Don't Measure Up," a woman Navy reservist wisely faults "Navy leaders who allow subordinates to continue doing jobs for which they are not qualified." These leaders, she says, are "perpetuating a terrible disservice to the poorer performers, who are allowed to continue in an atmosphere where they cannot compete safely."[88]

Feminists, however, believe that treating women in this fashion will help realize their vision of a good society. In this they are clearly correct, for denial of female preciousness well serves feminist goals. If women think of themselves and their children as precious, they will not as easily leave their children in surrogates' care, make sacrifices in their family life, and develop a hard competitive edge—all prerequisites of success in the very demanding and often high-aggression-level careers that the women's movement encouraged mothers to pursue in competition with men and childless women. It was to erode their feelings of preciousness—to bring them down from their pedestals, as it were, and make them fungible with males—that the movement encouraged women to adopt male sexual patterns, to view abortion as a necessary and acceptable component of their equality, and to declare themselves willing to be drafted and endure the horrors of combat service with the rapes, injuries, and deaths this service entails.

Women's Dissatisfaction with Casual Sex

In *Re-Making Love*, Ehrenreich et al. accurately describe the sexual revolution as a female revolution in which many young women postponed marriage and undertook "casual sexual adventures" on the same basis as men. At the same time, many teenage girls abandoned the role of "enforcers of purity," a role in which they had trod a path between being too cheap and too puritanical, while "drawing the line for overeager boys and ostracizing girls who failed in this responsibility."[89] Although male premarital sexual behavior changed very little since the 1930s, women's premarital sex rates "more than doubled between the 1930s and 1971, and sharply rose again to a new peak in 1976."[90]

But some feminists would like to deny responsibility for the sexual revolution and, as Ehrenreich et al. also correctly observe, would concentrate instead on "women's roles as bystanders or victims, not as instigators." Although Ehrenreich et al. claim that they themselves remain firmly committed to the revolution, this claim is contradicted by their depiction of the desirable dimensions of women's sexual experience, which will be considered later. Asserting that "feminism was strengthened by its appropriation of the sexual revolution" and lamenting that "feminism, which had helped initiate the sexual revolution in the first place, was now deeply divided over it," they plead that the revolution must not be seen as just "a victory for men and a joke on women . . . as victims."[91]

Yet clearly, women *have been* victimized. Those feminists who defend the sexual revolution are now divided from others who became hostile to it and regret or seek to deny feminism's responsibility for its success. Many feminists now actively oppose pornography,[92] and rarely mentioned is an earlier feminist argument that because women are no different from men in their sensual interests, pornography like that directed at men should be developed for women. Predictably, as Helen Hazen has noted, women's pornographic magazines with pictures of nude males have had little appeal to a female audience: "women may wish for the event to happen, but they do not want to see pictures of it."[93] Women, moreover, have always had their own version of pornography in which pictorial male nudity plays no part. Unlike male pornography, it is rarely visual, nor is it threatened by censorship under established obscenity law.

The gothic and romance fiction that can sexually excite women disturbs many feminists, however, because it depicts the kind of rape and other seemingly masochistic experiences that are often erotic stimulants for women.[94] Interestingly, the anti-pornography laws drafted by Catharine MacKinnon and Andrea Dworkin could, if enacted, possibly be interpreted to break new ground, in a radical departure from established obscenity law, by reaching some of women's romance fiction. Perhaps the writing that sexually excites women through its depiction of women's various submissions to dominant men is just as disturbing to these feminists as the pictures of naked female bodies that arouse men.

To the regret of Ehrenreich et al. the backlash against female promiscuity that began in the early 1980s undermined the "positive feelings of many who had enjoyed the freedom of casual sex." Typical of the backlash they criticize is a television documentary which implies that "women's primary goals are love and security": women "want to get married, they want a family," and said one of the sociological experts, "they won't get those things if they're sexually active, because 'men [don't] like them to be very sexually experienced.'"[95] Another expert stated that the biological basis of our sexual behavior impells men to "impregnate as many healthy looking females as possible," while women, who gained nothing from "random copulation," profited from monogamy and its protection against the hazards of pregnancy. Even *Cosmopolitan* magazine, which has promoted the sexual revolution with the "tough, sultry woman" who seems not to care that she "can't tell Tom, Dick or Harry apart," sometimes resembles a "fundamentalist tract on the wages of sin," with articles depicting how the single girl pays a heavy price for the sex from which she seems to derive little satisfaction.[96]

Among critics of the revolution are sex radicals like Erica Jong and Germaine Greer. Jong concludes that "the freedom to say yes to everyone and anyone was really another form of slavery," and sex "without commitment did not satisfy [women's] hunger for love and connection." Greer's revisionism has led her to denounce sexual permissiveness, extol the sexual power of the virgin, and express regret that "when I thought I could fit [a child] into my life I found out I couldn't conceive." Ehrenreich et al. find this a particularly distressing admission, since it came from one who has fought so hard for the uncoupling of a woman's sexuality from her reproductive capacity.[97] To admit that the sexual revolution has harmed women is to acknowledge a flaw in feminism's premise that there are no important differences between male and female sexuality. The essence of contemporary women's complaints about sex has been distilled in women's cry of outrage that they have different needs than men and those needs are not being satisfied.

Women have indeed been grievously injured. As a result of the sexual revolution, our population of well-educated, middle-class women has experienced an outbreak of sexually transmitted diseases never before seen save among prostitutes. The United States has the highest rate of sexually transmitted diseases of any developed country. If left untreated, these diseases "can cause infertility, cancer, birth defects, miscarriages and even death."[98] The Congressional Office of Technology Assessment has estimated that 20 percent of all cases of infertility is caused by sexually transmitted diseases.[99] These cases represent, the Office stated, the most preventable type of infertility, but two other causes— prior abortions and deferral of child-bearing to a later age—are also preventable. Because of the great increase in sexually transmitted diseases, ectopic pregnancies have surged sixfold in the last twenty years. This dangerous development of fetuses outside the uterus results when such diseases as chlamydia so scar the fallopian tubes that a fertilized egg cannot reach the uterus.[100] These same diseases are one factor explaining the significantly lower infant mortality rates among poor immigrant women, who do not have these diseases, than among better-off women born in the United States, many of whom now have them.[101]

The greatest damage to women's health results from obesity, smoking, drug use (including alcohol), and engaging in sexual intercourse with numerous men. Sexual activity at an early age or with multiple partners are risk factors for cervical cancer; the American Cancer Society includes as "high risk" any woman who has had more than one sex partner or who began sexual activity before age eighteen.[102] Abortion—the handmaiden of the sexual revolution—is now suspected to increase the risk of breast cancer. One study showed that women "45 years or younger who had had an induced abortion had a 50 percent greater risk of developing breast cancer" than those who had been pregnant and never had an abortion; about one in four women younger than forty-five have had at least one abortion. For women who had an abortion after the eighth week of pregnancy and were under age eighteen at the time, the risk of breast cancer went up 800 percent.[103] These conclusions were contradicted by a later study,[104] which was itself attacked as "a put-up job" because it used methods that would produce results understating the abortion risk.[105] Because feminists consider the right to a legal and unstigmatized abortion to be sacrosanct, this issue has now become thoroughly politicized. While they will march and rally against breast cancer, feminists also would like to see suppressed any evidence that might undermine abortion's acceptability. In this connection, it is of interest to note that the *The New York Times* article on the study showing a link between abortion and breast cancer appeared on page twelve, while the article on the study which denied the link appeared on page one.

Reality requires that we must be what feminists denounce as sexist. This highly charged word that they have made synonymous with racist means only that we must recognize the very real differences that do exist between men and women—differences, unlike that of skin color, of vast significance. On the issue of sexual promiscuity, evidence of one of these differences is the fact that female prostitutes have often been sterile and in poorer health than their clients. Unfair as it may seem to feminists, there are valid physical reasons for sexual reticence on women's part, whatever the case may be for men. Feminists are committed, nevertheless, to divorcing women's sexuality from any connection with reproductivity, and they have convinced many young women to engage "lightheartedly" in casual sexual intercourse "just for fun," as men have done. But our bodies always have the last word. Women's infertility has demonstrated the inextricable wedding of sex and fertility that feminist theory had neatly divorced.

Anne Taylor Fleming has written about the pain of such infertility, detailing her travails of having sex with a "syringe of sperm" and a petri dish in countless failed attempts to "trade a byline for a baby." She describes her generation of women, who rejected the "motherhood and dishes and diapers" of the "traditional wifely role," as "the golden girls of the brave new order": "We would do it differently, redefine the gender, fly free of our very own sex," becoming what she calls "the Sacrificial Generation."[106] And so they are. Why could she not conceive? Perhaps it was one of the trappings her body carried of being a golden girl of the brave new order—that conception-inhibiting scar tissue from sexually transmitted disease or an aging body asked too late to do the work of youth.[107] Or perhaps her aging husband's sperm was the culprit. Mrs. Fleming recalls, with seeming nostalgia, her college years with him when they blended into "a kind of permanent cloud of marijuana smoke" on the California coast so "redolent" with that aroma, and she also notes that after two decades of marriage he stopped drinking.[108] There are conflicting studies on whether there has been a marked decline in sperm counts in the past two decades due, perhaps, to environmental toxins or personal habits.[109]

In addition to physically harming their bodies, women who adopted male sexual patterns abandoned the bargaining power of the groined archway for themselves and compromised other women's ability to exercise that power. Female sexual reticence is integral to the matrimonial strategy that promotes the goals of marriage and family formation, the two achievements that embody what George Gilder calls the long-term horizons implicit in loving sexuality and women's procreative natures.[110] The incidence and durability of marriages and the creation of families will always decline when women adopt a masculine conception of sexuality that treats the sex act simply as a depersonalized and temporary "curious pleasure," sundered from the feminine gestalt of love and commitment, generativity and futurity.

As Richard Posner accurately observes, the "freer women are sexually, the less interest men have in marriage." Sexual permissiveness and readily available abortion are, therefore, always contrary to the interests of women who would choose to devote themselves to home and family rather than market production.[111] This was initially no matter for regret by women who subscribed to the feminist teaching that marriage and children were simply impediments to their career goals. An increasing number of these women, however, came to realize that careers cannot replace marriage and family.[112] For some, this insight arrived too late, as our own version of a lost generation faced the reality of another great difference between the sexes: the importance of youth in those seeking to become wives and mothers, in contrast to its relative unimportance, if not its negative worth, in those seeking to become husbands and fathers.

It is likely that many of the women who engaged in casual sexual intercourse never consciously adopted the view of feminist opinion makers that heterosexual "sex should have no ultimate meaning other than pleasure" and should be seen as the "sheer play" it was for homosexuals.[113] Midge Decter has observed that a young woman embarked on sexual adventure usually seeks a man "who will play husband to her."[114] The participants, however, often have widely varying views of what their premarital sexual relationships imply. A 1975 survey conducted at a midwestern university disclosed that while eighty per cent of the women engaging in sexual intercourse hoped to marry their partner, only twelve per cent of the men shared this expectation.[115] Young women should contemplate this study every day; nothing better demonstrates women's willingness to deceive themselves as to men's intentions.

Whatever interpretation promiscuous women put upon their own actions and whatever degree of male commitment their imaginations are able to invent—and in this area, women possess formidable imaginative powers—these women both decrease their own chances of marrying and undermine the ability of other women to compete for men without participating in casual sexual intercourse. In Gilder's very accurate words, "when there are many women easily available, men can more freely coax and bully reluctant ones into bed."[116] The girl or woman who stands out against the prevailing sexual mores and resists the coaxing will often find herself rejected for a dating relationship that could have afforded her an opportunity (provided by less permissive mores) to display qualities other than sexual availability which might encourage the man to accept deferral of sexual intercourse. Girls' felt need for help in rejecting boys' sexual overtures is evidenced by a survey of sexually active teenage girls, some of whom were already mothers. The information they were most likely to want was how to say "no" without hurting the boys' feelings.[117]

The newly permissive mores also undermined spouses' ability to enforce marital fidelity. By treating the sex act as merely a pleasurable physical activity that was, in Posner's words, "morally indifferent," sexual revolutionaries both increased the availability of single females in the sex pool and justified extramarital sexual relationships. Helen Gurley Brown, the editor of *Cosmopolitan* for thirty-two years and the paradigmatic sexual revolutionary, had advised men in 1965 to choose the unmarried career woman over the parasitic housewife. Although Mrs. Brown has been married for many years, she never had children, and one commentator has noted that her"distaste for motherhood is legend." Her revolutionary ardor has never slackened, and her latest book recommends that women look at their friends' husbands as potential lovers. "Husbands," she advises, "are a source of supply"; "I never feel guilt about the wife, if she can't keep him at home."[118]

In her tale of infertility's woes, Anne Taylor Fleming captures the ethos of the sexual revolution when she shares with us the fact that during college she lived with (and subsequently married) a man twice her age who, after meeting her when she was still in high school, had divorced the mother of his four children.[119] With the words "Sorry. Sorry. Sorry." Mrs. Fleming apologizes to the "station-wagon moms with their postpartum pounds who felt denigrated in the liberationist heyday by the young, lean, ambitious women like me." Is she speaking, one wonders, to the wife and mother that she supplanted, who was left "one of those heartland moms who ended up in a development of tract houses with four little blond boys"?[120]

Women began to sound a retreat from the battlefield of casual sex when, in Shere Hite's words, they grew dissatisfied with the results of their attempts to "have sex like men," devoid of a connection with "emotions or a relationship."[121] Many critics found the surveys on which Hite based *Women and Love* too flawed to support valid statistical inferences.[122] The complaints detailed in this book, nevertheless, indicate the depth of some women's disappointment and ring true to those not committed to a belief in the equivalence of male and female sexuality.

In their litany of grievances, women echoed what a Syracuse University Health Services physician had articulated twelve years earlier. Sexual promiscuity harmed many women, he said, because male and female sexuality are not the same: "to a man, sex can be an activity apart from his whole being—a drive related to the organs themselves," but in the woman, there is a "complex internal organization, correlated with her other hormonal systems." Thus, the "man is orgasm-oriented with a drive that ignores most other aspects of the relationship," while the woman is "engulfed in romanticism and trying to find and express her total feelings for her partner."[123]

This crucial difference between the sexes is pinpointed in Helen Hazen's comment that man's interest in woman usually begins with a sexual desire that love for the woman will cause him to direct so that "his passion for her is not pornographic."[124] Or as Roger Scruton cogently puts it, the man's sexual passion will be directed towards her with "individualising intentionality."[125] Woman's interest in man, on the other hand, usually begins with romantic feelings; with what is often, I believe, a continuing story that she constantly refines in her imagination and into which she trys to incorporate a particular man. In doing so, she must undertake to convert her diffuse romantic feelings into specific, concrete sexual desire.

Dr. James C. Neely elaborates these differences between the sexes in *Gender, The Myth of Equality*. For the man, he says, a woman is "the promise of release, the easing of his specific tension." The "driving force" of this tension is "physiological," but for its relief he can "be persuaded to do almost anything—including love." In contrast, the woman, "whose sexual reaction time is much more of an acquired taste than an intrinsic conditioned response," is more "diffusely aware" of her sexuality; she must be helped to discover "her specificity through a man's apparent awareness."[126] It is these basic sexual differences that help explain surveys showing that high school girls express lower levels of satisfaction than boys with their sexual experiences and that the girls much more frequently avow "love" for their last sexual partner.[127]

Women's disillusionment with the sexual revolution necessarily follows from the fact that casual sex is "sex without the emotions." As Steven Marcus details in *The Other Victorians*, that is the sex of pornography with its total concentration upon organs.[128] It is men, not women, who experience the visual pornography of naked, slippery bodies as lust-provoking. It is men, not women, who patronize prostitutes. If casual sex appealed to women nearly as much as it does to men, then throughout history the great bulk of prostitutes, both female and male, would not have been in the service of males.

THE VAST DIFFERENCE between male and female sexuality underlies those dichotomous attitudes of men and women that were encapsulated in Madame Germaine De Staël's observation: "Love is the whole history of a woman's life, it is but an episode in a man's."[129] It was this same truth that Lord Byron subsequently immortalized in *Don Juan*: "Man's love is of man's life a thing apart, 'tis woman's whole existence."

Contemporary feminism set out to prove De Staël and Byron wrong. Clearly, some women do fall outside their descriptions. Most women, however, fall within them—a fact that feminists find unbearable. But their own revulsion at the claims femininity exerts on women has never justified feminists in encouraging other women to adopt those male patterns of sexual promiscuity that are so contrary to the nature of most women.

4

The Mocking of Conjugal Sexuality

When a man sleeps with a modern woman, he actually gets into bed with all her lovers. That's why there are so many homosexuals today, because modern man is sleeping spiritually with countless other men. He constantly wants to excel in sex because he knows that his partner is comparing him to the others. This is also the cause of impotence, from which so many suffer. They've transformed sex into a marketplace with competitors. Today's man must convince himself that he is the greatest lover and that Casanova was a schoolboy in comparison. He tries to convince the female, too, but she knows better.

Issac Bashevis Singer[1]

Now, good-by. I thank God above all things that thou art my wife. Nobody but we ever knew what it is to be married. If other people knew it, this dull old earth would have a perpetual glory round about it.

Nathaniel Hawthorne[2]

𝒩O ASPECT OF THE FEMINIST SEXUAL REVOLUTION has contributed to women's sexual well-being. The revolution's substitution of pornographic desire for romance catered to men's, not women's, interests. Sexual relationships suffered, moreover, both from feminism's introduction of confrontation and competition into the sexual encounter and its distortion of sexual roles during that encounter. Feminist commitment to promoting its ideology of sexual equivalence required that women be encouraged not only to ape male sexual patterns by participating in casual sexual intercourse as freely as men do, but also to imitate male behavior in choosing the time for sexual activity and in becoming equally assertive throughout the sexual encounter. Denouncing as inferior all aspects of the traditional woman's existence, from her care of home and children to her behavior in the bedroom, feminism's supporters caricatured the marriages and daily lives of traditional women.

THE FEMINIST SEXUAL PRESCRIPTION

As Ehrenreich et al. explain in *Re-Making Love*, the feminist sexual revolution entailed women's exchange of "passivity and surrender" for "an interaction between potentially equal persons" who participate "with equal control" in the sexual activity.[3] Now, the phrase "potentially equal" can mean many things—of equal spiritual worth in the eyes of God, for example, or deserving of equal respect and consideration from one's fellow men. But to these feminists it means that sexual differences are trivial and that women should behave like men; that is, women should initiate sexual encounters and be as assertive throughout the encounter as men are. Thus, Andrea Dworkin approves the assertion by Victoria Woodhull, a nineteenth century feminist, that the "right of sexual determination" belongs to the woman: "When the instinct is aroused in her, then and then only should commerce follow." This means, says Dworkin, that "the woman's desire" should be "the desire of significance."[4] Where marital sex is involved, on this issue—like so many others—contemporary feminists could not be more wrong.

When genital intercourse is the goal of a sexual encounter, some assertiveness on the woman's part can, of course, be acceptable and even possess the attraction of any novelty. The woman's assertion of *equal* control, however, directly conflicts with the male's need for control. In George Gilder's accurate analysis, the "key contingent variable in sex is the male erection." By controlling the encounter, a man "can gain the sense of security that enables him to perform," but his security and confidence will usually be "undermined by female activity"; genital intercourse will usually not be successful if the woman's activity is such as to "upset the fragile male sense that he is in command."[5]

It is no challenge to the accuracy of Gilder's assertion that other paradigms may apply to the sexual activity of passive males who have forsaken genital intercourse for variants that mimic homosexual practices. Nor is the assertion rebutted by the depiction of sexually aggressive and predatory women in books, magazines, television, and movies. Much of this material has been created to express feminist ideology, and some of it is directed toward the passive male. It is no more likely that most men want or can function optimally in genital intercourse with sexually aggressive women, whom they perceive as matching their own level of sexual assertiveness, than it is likely that most women actually want to experience the rapes and other abuses that are erotic in fantasy. Very few of the women who find Pauline Réage's *Story of O* lust-provoking would willingly spend one instant in Sir Stephen's mansion.[6]

The vast bulk of heterosexual pornography makes clear what men want to deal with in bed. In "erotic representation aimed at men," Richard Posner has observed, the "male image desired . . . is one of effortless mastery, and the female image desired is one of youth, beauty, adoration, compliance, subordination, and admiration of stereotypical male characteristics such as strength and aggressiveness."[7] As Steven Marcus puts it, "[o]ne of the principal components in male sexuality is the desire for power, the desire to dominate."[8] While the challenge of a sexually aggressive woman may titillate a man, the ultimate end of male domination with effortless mastery is undermined proportionally to the degree of effort required for him to exceed her level of assertiveness.

One aspect of the equal control advocated by feminists (and likely the most counterproductive to successful long-term sexual relationships with genital intercourse as the goal) is equality in initiating the sexual encounter. Women—for whom sex is one of the least demanding activities—are equally entitled, feminists have argued, to designate the time of sexual performance for men—for whom it is one of the most demanding activities. Margaret Mead definitively disposed of this claim of female right when she said that since "receptivity requires so much less of [the woman]—merely a softening and relaxing of her whole body, and none of the specific readiness and sustained desire that is required of the male—she can learn to fit a simple compliancy ... into the whole pattern of a relationship." Beyond doubt, she asserted, "the male who has learned various mechanical ways to stimulate his sexual specificity in order to copulate with a woman whom he does not this moment desire is doing far more violence to his nature than the female who needs only to receive a male to whom she gives many other assents, but possibly not active desire."[9]

The importance sometimes placed on inhibiting female sexual assertiveness and the extreme measures that will be taken to accomplish this objective are evidenced by the practice of female genital circumcision in some African cultures. In *Prisoners of Ritual: An Odyssey into Female Genital Circumcision in Africa*, Hanny Lightfoot-Klein analyzes this custom that—in its most drastic but also most common form, the pharaonic circumcision—begins with excising the clitoris, the labia minora, and the inner layers of the labia majora. Then, in a procedure called "infibulation," the remaining skin of the labia majora is sutured together to form a bridge of scar tissue over the vaginal opening, with only a very small passage left for urine and menstrual flow. After childbirth, women are often "refibulated" by re-suturing the edges of the scar, usually to pin-hole size.[10] Refibulation renews their virginity, as it were, necessitating the often difficult, painful, and bloody re-penetrations which replicate the initial harrowing penetrations upon marriage that could take weeks, even months, to break through the scar tissue.

Many justifications are given for this custom: to "keep the sexual organs clean, prevent malodorous discharges, prevent rape, prevent vaginal worms, help women conceive, facilitate giving birth, make them less sexually sensitive before marriage, but more responsive after marriage."[11] There is an assumption "by African men that gross clitoral hypertrophy is common among African women, and that they have correspondingly insatiable sexual appetites"; uncircumcised girls are ridiculed for having "that thing dangling between [their] legs."[12] The chief justification given for the practice is to "attenuate or abolish sexual desire in women" who, it is believed, would otherwise "exhibit an unbridled and voracious appetite for promiscuous sex," women being considered "highly sexed and by nature promiscuous."[13] A doctor, who was married to two pharao-nized women and had four pharaonized daughters, explained that female circumcision, although without medical justification, was a response to the fact that "sexually sensitive women were a detriment to society." His wives' condition "made life smoother for him by removing sexual tensions"; "he could have sex with them when *he* wanted, but they made no demands on him."[14]

Lightfoot-Klein illustrates how the practice of female genital circumcision operates in Sudan both to meet the perceived necessity of bridling female sexual desire and to satisfy the custom that women should not only never initiate sexual intercourse but also should remain passive and immobile during the act, women's open expression of sexual interest and pleasure being considered "extremely shameful."

As part of this highly ritualized sexual drama there is a custom that enables the woman, nevertheless, to indicate her sexual desire, while not overtly demanding sexual performance. By engaging in the "smoke ceremony," which permeates her skin with sandalwood smoke and fragrant oils, she can convey an unmistakable signal of sexual receptivity.[15]

Descriptions of the ritual that imprisons these women are like a pornographer's creation. But while pornography is usually poorly written fantasy, Lightfoot-Klein's *Odyssey* is well written and appears to be an accurate presentation of facts. What is depicted in her book, nonetheless, resembles what Roger Scruton calls the Marquis de Sade's "dissolution" of the body of the "other" in "pain and mutilation."[16] The linkage of pain to eroticism defines the ritual.[17] Pain is imposed on the young girl through cutting and scraping away her external genitalia (often done without any analgesic), through burning urination that continues until her wound heals, and through infibulation that commonly causes painful and protracted urination and menstruation until the opening is finally enlarged through penetration upon marriage. This period of penetration is painful, bloody, and frequently lengthy, the husband sometimes eventually resorting to makeshift surgery with any available sharp instrument able to cut through what can be massive scar tissue.[18]

There is a Sadean honeymoon hotel located near a hospital in case of hemorrhaging or other complications. Its halls reverberate with the screams, whimpers, and pleas of the brides. They are encouraged by their husbands—often acting lovingly, tenderly, and sensitively, after the fashion of some accomplished inflicters of torture—to cooperate and endure. In words resonating with the image that entices women's so-called masochistic impulse, one prospective bridegroom explained that "he hopes to help her to understand that it must be this way."[19] It is a tableau with husband as ravager and wife as the ravaged. There is always screaming and pain, sometimes cutting; usually, the bride's tight infibulation guarantees a lot more blood in the wedding bed than could have ever been produced by a Western virgin. The pain, the screaming, the pleading, the moaning, the cutting, the bleeding are ritualized and institutionalized. They can be experienced without guilt.

Yet, these men are not evil, nor are the women stupid, and with respect to their postpartum refibulations, the women are not without choices. All who choose refibulation (and apparently the practice is growing) do so in order to increase their husbands' sexual pleasure; some do so to increase their own pleasure as well. And from their testimony it is clear that many do experience sexual pleasure and many do very much love their husbands.

The sexual drama they have created, like Western pornography, expresses men's felt needs and fears. Our revulsion at the bloody canvas painted in *Odyssey* cannot change the fact that palpable male anxieties impelled these men and women to construct, participate in, and then perpetuate such practices. They created rituals designed to ensure to the male what his culture perceives as the inestimable bounty of a virgin bride and to guarantee his status as the initiator of and manager throughout sexual transactions. Unless we are prepared to believe that we have nothing in common with these Africans, we must concede the likelihood that, to some degree, Western men possess corresponding needs and fears.

While we would like to tell Africans that these measures described in *Odyssey* are too draconian for the purpose, we cannot deny that some cultural imperative tells them the purpose must be served. It will not be served by following the prescriptions of Western feminism. African women can learn little from Western feminists who made fashionable the sexual promiscuity and single motherhood that characterize the ghettoes of all our major cities. Can we claim that—even though the women's genital organs are intact and their introitus uninfibulated—our single mothers and their children who have scarcely known a father have as good family lives as the African women and children of *Odyssey*?

We think of the African women as sexually mutilated—and surely they are that—but *Odyssey* also describes their "dignity, their insuppressible zest, their ability to experience joy, to express love, to speak of passion, and the amazing inner balance they projected." Sudanese families are characterized as "naturally loving and supportive of one another and especially of children in a major way that most Westerners can only marvel at and find enviable." Their children "grow up in an atmosphere of emotional security and acceptance," the girls being "able to effortlessly learn their role as mother and nurturer from many loving role models very early in life, and there is a smooth and pressureless transition into adult function."[20]

Instead of the mental pathology she had expected to find resulting from what she viewed as the incessant pain and brutality inflicted upon these women, Lightfoot-Klein was impressed with "the general aura of serenity and balance they far more commonly exude." They appeared to her "to be far more balanced and emotionally healthy than a lot of Western women." What she found most challenging in her study was that despite their acute physical suffering at nearly every point in their lives, these women "are able to survive and to remain emotionally relatively intact, apparently due to love and security they experience as children, and generally in their marriages as well."[21] Western women could, perhaps, learn something from these African women.

In depicting the institutionalization of rituals designed to ensure the dominance of male sexual assertiveness, *Odyssey* serves as a cautionary tale. It teaches us that women would find cultivation of the compliant perspective recommended by Margaret Mead more conducive to a successful marriage than the feminist sexual prescription. My experience of four decades' enjoyment of marital sex leads me to endorse this compliant perspective on the basis of the following assumption: within the parameters set by a standard of reasonableness, a healthy woman who uses a contraceptive method in which she has confidence, who has no emotional antipathy to sexual intercourse, who is not subject to undue stress, and who is married to a minimally competent lover should rarely find a sexual encounter anything less than pleasant. It not only will do no violence to her nature but will contribute to her enjoyment if she tries to think of herself as being always available for sex.

For a woman to believe she must decide each time whether or not she *really* feels like participating in a sexual encounter is akin to deciding at 2:00 a.m. whether or not one *really* wants to get up and begin a long hike. One is much more likely to join the hike in good spirits if one has already committed oneself to it and packed a lunch the night before. The fact is that, until they embark upon it, women really never know how much they will enjoy any particular encounter; it is sometimes when she is most tired that a woman can relax enough to be wiped out by the event. If a woman feels compelled in each instance to evaluate the height of her sexual desire, she finds it easy to conclude that tomorrow would probably be better. At the same time, the compliant perspective enjoins that while presenting herself as attractively as her capabilities permit—creating, perhaps, her own version of the "smoke ceremony"— the woman should try not to put her husband in the position where he must either comply with or refuse an overt demand for sexual performance, except in those circumstances where she can be confident that compliance will be willing.

The making, the refusing, the bargaining over demands for sexual activity has contributed to the confrontational setting in which many of the women who have experienced the so-called consciousness-raising of feminist teaching played out their sexual relationships. Another subject of contention has been the female orgasm and increasingly critical evaluations of male sexual performance. In a monumental falsification of reality, contemporary feminists credited the sexual revolution with establishing, as Ehrenreich et al. put it, that the woman's orgasm had to "count" as much as the man's.[22]

Valuing Female Sexuality

Each generation likes to think the world of sex is its own discovery, that others have never experienced or understood quite these same sensations; this is the childish naïveté that can scarcely imagine one's parents "doing it," much less enjoying it. Education and maturity should teach otherwise. Yet much of the recent writing on female sexuality assumes that the possibility of female sexual gratification was discovered at the end of the 1960s. Megan Marshall, for example, questions many feminist beliefs but—like Katherine Kersten—accepts this assumption in stating that "the research on orgasms helped women to think of themselves as sexual beings, rather than as the solely reproductive agents they'd been in the feminine mystique years."[23] Women like me, who attended college and married during those "feminine mystique" years, have been surprised to hear that we regarded ourselves as solely reproductive agents and not as sexual beings. Very few of us doubted our entitlement to sexual enjoyment, although some probably had unrealistic expectations as to the ease of obtaining it.

Re-Making Love expresses this same adolescent perspective that assumes women's sexuality had been repressed and their orgasms did not "count" prior to the very recent sexual revolution. This contention is simply silly. Any sexual encounter that does not involve a prostitute has usually had as one of its objectives (admittedly, not always a task easily accomplished) the woman aroused to provide her the greatest degree of sexual satisfaction of which she is capable. Women's orgasms have always counted: "the woman aroused" is the theme that has dominated literary and medical descriptions of sexual encounters, and her failure to experience orgasm has usually lessened satisfaction with the event for the man as well. That this is so is evidenced by the long held presumption of many women that it was desirable to fake orgasmic satisfaction. Granting that some men and women have been unconcerned with the woman's gratification or, being concerned, failed in the effort, it nevertheless does men an injustice and assumes that women have always been fools to pretend that the cultural teaching up until the late twentieth century did not consider women's sexual satisfaction to be important.

A plethora of material from literature and history—of which a few examples follow—rebuts the proposition that the sexual revolution was required to acquaint society with the possibility of female sexual gratification. Virginia Woolf's Mrs. Ramsay tells us: "Marriage needed—oh, all sorts of qualities . . . one—she need not name it—that was essential; the thing she had with her husband."[24] Encapsulated in this sentence is the essential Victorian morality that refrained from naming what was most certainly being done and often very much enjoyed. Queen Victoria herself acknowledged the delights of sex. After giving birth to her ninth baby at the age of thirty-eight, the Queen "longed for another child." Her physician warned against further pregnancies, however, "which led her to ask him with a sinking heart: 'Can I have no more fun in bed?'"[25]

As Steven Marcus has shown, Victorian pornography—which included all the sexuality that had to be omitted from the great Victorian novels—depicted women who, in the face of the socially accepted description of their nature, "have orgasms as quickly, easily, and spontaneously as men, and tend to be ready for sexual activity at almost any time. Their sexual needs are as impetuous as men's, if not more so, and there is the usual accompanying fantasy that they ejaculate during orgasm."[26] Victorian pornography indicated that men were well aware of women's sexual needs; indeed, the burden of adequate sexual performance must have weighed so heavily on Victorian men that they welcomed all reassurances of their ability to satisfy women.

One husband's pride in his sexual performance is reflected in a letter Fyodor Dostoyevsky wrote to his wife, Anna, in 1876, after ten years of marriage:

And, finally, how can you be surprised that I should love you as a husband and a man? Why, who ever made me feel as good as you have, who else ever succeeded in merging into one body and soul with me? And we do share all our secrets on *that score*. Is it any wonder, then, that I adore every atom of you and kiss *the whole of you*, never becoming satiated, as it actually happens? Why, you yourself have no idea what an angel of a wife you are in this respect! But I'll prove to you all the things I say as soon as I get back. Even assuming that I am a passionate man, do you really think that another man (even a passionate one) could love a woman so insatiably, as I have proved to you a thousand times already? Actually, all those past proofs of love were nothing; when I get back to you this time, I may very well eat you up! (No one else will read this letter and you must never show it to anyone.)[27]

One may feel some guilt at reading a letter Dostoyevsky wanted no one else to see yet still bask in a description of the sexual love this couple shared. Dostoyevsky's letter responded to one in which Anna had written that "I do not just love and respect you, I actually *adore and worship* you." Although many qualities in a husband may evoke his wife's love and respect, adoration and worship such as Anna expressed for Dostoyevsky usually derive from the satisfaction of being "a well-laid woman" (a phrase I have never found offensive but accurately descriptive of an enviable state).

Victorian Sexual Attitudes

Feminism's argument that it required the sexual revolution to rescue women from sexual neglect reflects an assumption, concurred in by Richard Posner, that Victorian public prudery meant private "sexual anesthesia" for the woman and that this anesthetic condition prevailed until the 1960s. This assumption ignores a wealth of evidence to the contrary.

An idea of female sexual anesthesia evolved out of the scientific discovery in the nineteenth century that conception was not dependent on female orgasm; as a result, says Posner, it was assumed there was no need for women's sexual pleasure. The link between female orgasm and conception, however, had always been questioned. Posner states that Aristotle denied the link, and the experience of at least some women, and even men, must have convinced them there was no link. Posner's assertion that "most women and many men" must have known there was no link assumes that most women were frequently inorgasmic and that many men would have had certain knowledge of this fact.[28] Neither assumption seems likely to be warranted.

Whether or not this scientific discovery did surprise many people, it is not credible that establishing the disconnection between female orgasm and conception caused men to lose interest in securing women's sexual pleasure. To make such an assumption requires believing, contrary to many women's experience, both that men's primary interest in sexual intercourse is reproduction and that most men do not want to think they are good sexual lovers. Rather than supposing that any significant number of men ever wanted to believe in the concept of female sexual anesthesia, the more accurate supposition is that most men would like to believe the proficiency of their sexual performance rises to the level of an art form—and they know the audience sets the value on a performance.

Far from harming women, the certainty that their orgasm was not necessary for conception was a great boon to them. For the woman who could neither conceive nor experience orgasm, it would have been a tremendous relief (and conducive to her ability to relax during intercourse) to know of the disconnection. And the enlightenment would have been truly redemptive for those women who deliberately refrained from orgasm as a means of birth control. Because some did so refrain, nineteenth century writers on contraception constantly stressed the disconnection, attesting to a recognition that women were expected to experience sexual pleasure.[29] To engage in sexual intercourse under the constraint of resisting the natural and longed for culmination of the event in the futile hope of preventing conception must have tormented women like a Sadean refinement of *coitus interruptus*.

Explanations abound for the nineteenth century development of a strict public sexual morality in the English-speaking world. Posner cites issues of health (a realization of the extraordinary prevalence of venereal disease) and concern for national power that underlay a determination to "channel sexual activity into marriage in order to encourage the procreation of numerous well-cared-for children." Also implicated was the common belief that ejaculation debilitated men, so that medical authorities recommended limiting sexual intercourse to once or, at most, twice a month.[30] In a discussion that must arouse a reader's compassion for Victorian men, Steven Marcus sets forth this medical opinion that expulsion of semen required "the expenditure of much vital force." This theory viewed the body as a "productive system with only a limited amount of material at its disposal"; the colloquial expression for orgasm was "to spend," a usage common throughout Victorian pornography.[31]

The damage to a man's mind and body that could be expected to result from excessive "spending" of semen capital (many doctors considered intercourse two or three times a week to be egregiously excessive) is reported in a medical description of one man's symptoms: "general debility, inaptitude to work, disinclination for sexual intercourse, in fact, he thought he was losing his senses." A "state of enervation produced, at least primarily, by the loss of semen" appeared to be an almost universal Victorian affliction that was seen as allied to "various forms of impotence." It was against this background that the Victorian male required reassurance that he "need not fear that his wife will require the excitement, or in any respect imitate the ways of a courtezan."[32]

Whether or not these gloomy pronouncements, like the herculean efforts to prevent masturbation, actually inhibited men very much, one impetus for imposing a stricter sexual morality that did succeed was Victorian feminism. The Victorian public commitment to chastity, propriety, and modesty, together with women's very successful evangelizing efforts to inculcate these bourgeois virtues, encouraged cultivation of the self-restraint that was required to exercise them. This achievement, as Marcus observes, was "a giant step toward the humanization of a class of persons who had been traditionally regarded as almost of another species." Life among the nineteenth century urban lower classes was "degraded and often bestial," characterized by "drink, violence, early and promiscuous sexuality, and disease"; elevation of this class required that its members learn to exercise an "immense effort of self-discipline and self-denial" and to accept the indefinite deferral of gratification.[33]

Strict Victorian sexual morality—in Gertrude Himmelfarb's words, "the morality that dignifies and civilizes human beings"[34]— was a boon to women, fought for by nineteenth century feminists and revoked by the contemporary feminism that encouraged women's return to early and promiscuous sexuality. Analyzing a Victorian pornographer's description of a young, lower-class girl's surprising attempt to summon the dignity to resist seduction, Marcus states that "in the degree to which that young girl succeeded in denying her sexuality to the author, and to other men, and in the degree to which she even made her own sexuality inaccessible to herself . . . might she have the chance of extending her humanity in other directions."[35] This chance was indeed the gift of Victorian sexual morality.

It was a morality, moreover, that did not prescribe repression and inhibition of female sexual enjoyment within marriage.[36] The testimony of women themselves and of medical books and marriage manuals shows, claims Himmelfarb, that in Victorian England both sexes might naturally expect "to experience the 'exstacy' of inter-course." Confirming that the "conventional view of sexual repression is much exaggerated," she notes that Evangelical writings in the latter part of the century "stressed the importance of conjugal sex for a happy and healthy marriage."[37]

Carl N. Degler has demonstrated that the American nineteenth-century literature in which women's sexuality was "either played down or virtually denied" was not describing actual practices and common beliefs, but presenting a "new ideology of sexual behavior." The purpose of this ideology was to help women gain a "certain moral superiority over men," so as to achieve "greater autonomy and self-respect within the family," in particular to gain female control over conception. Nineteenth century feminists promoted the ideology in order to bolster women's efforts to curtail the frequent child-bearing that damaged their health and the frequent intercourse during pregnancy that was believed to cause severe morning sickness, miscarriages, and unhealthy infants. Their depiction of husbands as inconsiderate satyrs forcing themselves upon reluctant wives was designed to increase women's control over conception by justifying their right to refuse intercourse. Thus, the Grimké sister's essay "Marriage" expressed the emerging feminist view that it was the woman's right "to decide *when* she shall become a mother, how often, and under what circumstances."[38]

In the nineteenth century, states Degler, "[t]he dubious reliability of the various methods of contraception threw a dark shadow over every act of intercourse."[39] Faced with this immutable fact, together with the harsh realities that women often died in childbirth and were commonly debilitated and disheartened by frequent and unwanted child-bearing, women could have felt themselves well justified in enforcing abstinence. Read against this background, there is merit in Victoria Woodhull's pronouncement that only when women so desired "should commerce follow." Absent the predicate of unreliable contraception, however, Woodhull's recommendation serves no valid objective, and its advocacy by contemporary feminists is a prescription for marital discord.

Promotion of an ideology that justified nineteenth century women's enforcement of abstinence upon husbands in order to curtail child-bearing was a feminist achievement, not a male patriarchal conspiracy to deprive women of sexual pleasure. As Degler observes, the new ideology of sexual control or denial was *contrary* to men's sexual desires, since "it usually resulted in limiting sexual satisfaction for men" who, medical doctors reported, "often de-

plored their wives' lack of sexual interest."[40]   Champions of the
ideology were not men in general, but women and those men who
sought its beneficial effects for women. The ideology was, moreover, completely consistent with the existence of a "clear recognition by male medical doctors, writers of advice books, and women
themselves" that women's sexual feelings required expression and
resolution—a recognition that negates any "notion that during the
19th century women's sexuality was generally denied or effectively
suppressed."[41]

   Writings from the period clearly recognize the reality of women's
sexual desire and the fact of its satisfaction.   An 1865 writer on
contraception noted that orgasm may be even more intense in the
woman than the man, "causing convulsive motions and involuntary
cries"; the woman sometimes "craves frequent and repeated intercourse, as the indulgence does not exhaust her as it does her partner."
Unlike the male orgasm (which was assumed to cause debilitation
by loss of the vital fluid), the female orgasm "not being produced
by any secretion, may be enjoyed without particular injury." Women
were acknowledged to be less easily exhausted sexually than men,
one physician advising in 1873 that the woman "await the advances
of her companion before she manifests her willingness for his
approaches," for a woman can ruin a man "of feebler sexual organization than her own." An 1886 marital guide for English workingmen's
families noted that women should know that "a man is sooner
exhausted by excessive indulgence than a woman. He should, therefore, never be encouraged to have connection unless he desires."[42]

   That women's sexual enjoyment was valued in the nineteenth
century is evidenced by the emphasis medical writers placed on
the "role of the clitoris as the center of women's sexual excitement
and satisfaction," the organ's sensitivity being explained by the fact
that it possessed "five times as many nerves as the penis." One of
the most outspoken doctors advocating birth control during the
1870s stressed how the "clitoris and the erectile tissue of the vagina
. . . induce sexual excitement." Almost all writers on birth control,

moreover, condemned *coitus interruptus* because, among other reasons, "it denied sexual satisfaction to women." One doctor referred to the method's "disastrous consequences, most particularly to the female, whose nervous system suffers from ungratified excitement." The method's effect upon the woman was criticized by another authority because the storm into which her genital organs enter "is not appeased by the natural crisis," and the "unreleased tension" is like that evoked when food that has been offered to a famished man is snatched away: "The sensibilities of the womb and the entire reproductive system are teased to no purpose."[43]

Beyond the evidence of medical writings and marriage manuals is the testimony of women themselves. A unique source on married women's sexual attitudes and habits during the last quarter of the nineteenth century is the Mosher Survey, conducted between 1892 and 1920 among women, of whom 70 percent were born before 1870 and a third before the Civil War. Degler's analysis of their responses to this survey demonstrates women's keen awareness of their own sexual feelings and needs. The great majority said they felt desire for sexual intercourse independent of their husbands' interest. From the form of the question on whether respondents experienced orgasm during intercourse, it was clear that Dr. Mosher assumed female orgasms could be expected, and the responses were about the same as those elicited in Kinsey's survey of women born between 1900 and 1920.[44]

Women's detailed responses to Mosher's questions demonstrated that most of them desired and enjoyed sexual relations, although a small minority only tolerated intercourse. Their responses attested to an enviable sexual satisfaction that starkly contrasts with the whining complaints of contemporary feminists. The contrast gives the lie to feminism's claim that it has contributed to women's sexual well-being and should give pause to anyone who is evaluating the feminist sexual prescription. What possible enlightenment could discontented feminists have bestowed on Sophia Peabody Hawthorne, the wife to whom Nathaniel addressed the sentiments expressed in this chapter's epigraph. Contemporary feminists—especially disappointed sexual revolutionaries—could, on the contrary, take inspiration from Sophia's homage to sexual intercourse: "the truly married alone can know what a wondrous instrument it is for the purposes of the heart."[45]

In the Mosher study, a woman born in 1857 wrote that sexual intercourse "makes more normal people," and even "if there are no children . . . men love their wives more if they continue this relation, and the highest devotion is based upon it, a beautiful thing, and I am glad nature gave it to us." Married people's relationship, said a woman born in 1855, "cannot exist in perfection without sexual intercourse to a moderate degree." Another respondent, writing in 1913, stated that at age fifty-three "my passionate feeling has declined somewhat and the orgasm does not always occur," but intercourse is still "agreeable" to her.[46]

Some of the responses specifically rejected reproduction as a sufficient justification for intercourse. A woman born before the Civil War denied that reproduction "alone warrants it at all; I think it is only warranted as an expression of true and passionate love." Another woman born before 1861 stated in her response in 1893 that "the desire of both husband and wife for this expression of their union seems to me the first and highest reason for intercourse. The desire for offspring is a secondary, incidental . . . motive, but could never to me make intercourse right unless the mutual desire were also present." She then elaborated: "My husband and I believe in intercourse for its own sake—we wish it for ourselves and spiritually miss it, rather than physically, when it does not occur, because it is the highest, most sacred expression of our oneness. On the other hand, even a slight risk of pregnancy, and then we deny ourselves the intercourse, feeling all the time that we are losing that which keeps us closest to each other."[47]

This sentiment is echoed in the Grimké sister's argument endorsing intercourse when the woman was no longer capable of having children: "To me that embrace is as spontaneous an expression of love in husband and wife after that period as before it." She then queries, "why repress this mode of manifestation which will never cease to be natural until disease or the infirmities of age have deadened all physical susceptibilities." "The desire for children" as a "natural incitement to the sexual act," she comments, "is weak in comparison with that yearning for *mutual absorption* into each other, which alone gives vitality to every true marriage."[48]

Such are the sentiments expressed by the women who, contemporary feminists and Richard Posner would have us believe, regarded themselves solely as reproductive agents without sexual feelings.

Women's Sexual Knowledge

By their testimony, nineteenth-century witnesses give the lie to contemporary feminism's myth that a sexual revolution was necessary to rescue women from Victorian sexual anesthesia and teach them that sex can have a purpose other than reproduction. Fabrication of this, as well as other feminist myths, demonstrates how little respect feminists really have for the intelligence of most women and how ignorant they believe women were prior to feminist "enlightenment" in the 1960s. Thus, Katherine Kersten wants to credit 1960s feminism for her "intellectual communion" with other women as a member of "the first generation of 'liberated' women."[49] What, one must wonder, can she possibly think they were actually liberated from, other than from a sense of honor, decency, and responsibility to someone other than themselves. Does she really believe that women were not serious students until the 1970s? In fact, many women had been well-educated for generations before hers; history and literature demonstrate that women's intellectual communion with each other long preceded the most recent feminist revival.

Virginia Woolf's *A Room of One's Own*, for example, was based upon papers read in 1928 at Newnham and Girton, two of the women's colleges at Cambridge University, where many of the residents certainly believed themselves to be in a ferment of shared intellectual communion.[50] In *Testament of Youth*, Vera Brittan provided eloquent testimony to university women's intellectual fervor in her descriptions of the period before and after the First World War when she was a student at Somerville, one of the four women's colleges at Oxford University.[51] Those of us who attended high school and college during and after the Second World War never required the enlightenment of contemporary feminism to appreciate the intellectual acumen of our female peers. It was almost always with other women that we *did* have intellectual communion. The communion that our male peers most desired with us was usually of a different sort.

Wherever one looks evidence appears that women have never been as ignorant or victimized as feminist mythology would have us believe. An exhibit at the Cape Cod National Seashore on nineteenth-century fishing communities, for example, explains how the village girls usually were better educated than the boys, who had to leave school at an early age in order to work on the fishing boats. In my own family, a common practice of the early twentieth-century working class permitted my mother to remain in high school, while her younger brother was legally removed from school at the age of fourteen and apprenticed to a printer in order to help support the household.

Among Charles Dickens's most bitter memories was the enrollment of his sister Fanny as a pupil and boarder at the Royal Academy of Music to study piano, grammar, moral and religious education, arithmetic, and Italian. His biographer remarks that while Dickens's sister was "taken out of the home to be properly educated," Charles's own "hopes and ambitions had been destroyed" when, two days after his twelfth birthday, his education ceased and he was sent to work for ten hours a day in a boot blacking factory. Even after their father was sent to debtors' prison, Fanny remained at boarding school, while Charles kept working at the factory rather than attending the school that was maintained for prisoners' children.[52]

Virginia Woolf has famously bemoaned the sacrifice of sisters since the year 1262 that enabled their brothers to be educated—she called it stocking "Arthur's Education Fund."[53] Norbert Elias, on the other hand, has pointed out that in the history of the Western world it was often not men but women of high class who were first liberated for reading and other intellectual development. It was around women who attracted poets, singers, and learned clerics that the first circles of peaceful intellectual activity were established: "In aristocratic circles in the twelfth century the education of women was on average more refined than that of men."[54] The prominence of learned women in eighteenth century China caused a debate about "women's learning," which was defended as having "deep roots in antiquity": in the classic *Book of Odes*, for example, more than half of the three hundred poems were written by women.[55] And in nineteenth-century England, more novels were published by women—writing under their own names, contrary to the myth that women were obliged to take male names—than by men.[56]

Contrary to feminist mythology, women were not so ignorant and victimized at the end of the 1960s that they required the enlightenment of feminist sexual revolutionaries. Rather, it was the feminist sexual teachings encouraging female pursuit of casual sex that themselves became the source of women's victimization. The reality of their sexual desire and the awareness of how to gratify that desire come early to women from their own bodies and are then elaborated through education and experience. Most women born in the first half of the twentieth century did not view the residual constraints of Victorian sexual morality as a token of our sexual anesthesia; we welcomed them as protection against men's sexual demands. Our bodies, our fantasies, our knowledge of history and literature all belied the anesthetic possibility. It was the rare adolescent girl who had no glimmerings of sexual passion, and most with a high school education knew it was this passion that had pinned the fiery letter to the breast of Hester Prynne.

There is no basis for believing that it was common at any time in history for women to doubt the female capacity for sexual passion or believe that their orgasms did not "count." The physiological theories of the Middle Ages "held that women were more capable of sexual pleasure than men," and American marriage manuals in the seventeenth and eighteenth centuries emphasized "the sexual arousal, pleasure, and satisfaction of women," advising use of the clitoris to encourage "the action excited in coition." Manuals written at the beginning of the nineteenth century considered normal sexual relations for a married couple to be four to five times a week and recommended that the wife experience an orgasm. Suspicion that women's sexual desires were insatiable apparently underlay the advice that a wife display "effeminate decorum" and not "play the harlot," although "she ought not to be denied what a healthy husband ought to be able to give."[57]

Part of our cultural knowledge is the tragic plight of the twelfth century's Héloise set forth in her paeans to sexual passion in the anguished letters she wrote from the convent to her husband, Abelard, from whom she had been forever separated. In an early instance of sexual harassment by an academician, Abelard—the most famous moral philosopher and logician of his century—seduced his pupil Héloise—probably the most brilliant woman of that century—whom he had been retained to tutor in her home. Although they subsequently married, her guardian retaliated by having Abelard castrated, and Héloise then retired to a convent for the remainder of her life.

It was not longing for the stimulation of his intellect (Héloise would have agreed with me that discussing the First Amendment is not life's greatest pleasure) that led Héloise to recall and express gratitude to Abelard for the monumentally delightful sexual experiences they had shared: "I never sought anything in you except yourself; I wanted simply you, nothing of yours. . . . The name of wife may seem more sacred or more binding, but sweeter for me will always be the word mistress, or, if you will permit me, that of concubine or whore." Recalling that "queens and great ladies envied me my joys and my bed," Héloise laments that—unlike Abelard whose castration has freed him "from these torments"—for her, "experience of pleasures which were so delightful intensify the torments of the flesh and longings of desire"[58]:

> In my case, the pleasures of lovers which we shared have been too sweet—they can never displease me, and can scarcely be banished from my thoughts. Wherever I turn they are always there before my eyes, bringing with them awakened longings and fantasies which will not even let me sleep. Even during the celebration of the Mass, when our prayers should be purer, lewd visions of those pleasures take such a hold upon my unhappy soul that my thoughts are on their wantonness instead of on prayers. I should be groaning over the sins I have committed, but I can only sigh for what I have lost. Everything we did and also the times and places are stamped on my heart along with your image, so that I live through it all again with you. Even in sleep I know no respite. Sometimes my thoughts are betrayed in a movement of my body, or they break out in an unguarded word.[59]

When we read about Héloise, few of us believed ourselves to be so corseted by Victorian sexual restraints that we did not hope someday to echo her homage to sexual pleasure. And even the least educated women had access to one of the best known and beautifully erotic negations of female sexual anesthesia. The reality of woman's sexual desire and promise of its gratification pervade the "Song of Solomon,"[60] which begins with the Woman:

> Let him kiss me with the kisses of his mouth; for thy love *is* better than wine (1:2) ... A bundle of myrrh *is* my well-beloved unto me; he shall lie all night betwixt my breasts (1:13); ... He brought me to the banqueting house, and his banner over me *was* love (2:4) ... His left hand *is* under my head, and his right hand doth embrace me (2:6) ... My beloved *is* mine, and I *am* his: he feedeth among the lilies. Until the day break,

and the shadows flee away, turn, my beloved, and be thou like
a roe or a young hart upon the mountains of Bether. (2:16-17).
. . . [The Man replies:] Thy two breasts *are* like two young
roes that are twins, which feed among the lilies. Until the
day break, and the shadows flee away, I will get me to the
mountain of myrrh, and to the hill of frankincense (4:5-6); . .
. Thy lips, O *my* spouse, drop *as* the honeycomb: honey and
milk *are* under thy tongue; and the smell of thy garments *is*
like the smell of Lebanon (4:11). . . .[Later, the Woman says:]
My beloved put in his hand by the hole *of the door*, and my
bowels were moved for him (5:4).

Some modern versions of the Bible translate this last verse with
variants of the less specific phrase "my heart thrilled for him." Now,
hearts may thrill for many reasons but, in the context of this poem,
the original phrase of "bowels were moved for him" clearly signifies
the fluttering anticipation of orgasmic delight.

Marriage in Caricature

Contemporary feminism's baseless claim to have rescued women
from sexual anesthesia and its depiction of traditional wives as dull
and uninteresting in contrast to titillating sexual revolutionaries
have been echoed by Richard Posner. His analysis of marriage in
ancient Greece mirrors feminist ideology and lays a veneer of
respectability over this ideology's caricature of traditional women.
Speaking like a contemporary feminist, he asserts that within Greek
marriages sexual intercourse occurred only occasionally and then
solely for the purpose of insemination. Men's sexual passion, says
Posner, was confined to pederastic relationships and those with
"cultured, witty courtesans (*hetairai*)."[61] Are we really to believe
that wit and culture were uniformly exhibited by elite prostitutes
and never by Greek citizen-wives? Granted these were arranged
marriages, does not all our experience confirm, nevertheless, that
the intimacy of sexual contact and the joy of creating children—

who were beloved even in a society which condoned infanticide—
could lay the foundation for growth of a loving, even passionate,
relationship?

The great Greek dramas belie Posner's caricature of wives, and
the epic poems would be senseless if marriages were unvaryingly
passionless. In *The Family in Classical Greece*, W. K. Lacey describes
Homer as "the basic educational medium in Greece." The Homeric
poems portrayed "a society which the Greeks of the classical period
believed to have been that of their ancestors," so that classical Greece
was shaped by the institutions and ideas of the Homeric society.
And within the society of the Homeric poems, "the ambitions,
hopes, desires and fears of the heroes are centred in their families."[62]

Analyses like Posner's cannot accurately describe a culture from
which came *The Iliad*'s depiction of the tragedy caused by Menelaus's
passion for his faithless wife Helen and the ten-year war waged to
retrieve her. When Achilles asks in *The Iliad*, "Why must we battle
Trojans, men of Argos?," the answer is "Why, why in the world if
not for Helen with her loose and lustrous hair?" Then, venting his
wrath at being deprived of his own beloved woman, Achilles rages,
"Are *they* the only men alive who love their wives, those sons of
Atreus [Agamemnon and Menelaus]? Never! Any decent man, a
man with sense, loves his own, cares for his own as deeply as I, I
loved that woman with all my heart, though I won her like a trophy
with my spear." If, as Posner would have us believe, husbands viewed
themselves as nothing but "financial protectors and occasional
inseminators," how could Achilles have so spoken and later envisioned
finding a "cherished wife" who will be "a fine partner to please my
heart, to enjoy with her the treasures my old father Peleus piled
high."[63]

Posner's derisive words "occasional inseminator" mock the depth
of emotions that endow with such overwhelming pathos the parting
of Hector from Andromache, his wife. Reminding Hector that he
is everything to her—"my father now, my noble mother, a brother
too, and you are my husband, young and warm and strong!"—

Andromache pleads with him to "take your stand on the rampart here, before you orphan your son and make your wife a widow." But Hector declines to "shrink from battle now, a coward." Foreseeing that "sacred Troy must die," Hector pours out his grief to Andomache at what the aftermath will be:

> it is less the pain of the Trojans still to come
> that weighs me down, . . .
> That is nothing, nothing beside your agony
> when some brazen Argive hales you off in tears,
> wrenching away your day of light and freedom!
> Then far off in the land of Argos you must live,
> laboring at a loom, at another woman's beck and call,
> fetching water at some spring, Messeis or Hyperia,
> resisting it all the way—
> the rough yoke of necessity at your neck.
> And a man may say, who sees you streaming tears,
> "There is the wife of Hector, the bravest fighter
> they could field, those stallion-breaking Trojans,
> long ago when the men fought for Troy." So he will say
> and the fresh grief will swell your heart once more,
> widowed, robbed of the one man strong enough
> to fight off your day of slavery.
>   No, no,
> let the earth come piling over my dead body
> before I hear your cries, I hear you dragged away!

Then Hector kisses his son and "tossed him in his arms," praying to Zeus that he "may be like me, first in glory among the Trojans" and "one day let them say, 'He is a better man than his father!'" So praying, Hector "placed his son in the arms of his loving wife." When Hector took up his helmet, "his loving wife went home, turning, glancing back again and again and weeping live warm tears."[64]

It is precisely Hector's role as husband and father, depicted in his devotion to Andromache and their son, that established his image as the premier defender of a peaceful civilization. This role assured him moral superiority over Achilles, who fought only to secure revenge and personal glory. The role of "occasional inseminator" is too slight to bear the weight of Hector's noble reputation as the champion of loyal wives and helpless children, nor can it encompass the marital relationship that evoked Andromache's tragic monody for Hector: "O my husband . . . cut off from life so young! You leave me a widow, lost in the royal halls—and the boy only a baby, the son we bore together, you and I so doomed. . . . you who always defended Troy, who kept her loyal wives and helpless children safe . . . . my Hector—you've brought your parents accursed tears and grief but to me most of all you've left the horror, the heartbreak! For you never died in bed and stretched your arms to me or said some last word from the heart I can remember, always, weeping for you through all my nights and days!"[65]

In questioning analyses similar to Posner's, Jasper Griffin relies on Homer's depiction in the *The Odyssey* of the heroic Odysseus who "endures all perils and resists all temptations—even that of immortality—to get back to his wife, Penelope, his reunion with whom is the climax of the poem."[66] That Greek men sought pleasure in pederasty (although usually only for a short period of their lives prior to marriage[67]) and in the services of *hetairai*, we cannot doubt. But neither can we doubt that the cultural knowledge which informed not only the creation of Penelope, Andromache, and Helen but also the expectations with which Greek men and women entered into and conducted their marriages assumed that wives would afford and receive all possible satisfactions of the marital relationship. It was these marital relationships—not the extramarital indulgences—that were celebrated in the masterworks of the age.

The family, says Lacey, was "the most central and enduring institution of Greek society." To enhance the ability of Athenian citizen women to secure husbands, the law provided that a child could be a citizen only if both parents were citizens, and the status of citizen wives as the sole producers of legitimate citizen children was zealously defended. Thus, in his famous speech demanding that Neaira be condemned for usurpation of citizenship because she was a courtesan of unknown parentage, the orator Apollodorus argued that acquittal would constitute approval of such careers, and "the high regard we have for free women will be transferred to courtesans if they gain leave with impunity to breed children as they please and have a share in the religious life of the state and its honours."[68]

Illegitimate Athenian children lacked rights of succession, were excluded from family religious observances, and lacked citizen-rights. This is the context of what Lacey describes as the "often misquoted dictum" that "we have courtesans for pleasure, concubines to look after the day-to-day needs of the body, wives that we may breed legitimate children and have a trusty warden of what we have in the house." The orator, Lacey observes, was not saying that "we cannot have either pleasure or care of our persons from our wives—quite the reverse; the services to a man of the three classes of woman are intended cumulatively, and it is the purpose of the argument merely to stress that you can beget legitimate children only from a properly married wife."[69]

Whether in the Homeric poems or the speeches of orators in classical Athens, wishes for good and ill were always expressed in terms of the welfare of family members. When Odysseus prepares to return home, he prays that he will "find my good wife at home and my dear ones all safe and sound." Demosthenes pleaded with the jury "by your children, by your wives, by all the good things you possess," and Apollodorus told the jury of his longing to see his children, wife, and mother: "What is sweeter than these to a man? or what would a man want to go on living for if he should lose them?" Herodotus tells of the man who hunted the savage boar which was ravaging the kingdom because if he did not, "what sort of a man would his wife think him." And the jury is admonished that if Neaira is acquitted "your wives will be furious with you."[70]

These expressions of devotion and homage cannot be dismissed as merely conventional. The very fact of their conventionality is evidence of the loving bonds between family members that gave rise to such conventional invocations of familial concerns. If only catamites and courtesans were loved, expressions of devotion to them would have, instead, become conventional. But great poets and orators did not express longings to return to their catamites or seek to soften jurors' hearts with avowals of love and devotion to a courtesan. On the contrary, the allegation that one's family members belonged in these categories was part of the language of insult in which a man could be attacked on the grounds that his children's mother was a whore or his father had been a catamite, or because he associated with *hetairai*, or had never married.[71] While not illegal (although Plato made it so in the *Laws*[72]), sodomy was thought reprehensible for older men, even when the catamite was not a citizen, and adult Athenians who acted as catamites were excluded from all offices in public life, not even being permitted to address the assembly.[73] A relationship so circumscribed with guilt and interdiction was ill-suited to sustain all man's passion.

It defies logic that married men living in a society which above all else valued perpetuation of the family through legitimate progeny would view themselves as nothing more to their wives than "occasional inseminators." As Lacey notes, Plato and Aristotle believed "marriage was intended to promote happiness." Because wives were so young at marriage (about age sixteen compared to age thirty for men), Xenophon counseled the man to teach his wife because "she is entrusted with more of his valuable possessions than anyone else"; "a wife who is a good partner in an *oikos* [a family, including its property] is in every way as important to its well-being as her husband." Xenophon instructed his own young wife "not to sit still at home herself all day, but to take part in the housework and keep her youthful beauty by getting some exercise"; she should learn from slaves who do something better than she and all this "improves the appetite" and "makes her more attractive (than the slave girls) to her husband."[74] Xenophon, it would appear, had an interest in his wife beyond occasional insemination.

In discussing the requirement in Sparta and Crete that a full citizen must belong to an *andreion* (a men's mess), Lacey comments that if membership continued throughout the man's life there would have been less possibility than in Athens for "that mutual association in marriage from which strong attachments could, and no doubt did, grow." How readily these attachments could grow in a culture that so highly valued a fertile wife appears from the testimony of Euphiletus, as he sought to convince an Athenian jury that he was a "reasonable, kindly man": "When I married, ... I looked after her as well as I could, and paid attention to her as was reasonable. But when a child was born, I at once began to trust her entirely and handed over to her all I possessed." Euphiletus then described a scene of teasing interaction between himself and the new mother one night after they had had supper together.[75] The authenticity of his description of what we would today consider a loving marital relationship indicates that both speaker and jurors thought such relationships to be desirable and possible.

Only cognizance of the fact that marriages could be loving gives meaning to Lycurgus's statement that "when a woman loses sympathy with her husband, life becomes not worth living." A loving marital relationship must have been known to Anaxandridas, a sixth century king of Sparta, for when he was urged by the magistrates to divorce his wife who had borne no children, he refused because he loved his wife. The magistrates then told him he could continue "to treat the wife you have as you have always treated her and take another wife besides to bear you children." This he did and lived in two houses in what Herodotus described as "a thoroughly un-Spartan fashion,"[76] an arrangement necessitated precisely by the fact that King Anaxandridas perceived his relationship with his first wife to encompass far more than being an "occasional inseminator."

It seems hardly possible to view Greek funerary sculptures from the fifth century B.C.[77] without concluding that those depicted had played an important part in the intimate life of the survivors who memorialized them. Are we to assume that the artists who carved these sculptures (some of whom are thought to have worked on the Parthenon, attesting to the sculptures' importance) were instructed to create a mere sham of affection? One grave stele depicts a little girl holding two pet doves; the beak of one dove seems to touch her lips as if giving her a parting kiss. Would an artist from a society in which daughters were not also well-loved have portrayed a farewell so moving that it can wrench one's heart from across the centuries? That daughters were indeed well-loved is evidenced by Athenian legislation enhancing their marriage opportunities and guaranteeing married women more economic security than our supposedly enlightened society provides for wives today.[78]

Commenting on the suggestion that Romans regarded marriage merely as a social duty, Jasper Griffin has observed that to make this claim "is to disregard such evidence as the thousands of tombstones and epitaphs still extant on which husbands and wives asserted their devotion."[79] The Greek grave stele of Ktesilaos and Theano stands as a similar memorial to devotion. It depicts a husband and wife gazing at each other with what appears to be serene confidence in one another's affection. Are we to believe the sculptor dissembled? Why *should* we choose to interpret this gaze that the sculptor created for the husband as merely that of an occasional inseminator? Is it not quite clearly intended to be the gaze of a man who has known happiness, love, and—unless we are to discount all of Greek drama and epic poetry and believe Greek men a thoroughly different breed from us—passion, as well, with this woman whose shared life with him the sculpture commemorates?

The social documentation found in gravestones, boundary markers, wills, and marriage contracts establishes, claims Mary Lefkowitz, that strong ties existed between Athenian husband and wife. Family members, for example, wished to be buried near each other, even when this necessitated moving established graves. Greek men, Lefkowitz observes, may have been less concerned with repressing women than protecting them, for why else would their two most important epics depict a war fought on behalf of a woman. And why, moreover, would Menelaus forgive Helen and resume life with her rather than repudiate or kill her?[80]

"Upper-class women in all periods and places in the Greek world had the opportunity to be educated," observes Lefkowitz, while the lives of lower-class women closely resembled those of men. Nor was repression through sexual deprivation in their marriages considered the fitting lot of women, as is demonstrated by the evidence Lefkowitz marshals "lest anyone . . . argue that Greek men got their sexual pleasure from extra-marital or homosexual relationships." While certainly not always honored, the applicable standard counseled that a husband who desired a happy home would attend to the sexual relationship in his marriage, and a wife should never cease doing what brings her husband pleasure.[81] Confirming the existence of marital sexual passion is the fact that Greek and Roman medical writers extensively discussed artificial methods of contraception, and literary texts assumed that contraception was well known and widely used.[82] Substantial development of folk remedies for contraceptive and abortifacient purposes and dissemination of this knowledge across generations of women would have been unnecessary in a society where husbands confined marital sexual activity to occasional insemination.

At the Freer Gallery of Art in Washington, D.C., there is a silver and gilt bowl from the seventh century A.D., believed to come from Iran or Afghanistan. This richly decorated bowl celebrates the marriage contract of the banqueting couple depicted in its primary scene. The man and woman are seated on a couch facing one another, each grasping the wreath held up between them.[83] Like Ktesilaos and Theano, they also gaze at each other; perhaps somewhat appraisingly, not yet confidently. It was the significance of their impending marriage that prompted creation of this magnificent work of art. Their naturalness and immediacy bring the figures alive for the viewer who can easily believe they depict a man and woman who were once flesh and blood. And all our experience suggests that this strong, healthy-looking nobleman—leaning back almost sensuously against the banqueting couch—promises affection as well as sexual passion in the look conferred upon the woman who returns his gaze from the other side of the wreath.

We have no reason to doubt that the cultural expectations which informed creation of both grave stele and silver bowl contemplated that the provision of affection and physical pleasure for both husband and wife were part of the marital relationships that the stele commemorated and the bowl anticipated. There has been no time in the history of civilization when this cultural knowledge was completely lost, though it may sometimes have been obscured. And even then, as in the Victorian era, the obscurity was much more apparent then real. Far from obscure to Victoria was either the fun she had in bed or the "wild longings" and torments of unsatisfied sexual desire that she suffered after the death of her husband, Albert.[84]

No grounds exist that would justify feminism's appropriation of the sexual revolution as a means to acquaint women with the possibility of sexual fulfillment or to resurrect women's sexual passion. Women have always been well aware of their entitlement to sexual gratification, and their passion has never died.

THE CASUALTY OF THE CASUAL ORGASM

It was not because, as Ehrenreich et al. believe, women's sexual satisfaction had not counted earlier that female sexual revolutionaries became obsessed with the topic of their orgasms. Rather, the attempt to imitate stereotypical male sexual activity—sex without the magic and mystery of romance—entailed casual sexual relationships in which nothing counted but the orgasm. At the same time, the casualness of these couplings was inconsistent with female orgasmic satisfaction, a more complicated goal than male ejaculation and far less attainable from this sex without emotion that is the hollow core of pornography. Women's dissatisfaction with the jejune fruits of loveless sex led to great demands on their part with respect to men's sexual performance. And from the men's perspective, women's demanding approach was particularly pernicious because women's increased participation in promiscuous sex invited knowledgeable comparisons of men's sexual performance.

The traditional dating system prevailing before the sexual revolution had always fostered a certain antagonism between men and women. As Christopher Lasch noted, the system involved a solidarity between members of the same sex combined with an attitude of ridicule toward, and a cynical willingness to exploit, the opposite sex. College students were inclined to "pretend a ruthlessness toward the opposite sex which they do not feel."[85] After playing out this dating ritual, the participants usually found someone who convinced them to abandon the emotional defense of ridicule and acknowledge an incipient love. Throughout the enterprise, wherever she drew the line within the range of sexual possibilities, a woman usually held herself unavailable for sexual intercourse, at least until marriage was imminent. This unavailability had the benefit, despite his complaints, of freeing a man from the full obligations of sexual performance until a time when he could feel more secure in the woman's affections. At that time, he could still be fairly certain that—whatever his capabilities as a lover—the woman would not have much experience on which to base comparisons.

The new sexual ethos created by the sexual revolution exacerbated the antagonisms of traditional dating relationships and—as Issac Bashevis Singer powerfully puts it in his condemnation of this ethos in the epigraph to this chapter—"transformed sex into a marketplace with competitors." Ehrenreich et al. acknowledge men's sense of injury, citing critics who characterized as "frightening" this "focus on the female orgasm and performance evaluation" of the male, who believed that men do not want women "to be very sexually experienced," and who speculated that "women's clitoral obsessions were driving men to homosexuality." Many surveys, these authors note, show "a large majority of men who did not think women should engage in premarital sex or have extramarital affairs."[86]   Midge Decter describes the sexual pursuits of college students as causing the girls to feel "themselves manipulated and mistreated by males," and the boys to line up "in droves at the student health services seeking help with a problem" that "once unmasked, is either the fear of, or the actual onset of, impotence."[87]

Charles Winick suggests that contemporary men's greater misgivings than their ancestors had about their sexual performance may be partly due to women's attitude that their failure to obtain orgasms meant they were being cheated by men.[88]   Compounding the pressures of coping with sexually aggressive, demanding, and experienced women was the new competition men faced as increasing numbers of women entered the workplace. The toll these pressures took helps explain those effete, attenuated males whose sexual fires, in my husband's description, appear to have been banked without ever blazing forth. It seems unlikely that any woman could evoke a spark from these men who reached middle age without marrying and reproducing.

Men's predicament reminds me of a Labrador Retreiver we once had who growled so ferociously whenever someone rang our doorbell that we held her collar to prevent her from lunging at the screen door. Late one night, when two threatening men stood outside the screen door, my husband let go of her collar. Instead of lunging, she stopped growling and looked up at him as if to ask why he was no longer holding her back. The collar of traditional sexual morality, with its expectation of greater sexual reticence on the woman's part, was always slipped by those sufficiently determined to gain release. Many women, however, welcomed the support of this restraint in resisting demands for sexual intercourse, while hoping to retain the man's interest in a dating relationship. For a man, the collar of traditional sexual morality provided welcome validation of his potency through its recognition that his rather awesome masculinity required curbing: he was given a reassuring aura of dominance as the potential sexual aggressor, yet unless he chose to, he would usually not be called upon to prove it.

On the basis of his studies of human mating behavior, David Buss concludes that American men "view the lack of sexual experience as desirable in a spouse." This is so because men "place a premium on fidelity" and "the single best predictor of extramarital sex is premarital sexual permissiveness." Men rank "faithfulness and sexual loyalty" as a wife's "most highly valued traits" and "abhor promiscuity and infidelity in their wives."[89] When a sexual relationship is threatened, claims Buss, women are more likely to feel sad and abandoned, and men to experience rage: "Male sexual jealousy is the single most frequent cause of all types of violence directed at wives," and most spousal homicide is "precipitated by male accusations of adultery or by the woman's leaving or threatening to leave the husband."[90]

These facts of life, which are now documented by evolutionary psychologists, were always part of our cultural knowledge. They are facts that feminist sexual revolutionaries chose to ignore. While they and the women who followed their lead obtained what they viewed as sexual freedom—that is, the freedom to imitate male tom cat behavior—they jeopardized their chances of marrying and, once married, of remaining so. Zora Neale Hurston showed far greater understanding than did feminists of men's needs and fears when she created John Pearson's response to a threat of infidelity from his wife, Lucy:

> "... Ahm goin' tuh kill yuh jes' ez sho ez gun is iron. Ahm de first wid you, and Ah means tuh be de last. Ain't never no man tuh breathe in yo' face but me. ... Don't keer whut come uh go, if you ever start out de door tuh leave me, you'll never make it tuh de gate. Ah means tuh blow yo' heart out and hang fuh it. ...
>
> "Don't tell me 'bout dem trashy women Ah lusts after once in uh while. Dey's less dan leaves uh grass. ... Look lak Ah can't git useter de thought dat you married me, Lucy, and you got chillun by *me*!"
>
> And he held Lucy tightly and thought pityingly of other men.[91]

John Pearson, unfortunately, never does stop lusting after "dem trashy women" who were "less dan leaves uh grass" to him, and Lucy, like many heroines before her, suffers until she dies. Not all stallions can be kept in harness, but the feminist response was to abandon the attempt and run wild with the stallions. For women to run wild, however, can be very costly, as many have learned to their regret.[92]

A FEMINIST VERSION OF CHASTITY

As discussed earlier, Ehrenreich et al. lament that some feminists have sought to dissociate themselves from responsibility for the sexual revolution, rather than justly claiming it as their own. These authors' own depiction of women's ideal sexual experience, however, demonstrates that they also reject the real sexual revolution. They endorse what they have merely redefined as revolutionary, although it is only prosaic.

Midge Decter observes that participants in the women's liberation movement often reacted to their experiences with casual sex by seeking "to repeal the sexual revolution altogether." Women, she says, found that the quest for sexual equality with men had made sex an "unmanageable realm" in their lives; they had "lost the sense of their peculiar womanly power to control the terms of the relations between themselves and men" and, in return, had "received nothing of any truly central value to them."[93] Believing that all aspects of traditional femininity denoted their inferiority, liberationists who wished to return to chastity in fact were unable to embrace it in theory. They instead adopted a version of chastity that either rejected sexual intercourse in all heterosexual relationships or dispensed with men altogether by endorsing the "larger, freer, and 'better' sexuality" of lesbianism.[94] This escape to lesbianism is described by Megan Marshall as a way of making a radical political statement while finding a "refuge from the heterosexual power games."[95]

Retreat from Sexual Intercourse

Re-Making Love is a textbook illustration of this retreat from sexual intercourse, an activity the authors describe with antipathy:

> Heterosexual sex, and especially intercourse, is a condensed drama of male domination and female submission. The man "mounts" and penetrates; the woman spreads her legs and "submits"; and these postures seem to ratify, again and again, the ancient authority of men over women.
>
> To put it another way: Heterosexual sex has had many uses, but it has had, over and over, one social meaning, and that is male domination over women . . . . Sex, or women's role in it, is understood as a humiliation no man would want to endure.[96]

Yet, while denouncing sexual intercourse, the authors claim, nonetheless, to endorse the sexual revolution.

Now, what the sexual revolution was all about was sexual intercourse and women's willingness to engage in it promiscuously, not their willingness to engage in that broad range of sexually stimulating and satisfying activities that my generation referred to as "necking" and "petting," premarital participation in which was hardly revolutionary. The authors contend, however, that the sexual revolution they championed was the alleged rediscovery of the supposedly lost art of what I—not they—call "heavy petting" and their discovery that this is actually the only worthwhile sexual experience for women. In other words, what the authors have decided they really wanted is what women in the supposedly sexually repressed pre-revolutionary period always had when they engaged in sexually satisfying activities without—in another phrase of my generation—"going all the way." The only revolutionary concept is feminism's alleged discovery that the "way" which we refrained from going leads nowhere that women would find worth reaching.

Ehrenreich et al. claimed that the real sexual revolution was the resurrection of the "long repressed" clitoris as "visible proof of women's sexual autonomy from men." They refer to "rediscovery of clitoral sexuality" and describe the clitoris as "our rediscovered magic spot."[97] They do not tell us at what period in history the clitoris was repressed or how the alleged repression had been accomplished, thus necessitating the rediscovery they celebrate. We have seen how the evidence refutes their theory of clitoral repression. Short of excision in clitoridectomy, moreover, it would seem to be well nigh impossible to repress the clitoris, an organ that is not only very tactilely responsive but announces its presence in response to sights, sounds, smells, and thoughts. One must query exactly how this organ *could* be successfully repressed during the nitty gritty of sexual activity, sitting, as it does, at the very threshold of the enterprise. The organ is readily available without lengthy or hazardous search; its usage has never been an obscure part of our cultural knowledge.

What explains this apparently counterfactual feminist analysis? While it is simply silly to say that the clitoris was repressed and then rediscovered, perhaps in the experience of sexual revolutionaries, the organ was somewhat ignored. When women present themselves as fortresses meant for storming, men will be extremely resourceful in their sallies against the citadel. The contribution of the clitoris in endeavoring to arouse a female was hardly arcane knowledge among boys and men in what feminists choose to call the sexually repressed period before their "revolution"—it was usually the focal point of the offensive. If this cultural knowledge was lost to, or purposely ignored by, a significant number of men, an important contributing factor would have been the changed dynamics of sexual encounters, as women undertook to ape the undifferentiated lust that characterizes male sexuality. Confronted with women who avowed an equal desire for casual sexual intercourse, some men may have taken these women at their word and neglected the clitoral attentions so helpful in securing women's sexual gratification.

Such neglect would not be surprising when one considers that, as Posner notes, "prostitutes are becoming more like other women," while at the same time the sexual revolution "has vastly increased the number of women available for casual liaisons." As a result, prostitutes, who in earlier times provided "normal," "ordinary" sex, have been replaced in that market by ordinary women whose services are relatively costless. Prostitutes must now specialize in servicing men who want "kinky" sex and men with physical or emotional disabilities, categories that do not fare well in the free market of casual sex.[98]   Some indication of the degree to which ordinary women have replaced prostitutes appears from the situation in Paris where about 20,000 persons now serve as prostitutes, and many of these are men. In 1890, when the population was one fifth of its present size, Paris was served by 100,000 prostitutes.[99]

Thus have young women been convinced to play the whore for their male peers. In the United States today, an adolescent high school male can find at the desk next to him a young girl equipped by their high school clinic with the latest birth control device ready to provide him with the sexual services that, in an earlier time, he would have received, if at all, from a prostitute.[100] The "soaring pregnancy and abortion statistics on many campuses across the country" that Thomas Sowell has deplored confirm the condition of sexual servitude to which our sexual revolution consigned the best educated segment of our female population.[101] And just as liberated female sexual revolutionaries replaced prostitutes by creating a competing market of free sex, it should not be surprising if they shared the prostitute's dearth of sexual pleasure. A man's sexual encounter with a prostitute is intended to secure his, not her, enjoyment; clitoral fondlings for her benefit usually play no part in the transaction.

An indication of some cultural memory loss in this regard appears from the reference in Ehrenreich et al. to "femoral intercourse." This technique of holding the penis between the thighs so that the penis thrusts laterally between the labia is correctly described by the authors as a technique which maintains virginity. They also refer to it as an "extremely idiosyncratic" and "obscure" practice.[102] Their description would surprise the many individuals who, although they probably did not know the name, were quite familiar with the practice in the pre-revolutionary period, when a high value was placed on the maintenance of virginity and the certainty of avoiding pregnancy. As the authors note, this technique can provide greater clitoral stimulation than is achieved by vaginal thrusting. For this reason, the technique can be a useful part of the repertoire of the course of arousal. Ironically, those allegedly sexually repressed women of the pre-revolutionary period again enjoyed a clitoral stimulation that was apparently denied to the liberated women who engaged in casual sexual intercourse.

Who Enjoys Sexual Rewards?

In discussing women's sexual dissatisfactions that Shere Hite details in *Women and Love*, Connaught Marshner states that men must be motivated and taught to achieve emotional intimacy: "If a man knows he can get you to go to bed with him, he's not going to bother to be interested in your personality."[103] While true, this appraisal applies even more appropriately to men's efforts to be good sexual lovers, a more achievable goal than the type of emotional intimacy many women seek.

Women are often quite unrealistic in their emotional demands upon men. As Virginia Woolf expressed so movingly in *To the Lighthouse*, in the realm of emotional intimacy it is more often the woman who must give and the man who will take.[104] Although men can learn to articulate an interest in the other, they are usually, in their hearts, more absorbed by their own than the other's personality. The efforts of women, encouraged by the women's movement, to try to make men more like women—more sensitive, caring, nurturing, and analytical of their emotional relationships—are largely

doomed to fail. It is homosexual men who are most likely to resemble women in being sensitive, overtly caring, and nurturing,
which is probably the basis of their attractiveness to some of those
women who think an abundance of these qualities is either possible
or desirable in a man.

When they are not given bad advice—as they have been by
contemporary feminism—women are usually capable of providing
the bulk of whatever sensitivity, caring, nurturing, and reflection
their marital relationship requires. And for those who exercise
this capability, the rewards can be great. In Virginia Woolf's description, the "giving, giving, giving" to the man can produce "the
glow, the rhapsody, the self-surrender" that was "on so many women's
faces (on Mrs. Ramsay's, for instance)" and that was "a rapture of
sympathy, of delight in the reward they had," a reward which "evi-
dently conferred on them the most supreme bliss of which human
nature was capable."[105]

With these words—apparently tinged with uncomprehending
ridicule—Virginia Woolf has Lily Briscoe, an unmarried artist,
describe the Mrs. Ramsays of the world. Like Woolf, who created
her, Lily possesses "weak and muffled sexual instincts" that experience
real sexuality as "something loathsome."[106] Virginia Woolf's biographer refers to Virginia's "deep aversion to lust" and "disposition
to shrink from the crudities of sex," which she regarded "not so
much with horror, as with incomprehension." When Leonard and
Virginia Woolf discussed Virginia's sexual frigidity with her sister
Vanessa, she commented that Virginia "never had understood or
sympathised with sexual passion in men." Although Virginia
expected to have children, Leonard persuaded her that it would be
too dangerous (presumably because of her mental health). This
lack "was to be a permanent source of grief to her and, in later
years, she could never think of Vanessa's fruitful state without misery
and envy."[107]

Lily Briscoe and Mrs. Ramsay represent two kinds of women.
Mrs. Ramsay's rewards are very different from the rewards of Lily

Briscoe and Virginia Woolf. Lily is honored by a contemporary feminism that has sought to extinguish "the glow, the rhapsody," and the "supreme bliss" in any woman who would be a Mrs. Ramsay— "giving, giving, giving" to husband and children. It should, however, give pause to feminists to consider that Woolf depicts Lily Briscoe as honoring Mrs. Ramsay for what she means to those around her; Mrs. Ramsay is far more important to Lily Briscoe than Lily is to her. Lily knows that Mrs. Ramsay is the godhead of her domestic universe. "Life stand still here," Mrs. Ramsay says. In this declaration, as Lily perceives, Mrs. Ramsay produces little, daily miracles by imposing shape and stability upon life's chaos. For her husband, her children, and those who might join her family circle, Mrs Ramsay calms the whirlwind, stops time, and with the gift of her attention, structures for others a moment to share with her, a moment that they would never experience without her mediation. In these moments of permanence, Mrs. Ramsay teaches others that they count for something in this life. Lily values, as feminists do not, how Mrs. Ramsay does all this—almost unnoticed, like Sartre's "useless marvel," the housewife of Rouen—and thus she shapes the lives of other human beings by creating the very moment of permanence that Lily tries to create on the canvas she is painting. In homage to Mrs. Ramsay, Lily acknowledges—what feminists will not— that she "owed it all to her."[108]

Feminists are wrong to teach that Mrs. Ramsay's is a lesser life than Lily's. They would be wrong even if Lily were to receive recognition comparable to that conferred on her creator, Virginia Woolf, instead of having her pictures end up "hung in the attics" and "flung under a sofa." For those individuals who have no Mrs. Ramsay in their lives, there may well be no moments of permanence in which they know that they count. They will be like unfinished canvases with a "centre of complete emptiness," without shape or stability. What is there in life that can replace the woman who "resolved everything into simplicity" and made "of the moment something permanent?"[109] Mrs. Ramsay is neither writer nor painter, but she orchestrates the well-being of her family and turns into works of art the daily lives of those to whom she is committed. Contemporary feminists drape themselves with shame when they teach that there is greater value in putting words on paper or paint on a canvas than in serving one's family and mediating life to its members.

Women who withstand the feminist attack and assume the role of a Mrs. Ramsay can find that an important component of their reward (which Virginia Woolf could exquisitely describe, while never herself experiencing it) is enjoying one of the things hetero-sexual men can be and most mature women do want: a good sexual lover. Because the sexual revolution was an obstacle to achieving this goal, feminism's endorsement of the revolution was, among other things, an attack on the sexual rewards of a Mrs. Ramsay. Sexual enjoyment plays a much larger role in Mrs. Ramsay's life than in Lily Briscoe's. Diminishing that pleasure can be a significant step towards accomplishing feminism's aim to extinguish "the glow, the rhapsody," and the "supreme bliss" from Mrs. Ramsay's life.

Sex Without Intercourse

By falsifying the reality of women's experiences, the claim of clitoral suppression promoted the acceptance of feminist ideology. Essentially, Ehrenreich et al. credit the sexual revolution with revealing to women that men are unnecessary for sexual gratification because the clitoral orgasm is all that counts. Solitary masturbation or stimulation by other women will do just as well as—and actually better than—sexual intercourse with men.

In typical feminist fashion, this analysis underestimates women, viewing them as oppressed victims who understand little about themselves or the world at large and, therefore, consent to sexual intercourse only because they are unaware of the alternatives. Once feminism had resurrected the clitoris as "proof of women's sexual autonomy from men," however, "women could now be sexual, fully orgasmic beings not only outside of marriage but apart from men." "Masturbation," assert Ehrenreich et al. was "reclaimed" by feminists as a "legitimate sexual alternative," while oral sex (described by the authors as the "most significant 'innovation' to enter the sexual mainstream in the seventies") by obviating the need for intercourse, "dispensed with the relatively inert vagina."[110]

This sexual analysis tracks feminism's explanation of why women chose to stay at home and care for their children, rather than pursue careers. Feminists always claim that prior to their movement women had no choices to make, because they were oppressed and discriminated against in their quest for both educational and employment opportunities; women cared for their children by default, as it were. Similarly, they argue that feminist sexual analysis was required to acquaint women with the possibility of clitoral orgasm through masturbation and manual or oral stimulation by men or other women.

On neither count was feminist intervention necessary. Women have always had choices as to how they would organize their lives—even though those choices, like men's, were often constrained—and women have always known of the alternative possibilities of sexual stimulation. What is revolutionary is not discovery of the possibility of choice, but how these feminists have encouraged women to exercise their choices: in the one case, by preferring pursuit of a career over care of one's children and, in the other, by preferring masturbatory techniques over sexual intercourse. Not by accident are these choices in juxtaposition, for they are mutually reinforcing.

It is a woman's ability to experience vaginal softening and feelings of passivity, receptivity, yieldingness, and finally, loss of control that will bring alive through genital intercourse what these feminists characterize as the "relatively inert vagina." This ability depends, in turn, upon the flourishing of that aspect of a woman's nature connected with her reproductivity and close nurturing ties to her children. Conception, gestation, birth, suckling, and perhaps most important, long periods of relaxed, intimate interaction with her children are, I have found, the most significant factors in preparing a woman to be readily capable of the vaginal orgasmic responsiveness that, while usually building upon, will transcend the very specific, localized sensation of the clitoral orgasm. A woman's responsiveness to vaginal sex is closely related to her acknowledgment of the indissoluble connection between genital sexuality and her reproductivity. Whether or not she has yet conceived or will ever conceive, her ability to experience fully the pleasures afforded by genital intercourse requires viewing herself as, in some sense, a reproductive being and feeling happy with that perception of herself.

The vagina will, of course, remain relatively inert for women whose ideology requires severing woman's sexuality from all connection—actual or symbolic—with her fertility. They recommend lesbian sex or what might be described as homosexual heterosexual sex that, dispensing with the vagina, consummates a sexual encounter through manual or oral manipulation. These women reject vaginal sex and celebrate homosexual sex as the paradigmatic sexual experience. Sex as "intercourse, with the possibility of pregnancy" is "frightening," to them, for it "imitate[s] rape" and is "symbolically (if not actually) tied to the work of reproduction." Homosexual sex, by contrast, being "utterly freed from the old reproductive 'work ethic' that haunts heterosexuality," is "sheer play," "without a trace of the heterosexual drama of male power and female subordination."[111]

If this feminist recommendation as to the paradigmatic sexual experience were confined to premarital sex play, I would heartily endorse it. The prescription would rescue girls and women from their current premarital sexual servitude, in which they service men as receptacles for semen in genital intercourse and then often serve time on the cross in the abortion clinic.

Adoption of a sexual prescription that rejects premarital genital intercourse and confines premarital sexual activity to necking and petting (now sometimes called "outercourse"[112]) would be a boon to girls and women alike. The recent success of a self-help primer called *The Rules* indicates that women are finally becoming willing to assert control over their dating relationships by returning to the pre-feminist matrimonial strategy of strict mores.[113] Men might initially shun dating relationships with females who do not behave as sexual revolutionaries and service them with genital intercourse. That male resistance could be intense is suggested by Robert Wright's anemic recommendation to counter what he has shown to be the serious harm that the sexual revolution has done to women: women, he suggests, might try imposing "austerity" for the first two months of an acquaintanceship. What he considers the "extreme" strategy of deferring coitus until marriage will not work, he argues, because so much sex is available to men that "if any one woman cuts off the supply, alternatives abound."[114] Perhaps.

But why should women be so desperate? In the eyes of a man who would turn from her to what Wright calls the abounding alternatives, a woman is not a unique individual whom he approaches with what Roger Scruton calls "individualising intentionality," but simply an object to be used for coital sexual servicing. Girls and women with enough dignity and self-respect to recognize and then resist their sexual servitude should ultimately win the day. Until they do, it would be better to forego male companionship than continue to serve as surrogates for prostitutes, or in Camille Paglia's inelegant but accurate description, as "sperm spittoons"[115]—the function to which the sexual revolution consigned them.

Beyond the Clitoris

This feminist sexual prescription, however, is not confined to pre-marital sexual relationships, but is offered as a paradigm for all sexual activity. In marital relationships, it should play only a supporting, not a leading, role. While clitoral stimulation without genital penetration serves the purpose in a premarital context, it cannot encompass the potential dimensions of female sexual gratification. The prescription is, nevertheless, wholly consistent with an ideology that promotes equivalence of the sexes and women's abandonment of their traditional roles in favor of career pursuits. These two feminist goals are not only facilitated by, but also are most compatible with, abandonment of the traditional female sexuality that is "passive and vaginally centered" and the cultivation of "active, clitoral sexuality."[116]

Feminists are correct that the active, clitoral sex they advocate is available "without the price of lifelong subordination to one man," "without the exclusive intensity of romantic love," and "without the punitive consequences" (presumably meaning reproduction).[117] They are absolutely incorrect, however, in their claim that this active, clitoral sexuality is either revolutionary or capable of exhausting the possibilities of woman's sexual fulfillment. There is nothing revolutionary about the "curious pleasure" of the masturbatory clitoral orgasm. Grown women have always been free—and some have so chosen—to confine their sexual experience to self-stimulation, or to diddling each other in the manner of schoolgirls, or to engaging in heterosexual relations that consist entirely of forms of mutual masturbation without vaginal penetration. But it is outrageously misleading for women, who admittedly do not enjoy vaginal sexuality, to announce that this variety of masturbatory stimulative activities—to which they are themselves confined—qualifies as mature sexuality for all women and to deny that vaginal intercourse can provide a further and different gratification.

Those who believe that the possibility of sexual fulfillment is exhausted by clitoral stimulation would find informative the interviews by Hanny Lightfoot-Klein of pharaonically circumcised women who described what can only be vaginal orgasms. Most of the women believed clitoridectomy was wrong and it is, therefore, doubtful they lied to vindicate the practice, although they may have exaggerated their responsiveness out of loyalty and love for their husbands. The interviewer, who clearly despised the practice, would not have sought to minimize its horror. The testimony is clear that many of these women experienced sexual satisfaction.

A founder of the Sudanese women's movement said "it was difficult for a man to satisfy a pharaonized woman sexually, but that with patience, effort, and understanding, it definitely could be done," an observation commonly made about satisfying Western women with their external genitals intact. Western women who complain about five-minute quickies would find impressive the extended performances of the men whose patient efforts must accomplish the goal without clitoral assistance (although many interviewees did speak of pleasurable sensations in the area of their scars as well as in non-genital erogenous areas).[118]

Lightfoot-Klein concludes that "orgasm exists even among these drastically mutilated women to a surprising extent, and it is far from being rare." Many appeared to be "lusty, sexually fulfilled women" who discussed "what they described as orgasm, under what circumstances they did or did not attain it, and how long a period of foreplay and intercourse it required." The following brief excerpts confirm her statement that the women's descriptions have "the ring of truth and familiarity." It would take a lot of imagination for a Western woman to identify the described sensations as the ones she experiences from mere clitoral stimulation without penile vaginal penetration:

I feel, as if I am trembling in my belly. It feels like electric shock going around my body—very sweet and pleasurable. When it finishes, I feel as if I would faint.

(*This description by a Director of Nursing.*) I feel as if I have had a shot of morphine. My body vibrates all over. Then I feel shocked and cannot move. At the end, I relax all over.

All my body begins to tingle, then I have a shock to my pelvis and in my legs. It gets very tight in my vagina. I have a tremendous feeling of pleasure, and I cannot move at all. It seems to last for about 2 minutes, and I seem to be flying, far,

far up. Then my whole body relaxes, and I go completely limp for about 15 minutes.

I feel as if I am losing all consciousness, and I seem to love him most intensely at that moment. I tremble all over. My vagina contracts stongly, and I have a feeling of great joy. Then I relax all over, and I am so happy to be alive and to be married to my husband.

I feel shivery, and as if I had had anesthesia (*this description by a nurse*). I feel very happy, and I want to swallow him inside of me. It is a very sweet feeling that spreads until it takes hold of my entire body. I feel very light, and seem to float up into the air. Then I go to sleep.

I feel as if I am losing all consciousness, it is such a strong feeling. I hold on to my husband very, very tightly, and if the baby fell out of the bed, I would not be able to pick it up.[119]

These may fairly be called descriptions of ecstatic sexual experiences. Yet, feminists exhort women to learn masturbatory techniques rather than counting on "male partners to lead the way to ecstasy."[120] Attached as we women may become to the easy masturbatory clitoral orgasm, it is hyperbolic to call the sensations it produces "ecstasy." Only limited expectations, I suggest, make the nervously excited and explosive vibrations of clitoral orgasm seem an ecstatic experience. On the contrary, unless experienced as some part of genital intercourse (as incorporated, perhaps, into the course of arousal that culminates in genital intercourse), the sensation produced by the clitoral orgasm is, essentially, one of loneliness. Absent genital intercourse, clitoral orgasm leaves the woman dangling, without the unity and completion that are the intended culmination of the sex act.

The essence of genital intercourse is completion, the uniting of opposites that only heterosexual intercourse can accomplish. It is this union that can produce ecstasy, as the woman delights in the male power taking pleasure inside her and rejoices in his filling the empty space of her womb. This union—not the throbbing clitoris—makes a woman feel as if she is losing consciousness, flying far, far up, relaxing all over and going completely limp. Union makes a woman "so happy to be alive and to be married to my husband"; makes her "want to swallow him inside of me." In the ecstasy of union, the woman may even agree with George Eliot that the sexual relation is the frankest recognition of the divine in Nature.[121]

Feminists deride any concept of the empty womb. Admission of woman's longing to fill her interior emptiness presumes a need for phallic penetration to make her whole that feminists resist, and it implies the female dependence upon males that feminists set out to eliminate. But the need asserts itself, no matter how vigorous the denial. A woman can arduously prepare herself for the marketplace, work as hard as men, earn as much, become as successful, and still feel empty and suffused with an obscure longing. What was obscure becomes clear to the woman who sees herself in Erik Erikson's description of the empty space of the womb: the "inner productive space" that "exposes women early to a specific sense of loneliness" or emptiness that "is the female form of perdition."[122] The filling of that space in genital intercourse—with its celebration of the fact, or promise, or remembrance of her reproductivity—can produce an ecstasy that, in comparison, renders pitiful the solitary clitoral orgasm. It is this substitution of the ersatz for the real thing that infuses masturbatory and homosexual activities with profound sadness.

D. H. Lawrence described "the entry into the body of a woman" as "the moment of pure peace," as the entering into "the peace on earth of her soft, quiescent body."[123] A woman like me, whose own experience is reflected in his description, appraises Lawrence's characterization against an event far different from the paradigmatic feminist sexual encounter. Feminists reject Lawrence's sexual vision of a phallic power "entering"—a word and concept they particularly dislike—the soft, quiescent female. The scope of female sexuality, they say, is encompassed within the hardened clitoris of the perennially adolescent, assertive, aggressive, striving girl.

Although feminists scoff at the concept as ludicrous, sexual maturity *can* take a woman beyond the hardened clitoris to the softened vagina which responds to her yearning for unity with the male and her delight in, rather than fear of, the claims exerted by her reproductivity. This woman neither envies nor fears but, in the words of Anna Dostoyevsky, adores and worships the male phallic power and exults in the knowledge of what that male power has done, or will now do, or may someday do for her. An event made trivial by the sexual revolution is, to this woman, a repeated miracle of resurrection that does indeed make her whole.

Because it pervades our society, this feminist version of female sexuality cannot be dismissed as the view of a small minority. A reviewer in the *Wall Street Journal*—hardly a bastion of radical feminism—described George Gilder's work as "profoundly misogynist" and "half-baked propaganda" in contrast to *Re-Making Love* which, she claimed, had "the advantage of making sense."[124] As Brigitte Berger has noted, the views of radical feminism—the views that "biology is the source of the systematic oppression of women," that women should be relieved of "the burden of childbearing," and that there should be "an end to exclusive heterosexuality"— have dominated academic feminism and "subvert academic life and academic disciplines to a degree unknown in the history of science."[125]

Most important, the feminist sexual analysis cannot be dismissed precisely because it can meet the needs of the prototypical woman of feminist ideology. The prerequisites for her fullest enjoyment of vaginal sexuality may often be unattainable for such a woman. She is commonly overworked, worried, and exhausted. Having been encouraged by society to denigrate and sublimate the claims exerted by the reproductive dimension of her nature, she is absorbed in her career and can enjoy only minimal contact with her children. If, as our society now socializes her to do, she is trying to compete with men in careers that require high levels of aggression for optimal performance, then she must often exert great will power to force herself into the mold of a tough, competitive, hard-driving person who is quite alien to her innate feminine nature.

That this is what many women are trying to do today is evidenced by the phenomenal growth of "cosmetic pharmacology," particularly in the use of the anti-depressant drug Prozac. As Peter Kramer's *Listening to Prozac* makes clear, the use of this drug is no longer confined to patients who are sick by standard psychiatric classifications. Kramer justifies prescribing Prozac for the cosmetic aim of giving "social confidence to the habitually timid, to make the sensitive brash, to lend the introvert the social skills of a salesman." Most of Kramer's case histories involve women (about two-thirds of clinically depressed patients are women), and he calls drugs like Prozac "feminist drugs." Prozac, he says, "allows a woman with the traits we now consider 'overly feminine'" to achieve "a spunkier persona" by "'curing' women of traditional, passive feminine traits."[126]

In criticizing this cosmetic use of Prozac, David J. Rothman notes that such usage is designed to enforce "the values of aggression and self-seeking ambition." Prozac, he says, is an "office" drug that "promotes adroit competitiveness." It is the answer to Henry Higgins's question in *My Fair Lady*, "Why can't a woman be like a man."[127] With Prozac, maybe she can. But after trying all day to compete like a man, can she stop being like him when she lies down in bed, tries to forget all she must do tomorrow, and seeks, somehow, to attain the calm and relaxation—the feminine passivity—that are prerequisite to the fullest enjoyment of vaginal sexuality? Or will her mind keep racing, as she lies there plotting out tomorrow's too many activities, inventing new arguments and re-arranging paragraphs in the legal brief that is soon due.

Whither Feminist Sex?

The results of this feminist sexual prescription are ironic. First, to abandon what they call the "relatively inert vagina" is to abandon the one means of sexual satisfaction that only women can offer men. Ehrenreich et al. state that the "most significant 'innovation' to enter the sexual mainstream in the seventies was oral sex,"[128] but as Charles Winick notes, surveys in the 1940s had shown participation in oragenitality by three-fifths of those surveyed. What was *actually* significant in the 1970s was the radical shift that did occur from the use of oragenital contact during the course of arousal to the complete replacement of coitus by the use of genderless organs. Oragenital contact that is confined to foreplay remains a "tributary to genital sexuality," with its reflection of the "complementary roles" of the sexes. But when oragenitality replaces coitus, genital sexuality and complementarity of the sexes are completely bypassed.[129]

To Winick, this crucial change suggests "an increased passivity and fear of the vagina in many men."[130] However explained, the change seriously threatens women's ability to attract and hold men's interest. And the message of those feminists who welcome and celebrate this development should be acknowledged as the threat it is to those heterosexual women who *do* want to attract and hold the interest of men. These are women in whose behalf feminists are most definitely not speaking.

A second irony lies in the alternative offered to heterosexual women. Ehrenreich et al. reject the "narrow, heterosexual definition of sex as the touchstone and standard for sexual experience" with its "ancient consequences of pregnancy and dependence on male support" and its "great drama of domination and submission." But they found "profoundly" significant the sexual diversification of sado-masochism which "mock[s] the old and presumedly natural meanings" of sex "by making domination and submission into a consciously chosen and deliberately scripted ritual."[131] In their view, the rewards of sado-masochism apparently outweigh its drawbacks of being "overtly anti-egalitarian" and ruling out "spontaniety and any casual promiscuity," since a "woman would have to genuinely trust a man before allowing him to use handcuffs or leather straps."[132]

In most cases, as these authors are aware, indulgence in sado-masochism returns by the back door the male dominance and female submission they threw out the front door. They quote a woman's statement that, as a result of being forcibly tied to the bed by her husband, her "strongest desire at that moment was to surrender—give in totally to the sexual experience."[133] Granting the importance that a feeling akin to surrender plays in achieving woman's gratification in genital intercourse, it is undesirable, and should be unnecessary, to evoke the feeling by means of activities properly defined as sado-masochistic.

Roger Scruton has distinguished between normal and perverted sado-masochism. The first enables one "to cross the barrier of inhibition" that prevents "one person from being 'overcome' by his body." The second is de Sade's "dissolution" of the body of the other in "pain and mutilation," which is the "sexual embodiment" of slavery.[134] Scruton defines the content of normal sado-masochism only by referring to "the lover's pinch"—quoting from *Antony and Cleopatra*: "A lover's pinch, that hurts, and is desir'd"—and to "the love bite"—"a wound that is both a mark of affection and an invitation to desire."[135] But describing these activities as sado-masochistic broadens the word's meaning beyond usefulness, making most of us sado-masochists.

The "deliberately scripted ritual" of sado-masochism recommended by Ehrenreich et al. does not refer to the ordinary and pleasurable lover's pinch and bite. When that ritual involves artificial devices or "cruelty" (something inflicting significantly more pain than that ordinary lover's pinch and bite), the complementarity that is the goal of genital intercourse is again bypassed. The woman's response to the body of the other is superseded by her response to the acting out of her own masturbatory fantasies; such an act is akin to solitary masturbation. Whatever the orgasmic outcome, the sexual encounter's integrity as an act of genital complementarity is compromised.

It is not surprising that the feminist sexual prescription leads to sado-masochism. Feminist ideology has left little else to substitute for the male dominance that animates female sexual responsiveness. In order for sexual intercourse to evoke in the woman a feeling of total surrender—of being overwhelmed in her body by the encounter—she must feel, in some sense, dependent upon the man and perceive him as dominant, powerful, and reliable. Seymour Fisher's studies of women's sexual responsiveness show that a woman's orgasm potential is correlated with two factors: first, a dependable childhood relationship with a father who was seen as "strict controlling" rather than "casual permissive"[136]; second, assurance that her husband is "a dependable love object (that he can be counted upon to remain with her)" and "to be loyal and to maintain steadfast interest in her."[137]

In discussing what they call the "fundamentalist sex" of traditional marriages, Ehrenreich et al. recognize the role of male dominance and reliability in securing women's sexual gratification. Apparently conceding that the institutional framework of such marriages can provide "better orgasms and more sensitive partners," they find the price too high for the woman because it requires "accepting a slave mentality not just for a finite sexual encounter but for an entire life."[138] Relevant to their attribution of "better orgasms" to the "fundamentalist sex" of traditional marriages is the finding of the 1994 comprehensive sex survey that the "women most likely to achieve orgasm each and every time" are conservative Protestants.[139]

Comparing the status of slaves to that of wives within traditional marriages is one of the most offensive feminist falsifications of reality. Hillary Rodham Clinton concurred in the comparison, writing as a representative of the Children's Defense Fund.[140] Depicting wives in traditional marriages as slaves, uneducated, without worldly experience, and less desirable and interesting because of their failure to pursue independent careers was part of feminism's assault on traditional women that was discussed in Chapter 2.[141] By undertaking the assault, feminists can be seen to have engaged in one of the oldest sexual strategies—what David Buss calls "status derogation"— whereby "members of one sex degrade, denigrate, slander, defile and generally impugn the character of members of their own sex to make them less desirable to members of the opposite sex."[142] Not only did feminists derogate the housewife's status in this fashion, but through the sexual revolution they attacked the traditional sexual mores by which she had lived, and as Anne Taylor Fleming has showed us, sometimes took away her husband as well.

WITH RESPECT TO SEX, no further argument is required to establish that at all stages of the sexual revolution feminism's vision for heterosexual women was corrupt: first, when feminists encouraged women to engage in promiscuous sexual intercourse; and second, when some of them rejected traditional heterosexual intercourse, advocating withdrawal to the barren wasteland of masturbation, lesbianism, and such so-called diversifications as sado-masochism.

That its sexual prescription could bring women to rest on the bed of de Sade and in Sir Stephen's mansion is feminism's recognition of the female desire for some dependence upon a powerful and dominant male. The male's status as breadwinner within the traditional family creates an archetype of male dominance and female dependence. But feminism has rejected the benign dominance and dependence institutionalized in traditional marriage. Taking their cue from the homosexual men they so much admire, some feminists choose to retreat instead to the malign dominance of rough sex with leather and chains.

5

Feminism's Totalitarian Impulse

It is because it was not dependent on organization but grew up as a spontaneous order that the structure of modern society has attained that degree of complexity which it possesses and which far exceeds any that could have been achieved by deliberate organization. In fact, of course, the rules which made the growth of this complex order possible were initially not designed in expectation of that result; but those people who happened to adopt suitable rules developed a complex civilization which then often spread to others.

F. A. Hayek[1]

In states there are often some obscure and almost latent causes, things which appear at first view of little moment, on which a very great part of its prosperity or adversity may most essentially depend. The science of government being, therefore, so practical in itself, and intended for such practical purposes, a matter which requires experience, and even more experience than any person can gain in his whole life, however sagacious and observing he may be, it is with infinite caution that any man ought to venture upon pulling down an edifice which has answered in any tolerable degree for ages the common purposes of society, or on building it up again without having models and patterns of approved utility before his eyes.

Edmund Burke [2]

The revolutionary heart of Communism . . . is a simple statement . . . : Philosophers have explained the world; it is necessary to change the world. . . . The Communist vision is the vision of Man without God. . . . It is the vision of man's liberated mind, by the sole force of its rational intelligence, redirecting man's destiny and reorganizing man's life and the world.

Whittaker Chambers [3]

WHAT ARE PERCEIVED as contemporary feminism's failures are denounced by its critics[4] and deplored by its advocates.[5] Perceptions of failure, however, are largely expressions of dissatisfaction with the results that followed from the *achievement* of feminist goals. Far from being a failure, the women's movement has worked a revolution in our society. Having already successfully undermined the traditional bourgeois family, the movement is well on the way towards achieving its primary goal of destroying that institution. Articulating and acting upon its totalitarian impulse to pull down the edifice of the traditional family, feminism has impelled many members of our society to redirect and reorganize their lives along pathways that have already been charted by collectivist nations.

To understand feminism's success, I have examined the social conditions that fostered acceptance of its ideology and the methods employed to achieve its goals. In evaluating the movement against this background, it is crucial to recognize that—contrary to the way feminists often seek to present themselves—they have never tried merely to shape their own destinies. They believe their goals are not attainable unless most women adopt these same goals. And so they have set out to remold society. Their lodestar is Lenin's directive: "Those who are really convinced that they have made progress in science would not demand freedom for the new views to continue side by side with the old, but the substitution of the new view for the old."[6] Like the collectivists they are, feminists have been willing to exert considerable force to secure other women's conformity.[7]

The next chapter will discuss the harmful changes in society that have followed feminism's assault on traditional family institutions and the values they embody. While feminist apologists acknowledge seeking drastic changes in traditional families, they deny having anticipated many of the consequences. In *The Divorce Revolution*, for example, Lenore J. Weitzman discussed Betty Friedan's explanation of feminist divorce policy. The movement, said Friedan, was so concerned that "equality of right and opportunity had to mean equality of responsibility, and therefore alimony was out— that we did not realize the trap we were falling into . . . . We fell into a trap when we said, 'No alimony,' because housewives who divorced were in terrible straits."[8] Thus, Friedan grounded the movement's support of no-fault divorce in the fundamental tenet of feminist dogma that a woman who devotes herself to care of home and child is *not* assuming equality of responsibility and must be forced to do so by a threat of financial hardship if she is divorced. Having undertaken a "reform" that would inevitably enhance the financial interests of divorcing husbands, the movement, explained Friedan, simply did not foresee that divorced housewives would be "in terrible straits" when deprived of alimony.

It requires little foresight to know that a woman who spends any substantial portion of her life out of the workplace (as many divorced housewives will have spent most of their adult lives) is at an overwhelming disadvantage when she is required to re-enter the job market in order to assume what Friedan characterized as "equality of responsibility." But the movement was "trapped," said

Friedan, into opposing alimony (one wonders by whom; possibly, evil men?), an excuse that exemplifies the movement's willingness to assume a posture of irresponsibility when faced with the consequences of its actions, as if it should not have been taken seriously. Most of the movement's leaders, who were certainly not unintelligent, no doubt knew full well the easily foreseeable results of their divorce policy. They were crystal clear to me the first time I considered the concept of no-fault divorce. Friedan's exculpatory explanation reflects either the disingenuity or stupidity of activist feminism.

Divorce reform had precisely the outcome contemporary feminism sought: to instill in women distrust of their husbands and reluctance to leave the work force for fear of financial privation in the event of their divorces that "reform" had made more likely. Feminism's support of this reform exhibited its totalitarian impulse to use the institutions of government to force all women to live according to the feminist script or face dire consequences. To feminists, such consequences are simply the price other women must pay so that the movement may achieve its goals. The prevalence of these consequences has been accelerated by feminism's promotion of the sexual revolution which markedly increased women's willingness and ability to destroy other women's marriages.

But not all outcomes of the feminist revolution were so easily forseeable. As Hayek and Burke stated so well, our limited knowledge of cause and effect within the complex ordering of society rarely provides us the information necessary to predict all outcomes of proposed changes to that ordering. It is wise, therefore, to treat with great respect the various accommodations to which the process of trial and error has led society. For this reason so-called reform movements must exercise great care lest they make matters worse instead of better. A remarkable degree of hubris is required to do otherwise and undertake, as the women's movement has, a thorough restructuring of the most important aspects of society—family life and the relations between the sexes.

FEMINISTS AS REMOLDERS OF SOCIETY

The point of view from which I criticize contemporary feminism is the conservative view that one should advocate change with humility; that it is dangerous to seek to destroy an edifice such as the traditional family which, in Burke's words, "has answered in any tolerable degree for ages the common purposes of society." This impulse to override our traditional accommodations with each other by tearing down society's edifices is what Whittaker Chambers identified as the totalitarian impulse to change the world. When men in their hubris seek to act like gods by reorganizing other men's lives in order to redirect their destinies, the results are often unpredictable and undesirable, sometimes even horrific.

A forceful exponent of this impulse to reshape society has been that most powerful feminist, Hillary Rodham Clinton. She has been described as motivated "by the conviction of her generation that it was destined (and equipped) to teach the world the error of its ways." In her own words, she exhorts us "to remold society by redefining what it means to be a human being in the 20th century, moving into a new millennium."[9] This is the language of Rousseau and Robespierre, the language of certitude that one knows what is best for all and willingness to enforce that vision. It is what Simon Schama has described as "the intensely moral politics recommended by Rousseau" and acted upon by Robespierre on the theory that "the reforming state must needs be a school of virtue, one capable of bringing about a great moral regeneration in individuals and in its collective life."[10]

The crucial role this opportunity to remold society plays in the lives of those with the reforming impulse can be gleaned from Hillary Rodham's student commencement address at Wellesley. Rejecting the "prevailing, acquisitive and competitive corporate life," she advocated a "more immediate, ecstatic and penetrating mode of living."[11] By this she could, of course, have meant that her classmates should seek a more personal penetrating ecstasy in the domestic arena, not ecstasy through market production in the public arena. But she did not. The "ecstatic and penetrating mode of living" she recommended was a life in the public arena dedicated to remolding society according to one's vision of the common good.

Ecstasy so defined is a very dangerous thing. I am familiar with ecstasy. It has been a gift of my marital relationship and the birth and rearing of my children. In the public arena of market production, on the other hand, I have found only the calm satisfaction of doing a workmanlike job. Ecstatic experience more appropriately springs from personal relationships; for some, perhaps, from religious ones. To seek ecstasy in the public arena is to look where it cannot be found; like all surrogate activities, the experience will never satisfy. Mrs. Clinton concedes as much. Leon Wieseltier observed that she "prospered handsomely during the last decade," once explaining that "you can't be a lawyer if you don't represent banks"[12]—a rather curious statement since, while there is nothing wrong with representing banks and most major law firms do so, many lawyers do not work in these firms and never represent a bank. Yet, where did representing banks—a highly profitable and respectable market activity—leave her? Apparently, it left her feeling that "we lack at some core level meaning in our individual lives and meaning collectively," that we are in "a crisis of meaning"; not knowing what it means "to be human," we need "a new politics of meaning" and in seeking it, "we are breaking new ground."[13]

And so she will till the fields of social reform. But ecstasy will not lie at that row's end either. The furrow of social reform is limitless; a search for ecstasy through the process of remolding society is never-ending. Declaring a goal achieved and pronouncing some aspect of society to be finally good simply diminishes opportunities for the ecstatic experience of doing good. For this reason, reformers must constantly redefine what constitutes the common good so they can continue this remolding process through which their own lives derive meaning. And those who are being remolded according to a vision of the common good they may not share must continue to serve the ecstasy of these remolders. Thus, Mootfowl—a character in Mark Helprin's *Winter's Tale* who is devoted to re-molding society—reconciles his colleague to the likely failure of their scheme for "eternal salvation" and "heaven on earth" by noting what their success would actually mean to them: "We'd be out of a job. If everything were bliss, there'd be no need for us, would there?"[14]

But should not a conservative who criticizes the now regnant feminist dogma be rebuked for violating conservatism's standard of respect for tradition? Am I not also seeking to remold society? I would answer that feminist ideology has reigned only a brief time; it hardly constitutes a tradition. Nor is defense of a family arrangement common only a few decades ago comparable to femi-nism's revolutionary denial of basic differences between the sexes, or to its denial of the worth of woman's role as wife and mother, or to its super-materialistic and individualistic elevation of market production as the primary activity in life.

Furthermore, I have no worldview to impose. I do not claim to know how to follow Hillary Rodham Clinton's exhortation to "remold society by redefining what it means to be a human being in the 20th century, moving into a new millennium." But I do know how dangerous is the concept these words suggest; through-out history, humanity has suffered greatly from those seeking to move it into new millennia. *The Pursuit of the Millennium*, Norman Cohn's study of revolutionary millenarianism and mystical anar-chism, shows that usually "the route to the Millennium leads through massacre and terror."[15] History as set forth by Cohn disproves Mrs. Clinton's claim to be "breaking new ground" when question-ing the meaning of life; as Leon Wieseltier has noted, there "is no older ground."[16] If social reformers absorbed the lessons found in that old ground, they might be much less confident of their own ability to tell others how to live. Cohn's study shows that the "aims and premises" of those reformers seeking to move society into new millennia are "boundless"; they do not seek to accomplish "specific, limited objectives" but to create a world that is "totally transformed and redeemed"—"a perfect world from which self-seeking would be for ever banished."[17]

These quests—all reflecting the totalitarian impulse—have always failed, with misery and suffering as their legacy. To resist them does no violence to conservative principles. I do not seek to remold feminists. They have sought to remold me and to prevent other women from living the kind of life I have led. Towards that end they have deliberately and successfully remolded our society into a very inhospitable place for a woman like me, an awakened Brünnhilde who seeks her ecstasy outside the marketplace and does not want to turn her children and home over to others so that she can live feminism's version of the good life. Nor does she share Mrs. Clinton's feeling that "we lack at some core level meaning in our individual lives." That core meaning is readily apparent to Brünnhilde all day, every day, as she nurses her baby, rocks it to sleep, reads to her children, and prepares dinner for her family.

In resisting the feminist redefinition of what it means to be a human being, it is appropriate to argue that results *must* count. The pathologies described in the next chapter reveal that something went very wrong after our society adopted the feminist perspective. While correlation does not prove causality, it warrants careful inquiry into the causes of our families' distress. Such inquiry could justify societal changes, a conclusion scarcely called for by analysis of the much healthier family institution of the 1950s and 1960s that feminists targeted as their enemy. Because we live in a community, holding each other's fortunes in our hands, changes we seek in the conditions of our own lives do often affect others. It is compatible with conservatism to pursue change through democratic means and with a constant awareness of human fallibility.

The best protection against making extreme reforms—all the outcomes of which can rarely be foreseen—is the humility to recognize how little we can ever know and how vulnerable we are to being swayed by passion and unreason. Two salient characteristics of contemporary feminism are its lack of humility and the passionate earnestness with which its adherents believe they have been terribly wronged by society, particularly by males. An apt characterization of the movement's earnestness can be taken from Benjamin Disraeli's comment about the Bishop who "sympathises with everything that is earnest; but what is earnest is not always true; on the contrary error is often more earnest than truth."[18]

The Spontaneity of the Civilizing Process

Its totalitarian impulse becomes apparent when the doctrines and actions of the women's movement are viewed against a description of political and cultural developments that evolve through the undirected, spontaneous activities of individuals. Norbert Elias provides such a description in the two volumes of *The Civilizing Process,* where he analyzes processes like emergence of the French State through consolidation of regions around the duchy of Francia and the evolution of regularized taxation out of occasional levies by lords of estates.[19] His analysis demonstrates that "from the interweaving of countless individual interests and intentions— whether tending in the same direction or in divergent and hostile directions—something comes into being that was planned and intended by none of these individuals, yet has emerged nevertheless from their intentions and actions."[20]

Thus, says Elias, the modern French state resulted not from a "prophetic vision or a rigorous plan" but from a series of elimination contests in which the domains of numerous feudal lords were consolidated, the players in this drama seeing only the next few steps as they acquired land to prevent a threatening neighbor from growing any stronger. The lesson Elias teaches is that enduring and effective social institutions are not imposed by powerful visionaries but are an outgrowth of the "goals, plans and actions of individual people constantly intertwin[ing] with those of others." Such institutions do not result because some people in the past, "understanding the usefulness of these institutions, once took a common decision to live together in this way and no other."[21]

Like Elias, Friedrich Hayek also rejected the utility of achieving economic, political, and social goals through centralized government control; in his view, spontaneous growth, not organized planning, produces freedom and prosperity. If Elias is correct that the "order of interweaving human impulses and strivings" best determines "the course of historical change" and "underlies the civilizing process," the reforming visionary will usually impede that process.[22] Reforming visionaries created our modern collectivist states which, by fiat from their centralized governments, prohibited spontaneous growth, controlling all institutions within their societies and leaving little room for individual human impulses and strivings to affect those institutions.

This is the critical difference between a communist society and the civil society of a Western democracy that Ernest Gellner elaborates in *Conditions of Liberty*.[23] A "civil society," as Kenneth Minogue so well puts it, "is not the sort of thing any single power can create," for it "bubbles up from below."[24] In the wake of near global discrediting of overt collectivism, Western feminism is one of the last strongholds of the collectivist viewpoint. Like collectivists, feminists are committed to imposing their own version of the common good upon society. They have well-defined goals and a vision of the new androgynous man and woman to be created by remolding society through so-called reforms that are the antithesis of spontaneous growth.

COLLECTIVIST CHILD-REARING

The women's movement shares with totalitarian collectivism contempt both for the theory of spontaneous evolution of a civilized society and for the traditional bourgeois family, an institution that is among the great achievements of the civilizing process. Feminism's collectivist affinity, as well as the fact of its great success, is evidenced by the immense change that has occurred in the institution that feminists most wanted to destroy: the family with a stay-at-home mother. To the degree that institution has been modified, our society has come to resemble a collectivist state. Under collectivism, almost all women work outside the home. Mothers return to work shortly after giving birth, and children, including very young infants, are generally cared for during most of each day in institutional settings outside the home.

Thus, when the women's movement first articulated its vision of the new American family, an observer in mainland China noted that in the cities you rarely see mothers with their children: "A wife is granted two months' paid leave for each pregnancy but she is expected to lodge the child in a nursery as soon as it is weaned. From then on, the mother has her child home only at weekends."[25] At the same time in the former Soviet Union, it was the common practice for mothers to return to work two months after giving birth. From then on, unless there was an available grandmother, the child was usually cared for in state institutions; if desired, children could be left at the state nursery for the entire week, spending only Saturday afternoon and Sunday at home. The objective was to create conditions that would prevent children from being regarded as a burden on parents. This was part of an effort to stem the declining Soviet birth rate which had been a source of great official concern since before 1971, when 40 percent of couples desired only one child, and only eight percent desired the three-child family encouraged by government authorities.[26]

Such was the vision of a good society propounded by feminist Kate Millett, who endorsed Engels's theory that with "transformation of the means of production into collective property, the monogamous family will cease to be the economic unit of society" and the care of children "becomes a public matter." While assuming that this "most crucial of Engels' propositions" would meet with the greatest resistance, Millett endorsed the recommendation as logical and inevitable: so long as the female is the "primary caretaker of childhood, she is prevented from being a free human being." Although "middle-class Americans," she argued, "infer that childbirth must mean child care," intellectuals understand that "the assignment of child care is cultural rather than biological." It is, Millett concluded, "one of conservatism's favorite myths that every woman is a mother."[27]

There is no better example of feminist hubris than this arrogant assertion of authority to explain to child-bearing heterosexual women what *soi-disant* intellectuals understand about the role biology plays in the decision that mothers make to care for their children and how that decision affects mothers' status as human beings.[28] Contrary to Millett's assertion, few conservatives would claim that every woman is suited for motherhood. But those women who do undertake a mother's role in the belief that, for them, Millett's vision of motherhood would be the worst way of performing the role should not be denigrated and disadvantaged by a women's movement that is dedicated to promoting Millett's vision. That her vision has been successfully promoted is evidenced by the fact that, despite Millett's prediction of great resistance, Engels's proposition on child care has been readily embraced through a relinquishing of infants and young children to surrogate child care to the greatest extent this country has ever experienced.

While feminists and Marxist-Leninists have shared the goal of destroying the traditional bourgeois family, they usually have different motives. Feminists' major concern is women's independence from men, not the nature of a society's economic organization. As discussed earlier, feminism, in the words of Jane Mansbridge, "was profoundly opposed to traditional conceptions of how families should be organized," because the "very existence of full-time homemakers was incompatible with many goals of the women's movement," especially the goal that women hold half the economically and politically powerful positions in the country.[29] Simone de Beauvoir stated in a discussion with Betty Friedan that society should not allow any woman to be a full-time homemaker: "No woman should be authorized to stay at home to raise her children. Society should be totally different. Women should not have that choice, precisely because if there is such a choice, too many women will make that one. It is a way of forcing women in a certain direction."[30]

In de Beauvoir's view, "as long as the family and the myth of the family and the myth of maternity and the maternal instinct are not destroyed, women will still be oppressed."[31] Although de Beauvoir had long been a socialist, her views on feminism and the family were not specifically grounded in her socialist theories; Friedan noted that de Beauvoir had only recently embraced the women's movement, finding in "radical feminism an ideological blueprint superior to Marxist-Leninist-Stalinist communism."[32] De Beauvoir's embrace of radical feminism's ideological blueprint with her ringing declaration that no woman should be authorized to stay home to raise her children—"women should not have that choice"— unmistakably gives voice to feminism's totalitarian impulse. In *The Second Sex*, de Beauvoir had already laid out what was to become this fundamental tenet of the movement, grounded in the collectivism of the Soviet Revolution: "A world where men and women would be equal is easy to visualize, for that precisely is what the Soviet Revolution *promised*; women raised and trained exactly like men were to work under the same conditions and for the same wages. . . . [P]regnancy leaves were to be paid for by the State, which would assume charge of the children, signifying not that they would be *taken away* from their parents, but that they would not be *abandoned* to them."[33] Just as Charlotte Perkins Gilman had made clear at the turn of the century, the goal was to make all women abandon the domestic role; it simply should not be an option.

Certainly, a feminist might prefer free market capitalism to socialism, even though she also believes that the traditional family must be destroyed before women can be fully competitive with men in economic and political arenas. In this latter belief, she is correct. Absent significant preferential treatment, women as a group will never exercise economic and political power equally with men so long as any but a most minimal proportion of women devote any more than a most minimal amount of time to the responsibilities of motherhood and homemaking. The evolution of feminist demands has reflected women's dissatisfaction with such stringent curtailment of their domestic activities. As an alternative, feminists would rely on government-imposed market interferences through discrimination against men (which, it cannot be emphasized too often, also injures the women for whom these men are or may become breadwinners) and the conferral of various benefits on working mothers (and fathers).

Thus, whatever theoretical appeal a free market economy might have to some feminists, in practice its operation is inconsistent with the feminist solution of preferential treatment for women. Women like me do not, of course, share the feminist goal of achieving sexual equivalence by this or any other means. We reject displacing merit-based decisions with the preferential treatment without which women must essentially become male clones in order to achieve economic and political equivalence with men. And even if we did accept preferential treatment, this goal of equivalence—despite such assistance—would still require us to curtail drastically those domestic commitments that we find extremely gratifying and of greater value than the market activities replacing them.

THE TRADITIONAL FAMILY'S CONTRIBUTION TO CAPITALISM

Whether or not the goal of sexual equivalence is desirable or possible, there is serious doubt that destruction of the traditional bourgeois family is consistent with continuation of a free market economy. This should concern those who, while championing the free market, have joined feminists in welcoming demise of the traditional female role. For example, Judge Richard A. Posner criticizes the traditional female role with its emphasis on premarital virginity and marital chastity, yet he is one of the leading exponents of the free market. Unlike Posner, I value the traditional female role within the traditional bourgeois family. If faced with a "Sophie's Choice" between that family and the free market economy that we both value, I would choose the former. Formation and maintenance of a stable family are, in my view, the goals that give the fullest meaning to our lives. Women who seek their ecstasy in performing these tasks may well contribute the most to society, and certainly are less likely to harm it, than those who seek ecstasy in remolding humanity.

By providing the best livelihood for the greatest number of people, a free market economy is most valuable as a servant to our families. But the fortunes of both are so interconnected that there can probably be no choice between them. Because the costs and inefficiencies inherent in a socialist economic structure usually require full-time employment of both mother and father outside the home, it is doubtful that any substantial number of traditional families can be long maintained in highly socialized economies. (Insofar as perceived economic necessity is the factor motivating women in two-parent families to remain employed in our own country, much of the blame may lie in the degree to which our economy has suffered from abandoning free market principles in favor of increasingly burdensome government regulation.) It is also doubtful that a free market economy can function optimally in a society peopled by products of the institutional child-rearing that inevitably follows destruction of traditional families. Acknowledging the interdependence of family structure and economic organization should lead those who value the free market to be wary of championing the cause of those who have attacked traditional families.

Social conservatives, who are among the staunchest supporters of the traditional family, usually favor restricting abortion, controlling distribution of pornography, inhibiting easy divorce, retaining and better enforcing laws against drug use, and recognizing that the status of homosexuals is not simply a civil rights issue analogous to the status of a racial minority. Since economic conservatives may reject many of these propositions (many Libertarians reject all of them), they may have little desire to cooperate with social conservatives. Yet these two groups have cooperated to promote a free market economy through economic deregulation and tax revision. Libertarians and other economic conservatives should realize that by rejecting traditional conservatism's pro-family cultural premises, they are aligning themselves with the cultural values of modern liberals. These are the values embodied in an ideology that Gertrude Himmelfarb has described as insisting "upon the largest measure of individual liberty in one area—the freedom to see, read, say, and act as they please, to be free of moral restraints and social conventions," while also insisting "upon the largest measure of social and government controls in other areas—to provide for economic security, racial equality, social justice, [and] environmental protection."[34]

Economic conservatives might find value in social conservatism if they recognized that liberalism's subversion of the traditional bourgeois family has undermined an institution that significantly contributes to a successfully functioning free market economy within a civil society. Even those with no personal interest in establishing a family should concede the need for an orderly and stable society which sustains a birthrate sufficient to maintain its population and produces individuals who are, in large part, happy, well-adjusted, and productive. Such does not seem to be our present society.

On the contrary, our culture is more accurately described in Amaury de Riencourt's observation that—in our acceptance of androgyny and unisexual values, our emphasis on the seductive attributes of women rather than their worthiness as mothers, our devaluing of maternity, our sanctioning of abortion, and our declining birth rate—we resemble the Greek and Roman Empires in their decline. Documenting how triumph of the first full-fledged feminist movement led Roman women to scorn child-bearing as "unworthy of their talents," de Riencourt concludes that with the decline in marriages and fertility, Romans committed ethnic suicide. Similarly, Greece was described by Polybius in the second

century B.C. as "subject to a low birthrate and a general decrease of
the population. . . . Men had fallen into such a state of luxury,
avarice and indolence that they did not wish to marry, or, if they
married, to rear the children born to them . . . and by small degrees
cities became resourceless and feeble."[35]

Totalitarian movements always seek to weaken family institutions
so that men, women, and children will become equally subordinate
to the State. De Riencourt has described how, from the Spartan
dictatorship through Leninist Russia to the National Socialism of
Hitler's Germany, the patriarchal autonomous family was attacked
as a dangerous barrier protecting individuals against an all-powerful
government.[36] Although their propaganda may stress family sanctity,
as Christopher Lasch observed, totalitarian regimes depend on the
"decay of patriarchal authority"; a society in which "the few tyrannize
over the many" follows the collapse of that familial authority.[37]
Unfurling its totalitarian colors, contemporary feminism has similarly
feigned concern for families while denouncing as women's worst
enemy the patriarchal authority most likely to produce strong and
enduring families.

Today's patriarchal decline under the aegis of a triumphant feminism has resulted in the sanctioning of single motherhood and its
encouragement by a welfare system that has effectively displaced
husband and father. This system recalls Margaret Mead's discussion
of the practice in Nazi Germany of rewarding illegitimacy with
especially sunny nursing homes for mother and child, a step the
state took towards complete severing of the male's bond with woman
and offspring. Thus Mead concluded, "the most successful large-
scale abrogations of the family have occurred not among simple
savages, living close to the subsistence edge, but among great nations
and strong empires."[38]

To contemporary feminists, the traditional family is the same
obstacle to women's freedom and equality that Russian Bolsheviks
believed it was to Communism. Bolshevism's attitude towards the
family was described by Crane Brinton in *The Anatomy of Revolution*:

It was an institution of the old regime, interwoven with all sorts of religious elements, inevitably conservative in its social action. The family was a stuffy little nest breeding selfishness, jealousy, love of property, indifference toward the great needs of society. The family kept the young indoctrinated with the stupidities of the old. The Bolsheviks would break up the family, encourage divorce, educate the children to the true selflessness of Communism, get them used to collective enterprises and collective social life, get rid of the influence of the Church in family relations.[39]

Because the disastrous results of those early Bolshevik policies required modifications, the former Soviet Union experimented with varying degrees of control over abortion and divorce and with varying levels of commitment to institutional child-rearing.[40] Its experimentations did little, however, to raise the birth rate, increase life expectancy, or curb alcoholism. Such results, it is now hoped, will follow in Russia once a free market economy has been successfully instituted. Among its other benefits, this is the only economy that has ever produced enough wealth in an advanced industrial society to support a large female population sufficiently freed from labor outside the home that it will *willingly* choose a high rate of reproductivity.

Francine du Plessix Gray has painted a devastating picture of life for women in Russia, where the entire female population seems to reject Western feminism and long for the return of the traditional family. They are dumbfounded that Western feminists think this arrangement oppressive, for it is the dream of Russian women not to have to work. Russian women writers present the bleakest picture of Russian society, where the Bolshevik conferral of "equal rights" on women by pushing them into market production simply meant women assumed greater obligations disguised as increased benefits. These writers depict a disintegrating family life and women who must daily contend with debasing indignities.[41] It is only Western feminists who retain that Bolshevik antipathy towards traditional families which, when put into practice, leads to low birth rates, institutional child-rearing, and high abortion and divorce rates.

Feminists accept these conditions as the necessary price of achieving male-female equivalence. But for those who do not share this goal of equivalence, nothing is gained to compensate for the resulting erosion and distress of the family. The damage to our families, moreover, has weakened a major bulwark against totalitarianism and undermined the agency that is best able to produce children who will grow up to be independent and willing to take the risks required for entrepreneurial success within a free market economy. The products of communal child-rearing will more easily fit within the mold of tomorrow's bureaucrats: risk-averse, conforming, non-individualists, well-suited to perform in a welfare-state bureaucracy.

A free market economy requires the energy and initiative of an individualist who is an entrepreneur who takes responsibility for his actions, is willing to take charge and take chances, and has the courage to make his own decisions, acting if necessary, without the security of peer group approval. We once fearlessly described this person as "a real man" (being aware, of course, that a woman can also fill the entrepreneurial role). As shown in Patricia Cayo Sexton's *The Feminized Male*[42] and George Gilder's *Sexual Suicide*,[43] it is precisely these qualities—once possessed in abundance by many men—that make men less suited to work in a bureaucratic environment.

It is male individuality, exuberance, and aggressiveness that must be most stringently curbed and disciplined to meet the requirements of bureaucratic success. Bureaucracies are more hospitable to the effete, androgynous male who fits the feminist mold of manhood. Women, on the other hand, are generally as well suited to bureaucratic action as they were suited, when young girls, to the largely female-administered elementary school which, in Sexton's very accurate description, rewarded all the behaviors that come so easily to most of us who were little models of self-control and stressless conformity. While usually more risk-averse than men, women will, with bureaucratic sanction, happily cast a wide net in deploying their aptitude for nurturing, caring, and empathy to organize and direct the lives of others. Being willing and often very competent to institute and enforce a minute regulation of other people's affairs, women thrive in the security of a bureaucracy, the bastion of females and feminized males.

That males have been substantially broken to fit the feminist bureaucratic mold is evident from what Leon Wieseltier has described as the current eclipse of individual initiative by collective activity. This eclipse is indicated by the pervasiveness within both business and government bureaucracies of theories like "Total Quality Management" which promote cooperation rather than competition as the desirable workplace modus operandi. Accompanying this devaluation of individualism has been a feminization of the workplace designed to make it less a hierarchical and more a cooperative enterprise. The theory is that "individuality is a failing, and the individual should be buried in the group"; the goal, in the words of then Secretary of Labor, Robert B. Reich, should be "collective entrepreneurialism."[44]

In discussing the effects of these changes on business management (while not necessarily criticizing them), Walter Kiechel III has described the young generation of managers as committed to the "sharing of responsibility" while being "thoroughly uncomfortable with" "the leader's role." They display "what can look a lot like an unwillingness to assume responsibility for others." Hierarchy is unfashionable: "Nobody gives orders"; "It feels more like we're equals." In one psychiatrist's view, the "baby-boom generation consider their peer bonding one of the most important parts of life [perhaps, says Kiechel, because of all the time spent in school and camp]. They feel uncomfortable in organizations hierarchically arranged, and approach things laterally." A comparison of tests given first level managers in the 1950s with those given in the 1970s showed the biggest difference was that the "boomers scored much lower on a measure social scientists call dominance, approximately the willingness to assert oneself and exert power with peers and subordinates."[45]

The view that individuality is a failing and must be subordinated to group action is antipathetic to free market capitalism and integral to totalitarian collectivism; it was part of the bedrock on which the Soviet Union built its economic disaster. Insofar as the traditional bourgeois family was a precondition of free market capitalism, the family's decline could be expected to result in a work force apprehensive of individuality and receptive to an emerging welfare state socialism. This relationship between traditional families and democratic capitalism has been ably described by Brigitte and Peter L. Berger. The patterns of socialization within the nuclear family, they argue, produced the "mind-sets and values" which were a precondition of the industrial revolution and modernization. This socializing process resulted "in the closer relationship between parents and children, in greater parental influence, and in greater individuation." The bourgeoisie of the industrial revolution sprang from the combination of this distinctive family relationship with the new ideas of private property and individualism. They were "a community of dissenters" with a single-minded devotion to "hard work, simple living, and moral propriety"; most important, they produced children characterized by "an inner resilience."[46]

From this bourgeois family came individuals "with singularly stable personalities" who were uniquely capable of the innovation and risk-taking that are the critical preconditions of entrepreneurship and capitalist enterprise. It is this ability to raise children who combine the qualities of stable characters and reliable habits with the capacity to display individual independence and initiative that is the distinctive contribution of traditional bourgeois families in a democratic, capitalist society.[47] Totalitarian collectivist states saw very clearly that this family and the children it produces constituted a primary obstacle to collectivism's success. Regimes, such as the liberated states of the former Soviet Union, that undertake to remake collectivist systems may also come to realize the crucial role this family and its children play in creating and maintaining a democratic, capitalist society. Their success may well depend upon that realization, as may the reversal of our own decay.

It is our traditional bourgeois families, say the Bergers, that are "the one great barrier against an all-embracing bureaucratization of life," the one means of producing "autonomous, independent-minded individuals" fit for an entrepreneurial rather than a welfare-bureaucratic society. Confirmation of their analysis comes from the many studies of the children who were raised under communal conditions in the Israeli kibbutz system and developed personalities and value systems that "are emphatically collectivistic and conformist." Those raised in the kibbutz become individuals who "find it extraordinarily difficult to stand up against their group, who find it difficult to develop an inner life outside the sphere of collective activity, and who very often find it hard to exist in any less-collectivistic situation."[48]

Similarly, Chinese communal child-rearing practices are designed precisely to obviate any display of that inner resilience and individual independence and initiative that characterize the children of traditional bourgeois families. The goal of China's communal techniques (which still commonly include placing infants and young children in full-time boarding schools with home visits on Wednesday and Saturday) is to instill obedience and conformity. From the moment of birth, "Chinese babies are conditioned to conform" so that individualism will never take root. It is a child-rearing philosophy most likely to "teach children to rely not on themselves, but on an outside power, whether their parents or society."[49] In this, of course, the Chinese are implementing what has always been the child-rearing philosophy of totalitarian states.

That children raised largely in a communal setting become collectivistic and conformist accords with the teachings of child specialists Erik Erikson and John Bowlby; it is, they observe, through close and fairly continuous contact with the mother during the early years of life that a child gains a sense of basic trust. Out of this basic trust can develop the self-confidence, self-esteem, and independence required to become a fully autonomous individual, independent of a peer group, and capable of introspection and the ability to develop an inner life.[50] Over the past three decades, our families have moved ever further from the paradigm of child-nurturing elaborated by Bowlby and Erikson. As traditional family structures have weakened, the individual, personal care children once received from their mothers has been replaced by communal, impersonal care from mother-substitutes—a care most likely to fit them for collective conformity rather than independent individualism.

Confirming the analyses of the Bergers, Bowlby, and Erikson are the fruits of these familial changes. They were documented in a report of the United States Department of Education, *Youth Indicators: Trends in the Well-Being of American Youth*: Young people are living with their parents longer and, by delaying marriage to significantly later ages, are slower to form their own families and become self-sufficient. Youth, said the report, are "staying younger longer" and "seem to be becoming autonomous, self-supporting individuals at a slower rate than was once the case"; "the transition from childhood to adulthood is taking longer and presenting more pitfalls."[51]

Growth of the societal conditions that necessitate communal child care is accelerating, not abating. Over the last decade, for example, the number of women who have become mothers without marrying has increased almost 60 percent to nearly a quarter (23.7 percent) of unmarried women. The increasing social acceptability of unwed motherhood is evidenced by the fact that, among those who have become mothers without marrying, the percentage of white women and women who have attended college more than doubled and the percentage in the case of women with professional or managerial jobs nearly tripled.[52] In this, we are now walking in Sweden's footsteps.

Sweden has the lowest marriage rate and one of the highest illegitimacy rates in the industrialized world (over 50 percent of

its births are out of wedlock); it also has one of the highest employment rates of working-age women in the Western world. These
outcomes result from a deliberate government policy to discourage
maternal care of children and force all women to work so that they
will achieve economic independence from men.[53] Given this policy,
there is indeed a logic in Swedish women's choice of unwed
motherhood, a choice which increasing numbers of American women
are making. By forcing a woman to work and commit her children
to surrogate care, her society not only destroys what is probably
the marital home's most important function, providing the primary locus of child-rearing, but it also forecloses a major contribution a husband can make to his wife's life through enabling her
to provide the full-time care of their children within that marital
home.

Some in Sweden have begun to reexamine its social welfare
state. At the foundation of their system has been the ethic: "To be
average is good"; "To be different is bad." Infusing all aspects of
Swedish life, this ethic "makes for an orderly society" but, when
"combined with an educational system that stresses uniformity,"
the ethic "discourages the best and the brightest—the smartest
kid in class, the entrepreneur, the risktaker, the artist, the inventor—
in short, the very kinds of people Sweden needs now."[54] And, one
might add, the very kinds of people every country needs.

CHINESE WOMEN AND THE "RETURN HOME"

Telling evidence has recently appeared that a society striving to
develop a more competitive economic system does discern some
connection between such a system and family structure. Thus, the
desire of some Chinese women to cease market production and
return home is being sanctioned in some areas, and even encouraged.
That these women are revolting against the communal child-rearing
which was integral to their collectivist system should give pause to

those who would structure our own society so as to push American women into leaving home for marketplace.

Women in China began to echo the complaints of Eastern European women that they are forced into market production and denied the enjoyment of a domestic life. Expressing her "aversion" to a Western feminism that would "deny the distinction between men and women" and would instead claim it to be "entirely socially constructed," writer Wang Anyi states that Chinese women are just beginning to have "the luxury to talk about the differences between men and women, to enjoy something that distinguishes women from men." "Children in the nursery school are pitiable enough," she says, while parents "are crushed on the bus holding their children every morning." Female factory workers are so "tremendously fatigued" from doing the same physical work as men that "many women have difficult labors and few have milk." Observing that "many female workers would like to stay at home and do the housework if their husbands made higher salaries," she complains that "women's health is deteriorating" and "our energy has been totally exhausted."[55]

A whole genre of contemporary Chinese women's writing has developed to express women's fatigued despair through metaphors of illness and hospitalization as a result of which "women have ceased to function, not only in a social, political, or domestic capacity, but even as sexual beings." These stories use images of "ugliness, pain, and dirt" to describe these women, symbolizing the "injustice and frustration that bear down on them and threaten to ruin them"—reminiscent, I suggest, of the woman I describe as Andrea Dworkin's spiritual virgin. The character of Lu Wenting in one of these stories is called the Everywoman of contemporary Chinese fiction: she is a doctor who has collapsed from overwork, the emblem of female victimization by the demands of society and the "added burdens a woman has to bear if she wants to be a good citizen, a good professional, a good wife, and a good mother."[56]

The writer Dai Qing tells us that the question facing China is "whether women should return to the home rather than the question of how to leave the home." "In some rapidly developing rural areas, like Daqiu Village," she says, "the women have all gone home": "So Chinese women have no reason to be interested in feminism abroad." Feminism, she states, "is not the force to push China forward," for "many women want to stay home these days."[57] Another commentator describes the phenomenon of Daqiu Village as existing "in newly prosperous rural households in every region." Noting that women's work force participation under collectivization was not by choice but because of "subsistence needs and administrative initiative," when the village grew wealthy and "adminstrative preference reversed, women themselves were willing to 'return to the home.'" This is an unfortunate outcome, she says, because it means the sacrifice of women's "individual development in exchange for men's realization of their greatest social value,"[58] an appraisal that rejects the more realistic conclusion of another commentator that women's "reproductive and household labor" are roles "much more important than women's participation in society and government."[59]

A university head of women's studies, Li Xiaojiang, has described women's return to the home as a part of an economic reform that "lightens the burden for industry of tasks not oriented toward production [that is, providing the various benefits related to women's reproductive requirements] and supports social stability and enterprise development." Although the return home "allows men to work to their utmost capacity and alleviates the pressures in women's lives," Li Xiaojiang notes that some resist it as inconsistent with their individual "self-development." But in light of the heavy burden inflicted on women by over "forty years of mental and physical exhaustion caused by the extraordinary stress of a double role," she understands why many women have willingly returned home. "The life of a beast of burden," she says, "is certainly not the liberation which Chinese women have so painstakingly sought." In developing a new feminist ideology that would support women's escape from the marketplace (precisely the old social feminism of our own New Deal liberals who opposed sending mothers into the workplace),

Li Xiaojiang reasons that because sex difference is not "a gap that can be bridged by human effort," the goal of "formal equality between men and women" places "excessive demands on women" by requiring them to take on the "risks and burdens of competition in a male-centered society" as well as "their mission of human reproduction." And so women's liberation, she concludes, must mean "giving a good name to the 'incurably' petty qualities of femininity" and promoting "those valuable human characteristics that have long been undervalued by the standards of civilized society."[60]

That Li Xiaojiang speaks from her own experience appears from an autobiographical work in which she depicted herself "as a girl who had excelled in a meritocratic world because she possessed a wholly androgynous will . . . and could expend heroic effort in pursuing her goals." In motherhood, however, "she confronted the 'typical eastern woman's fate' of selfless domestic sacrifice on top of the burden of her salaried work." All her reading, she said, had never taught her what it was to be a woman whose double roles made it impossible "to find a relaxed, real sense of self . . . in the home or outside in society."[61] Her own experience no doubt evoked sympathy with the young generation of workers who, like Xiao Bo, the silk factory worker described by Lisa Rofel, was so pleased to embrace motherhood that, having already extended her maternity leave, she intended to stay home "as long as possible," although "abandoning the lifetime security of a state-run factory job also meant giving up one's food rations and child supplements." As these women are "becoming more strongly tied to domesticity and motherhood," says Rofel, "their activities in the home are no longer condemned as feudal social arrangements" but are seen as "a natural expression of the female self."[62]

These are the views of the women whom Lisa Rofel describes as the "younger generation of women workers" who have rejected "state-induced feminism" in their "search for a meaningful sense of womanhood," having found that "they were not liberated by 'work' but were instead now doubly burdened by a socialist state's demands."[63]   It is these feminine yearnings that Chinese women writers have expressed in their stories of women who believe they have lost their "very nature as a woman" and strive "to take back the femininity of which women have been robbed," a femininity that they would "reclaim as part of a woman's right."[64] The evil identified by these criticisms, explains Tani Barlow, was the Maoist effort to obliterate natural sex differences by "stripping women of their female nature and by default masculinizing the feminine."[65]

In his discussion of Chinese feminism, Jonathan Mirsky concludes that the reactions of the women who chose to return home showed "how deeply the hopes for women's emancipation have been disappointed."[66] But perhaps they show that emancipation from child-rearing and domesticity can never serve the interests of all women. For some of us, such emancipation is like freeing a camel from the burden of his hump—if you do so, you may, as G. K. Chesterton told us, only free him from being a camel.[67]

Before we continue any further down the path blazed by the world's collectivist societies, we should heed the example of women in those societies who have forsaken that path. The lesson they teach us is that not all women consider child-rearing and domesticity to be burdens of which they want to be relieved. We should ask ourselves whether it is just or prudent to adopt policies designed to force all women into the feminist mold. We should also consider how great is the cost of losing those autonomous, independent-minded individuals once produced by traditional families. Insofar as such individuals are necessary to the optimal functioning of a free market economy, feminism's attack on the traditional family must be recognized as an attack on democratic capitalism as well. And defense of the traditional family must also be seen as a defense of democratic capitalism.

6

A Tangle of Pathology

Turning and turning in the widening gyre
The falcon cannot hear the falconer;
Things fall apart; the center cannot hold;
Mere anarchy is loosed upon the world,
The blood-dimmed tide is loosed, and everywhere
The ceremony of innocence is drowned;
The best lack all conviction, while the worst
Are full of passionate intensity.

William Butler Yeats
The Second Coming

IN 1965, SENATOR DANIEL PATRICK MOYNIHAN, then an assistant secretary of labor, wrote a report detailing the "deterioration of the fabric of Negro society," the primary cause of which was "the deterioration of the Negro family": "the family structure of lower class Negroes is highly unstable, and in many urban centers is approaching complete breakdown." "The white family," his report stated, "has achieved a high degree of stability and is maintaining that stability." In contrast, urban black family life involves rates of divorce, desertion, female-headed families, and illegitimacy that render it a "tangle of pathology." "The Negro community," he concluded, "has been forced into a matriarchal structure which ... seriously retards the progress of the group as a whole, and imposes a crushing burden on the Negro male and, in consequence, on a great many Negro women as well."[1] Under this matriarchal structure, the roles of husband and wife are often reversed, with the largest percentage of black families being dominated by the wife. Black females are better students and better educated than black males, have higher aspirations than males (one study showing that from 75 to 90 percent of all black honor students in high schools are females), and have much higher representation in white collar and professional employment than males.[2] Moynihan concluded that "Negro children without fathers flounder—and fail," in large part because of the importance of a father in the home for successful socialization of children and the fact that children from homes where fathers are present have significantly higher intelligence scores than children in homes without fathers.[3]

Twenty years later, in the 1985 Godkin lectures, Senator Moynihan announced that, although single-parent families were still more common among blacks than whites, the phenomenon now pervades white as well as black society—"single parenthood is now a fact of life for all classes and for all races."[4] Children, he noted, constituted less than 27 percent of our population but 40 percent of those in poverty and were the only age group over-represented in the poverty population. The United States had become "the first society in history in which a person is more likely to be poor if young rather than old."[5] The number of single-parent families had increased 124 percent since 1970, he observed, in contrast with an increase of only 12 percent in the number of all families with children and a decline of 4 percent in the number of married-couple families with children. Eighty-nine percent of these single parents were women, and 54 percent of the children in these female-headed families were in poverty, in contrast to 12.5 percent of the children in all other families.[6] By the end of 1986, 26.3 percent of all families with children were single-parent families, up from 12.9 percent in 1970. Sixty percent of black families with children were maintained by a single parent, up from 35.7 percent in 1970, and 20.8 percent of white families with children were headed by a single parent, up from 10.1 percent in 1970. Single-parent families had increased to 28.6 percent of all families with children in 1991.[7]

Moynihan was attacked as a racist in 1965 for viewing the matriarchal black family structure as deviant, but he noted in his 1985 lectures that the black community had with great concern begun to acknowledge black family disintegration. He was also attacked for commending the stability of traditional families which predominated among whites, a stability described as a "sentimental myth" by one commentator who endorsed the "destruction" of this "impossibly overloaded and guilt-creating social unit, the family."[8] In The Feminine Mystique, Betty Friedan had two years earlier denounced women's oppression by this traditional family which, she claimed, prevented them from growing as human beings and finding self-fulfillment. Very quickly, traditional families had come to be seen as the chief impediment to feminist aims. Sociologist Jessie Bernard characterized the "family as the major roadblock to the full emancipation of women"; other feminist commentators speculated that "the conjugal model may be outmoded" and that "in order to establish and maintain a status equal to her husband's, a woman needs to remain childless."[9]

Critics who defend a matriarchal family structure and believe the traditional family has hindered women's "full emancipation" may celebrate the developments Moynihan deplored. But much of society claims to be appalled that the conditions which Moynihan observed have greatly worsened for urban blacks and became much more prevalent among whites. If Moynihan correctly described the urban black family as a tangle of pathology in 1965, then as he recognized in his 1985 lectures, this description now applies to a large portion of all families—black and white—that more closely resemble 1965's unstable black ghetto family than 1965's stable white suburban family. This twenty-year period that Moynihan analyzed in his Godkin lectures bore the impact of the most strident feminist activism. Public awareness of AIDS and female doubts about the sexual revolution had not yet provoked significant reexamination of sexual mores, and women who had entered the work force had not yet begun seriously to question the compatibility of career achievement with family commitments. These two decades witnessed a startling deterioration in what are generally recognized to be crucial determinants of familial health and stability. To consider and acknowledge the extent of the deterioration that occurred over these two decades must raise grave doubts about the appropriateness of the path down which feminists led our society. Each of the areas in which the condition of families has worsened is an area that was affected by feminist initiatives. The tangles of pathology that so many of our families have become are, in part, the price that has been paid to achieve feminist goals.

DIVORCE

Moynihan's 1965 report was based on the 1960 census figures showing that 22.9 percent of urban black women and 7.9 percent of urban white women who had ever married were divorced, separated, or living apart from their husbands.[10] By 1986, of the women who had married, 30.6 percent of the black and 26.7 percent of the white were divorced. In 1985, nearly one-third of women, aged 35 to 39, who had ever married had been divorced, and since 1960 the divorce rate doubled for men and women who were 45 and over, contrary to the previous expectation of stability in longer term marriages.[11] The divorce rate (the number of couples divorcing per 1,000 population) in the United States is by far the highest in the world and more than doubled between 1965 and 1980. One-half of marriages contracted in 1986 are predicted to end in divorce,[12] and it is estimated that close to two-thirds of all marriages that occurred in 1988 will result in separation or divorce.[13]

Concomitants of increasing divorce rates are an increase in the number of single-parent families and what has come to be called the feminization of poverty. Between 1970 and 1981, the number of families headed by divorced women increased from 956,000 to 2.7 million.[14] Over one million children have been involved in divorce each year since 1972; by 1984, one of every five American children lived in a single-parent home, and by 1986, 24 percent of all children under age eighteen lived in single-parent homes, compared with 9 percent in 1960. It is predicted that more than one-third of the stepfamilies in which four out of seven white children and one out of eight black children lived in 1989 will themselves dissolve.[15] Three-fifths of the children born in 1986 are expected to spend at least part of their childhood in a single-parent family. Moynihan's Godkin lectures projected that 46 percent of white and 87 percent of black 17 year olds living in 1994 will have spent some portion of their childhood in a broken family.[16]

The number of families in the United States are projected to increase by 13 million between 1980 and 2000. Of this 13 million, 5.9 million are expected to be husband-wife families, 5.8 million will be female-headed, and 1.3 million male-headed. The number of female-headed families will increase at more than five times the rate of husband-wife families, and the number of male-headed families at more than six times the rate of traditional families.[17] In 1984 for the first time, the number of poor female-headed families exceeded the number of poor married-couple families. The great majority of poor adults were women—almost two out of three— and more than three-fourths of all the poor were either adult women or children under eighteen. Sixty-five percent of the increase in the number of children living in poverty between 1970 and 1983 occurred in female-headed families. It is projected that if the proportion of the poor who are in female-headed families were to increase at the same rate it did from 1967 to 1977, by the year 2000 the poverty population would consist solely of women and their children.[18]

A primary factor contributing to the feminization of poverty has been the change to a system of no-fault divorce under which divorce is easily obtained, even when opposed by one of the parties, and men are often able to terminate marriages without providing adequate alimony or child support. The feminist quest for female fungibility with males has led the women's movement to support the invalidation of laws benefiting and protecting women. This was the thrust, for example, of litigation directed by Ruth Bader Ginsburg when she was director of the Women's Rights Project of the American Civil Liberties Union and, often using male plaintiffs, secured invalidation of laws that favored women.[19] The theory was that obliteration of all legal sex distinctions would ultimately be in the best interests of working women; those women, including homemakers, who wished to retain the benefits of protective legislation were never the women with whose rights the Project was concerned. In the area of divorce reform, one of the benefits women have lost is the maternal preference which favored awarding custody to the mother. Almost all states now grant men and women a statutory equal right to custody. While mothers still gain custody in the vast majority of cases, loss of the maternal preference has seriously affected the bargaining process. In order to secure custody many women will drastically compromise their financial interests: "Women who are scared to death of losing custody will trade away anything else—child support, property, alimony to keep it from happening."[20] Again, the one most grievously injured by this so-called reform grounded in feminism's commitment to sexual fungibility is the homemaker who is most devoted to her children.

Among the greatest harms done by contemporary feminism has been its support of no-fault divorce laws that enable men to abandon wives and children with minimum guilt and little monetary compensation. It may seem ironic that through its divorce policy a movement supposedly devoted to women's interests disadvantages women who are homemakers and favors the interests of males who abjure responsibility for wives and children. But it is also consistent, for through no-fault divorce society has institutionalized the movement's diktat that women must abandon homemaking for full-time marketplace activity. As Mary Ann Glendon accurately states, our "divorce law in practice seems to be saying to parents, especially mothers, that it is not safe to devote oneself primarily or exclusively to raising children."[21]

As mentioned earlier, feminists nevertheless often try to disclaim responsibility for no-fault's results. Liberationists of the 1970s blathered mindlessly about the oppressiveness of the family, exhorting women to break the chains of their confinement, to cease being parasites in their suburban havens, to cease holding husbands in marriages the men no longer wanted, and to set out on the road to true fulfillment and equality by finding some rewarding career. Yet, having been taken seriously by every state legislature in the country and with the divorce revolution accomplished, feminists seek to absolve themselves from blame, as if society should have known better than to listen to them. No longer concentrating on the oppressiveness of home and family for women, feminists argue instead that, unfortunately, married mothers must remain in the work force to protect themselves from the very likely possibility of becoming single-parents impoverished by divorce. This is a likelihood, they choose not to remember, their movement was highly instrumental in creating.

The deplorable results of no-fault divorce were extensively documented by Lenore J. Weitzman in *The Divorce Revolution*. Concluding that no-fault had made divorce too attractive to men and impoverished large numbers of women and children, she stated that the average divorced woman and her minor children experience a 73-percent decline in their standard of living in the first year after divorce, while the former husband's standard of living increases 42 percent. The magnitude, but not the fact, of a great disparity has been questioned in subsequent studies.[22] Less than one-half of all divorced mothers are granted child support, and of these less than one-half actually obtain the full amount that was granted— about 30 percent receive partial payments and 25 percent receive nothing. In 1986, the average annual payment to mothers who did receive child support was $710—less than $14 per week; including divorced, separated, and never-married women, nearly 8.7 million American women were raising children without fathers in the home, and 53 percent of these received no money from the fathers; about 3.7 million of these women had not been awarded child support and 958,000 were unable to collect their award.[23] Census Bureau data for 1970-79 showed that the median income in families headed by women with children under the age of six was only 30 percent of the median income for all families with children under six.[24]

ILLEGITIMACY AND TEENAGE PREGNANCY

Moynihan's 1965 report revealed that the illegitimacy rate among whites had increased from 2 percent in 1940 to 3.07 percent in 1963; the rate among blacks had increased from 16.8 percent to 23.6 percent.[25] At the time of his 1985 lectures, 20.2 percent of white births and 74.5 percent of black births were illegitimate.[26]

Between 1960 and 1980, the birth rate of single white women aged fifteen to nineteen increased from 6.6 to 15.9 per 1,000, an increase of 140.9 percent.[27] In 1980, 82 percent of all births among black women aged fifteen to nineteen were illegitimate. As Charles Murray noted, a study of fertility among thirty-two populations in developed nations showed that the 1980 teenage fertility rate for blacks in the United States was the highest of all thirty-two and was 37 percent higher than the next highest rate. The next highest rate occurred in a traditional population of women who marry at a very young age, and if the study had been limited to illegitimate births, the fertility rate of American black teenagers would have appeared even more disproportionate than it did. Most striking is the inconsistency between teenage behavior and that of all other women, illustrated by the statistics for the period from 1965 to 1970: an increase in birth rate in the United States occurred only among single teenagers, both black and white, and to a fractional extent among single white women aged twenty to twenty-four, while the rate declined among every other segment of the population.[28]

As noted by Moynihan in his 1985 lectures, teenagers in the United States are "much more likely to become pregnant than are teenagers in other Western nations," and ours is the only developed nation where rates of teenage pregnancy have been increasing. In 1985, 1.1 million American teenagers became pregnant. The rate of pregnancy among American women aged 15 to 19 was 96 per 1,000; in Canada the rate was 44 per 1,000, and in the Netherlands it was 14 per 1,000. In one-half of our states in 1982 more than 50 percent of births to women under age twenty were illegitimate: the illegitimacy rate was 71 percent in New Jersey and 88 percent in the District of Columbia; in only ten states did such illegitimate births constitute less than 40 percent of all births.[29]

By 1984, over 90 percent of births to black women under age twenty were illegitimate.[30] As the president of the National Council of Negro Women noted in 1985, although early marriage and the resulting early motherhood were once common among blacks, today the overwhelming majority of all black babies are born to unwed teenage mothers—a situation described by Eleanor Holmes Norton as a "natural catastrophe in our midst, a threat to the future of Black people without equal." In 1985, the Children's Defense Fund described marriage as a "forgotten institution" among black teenagers, when the adolescent single mother had become the rule, rather than the exception that she was in the black community in the 1950s.[31]

POVERTY

One result of divorce and illegitimate birth is the number of children living in single-parent homes, 90 percent of which are headed by women; many of these women and children live in poverty. In 1985, the lowest median family income occurred in female-headed families ($13,660).[32] More than one youth in five (21.3 percent) lived below the poverty line in 1984, compared to 11 percent of adults. Taking into account the market value of food stamps, school lunches, subsidized housing, and medical benefits, the poverty rate for children under eighteen declined to 14.9 percent, compared with a similarly adjusted rate for the elderly of 2.6 percent. For children under six, this adjusted poverty rate was 17.5 percent, almost seven times the elderly rate. It is projected that by the year 2000 one-half of all American children will have lived some part of their lives in poverty.[33]

Female-headed families are not the sole cause of child poverty, however. Economist Victor Fuchs has shown that excluding such families from the analysis still left a poverty rate in 1984 of 14 percent for children and 8 percent for adults. This was because 40 percent of all children and only 9 percent of all adults lived in households that had three or more children, and the average income of such households is well below the national average. Fifty-seven percent of all adults lived in households that contained no children; the average income in these households was almost as high as in households with children and, as a result, the per-capita income was much higher. During the 1980s, only those 65 and over experienced a gain in per-capita income, mainly because of an increase in non-labor income such as Social Security, pensions, and interest, but only 5 percent of the elderly live in households with children. Children are supported by the income of a relatively small number of young and middle-aged adults, and the per-capita income of this group declined in households with children during the 1980s.[34]

It should be noted that, unlike the other factors that have adversely affected the quality of family life, child poverty has decreased over the past three decades. The child poverty rate was 26.9 percent in 1959, compared to an elderly poverty rate of 35.2 percent. Both rates then declined, but while the child poverty rate stayed in the range of 15 percent until 1979 and then rose sharply until it reached 21.3 percent in 1984, the elderly poverty rate continued to decline, reaching 12.4 percent in 1984.[35] Thus, although the child poverty rate is lower than it was in 1959, poverty occurs disproportionately among families with children.

CRIME

Rates for both violent and property crime were low and generally constant during the 1950s and early 1960s. Between 1963 and 1980, however, the rates soared for both types of crime, with percentage increases of 122 for murder, 287 for rape, 294 for robbery, 215 for assault, and 189 for burglary. Males accounted for 89 percent of arrests for violent crimes in 1954 and for 90 percent in 1974. There was a change in the age of criminals, however; in 1954, 40 percent of those arrested for violent crimes were under 25, while in 1974, that proportion had increased to 60 percent.[36] The growing frequency of crime among the young is illustrated by a comparison of the homicide rates between 1964 and 1976 when the rate per 100,000 population for men aged 15 to 24 more than doubled—from 7.2 to 14.7—while the rate for men aged 45 to 54 rose only from 3.5 to 4.7.[37] Official delinquency rates for youths aged 10 to 17 increased 130.8 percent between 1960 (20.1 per 1,000) and 1980 (46.4 per 1,000).[38]

IT CANNOT BE DISPUTED that in the four categories of divorce, illegitimacy, poverty, and crime, to which Moynihan directed his attention in 1965, the situation of the family and its children had significantly worsened by 1985. Since then, this situation has continued to worsen, but at a slower rate.[39] While some find hope in this fact, others have little faith that our society can much improve. In *Slouching Towards Gomorrah*, Robert H. Bork concludes his masterly depiction of society's distress with the thought that "the pessimism of the intellect tells us that Gomorrah is our probable destination"[40] Similarly, Leon R. Kass has expressed grave doubts that we can attain the most crucial prerequisite of our moral renewal: "a restoration of sexual self-restraint generally and of female modesty in particular."[41] I do believe that society will find what Bork calls the "optimism of the will" to pull back from its self-destruction. How difficult the fight will be, however, is indicated by the vast changes that have also occurred in aspects of family life other than those considered by Moynihan. These include changes that are universally deplored as well as changes that some deplore, but others herald as evidence of women's liberation and equality.

CHILDREN AND ADOLESCENTS

The youth suicide rate (15 to 24 year olds) increased from four suicides per 100,000 population in 1954 to 13.6 in 1977, a rise of 240 percent, while the suicide rate of the general population rose 32 percent. Suicide is the second leading cause of death among adolescents, between 5,000 and 6,000 young people taking their lives each year. This number would be significantly higher if it were known how many supposed accidents are, in fact, suicides.[42] Sociologist Steven Stack has related the rise in youth suicides to three factors: an increase in family disorganization, a glutted labor market, and a diminished religious orientation among the young.[43]

Analysts in communities experiencing epidemics of "cluster suicides" by teenagers often focus on the impact of increased family disorganization as a cause. Thus in 1983, the Dallas area had one of the nation's highest divorce rates and the second highest suicide rate among adolescents, reflecting a consistent correlation between high divorce and high suicide rates in the same regions.[44] The Centers for Disease Control responded to the problem by issuing recommendations to help communities prevent these "cluster suicides" among teenagers.[45] Suicide rates have continued to rise steadily for teenagers, while declining or holding steady for all other age groups. Part of the explanation, says the director of the American Association of Suicidology, is that "there are more depressed kids."[46] A 1986 survey of high school students disclosed that 46 percent of respondents knew a young person who had committed or tried to commit suicide; the three major causes of teenage suicide were listed as "a feeling of personal worthlessness," "a feeling of isolation and loneliness," and "pressure to achieve." It has been estimated that for every successful adolescent suicide there are fifty to one hundred attempts.[47]

The National Institute of Alcohol Abuse and Alcoholism reported in 1974 that 40 percent of male and 21 percent of female high school seniors had drinking problems, compared to 5 percent or less in 1960.[48] Another study showed that among high school seniors in 1980, 88 percent had used alcohol within the past twelve months, 49 percent had used marijuana, 21 percent had used non-prescribed stimulants, and 12 percent had used cocaine. Between 1972 and 1979 the proportion of white twelve-to-seventeen-year-olds using drugs increased 138.6 percent, and the proportion using alcohol increased 56.2 percent.[49] Adolescent drug use has declined since its peak in the early 1980s, but the 1987 annual survey of drug use by students in the United States conducted by the Institute for Social Research at the University of Michigan showed, nonetheless, that young Americans had "a level of involvement with illicit drugs which is greater than can be found in any other industrialized nation in the world."[50] The Institute's 1994 survey confirmed that increases in teenagers' drug use over the past few years are continuing, a trend attributed to "glamorizing of drugs by the entertainment industry.[51]

As Senator Moynihan noted in his 1985 lectures, our cities have been "flooded with narcotics smuggled past [our] borders." In addition to the use of these drugs by youth themselves, the harmful effects of drug use have blighted many families through the birth of addicted babies, the influence of drug-abusing parents, and the hideous environment created by a pervasive drug culture, particularly in the ghettos of our major urban areas.[52] Disclosing far more pervasive drug abuse during pregnancy than had been suspected, a survey by the National Association for Perinatal Addiction Research and Education showed that at least 11 percent of the women studied had used cocaine or other illegal drugs during pregnancy. Since a wide spectrum of injuries can be caused by even brief fetal exposure to cocaine, the result has been an epidemic of damaged infants.[53]

Between 1976 and 1986, the number of reported child-molestation cases had increased seventeen times to reach more than 100,000; the number of reported child abuse and neglect cases rose 55 percent between 1981 and 1985, and deaths from such abuse increased by 23 percent between 1985 and 1986.[54] Citing an "alarming increase in the number of day-care center sexual abuse cases," the American Bar Association's Criminal Justice Section undertook the first nationwide project to study the sexual abuse of children in such centers and to seek ways to make day care centers safe for very young children.[55] Psychiatrists have observed an increase in the incidence of depression in children, and the problem of "stress" in children has received increasing attention. An organizer of workshops on relieving children's stress reported that the biggest social problem leading to stress in children is the increasing number of working mothers who use child care. The Center for Studies of Suicide Prevention and the National Institute of Mental Health have issued advice on how to "de-stress" one's children, including the suggestion that the parent spend one-on-one time with the child every day.[56]

The chairman of the American Academy of Pediatrics' committee on sports medicine reported that children were less fit in 1985 than they were in the 1960s: while the "fathers are jogging," the sons are "sitting home watching television." About one-third of all children over age twelve had elevated levels of blood cholesterol, and boys and girls were significantly fatter than those studied in the 1960s. Between 1963 and 1980, the number of fat children aged six to eleven increased by 54 percent and obesity in twelve-to-seventeen-year-olds rose by 39 percent, while children's performance on physical endurance tests had declined.[57] A 1989 report by the National Association of Children's Hospital and Related Institutions concluded that the gains achieved in fifty years of marked improvement in children's health had begun eroding in the 1970s and had reached a state of crisis. This was confirmed by a finding that Army recruits in 1989 were in the worst condition in twenty years, a fact attributed to the physical inactivity of high school students.[58]

Academically, the SAT score averages for college-bound high school seniors declined 11.1 percent on the verbal and 6.4 percent on the math between 1960 and 1980. The proportion of eighteen-year-olds who were high school graduates declined 5 percent between 1970 and 1980 and was lower in 1980 than in 1960.[59] Citing a 1986 Louis Harris poll, Senator Moynihan concluded that "the United States in the 1980s may be the first society in history in which children are distinctly worse off than adults." The poll disclosed that three out of four American adults thought children faced more severe problems than children encountered when the adults were growing up. The problems cited included drug abuse, viewed as the most serious, hunger, kidnapping, sexual assault, parental abuse, suicide, and prostitution. Only 48 percent of adults believed that most American children were basically happy, only 40 percent believed most children got a good education, and only 53 percent believed that most children had loving parents.[60]

A 1986 Louis Harris survey disclosed that 46 percent of sixteen-year-olds and 57 percent of seventeen-year-olds had had sexual intercourse. Another survey of high-achieving high school students, however, showed a rate of 23 percent, and 63 percent of these respondents said sex "is not expected in a steady romance."[61] Surveys of females aged sixteen to seventeen found that the proportion who reported having had sexual intercourse doubled between 1971 and 1979. The result was vast increases in teenage pregnancies, in the number of adolescents contracting syphilis, gonorrhea, genital herpes, and other venereal diseases, and in the number of teenagers having abortions. For all women aged fifteen to nineteen the proportion of pregnancies terminated by abortion increased from 28 percent in 1973 to 44 percent in 1980. The number of white women aged fifteen to nineteen having abortions increased 58.6 percent between 1973 and 1979.[62] Although there was little change in the teen population between 1971 and 1981, the number of teenagers having abortions increased during this period from 190,000 to 430,000 per year.[63] Forty percent of all pregnancies in American teenagers were terminated by abortion in 1986. Sixty of every 1,000 American women under age eighteen had abortions, compared with eighteen in Canada and seven in the Netherlands.[64]

Working Mothers and Declining Birth Rates

The percentage of married women with children under eighteen who worked outside the home increased from 18 to 54 percent between 1950 and 1980, and was 62 percent in 1986. The percentage of those working who had children under the age of six increased from 12 to 45 percent,[65] and was 57 percent in 1988.[66] A 1984 study disclosed that women who needed to work the least in terms of family incomes were those returning to work first after birth of a child: 65 percent of the women with family incomes of $45,000 or more planned to return to work, while only 49 percent of those who earned less than $15,000 intended to do so. Moreover, in the higher-income group, many of the women were returning to work when their children were six months old or less, whereas ten years earlier working mothers usually waited until their children were three years old before resuming work. Numerous studies have confirmed this pattern, one in 1988 showing that almost two-thirds of a large nationally representative sample of young women worked into their last trimester and almost two-thirds of those women resumed working in the first three months after giving birth; the higher paid or better educated women were likely to continue working the longest during pregnancy and to return to work the soonest.[67]

By 1986, the fertility rate in the United States had fallen to the lowest rate ever recorded—1.74 children per woman of child-bearing age—continuing a trend begun in 1972, when the rate first fell below the 2.1 rate required to maintain a stable population. This birth rate is 54 percent lower than the rate of 3.77 children per woman at the height of the baby boom in 1957, when 36 million women aged 15 to 44 produced more babies than the 58 million women in this age group produced in 1986.[68] Although the number of adult men in the United States grew 33 percent since 1970, the number of fathers living with their children declined by 3 percent. Several million men who would have been expected to become fathers have not: more than one-third of American men in their twenties continue to live in their parents' home, double the number in 1970, and the percentages of both men and women aged 18 to 24 still living in their parents' home have been steadily increasing since 1960. The percentage of Americans in their early thirties who have never married has more than doubled since 1970, and families now constitute 71.5 percent of all households, a decline of one-fifth from 90.3 percent in 1948.[69]

If as Ben J. Wattenberg has predicted, the American birth rate continues its decline, one result will be—as in the nations of the European Common Market—increasingly higher social security costs of an expanded elderly population which must be borne by a declining cadre of young people.[70] The low European birth rate has been described by European government officials as indicative of "the tendency toward collective suicide" and a vanishing Europe. Wattenberg's projections are supported by a 1988 Census Bureau study predicting a shrinking American population with a doubling of the number of the elderly.[71]

Indicative of the fate of low birth rate countries is the prognosis for the former West Germany. If its birth rate remains at its low level of 1.27 births per woman, within fifty years its total population will decline from 61.7 to 39.4 millon, with 23 percent of the population over age 65 and only 13 percent under age 15. This trend is reflected in a fall in the European Economic Community population from 7.8 percent of the total world population in 1960 to 5.9 percent in 1980; it is expected to reach 4.9 percent in the year 2000. France has long regarded its low birth rate of 1.8 children per woman of child-bearing age as one of the country's major problems and has implemented a program to combat what it calls *dénatalité:* families are offered $125 a month for two years after the birth of a third child, in addition to an allowance to all families of about $85 per month from the third month of the mother's pregnancy until each child's third birthday. That something else will be required to encourage women to bear children is indicated by the fact that the French have steadily resisted inducements of family allowances, guaranteed minimum income, extended maternity leave, and government day care centers.[72]

The reaction was the same in the province of Quebec, Canada, where the attempt to increase its even lower rate of 1.4 children per woman by offering successive increases in its child allowances had no discernible impact on the birth rate.[73] And despite one of the most generous maternity leave and government-funded child care systems in the world, Sweden's birth rate has remained considerably below the rate necessary to sustain its population.[74]

THE DIMINISHED MALE

Columnist William Raspberry has observed that "Black men are fast becoming an endangered species." He cited as evidence a program for black high school journalists in which only three participants out of fifteen were boys, the campuses of black colleges—where female outnumber male students by three or four to one—and the rarity of black males in classes for gifted students. The young black male, often growing up in fatherless homes, falls prey to "crime, drug abuse, academic indifference (or outright hostility)—and more joblessness"; one result, Raspberry noted, is a depleted pool of marriageable black men for either the pregnant teenager or the professional woman.[75] Single black women now outnumber single black men in every adult age bracket—in the 25 to 34 age bracket there are 100 men for 111 women. Single black men, moreover, have about a 17 percent unemployment rate, a figure which does not take account of either those who have given up seeking work or the 500,000 black men in prison.[76]

These are the precise conditions that Moynihan's *The Negro Family* addressed in 1965. They have greatly worsened since then. The harmful effects that Moynihan attributed to life in fatherless homes have been corroborated by studies showing a particularly negative impact on the educational attainments of boys. A report of the American Council on Education showed that the number of black men enrolled in college declined "alarmingly" between 1976 and 1986, one factor in the widening disparity between black men and women in numerous measures of educational achievement. Contributing to this disparity was the decline by more than one-half in the number of doctoral degrees awarded to black men between 1977 and 1986, while the number awarded to black women increased slightly.[77]

In another column urging that civil authorities in Washington, D. C., employ troops to control the city's streets, Raspberry quoted a psychiatrist's query as to "what is happening to Black men, a large segment of whom are in a state of frustration and hopelessness."[78] Raspberry pleaded the necessity of further programs to alleviate joblessness among black males. The lack of these programs, however, cannot explain the great disparity in achievement between black men and women which must, in large measure, be attributed to the matriarchal structure prevailing in black ghetto families. It is the scant contact with their fathers or any acceptable male role models that deprives boys of the most important precondition of their successful socialization.

Abandoning the Black Male

More effective than further job programs (shown by a massive 1993 study to have increased employment of adult male participants by only 2.8 percent and to have had only a negligible effect for male youths) would be a school experience that helps compensate for the baleful lack of a constructive male influence in boys' lives. Efforts to institute all-male schools and classrooms to meet this desperate need of inner-city boys have, unfortunately, been successfully attacked by the National Organization for Women and the American Civil Liberties Union.[79] One such program that had encouraging results was halted because the United States Department of Education found it violated civil rights laws.[80] In contrast to all other groups (including women and recent immigrants), young black males "are now more likely than they were in 1960 to be unemployed, to be addicted to drugs, to be involved in the criminal justice system, to be unwed fathers, and to die from homicide or suicide."[81] Why, one wonders, do these organizations seek to deprive young black males of a possible solution to their woeful predicament?

Why, in particular, is this solution rejected to further the interests of women, when black women's achievement already greatly exceeds that of black men who must "compete for jobs with a labor force increasingly dominated by white women and immigrants."[82] Between 1982 and 1992, for example, the number of black professional women increased by 125 percent, reaching nearly twice the number of black professional men.[83] Those women who wish to construct a life with a man would do well to give credence to Zora Neale Hurston's acute observation: "I know now that it is a griping thing to a man—not to be able to whip his woman mentally. Some women know how to give their man that conquesting feeling."[84]

Except for the task of impregnating females, today's black ghetto males have become largely expendable. Black families, William Tucker has observed, are not really "breaking up" but are "no longer forming"; the black family in the ghetto "is simply kicking black men out of the house and taking in the government as the bread-winner."[85] As one such man described these women: "If it weren't for welfare, they'd need us men"; in the words of another: "Let's face it, society is basically set up for women."[86] This process by which our welfare system has enabled females to dispense with males for all purposes except stud service has been ably described by George Gilder and Charles Murray.[87] Marvin Olasky has cogently criticized the deficiencies of a government-administered welfare system and suggested ways to aid the underclass that will help its members develop the attitudes and values necessary for their self-sufficiency and upward mobility.[88]

Any initiative that will meaningfully help the underclass must enable its members to satisfy the prerequisites for escaping from long-term poverty set forth by the Working Seminar on the Family and American Welfare Policy: one should finish high school; obtain employment—even at the minimum wage—and remain employed; marry when an adult, and stay married—even when it takes more than one marriage to do so.[89] The critical importance of work and marriage in stabilizing men is confirmed by data collected over a forty-five year period showing that, for men aged seventeen to twenty-five, work and marriage are the two influences which turned them away from committing further crimes. Of the teenage delinquents who found a stable job, only 32 percent went on to commit crimes, as opposed to 74 percent of those without such jobs; of those who married a woman and supported her and any children, 34 percent engaged in crime, as opposed to 76 percent of those without such a strong marital bond.[90] The "pacifying effect of marriage," as Robert

Wright observes, goes far to explain why, between ages twenty-four and thirty-five, unmarried men are about three times as likely to murder another male as are married men.[91]

How far we are from achieving the Working Seminar's goals was demonstrated by the sharp acceleration in 1991 of the decade-long decline in marriage rates. Moreover, as a director at the University of Chicago's National Opinion Research Center noted, statistics on marriage, child-bearing, and child-rearing "indicate that recent trends among whites have been mimicking earlier trends among blacks," a continuation of the pattern Moynihan identified in 1985.[92] The destructive culmination of these living patterns is now thoroughly documented in David Blankenhorn's *Fatherless America*, where he examines today's absence of males from the lives of their children.[93]

More than the welfare reform that began in 1996 will be required to reverse these trends. Realization of the Working Seminar's goals will continue to be thwarted by the institutionalization within our society of cultural values that reflect contemporary feminism's hostility towards traditional sexual morality and the traditional family. This hostility is undiminished by the fact that it has become fashionable to pay lip service to the very family values that our laws and customs undermine. As Myron Magnet has demonstrated in *The Dream and the Nightmare*, the cultural views of our affluent opinion-makers who jettisoned traditional bourgeois morality have contributed to the demoralization and impoverishment of our underclass.[94] When these affluent opinion-makers traduced traditional marriage and morality and lived together without marrying and when they destigmatized illegitimacy and defended single-motherhood, their own children may have paid the price in psychiatrists' offices and in posh drug rehabilitation programs for the wealthy that became a growth industry. But when the underclass mirrored this abandonment of traditional morality, the price *their* children paid was to remain mired in poverty and crime.

The flouting by our affluent cultural elite of what it has derided as outdated Victorian sexual morality has helped to create our present underclass, which closely resembles the underclass in nineteenth-century England. This British underclass was itself largely transformed by adoption and successful promotion of that same, now scorned, Victorian sexual morality. Regeneration of our own underclass will very likely depend upon revival of those traditional bourgeois virtues that contemporary feminism led the fight to repudiate.

A Chasm of Rancor

Accompanying the expulsion of males from black ghetto families was growth of a chasm of rancor between black men and women which led one commentator to conclude that "black men and black women seem intent on destroying each other." Typical are one woman's statement that her "basic assumption is that men are damaged . . . they're mutants like a species that's got something missing" and a man's complaint that he is "fed up with the attitude of Black women and their money-hungry games."[95] In describing the "state of crisis" of black male-female relationships, Harvard psychiatry professor Alvin Poussaint noted that "black men and women have, for the past several decades, been mired in a never-ending battle."[96] That black women college graduates now earn more than black male graduates indicates one source of the friction.[97]

This conventional hostility along sexual lines was earlier documented by Helena Z. Lopata and linked to the fact that black women are much more likely than white women to be better educated than their husbands because, except in the black community, most men marry women with equal or less educational achievement. Lower class black women's hostility toward men reflected this view that men "do not take enough responsibility for providing money and help in the home" and "they make it necessary for the woman to work"—men have gotten "lazier over the last three generations" and "think women are work horses."[98]

Alice Walker's Pulitzer Prize–winning novel *The Color Purple* manifests the depths of this hostility against black men whom she usually depicts as vile, evil, and ineffectual, while women are consistently competent and good, and lesbian love is redemptive. "A girl child ain't safe in a family of men," observes Sofia. And in Celie's view, God has acted like all the other men in her life: "Trifling, forgitful and lowdown." She knows that "wherever there's a man, there's trouble"; "men look like frogs to me," she says: "No matter how you kiss 'em, as far as I'm concern, frogs is what they stay."[99] Only when stallion males have been gelded into feminine domesticity does Walker imagine some degree of reconciliation might occur between men and women. Darryl Pinckney describes Walker's view of men as "those boulders obstructing the path to glory": "The black men are seen at a distance—that is, entirely from the point of view of the women—as naifs incapable of reflection, tyrants filled with impotent rage, or as totemic do-gooders. Walker's cards are always stacked against them."[100]

The Color Purple typifies contemporary black female literature in portraying the black man as a despicable character who is "lazy, corrupt, lecherous, violent, despotic, and the chief exploiter of the black woman."[101] Its teaching that a "girl child ain't safe in a family of men" is propagated by feminists and many in the social service establishment, both concentrating on male perversity while overlooking women's complicity in their daughters' vulnerability. Women should conduct their lives in constant awareness of the fact that, as Richard Posner has noted, studies of child sexual abuse evidence a "substantially greater propensity of stepfathers to abuse their stepdaughters than of fathers to do so"; one study showed sexual abuse of daughters by stepfathers to be seven times more likely than by biological fathers. When father-daughter incest occurs, three factors usually are present: "marital discord and a poor sexual relationship between the parents"; a "role reversal between mother and daughter which makes the daughter the central female figure in the home with the responsibility of satisfying the needs of the father"; and "conscious or unconscious condonation on the part of the mother of the relationship between father and daughter."[102] All three factors are, to some extent, subject to a mother's control.

Women greatly contribute to their daughters' vulnerability when they put them in homes with stepfathers or, more dangerously, with the women's boyfriends (an unconscionable act that denies their daughters the protection of whatever institutional constraints a regularized marriage would impose). It is certainly the case that our no-fault divorce regime has drastically impaired women's ability to maintain their children in the marital home with their natural fathers. Nevertheless, when a woman is choosing how she will organize her life, the choices she makes should reflect her responsibility to protect her daughter. Her choices must always be informed by the warning of studies showing that "a child living with one or more substitute parents was about one hundred times more likely to be fatally abused than a child living with natural parents" and that children under ten were between "thirty and forty times more likely to suffer parental abuse if living with a stepparent and a natural parent than if living with two natural parents."[103]

Most feminists, however, would ignore women's failure to act responsibly; the problem, they want us to believe, is solely one of male perversity. They would better serve familial well-being by reminding a wife in a home with young females that she must resolutely assert her own authority as the female sexual protagonist of her household. It is up to her to control the sexual activity within that home and assume responsibility for keeping her husband sexually satisfied. She leaves her daughters hostage to her failure. Thus is Celie left hostage in *The Color Purple*. In describing Celie's travail, Walker touches the bases of incestuous dysfunction: Celie, her stepfather tells her, is to do "what your mammy wouldn't"; and when Celie fills her mother's sexual role in addition to assuming her other household responsibilities, the mother, despite her suspicions, is "happy, cause he good to her now."[104]

Celie's stepfather is certainly not redeemed—nor his guilt even mitigated—by the fact that her mother (who was ill both physically and mentally) failed in her responsibilities. But focusing exclusively on his degradation (as Walker does with venomous precision) without acknowledging that—whatever the justifications—the mother did fail, sets too low a standard for a wife's contribution to her family's well-being.[105] Feminism's willingness to concentrate on what it would depict as a male propensity for perversity, without recognizing women's complicity in family pathologies, has contributed to a perception of males as figures of diminished stature in our society. Women must sometimes share responsibility for scripting the role their men play.

Just as the white community followed earlier trends among blacks by producing more families that are, in Moynihan's words, tangles of pathology, it has also allowed the same chasm of rancor to open up between men and women. The rhetoric of white feminists has consistently depicted men as the oppressors of women, and it often delighted in belittling male sexual prowess. Tom Bethell ably described this common form of attack in his coverage of a 1984 campaign rally for feminist Sonia Johnson, presidential candidate of the Citizens Party.[106] Innuendoes in the speeches evidenced a morbid phallic preoccupation warranting a suspicion that some feminists enter the political arena freighted with hostility against males which can bias all their political endeavors. This feminist fulmination against males may have reached its apex in Andrea Dworkin's *Intercourse*, where women's participation in sexual intercourse is equated with their sexual abuse, different only in degree from rape.

But beyond rhetoric is the fact that six of every ten additions made to the work force in the United States since 1950 have been female, while in 1983 the proportion of the adult male population that held jobs fell to its lowest level since the Bureau of Labor Statistics began keeping such records in 1948.[107] By 1994, when women were graduating from college at higher rates than men, the labor force participation rate of men aged 25 to 54 reached a new record low.[108] At the same time that men's labor-force participation rates continued their long-term decline to reach 75.1 percent in 1994, women's reached a new high of 58.8 percent. Men's rates are now just 28 percent higher than women's, after a steady decline from 1962, when men's rates were more than twice women's (82 percent for men and 39 percent for women).[109] "The most stunning change" disclosed by numerous studies is "the shrinking share of men who serve as traditional breadwinners—the male who works full time, year-round." In the 1970s almost 80 percent of men aged 22 to 58 performed "that basic family role"; now only 70 percent are among these "hard-core employed." Men's experience, moreover, sharply contrasts with that of women, "who are working more and at higher pay."[110]

Thus have men been withdrawing from both the marital home and the labor market. Their withdrawal is one factor contributing to the homelessness that has been a continuing symptom of our societal dysfunction.[111] As Robert Wright has observed, in an earlier era with "more equally distributed female resources," some of our male misfits might have "found a wife and adopted a lower-risk, less destructive life style" that would have kept them from "crime, drug addiction, and, sometimes, homelessness."[112] In *Violent Land*, David T. Courtwright analyzes the propensity of single young males to engage in violent behavior that has disrupted society throughout the course of American history. The "male penchant for violent, disorderly, and sexually compulsive behavior," he notes, "can be observed throughout history, across cultures, and among different primate species." In recent decades, however, there not only were "more young and therefore trouble-prone men in the population," but also "more of these men were avoiding, delaying, or terminating marriages," as the number of men living alone roughly doubled between 1960 and 1983. Society, says Courtwright, "will always be more orderly and less costly if more of its male members are domesticated." His book ends with an observation that should be pondered by anyone who thinks ill of the 1950s traditional family: "Where married men have been scarce or parental supervision wanting, violence and disorder have flourished, as in the mining camps, cattle towns, Chinatowns, black ghettos, and the small hours of the morning. But when stable family life has been the norm for men and boys, violence and disorder have diminished. That was one important reason why, during the mid-twentieth-century marriage boom, violent death rates showed a sustained decline."[113]

The Maritally Unfit

Those who value highly the institutions of marriage and family must necessarily appraise men on the basis of their fitness for marriage. To the extent that men are so appraised, the increased visibility and social acceptability of homosexual men contribute to a perception of males as less maritally fit and, therefore, as diminished figures in society. Whether or not the number of homosexual men has actually increased (a recent study showed that 2 percent of the men surveyed had engaged in homosexual sex and 1 percent considered themselves exclusively homosexual), societal awareness of their existence surely has.[114] When my generation was growing up, heterosexuals (a term which we never thought to apply to ourselves) knew few, if any, admitted homosexuals. The concept of a socially acceptable alternative to heterosexuality, other than celibacy, was not part of our cultural vocabulary. The overwhelming majority of our acquaintances married and raised families, and women almost never complained, as they now do, of men's unavailability because of their acknowledged homosexuality.

Men apparently can and will respond to society's teachings on the appropriateness of homosexual activity. As Posner has observed, "the proportion of male homosexuals who marry is higher the more intolerant the society is of homosexuals." Since "most homosexual men are capable of vaginal intercourse, although they do not find it highly pleasurable or emotionally satisfying," they will, despite their preference, "substitute heterosexual intercourse when the benefit-cost ratio shifts far enough in favor of those relations."[115] For example, the singer Tom Robinson, who was "an openly gay punk rock rebel in the late 1970's," now has a son and lives with a woman with whom he has "a long-term sexual and emotional relationship," although he acknowledges that "I still find men more sexually attractive than women."[116]

The extensive sex survey by researchers at the University of Chicago, *The Social Organization of Sexuality*, showed that 6.2 percent of the surveyed males said they were sexually attracted to males, but only 2.7 percent had had homosexual sex in the past year.[117] This response is consistent with the assumption that not all men act on their homosexual impulse. Depending on many factors, including how severely society frowns on homosexuality, the benefit-cost ratio will shift enough for some men to function as heterosexuals, marrying and reproducing even though they prefer—and possibly sometimes engage in—homosexual activity. Such was the case in ancient Greece where pederastic relationships were tolerated for a short period in a man's life, but society expected men to— and almost all did—marry and raise families.

To a heterosexual woman who values marriage and family, the blanket rejection of her sex by homosexual men—now loudly announced and encouraged, sometimes with expressions of contempt for "breeders" and men who work to support women and their broods—can appear unsettling, even somewhat dangerous. Like the ancient Greeks, this heterosexual woman may well think that those men who decline to bond with a woman, reproduce, and work to maintain a family seem like perennial juveniles. In her eyes, males are diminished when society endorses homosexuality and these perennial juveniles become much in evidence; males' stature waxes when society validates her sexual function by encouraging heterosexuality.

In the wake of the sexual revolution, our society has demonstrated an increasing tolerance of marital infidelity and instituted a regime of easy divorce that has enabled men to leave their aging wives and marry young women. *Fortune* magazine coined the term "trophy wife" to describe the glamorous replacement wives of celebrity CEOs. Then in a few years, these particular trophies themselves went out of fashion as this "walking testament to her husband's virility" was swapped for the "newer models" who had the "brains" to be "an intellectual companion as well."[118] *Fortune* has told the story of how Bill Agee's "world was irrevocably altered" when, as CEO of Bendix, he hired as his executive assistant the "attractive strawberry blonde" Harvard business school student who later became his wife, after he obtained an annulment of his first marriage—an act that might seem a spiritual, if not a legal, bastardization of his three children.[119] In what sense, one must wonder, can contemporary feminism be said to have advanced the position of women in our society when it supported no-fault divorce, the sexual revolution, and the glamorizing of market production at the expense of domesticity, all of which have led to broken marriages, mothers who are devalued and abandoned, and young women who are regarded as the trophies—of either the bimbo or brainy variety—that advertise men's success?

George Gilder has analyzed how, under the aegis of the sexual revolution, we have instituted a form of polygyny in which virile and high-achieving males co-opt "the nubile years of many young women, in a succession of wives and mistresses." Then, the homosexual choice became more attractive, as it always will—for example, in a prison culture—when young women are unavailable.[120] That there is some truth in Gilder's analysis should be apparent to all who have watched over the past years as older men left wives and children to start new families with younger women. On the periphery of familial society were left the unattached males (many of them apparently asexual or homosexual), reminiscent of outcast juvenile anthropoid apes denied access to females by the dominant males. Insofar as they are disabled from or unsuited to creating and maintaining stable families, these perennially juvenile males contribute to our societal dysfunction.

Usurpation of females by dominant males cannot, however, entirely explain this phenomenon of the maritally unfit, peripheral males. Its cause must spring, in part, both from the climate of hostility between men and women that has been engendered by contemporary feminism and from the tremendous increase in competition between boys and girls and men and women which the women's movement encouraged. As Margaret Mead has told us, failure in this competition unsexes the male —and failure has not been rare.[121] What is the connection, we should ask, between this failure and the fact that since 1995 one million men in their prime working years have disappeared from the labor force—"a mass disappearance" of prime-age men, many of whom "are just sitting at home, too discouraged to hunt for a job."[122]

FEMINISM'S SUCCESS MUST BE JUDGED against the foregoing picture of societal distress. Clearly, the widespread institutionalization of feminist ideology within our society was accompanied by a marked deterioration in the lives of many individuals who were living within families as well as of many who were unable to form or maintain families. Irrefutable proof that societal acceptance and implementation of feminist ideology caused this deterioration is not required to conclude that these facts justify derailing the feminist engine of reform and re-examining the goals that the women's movement has so successfully promoted.

Such re-examination has begun, for example, with respect to our divorce regime. As the baleful results of no-fault divorce have become increasingly evident—with its great harm to long-term housewives and the children of broken marriages—it has come under increasing attack.[123] In undertaking this re-examination of our society's plight, the familial distress that has just been outlined should, at a minimum, win a hearing for an argument supporting those who would order their lives in accordance with the vision rejected by contemporary feminism.

7

The Awakened Brünnhilde

[To punish her disobedience, Wotan, ruler of the gods, declared his daughter Brünnhilde a Valkyrie no longer:] "No more farest thou forth warriors to seek; no more bringest thou heroes to fill my hall. [On a rock] defenceless in sleep bound shalt thou lie: that man shall master the maid who shall find her and wake her from sleep [and so mastered by a husband] by the hearth to sit and spin, to all mockers a sport and shame." [Brünnhilde, now a mortal, sleeps in her helmet and armor on a rock which, granting her plea, Wotan had surrounded by fire that could be braved only by the freest and greatest of heroes, Siegfried, who removes the helmet, cuts through the armor, and awakens her with a kiss.]

[Pointing to her weapons, Brünnhilde mourns:] "And there is the shield that sheltered heroes; beside it the helmet that hid my head. They shield, they hide no more!" [Siegfried, noting that for her he had fared through furious fire without breastplate or armor, pleaded] "that blaze which guarded Brünnhilde's rock now flames fiercely in my breast! O maid, you started the fire! You can extinguish the flame!" [But Brünnhilde repulses his embrace.] "No god dared to come near! The heroes bowed and knelt to the maiden: holy came she from Walhall. Sorrow! Sorrow! Woe for my shame, how keen my disgrace! Brünnhilde am I no more!" [Siegfried rejoins] "You are still to me that slumbering maid; Brünnhilde's sleep still binds her fast. Awaken, you are my bride!"

[Brünnhilde demurs:] "My mind's in confusion, my reason sways: must all my wisdom fail me? Do not come near me with passionate frenzy; do not pursue me with masterful might." [But, says Siegfried,] "I love you: did you but love me! Mine I am no more: were you but mine! End my doubts, let me be sure that now Brünnhilde's mine!" [And Brünnhilde succumbs to the logic of his plea:] "Godly composure, change into wildness; virginal light, flare into frenzy; heavenly wisdom, fly to the winds: love, love alone inspires all my heart! Laughing I shall love you, laughing, welcome my blindness, laughing, let us be lost together, in laughter die! Farewell, Walhall's bright glittering world! Your glorious halls now may fall to dust! Farewell, proud, radiant, godly race! I live by the light of Siegfried's bright star! He's mine forever, he is my joy, my wealth, my world, my one and all!"

Richard Wagner [1]

*I*N THE FACE OF A MONOLITHIC NEGATION of her worth as a full-time wife and mother who makes marriage her career— being told, in 1996, by a "moderate" feminist that domesticity cannot be the story of an intelligent woman's life—how can a woman explain her choice of domesticity?[2] Why does she stand out against the prevailing consensus and embrace a vision that contemporary feminism has ridiculed and rejected? The story of the awakened Brünnhilde, told in the epigraph to this chapter, captures the feelings that prompted my choice. Like the Valkyrie Brünnhilde, the maiden warrior astride her horse bearing fallen warriors to Valhalla, a woman can take great pleasure in her career and contemplate its end with trepidation. But if a Siegfried awakens her to another dimension of womanhood and she bears children, she may come to view the labor of the workplace—her version of bringing warriors to Valhalla—as part of what I consider a spiritual maidenhood that her awakened femininity leads her to abandon.

Such a response may be evoked at various times in a woman's life—or not at all. In my own case, I never intended to cease working for more than a few months, having planned to give birth to my first child during an extended summer vacation. I never did return to the workplace on other than an occasional, short-term basis. I had always thought my children would be raised by nannies so that I could continue pursuing what seemed my settled and agreeable destiny as a lawyer. Yet, when that first wave of queasiness signaled my pregnancy one morning, I was overwhelmed by a sense of spectacular accomplishment. The professional achievements I had known paled into insignificance—instantly and to my utter surprise. Dressing for work, I foresaw with epiphanic clarity that I would not continue working after my baby was born.

The passage of time only reinforced the realization that, absent dire necessity, I could never devote my best personal efforts to what now seemed the much lesser task of market production and leave to surrogates the care of my baby who had become the paramount obligation of my life. This response is one part of what I call Brünnhilde's awakening. When and why, if ever, a woman does so respond depends on many factors. Among the most important, in my experience, are the ways in which she has been molded by her marital relationship, her hormonal reactions, and her sexual encounters. The woman who, at some time in her life, experiences a similar response would probably agree with Margaret Mead's description of the solid sense of irreversible achievement conferred by childbearing. She might also see herself reflected in George Eliot's observation in *Middlemarch* that after Celia's baby was born

"she had had a new sense of her mental solidity and calm wisdom":
"It seemed clear that where there was a baby, things were right
enough, and that error, in general, was a mere lack of that central
poising force."[3] Women like us are sexists. I think of myself as
defined, most essentially, by being female and very different from a
male—different from years of menstruating, from the nature of
my sexual encounters, from the priming of my body by pregnancy,
from giving birth, from nursing my babies, and from my unique
maternal—not simply parental—interactions with my children.
These differences comprise my femininity.

I have never envied males, but always loved being female and
basked in the sensual satisfactions it affords me. Delight in my
distinctive femininity distinguishes a woman like me from those
feminists who claim that sexual differences are as inconsequential
as the color of one's eyes. At the same time, while I always believed
sexual differences to be important—and reveled in those differences—I never found being female incompatible with being a lawyer.
I did decide, however, that practicing law was incompatible with
being the kind of wife and mother I wanted to be. Nor did I ever
think men's greater strength and aggressiveness insurmountably
disadvantaged me in any of the things I set out to do. Though we
are all women, those of us who eventually find that our greatest
happiness comes from feminine domesticity, and not from market
production, are worlds apart from Charlotte Perkins Gilman, Simone
de Beauvoir, Betty Friedan, Gloria Steinem, Kate Millett, Carolyn
Heilbrun, Justice Ruth Bader Ginsburg, and Hillary Rodham Clinton. The movement they promoted derides our femininity and
denounces the dependency on our husbands that makes possible
our happiness in rearing our children at home. They would remold
society to compel us to become like them and to make our delight
impossible.

Just as the metaphor of the awakened Brünnhilde captures my
response to maternity, I see women who never experience a comparable response captured in Virginia Woolf's description of Clarissa

Dalloway who "could not dispel a virginity preserved through child-birth." Mrs. Dalloway's virginity lay in her inability to be touched by the heterosexual sexual experience: she knew the warmth that she lacked and that again and again she had failed her husband.[4] I use the trope "spiritual virginity" to describe what I consider a kind of "virginity preserved through childbirth" that characterizes women who see little value in domesticity and remain relatively unbur-dened by maternal longings. Such women can happily leave their children in others' care in order to pursue their careers. Theirs is like the virginity of spiritual maidens who are never unreservedly transformed by their sensual experiences—in particular, by child-birth and its fruits. The primacy of their commitment to market production is, like Mrs. Dalloway's virginity, preserved through childbirth. Their response to motherhood—which I had been certain would be my own—accords with the ideology of contemporary feminism that is now institutionalized within our society. This ideology teaches that maintaining the primacy of her workplace commitment is precisely the reaction women *must* cultivate as the only appropriate, even healthy, response to motherhood.

To its shame, contemporary feminism promoted the sexual revolution's disparagement of maidenly physical virginity, while it deprecated the woman who failed to maintain the spiritual virginity that would enable her to resist the seductive pull of her offspring and continue to perform as a market producer. Contemporary femin-ism encouraged this spiritual virginity through the efforts examined earlier to disabuse women of the quaint notion that being a full-time wife and mother is an attractive and worthy career. Feminists would derisively dismiss my reaction to motherhood as the mawkish sentimentalism of the uneducated and unintelligent. It was their mission to deny the force and worthiness of maternal yearnings to care for one's children. Upon these yearnings was based what Simone de Beauvoir denounced as "the myth of maternity" which had to be destroyed. The crux of de Beauvoir's argument, endlessly recycled by feminist writers, is that women must maintain a spiritual virginity—although they never used this term—so that maternity and devotion to children would not interfere with the worthier market production of their maidenhood.

There is little difference, feminists have assured society, between leaving your child with caretakers and having your house cleaned and grass cut by others. Women who deny that this is so or claim that, even if true, they still enjoy rearing their own children have been told that femininity and domesticity make women parasitic inferiors to men. If a woman does not become a wage-earner, admonished feminists, she stigmatizes herself as unintelligent, unworthy, and in sociologist Jessie Bernard's words, somewhat mentally ill. The force of law in the form of no-fault divorce and numerous preferences for working women at the expense of one-earner families has augmented this completely intentional *shaming* of women into the workplace.

The choice women have made to be primarily wage-earners rather than child-rearers does indeed reflect a realistic response to the fact that, as Margaret Mead long ago noted, women cease to enjoy being women when the home is undervalued. Women's acquiescence in the feminist ideology that only market production can confer status also confirmed Mead's conclusion that social arrangements—such as the valuing of rank above everything else—can break down a mother's nurturing ties to her child. Contemporary feminism has proved the truth of Mead's claim that women can be "taught to deny their child-bearing qualities." A "series of learning-outrages" must be perpetrated by society, said Mead, "before [women] will cease to want to provide, at least for a few years, for the child they have already nourished for nine months within the safe circle of their own bodies."[5] The essence of feminism has been to perpetrate such outrages.

These learning-outrages embodied in feminism's falsifications of reality, discussed throughout this book, helped mold women into the spiritual virgins who *will* "cease to want to provide" the · daily care of their children. A mother, said Erik Erikson, is both "a parturient creature" and a member of her family and society. She must, therefore, "feel a certain wholesome relation between her biological role and the values of her community."[6] The learning-outrages perpetrated by society's institutionalization of feminist ideology taught women that little *was* wholesome in the relation between their biology and the community's values. Society made clear that it disdained any more than minimal devotion by women to the responsibilities connected with their biological role and valued women almost solely to the extent that they played the same roles as men within the public arena.

Granting that abandonment of the child-nurturing role has been a realistic response to our cultural estimation of the role's unworthiness, nonetheless, this decision must also, in some measure, have reflected women's own desires. If women wished to, they could rebel against the culture. At a time when they had no formal political status, women secured the right to vote. Although now a majority of the electorate, women have made little effort to reform our no-fault divorce laws which imperil the homemaker. Women have apparently acquiesced in this societal mechanism calculated to compel their abandonment of domesticity, just as they have acquiesced in the stigmatization of marriage as a career for women and the denigration of their devotion to child-nurturing. They have, at the same time, championed female educational and job preferences and other market interferences that disfavor men who might become family breadwinners for women at home. Women would seem to have chosen the feminist way. *They cannot have it both ways* by then claiming that they really would like to stay at home, if only they had husbands able and willing to support them.

When the founding mothers of contemporary feminism broke the women's pact, many women agreed that they would rather be Valkyries than awakened Brünnhildes, and so they cantered off to their Valhalla, the marketplace. Most women are neither cowards nor impotent victims. When society tells them that the rank conferred by a career is all important and that maternal child-nurturing must be sacrificed to it, many will defy society if they believe this not to be so. It has been my experience both as a market producer and mother at home that determined women in our society are very successful at getting what they want. If women want to destroy the remnants of patriarchy and become virtually fungible with men, I believe that—unless a significant number of our effete, attenuated, androgynous males undergo a rapid metamorphosis—women can do so. But before they do, I would have women consider whether their acquiescence in the feminist ideology our culture promotes does not rest solely on an intellectual evaluation of its message. If women do not defy that ideology, it is partly because they do not *feel* it is wrong. And they do not *feel* it is wrong because many of them are responding with the constricted emotions of a spiritual virgin.

THE SEXUAL EXPERIENCE THAT OVERWHELMS

Feminism's goal that women hold one-half of the economically and politically powerful positions in the country requires women's full-time commitment to market production throughout most of their lives. But such a commitment precludes a woman's significant personal attention to child-rearing, domesticity, and cultivating her marital relationship. Spiritual virginity of a critical mass of women is, therefore, prerequisite to achieving the feminist goal. Andrea Dworkin's *Intercourse* graphically illustrates why this is so. Again, although I reject her ultimate conclusions, I find her writing on this subject to be a dramatic acknowledgment that an awakened Brünnhilde will not be inclined to assume her proportionate share of market production.

Dworkin expresses great distaste for heterosexual sexual intercourse. Discussing homosexual sex in a chapter entitled "Communion," on the other hand, she softens her tone as a certain tenderness replaces the vitriol. Sex as "communion" which brings peace and redemption can occur, she apparently believes, only between homosexuals. Contrasted with sex as communion, her chapter entitled "Stigma" examines the heterosexuality of Stanley Kowalski in Tennessee Williams's *A Streetcar Named Desire*: "He is the prototypical male animal, without remorse. Each act of sex or act of animal exhibition of virility is nature, not art." Stella, Stanley's wife, explains her reconciliation to his lower class crudity by saying: "But there are things that happen between a man and a woman in the dark—that sort of make everything else seem—unimportant."[7]

Now, Stella is right, Dworkin perceives that she is right, and this is why Dworkin counsels women to reject heterosexual sexual intercourse. But if they do not reject it, then like Blanche, Stella's sister, they should seek a sexuality of tenderness, as opposed to Stanley's animal sexuality: Blanche desired "a lover with a sensibility the opposite of Stanley's, not traditionally masculine, animalistic, aggressive." Repulsed by "ordinary masculinity," Blanche cherished the memory of love for her dead husband, a boy who "was gentle, nervous, beautiful, with 'a softness and tenderness which wasn't like a man's,'" a boy who killed himself after she found him in a room with an older man.[8]

The very popular movie version of *A Streetcar Named Desire* with Marlon Brando was released when I was in law school. In our discussions, residents of my graduate women's dormitory gave little indication that the boy Blanche chose could inspire their fantasies; most of us had not acquired the current feminist distaste for "ordinary masculinity." But we garnered fodder aplenty for our fantasies when Stella walked down the stairs, not into the arms of a gentle, nervous, beautiful boy of unmanly softness and tenderness, but into those of the traditionally masculine, animalistic, aggressive Kowalski in the torn undershirt. Tennessee Williams's stage directions for this scene are proof that one can surely teach what one does not do: "Stella slips down the rickety stairs in her robe. Her eyes are glistening with tears and her hair loose about her throat and shoulders. They stare at each other. Then they come together with low, animal moans. He falls to his knees on the steps and presses his face to her belly, curving a little with maternity. Her eyes go blind with tenderness as she catches his head and raises him level with her. He snatches the screen door open and lifts her off her feet and bears her into the dark flat."[9]

This is one of the film scenes women often say they find erotic; the obeisance Stanley pays to Stella's maternity is not the least important reason why this is so. Another favorite is the scene in *On the Waterfront* where Brando (again traditionally masculine and aggressive) breaks into his girlfriend's apartment, while she huddles on the bed in her slip waiting to see what he will do with her. That feminist bugbear, *Gone With the Wind*'s Rhett and Scarlett on the staircase, is somewhat deficient. Notwithstanding her smile the next morning, the suspicion lingers that Scarlett never did learn to enjoy sex with a masculine man like Rhett very much (she resembled Blanche in pining for someone with "a softness and tenderness which wasn't like a man's"—the wimp Ashley), and it won't make a good fantasy unless the woman likes it.

In our fantasies, most of us would probably have polished Kowalski's rough edges a bit and perhaps given him a higher standard of living; we were, after all, graduate students looking forward to professional careers and would not picture ourselves in the lower class. But in bed, Kowalski would do just fine; there, contrary to Dworkin, we believed it was nature and not art that would satisfy. Inelegance characterizes the nitty gritty of the sexual encounter. It is precisely a fleshly, not an artistic, endeavor, unless artistry simply means the man's ability to secure the woman's sexual gratification. So satisfied by his sexual artistry, a woman finds it easy to agree with Stella that a great deal *is* required to weigh in the balance "against the way her husband uses her in the dark."[10] Thus, Dworkin's erotic turn of phrase dramatically acknowledges—what one would think indisputable—that satisfying sex goes far to make a marriage worthwhile.

But Stella's perspective is fatally defective, Dworkin argues, precisely because her relationship with her husband makes everything else unimportant: "The wife, raised to be refined, wants the animal passion of her husband, not anything else that she has had or could be. All her past of sensibility and taste means nothing to her against the way her husband uses her in the dark."[11] While Scarlett's smile implied that her usage in the night afforded *some* glimmering of sexual delight, Tennessee Williams's stage directions for the next morning depict a Stella suffused with knowledge of transforming sexual satisfaction: "Stella is lying down in the bedroom. Her face is serene in the early morning sunlight. One hand rests on her belly, rounding slightly with new maternity. . . . Her eyes and lips have that almost narcotized tranquility that is in the faces of Eastern idols."[12] Thus she lies, serene and tranquil. What greater gifts can life afford than serenity and tranquility?

Stella is an awakened Brünnhilde who abandoned her own Southern Valhalla's bright glittering world, glorious halls, and proud, radiant, godly race for a husband who would be her joy, her wealth, her world, her one and all. For the passion of *her* Siegfried (in the less than heroic form of Stanley Kowalski) and for her expected child, Stella abandoned the "aspirations of her own" that have become a feminist cliché. Stella represents contemporary feminism's most dangerous enemy—the contented traditional housewife. A woman like Stella wallows (wallow: to indulge oneself fully with animal pleasure or luxurious enjoyment) in her contentment. Her husband takes her and, as her body overcomes her mind, she is transformed—wrung out, as it were. When he finishes and she lies in his arms—breasts still tingling, belly still exploding—her solace for the postcoital *tristesse* is the realization that in not too long a time the miraculous event will occur again.

Such a woman might be familiar with a response like Rebeca's to Jose Arcadio in Gabriel García Márquez's *One Hundred Years of Solitude*: "She had to make a supernatural effort not to die when a startlingly regulated cyclonic power lifted her up by the waist and despoiled her of her intimacy with three slashes of its claws and quartered her like a little bird. She managed to thank God for having been born before she lost herself in the inconceivable pleasure of that unbearable pain, splashing in the steaming marsh of the hammock which absorbed the explosion of blood like a blotter."[13]

When, with regularity, a woman experiences sexual pleasure that, as did Rebeca's, evokes her thanks to God for having been born, she increasingly delights in her femininity and feels herself to be precious. Ever softening, she becomes self-satisfied, less competitive, less aggressive, and she bonds more thoroughly to her husband and the children created and commemorated in these encounters. The women's movement will be hard pressed to send a Brünnhilde so awakened back to the Valhalla of the marketplace. This is why Dworkin knows that the woman must remain a spiritual virgin, largely unchanged by the sexual encounter. More conducive to this end, in all likelihood, will be the sexual ministrations of the gentle, nervous, beautiful boy, with the "softness and tenderness which wasn't like a man's"—the paradigmatic androgynous, sensitive male of feminist ideology.

How does Dworkin depict the experience of sexual intercourse for women like Stella and Rebeca? Women, she says, experience sexual intercourse "—when it works, when it overwhelms—as possession; and feel possession as deeply erotic; and value annihilation of the self in sex as proof of the man's desire or love . . . ; and sex itself is an experience of diminishing self-possession, an erosion of self." Then Dworkin very eloquently and dramatically asserts that "the physical rigors of sexual possession—of being possessed— overwhelm the body's vitality; and while at first the woman is fierce with the pride of possession—he wants her enough to empty her out—her insides are worn away over time, and she, possessed, becomes weak, depleted, usurped in all her physical and mental energies and capacities by the one who has physically taken her over; by the one who occupies her."

In the end, she concludes, the woman's "body is used up; and the will is raped."[14] Dworkin's is an excellent description of the effect which the sex that works, that overwhelms, can have on a woman's mind and emotions, but hardly on her body. Even granting Dworkin hyperbolic license, she cannot fairly claim that the average middle-class Western woman (who is rarely weakened by repetitive child-bearing with inadequate medical care) is made physically weak and depleted by sexual intercourse or that her "insides are worn away over time."

But Dworkin's words do accurately depict the emotional reaction of some women to the sexual experience "when it works, when it overwhelms." The woman she describes is like Ferdinand the Bull, smelling the flowers. Stella and Rebeca—luxuriating in what Tennessee Williams styled the "almost narcotized tranquility that is in the faces of Eastern idols"—wallow in their contentment, just as in the children's story by Monroe Leaf, Ferdinand blissfully lies in a field of flowers, having politely declined the bullring and confrontation with the matador. Read against this metaphor, Dworkin's shockingly dramatic words authentically depict the reality of some women's experience. Beginning her book prepared to scoff, I saw myself reflected in her words. While Dworkin shrinks in horror from the experience she describes, I attest to its delights and would see it shared by as many women as possible.

It is the awakened Brünnhilde whom Dworkin portrays. The self that is annihilated in the sex that works, that overwhelms, is the self of the maidenly Brünnhilde who energetically strived in the bullring of the marketplace. And the annihilation *is* indeed proof of the man's love, because loss of the maidenly Brünnhilde's will to strive in that marketplace requires a man to assume the husband's responsibility of providing and caring for her and their children. The woman, says Dworkin, feels that the man "wants her enough to empty her out." The man, however, often will scarcely understand what has happened. Women who experience this transformation must explain to men that, like Ferdinand amongst the flowers, the awakened Brünnhilde who takes delight in bearing children and nursing them and providing their daily care finds herself emptied of aggressiveness, competitiveness, and ambition to achieve in the workplace.

This woman's body, Dworkin laments, "is used up; and the will is raped." Dworkin's lament reprises the wail of the maidenly Brünnhilde who, when awakened by Siegfried's kiss, points to her broken breastplate and helmet and mourns "Brünnhilde am I no more!"; her mind is in confusion, her reason sways, all wisdom fails her. No longer would she be dedicated to the vocation of Valkyrie; she would expend herself in passion for Siegfried (although her death foreclosed fruition of that passion in childbirth). The Brünnhilde who is no more is the striving maiden with aspirations of her own. The will that Dworkin describes as raped is the will to achieve in the workplace. It is this will that keeps the woman's analytical mind racing, thus functioning to inhibit her body's response to sexual passion. It was this will's submission to the body that Brünnhilde invoked when she cried: "Godly composure, change into wildness; virginal light, flare into frenzy; heavenly wisdom, fly to the winds . . . . Laughing I shall love you, laughing, welcome my blindness." The blindness she welcomes is the freeing of her body from the inhibiting constraints of her analytical mind, the restless, questing mind that can muffle, even kill, sexual passion in women.

SPIRITUAL VIRGINITY

What is wrong with Brünnhilde's choice? In Henrik Ibsen's *A Doll's House*, Nora repudiates this choice because her Siegfried, Torvald, is not heroic enough. When tested in battle he disappointingly displays the human frailties of selfishness and cowardliness that prevent him from making the most wonderful thing in the world happen for her: "when the miracle failed to happen," Nora reproaches Torvald, "I realized you weren't the man I'd thought you to be."[15] Nora, a precursor of contemporary feminists, deems neither the flawed Torvald nor her children begotten by him to be worthy of her further devotion. Dworkin impugns Brünnhilde's choice by asserting that "the lover discards the body when it is used up, throws it away, an old, useless thing, emptied, like an empty bottle," a puissant argument, indeed, in an era of no-fault divorce and trophy wives.[16]

But even if all husbands were forever loyal, Dworkin's analysis cannot countenance the choice Brünnhilde makes. The sex that works—that overwhelms—is felt by the woman, says Dworkin, as being possessed by the man: "Each act of possession is a sensual derangement for the woman—physical, overpowering, consuming; and each act of possession illuminates the meaning of sex in which the woman is owned by the man, her body becoming his. The physical and spiritual impact of this sexual dominance is on the integrity of the woman."[17]

In succumbing to this sexual dominance, the woman compromises her integrity (that is, diminishes her wholeness) by accepting "tiny boundaries and degraded possibilities." Dworkin, therefore, counsels women to adopt the "rebel virginity" of Joan of Arc and her guardian saints, Saint Catherine and Saint Margaret. A woman like Joan "wants what men have," Dworkin declares, "and to have what men have one must be what men are"; to this end, Joan assumed a male vocation and male clothes that established the militancy of her virginity, "hostile to men who would want her for sex and hostile to female status altogether."[18]

Dworkin contrasts with the virgin Joan the adulterous Emma Bovary who, taking no delight in marital sex or its fruits, was surely no awakened Brünnhilde. But she well serves Dworkin's purpose of demonstrating the perils of "having a mind filled with fantasies rather than ideas or possibilities, having no purpose or commitment, having no action, no vocation, only the boring chores and obligations of domesticity." Lacking the power that men have, Emma does not live "in a wide world" and "she cannot make opportunities in her confined domesticity." Let women heed the message of Emma's suicide: "Romance was her suicidal substitute for action; fantasy her suicidal substitute for a real world, a wide world. And intercourse was her suicidal substitute for freedom."[19]

From Emma's tragic example, admonishes Dworkin, women should learn to preserve virginity. But it need not be the physical kind. Virginity can also be viewed as "not yet having been subsumed: one's being is still intact, penetrated or not."[20] What Dworkin terms the virginity of a woman whose being remains intact though she is penetrated is, of course, what I call spiritual virginity. It describes the woman for whom sex does not work in the sense that it never thoroughly overwhelms; the woman who is not transformed by the sexual encounter in the sense that neither her sexual experiences nor their fruition ever change the portion of herself that she holds separate and aloof. This portion which she keeps always intact—what Virginia Woolf called the "wedge-shaped core of darkness" of being oneself—is her maiden selfhood and identity as a market producer that will remain forever inviolate.

The appeal of Dworkin's book lies in its recognition that sexual intercourse is a momentous event, so much so that she urges women to resist its lure. Feminist sexual revolutionaries denied its importance and stood at the forefront of the sexual revolution to encourage women's participation in the casual sexual intercourse that it portrayed as a trivial event, little more significant than solitary masturbation. Allan Bloom's female college student who described sexual intercourse as "no big deal" had well absorbed this message. But on Dworkin's pages, sexual intercourse is a very big deal, a recognition that, in my view, represents one of the few steps a feminist activist has ever taken in the right direction. Her book has touched me more than any other feminist writing; reading it, I constantly exclaimed "she's absolutely right." I agree with Dworkin that sexual experiences can profoundly affect women. We agree also, I believe, as to what these effects can be: a dulling of the woman's competitive and aggressive drives; a lessening of her appetite for success in the wide world; and a turning inward to a circle of domesticity, often enlivened by fantasy and romantic dreams.

About the joys of a Brünnhilde who has been awakened by transforming sexual experiences—including the child-bearing and -nurturing that are the fruits of her sexual encounters—Dworkin does not speak. Hers is nonetheless a powerful testimony to the experience of the penetrated woman whose being remains intact, her maiden selfhood and identity unchanged, perhaps even untouched. Physical virginity should always be seen as an acceptable option for a woman, whether it is imposed by circumstance or reflects religious commitment, emotional dictates, or physical disinclination. Virginity was essential to Joan of Arc's success in the wide world. There is no reason to doubt that some of the women who place paramount importance on such success can also be well served by this choice, just as some of them can find that spiritual virginity serves their needs. It is clear, however, that there are other women who are not well served by spiritual virginity. Much of Dworkin's seemingly outrageous philippic is a vehemently, often eloquently, articulated demonstration of this fact.

Spiritual Virginity's Sometimes Painful Price

Dworkin's chapters entitled "Occupation/Collaboration" and "Dirt/ Death" are agonized cries of outrage from an unawakened female participant in sexual intercourse. Clearly, some—possibly many—women would scoff at and reject an experience like the one I describe as Brünnhilde's awakening, since it is a response that can seriously compromise the version of identity and selfhood most compatible with their market achievement. Yet even as Dworkin denounces the destruction of women's integrity by such an awakening, she powerfully voices the painful despair that can accompany its absence.

"Awakening," as I use the term, encompasses far more than the orgasmic outcome of the sexual encounter. It reflects Roger Scruton's perception that orgasm is not the ultimate end of sexual desire, but in "a very important sense, it is an *interruption* of congress, from which the subject must recover, as and when he can." To see orgasm as the aim of desire is as misguided, he says, "as to see the exultation experienced by a player upon scoring a goal as the aim of football, rather than as a pleasurable offshoot of an aim fulfilled." The aim of sexual desire is fulfilled, declares Scruton, by "union with the other."[21] Certainly, when one plays out the game of erotic love on the field of the bed, orgasm—whether viewed as an interruption or a facilitation (I think the latter term a better description)—is only one, and not the final, segment of the enterprise. Sexual encounters that fall short of this paradigm are often characterized by the woman's thwarted isolation and the man's self-deceiving ineptitude, plights described with stunning precision by Gabriel García Márquez in *Love in the Time of Cholera*: "She was left dangling, barely at the entrance of her tunnel of solitude, while he was already buttoning up again, as exhausted as if he had made absolute love on the dividing line between life and death, when in reality he had accomplished no more than the physical act that is only a part of the feat of love."[22]

What, then, beyond orgasmic explosiveness, is the content of the female's awakening through union with the other? It is to be assured that in her unique femaleness she is a delight. All of her is delightful: the smelly, bleeding parts, the parts swollen in pregnancy, the parts scarred from childbirth. It is to be enveloped by the secure confidence of knowing that simply her femaleness—not what she does or strives to do in escape from that femaleness—endears her to the man and secures his pleasure. It is to bask in the certitude that being female is a wonderful thing: she need not try to become like a male, because the femininity that makes her so very different from the male is a beautiful and worthy attribute that makes her precious. It is to be awash—on going to sleep, and on arising, and on going about her daily tasks—with an ever-present awareness that everything is "just right." This "just right" feeling, which may last, if she is lucky, until its renewal with the next sexual encounter, must be deemed the principal gift of her awakening.

How does Dworkin view femaleness? She tells us that because of the "slit between the legs" the woman's body has no integrity. The woman "is intended to have a lesser privacy, a lesser integrity of the body, a lesser sense of self, since her body can be physically occupied": "She is defined by how she is made, that hole, which is synonymous with entry; and intercourse, the act fundamental to existence, has consequences to her being that may be intrinsic, not socially imposed." The woman is "made for intercourse: for penetration, entry, occupation," "all of which are construed to be normal and also fundamental to continuing human existence," which is dependent on women's compliance.[23] On a single page, Dworkin thrice acknowledges that women *must* participate in sexual intercourse if human existence is to continue. And they must also (although this she never articulates) submit to the inevitability of the pain that childbirth usually entails.

Dworkin does not exaggerate the role a woman's biology plays in her life. Women's lives are defined by the knowledge that survival of our species requires us to submit to sexual intercourse and childbirth. This knowledge rivets our attention from our earliest years, and it is a frightening burden. Dworkin speaks the truth. Any woman who thinks about what she says must know it is true. No one should say it is not so. But they do. A reviewer of Queen Victoria's biography, for example, referred to the Queen's "genuinely Victorian ideas about sex," implying that her ideas were false and unenlightened.[24] They were not; Victoria, like Dworkin, spoke truly. Child-bearing, said Victoria, "was not only dangerous and agonising, but 'a complete violence to all one's feelings of propriety (which God knows receive a shock enough in marriage alone).'"[25]

Childbirth surely does do violence to one's feelings of propriety; the one benefit of the pain is that you lose all concern for propriety. The danger is still a reality for women, although no doubt now exaggerated through the etching in women's cultural memory of dangers past. The agony remains, especially when, in thrall to "naturalness" or in response to financial constraints, women are encouraged to endure as much as they can before using the pain relief that will be made available. To whoever questions Victoria's appraisal of childbirth, I commend the description, which seems accurate to me, from the poem "Parturition" by a feminist predecessor, Mina Loy:

> *I am climbing a distorted mountain of agony. . . .*
> *Something in the delirium of night-hours*
> *Confuses while intensifying sensibility*
> *Blurring spatial contours*
> *So aiding elusion of the circumscribed*
> *That the gurgling of a crucified wild beast*
> *Comes from so far away*
> *And the foam on the stretched muscles of a mouth*
> *Is no part of myself*
> *There is climax in sensibility*
> *When pain surpassing itself*
> *Becomes Exotic* [26]

In a society that grooms its women to work until giving birth, to toss off a baby and leave the hospital within two or three days, and then return to work within a few months, if not sooner, childbirth and children have become peripheral to what are considered the important activities of the marketplace. Women are expected to do it as quietly as possible, without any fuss; to dwell on childbirth's pain seems in unfashionably poor taste. But women are affected, nonetheless. Seymour Fisher's study of women's reactions to their birth experiences led him to query whether we "have underestimated the seriousness of the damage which may be done to a woman's personality defenses and control as the result of the delivery demands?" The average woman, he says, experiences "pain greater than that she has ever before encountered," persisting for "an extended period of time," and taking on an "intolerable intensity," so that she "begins to doubt that she can sustain it." What deeply impresses her is "the uncontrollable nature of her suffering" and the fact that it is "inevitable." However low the fatality rate today, women, nevertheless, experience a "buildup of anxiety about the possibility of serious injury or death": "Few women involved in the painful delivery sequence do not entertain some fantasies that they will be grossly injured ('ripped') or suffer a fatal complication."[27]

That many women still find childbirth agonizing helps explain their willingness to deliver by caesarean section, now the most common major surgery in the United States. Used in 5.5 percent of births in 1970, caesareans soared to 24.7 percent in 1988, about twice what is believed appropriate. It is estimated that 420,000 unnecessary caesareans are performed each year, a fact the American Hospital Association attributes to "women's preferences and the fear of malpractice suits."[28] These preferences reflect, in part, acceptance of a caesarean as the relief which "that blessed chloroform," as she called it, was for Queen Victoria.[29] Acceptance of a caesarean may also indicate a loss of the resilience which helps reconcile a woman to the pain and messiness that are among the trappings of being female. How does she retain this precious resilience when her society devalues femininity and affirms those women whose lives most closely approximate men's? When women are told that they must try with all their might to compete equally in the marketplace with men and childless women, some may find too great a discontinuity in undertaking the vaginal delivery where they would quintessentially act as female. This delivery's only perceived advantage may be that its shorter recovery period can enable her to resume market production sooner.

Neither did Victoria speak falsely in recounting the sexual encounter's initial shock to one's feelings of propriety. Indecorous is not an inapt description of what occurs in that encounter, a fairly messy and inelegant physical activity. When the educated woman of culture and refinement enters the sexual realm, the path may indeed be long that she must travel from inhibition to abandonment. The evidence is clear that Victoria, at least, successfully negotiated the journey. This is the fact that, as noted earlier, she most charmingly acknowledged when she responded to her doctor's warning against having further children by asking him "with a sinking heart: 'Can I have no more fun in bed?'"[30]

Women's recognition that they must submit to the inevitability of pain is like the grain of sand in an oyster. Nothing in men's experience is quite comparable. Even the spy who risks torture knows he can always confess. Confession will not release the woman from the agony of childbirth. In order to experience the full dimensions of female biology she must embrace inevitability. Her fear must be faced and in some way mastered. It will probably be tamed through incorporation as a component of her eroticism. How she does this helps shape the fantasies that may accompany her on the course of sexual arousal.[31] And how she does this also helps shape the kind of woman and wife and mother she will be.

Rare is the woman, I suspect, who does not recall something of herself in Dworkin's description of the little girl taking up a mirror and looking at the slit between her legs "to see if it *could* be true—is there an entrance to her body down there? and something big comes into it? (how?) and something as big as a baby comes out of it? (how?) and doesn't that hurt?"[32] The little girl knows it will hurt. What goes inside may fit, but she scarcely believes a baby can come out. Not out of there; maybe from the back where things already come out. Or maybe the button in her belly somehow opens up to let the baby out—a little girl's wishful fantasy that is realized in the caesarean section.

This frightened little girl must try to coat the grain of sand which is her shame and fear and transform the irritant into a pride and self-esteem in being female that will become the foundation for her sexual gratification. Such transformation is facilitated when a woman is assured by society and, especially, by the male to whom she submits (the male who masters the maid) that her femaleness is revered, that honor is *due and will be paid* to her distinctively feminine attributes: her menstruation, gestation, child-bearing, lactation, and child-nurturing endeavors. Thus, Stanley Kowalski's obeisance to Stella's child-filled belly engendered the scene's eroticism, as the predicate to Stella's sexual fulfillment.

For the spiritual virgin, however, no honor resides simply in being female. Society has taught her—often with the complicity of the male to whom she has submitted and for whom she has borne children—that although penetrated and a child-bearer, she is unworthy unless she also labors in the marketplace as the competitor of men, her femininity a burden of baggage, and its demands (including her children) only a peripheral aspect of her life that merit no more than her minimal personal attention. She has acceded to the lesson. Dworkin's writing is witness that for some of these women the grain of sand is never coated; the fear and self-loathing forever irritate, unassuaged. It is precisely such fear and self-loathing that is expressed, for example, in a "bleed-in" demonstration where college women litter the ground with used tampons.[33] Theirs is the action of women who are neither stupid nor crazy, but terribly anguished.

Yet Dworkin does not know how to assuage the pain. She knows why sexual intercourse is bad, but not how to go about making it good. It is bad, she says, because it does not matter to the man "that in entering her, he is entering this one, real, unique individual." It is bad because entry for the woman "is the first acceptance in her body that she is generic, not individual; that she is one of a many that is antagonistic to the individual interpretation she might have of her own worth, purpose, or intention."[34] Is not Dworkin rightly demanding that the woman be approached with what Roger Scruton calls "individualising intentionality?"

Assuaging the Pain

"In desire," says Scruton, "I wish to find a unity between your bodily and your personal identity, and to hold in your body the soul that speaks and looks from it." Sexual desire "is directed towards the embodiment of the other," with an "individualising intentionality" which makes "the perspective of the other" "real to us in his embodiment, and which provides our most immediate image of his irreplaceable individuality."[35] For Scruton, the proper objective of desire is not to regard the other as the "instrument . . . of sexual release," but "to know him from the inside, as a creature who is part of oneself." "I do not want to press against your flesh for the sake of whatever comfortable sensation this may provide," he says, "but for the sake of the consciousness with which your flesh is saturated": "The aim of desire is first to incarnate the first-person perspective (the for-itself) of the other; and secondly to unite with it as flesh."[36] Now this is the stuff of romance. It must be perfectly clear to any reader that Scruton is not talking about just getting laid; the casual sex of the sexual revolution is incapable of fulfilling the aim of desire as Scruton describes it.

Delineating a theory of sexual desire that views the woman as vastly more than an instrument for release of sexual tension, Scruton requires the male to comply with Dworkin's demand for acknowledgment that, when entering the woman, he is "entering this one, real, unique individual." But how does the woman know? Because he tells her so? Surely not. In sexual transactions—as in child-rearing—mere words of commitment and affection mean little. It is what one does all the time, every day, that counts. As Zora Neale Hurston's John Pearson so well put it: "You know better'n tuh b'lieve anything uh man tell yuh after ten o'clock at night."[37] A woman *can only* know through the life the man constructs with her, through how he makes her feel as a female, through what he is to her and does for her compared to what she does for him by bearing his children. It is easy for a man to give these assurances to Brünnhilde by assuming the traditional provider role, for that is what she wants from him. But what can a man do to assure the spiritual virgin? She largely does it all for herself.

Intercourse, Dworkin tells us, makes the woman feel that "she is generic, not individual; that she is one of a many." This is surely true of the casual sexual intercourse promoted by the sexual revolution. But what of marital sex? Midge Decter tells us that because of the male's undifferentiated lust for femaleness, each woman is "an undifferentiated member of a species," and must "establish herself as a differentiated individual." Since it is men who "have placed her in the crowd, they have a unique authority to single her out from it"; the woman must "use the power of her abstract desirability to wrest the acknowledgment of her concrete irreplaceability."[38] If Decter is right, far from making women generic, sexual intercourse can most surely establish their individuality.

Dworkin claims, however, that intercourse does not accomplish this goal for the woman who, entered, "finds herself depersonalized into a function"; entered, "she has mostly given something up."[39] She is speaking of a spiritual virgin, her being intact, untransformed by an act which she experiences as largely confined to providing what Scruton calls the "curious pleasure" of pressing against another's flesh. The Brünnhilde who is assured of her concrete irreplaceability by the loyal Siegfried sharing her life cannot possibly think she has given something up and, except for that "curious pleasure," gotten little in return. So great is Brünnhilde's delight in all she has gotten in return that she might echo Clarissa Dalloway's sentiment, which was evoked by what she perceived as the sacramental beauty of her life—although not of her marital sexual experiences: to "her husband, who was the foundation of it," Clarissa knew she somehow "must pay back from this secret deposit of exquisite moments."[40]

The woman pretends, Dworkin laments, that "pleasure is in being reduced through intercourse to insignificance": "Intercourse is the pure, sterile, formal expression of men's contempt for women." "When," she demands, "will they choose not to despise us?"[41] Certainly, the casual sexual intercourse to which women have submitted at the urging of feminist sexual revolutionaries is nothing more than an expression of men's contempt for them, because it is intercourse without commitment, the terms of which most women experience as contrary to their interests, but which sexually predatory men will always impose when they are allowed to. The abortions to which so many women have also submitted have guaranteed the sterility of these sexual encounters. Eloquently, Dworkin asserts that "it is a tragedy beyond the power of language to convey when what has been imposed on women by force becomes a standard of freedom for women: and all the women say it is so."[42]   But her words indict the wrong culprit if they allege that men imposed this so-called sexual freedom upon women. Men did not do this to women; women did it to themselves and to each other.

Dworkin's argument has been compared by Barbara Herman to Immanuel Kant's conclusion in *The Metaphysics of Morals* that sexual interest in another presents a moral problem, because "it is not interest in the other as a person" but only as a "body or body part." Kant concluded that the problem can only be resolved through the legal institution of marriage in which "sexuality leads to a union of human beings" where gratification of sexual desire depends upon the right of each of the spouses to dispose over the other's "person as whole: over the welfare and happiness and generally over all the circumstances of that person."[43]   This truth, to which the intellect of one of the world's philosophical giants led him, is one that Brünnhilde knows in her bones. It was also part of the cultural knowledge of the average, unsophisticated high school girl of my generation.

Brünnhilde also knows that men will stop using women with contempt only when women insist upon respectful treatment— insist, that is, on sexual treatment that is Kantian and morally based, not Posnerian and morally indifferent. It is probably towards the goal of demanding respectful usage that "rape crisis" feminists are working in their clumsy fashion. But a woman will never command respectful treatment from men if she thinks of herself as an op-pressed victim, or if she follows the injunction of feminist sexual revolutionaries to prove her equality with men by mimicking male promiscuity. She should decline to act like an ersatz male, view her femininity with pride, and shun the casual sex that proclaims contempt for femininity's distinctively diffuse sexuality. Without apology or diffidence, a woman can use her power of the groined archway to secure the male's affirmation of her individual worth as female by his honoring and accepting responsibility for all the feminine baggage that comes with being female.

In what concrete way does Dworkin claim men's usage of women in the sex act evidences contempt? She never explicitly tells us; the accusation is bald. But a coherent explanation may be found in her jeremiad. *Men show their contempt for women when they use us only for the purpose they could use another male.* Seemingly to scoff, Dworkin quotes Norman Mailer's reference to the "feminine male" in prison who is "despised" because he is used: "one is a woman without the power to be female." Again, she quotes Mailer on homosexual sex: "the result can be no more than a transaction—pleasurable, even all-encompassing, but a transaction—when no hint remains of the awe that a life in these circumstances can be conceived." He means, says Dworkin, that it is "the woman's potential to reproduce that distinguishes and affirms the real man": "Sensual pleasure is not what distinguishes homosexual sodomy" from heterosexual sexual intercourse: "the woman bearing the child does—in religion, in Mailer."[44] And I would add, in real life as well.

Simply bearing the child, however, does not encompass the full range of the power to be female and so does not necessarily affirm a woman as female. She has done that for him. What does he do for her? For some of us, femaleness will only be affirmed by dependence on the male, by the fact of his care of us, by the knowledge that because of what we, in our unique capacity as a female, do for him, he provides for us and our children. By so doing, he enables us fully to exercise the power to be female by developing the potentially vast child-nurturing dimension of femininity. Because it is never intended to accomplish any of these goals (not even childbirth, without more), casual sexual intercourse—whatever its orgasmic outcome—can never affirm our femaleness. *Casual sex constricts the woman's usage in sex to providing release of sexual tension, just as another man could provide.*

By the same token, to tell the woman that, though penetrated and a child-bearer, she must act like a man and devote herself to market production will, in the eyes of some women, so constrict the ability of the sex act to affirm her worth as distinctively female that, in its intentionality, her usage in sex will differ little from usage of another man. This is so because demands of marketplace performance must always diminish a woman's commitment to the responsibilities integral to her biological role. It is precisely for this reason that contemporary feminists consistently derided femininity. They rightly saw that femininity's demands—most especially, women's choice of domesticity in response to their maternal yearnings—are completely inconsistent with women's full-time commitment to market production that is necessary to make women equivalent to men.

To the extent, therefore, that her market activities prevent a woman from developing the distinctively feminine aspects of her nature and insofar as she is not dependent upon her husband, her role in sexual intercourse is logically akin to that of a male, who is defined by his lack of power to be female. Nature imposes his lack. Hers results from constriction of her distinctively feminine role, a constriction that must necessarily circumscribe the intentionality of the man's usage of her in sex. With her femininity so constricted by the demands of market performance, her usage in sex will differ from usage of another man largely to the extent of her service in giving birth. But such service clearly constitutes only a portion of femininity's potential dimensions. The soul that speaks and looks from her body in the sex act remains that of a market-producing co-worker of her husband: on her part, no dependency upon him; on his part, no dominance through assumption of responsibility for her.

Benefits accrue from this arrangement: for both, higher income; for him, freedom from the breadwinner's responsibility; for her, status in the public arena, divorce insurance, and whatever pleasure she derives from market production. To the man, she is precisely what contemporary feminism demanded she must be: a financially independent roommate who is a full-time market producer, much like himself. Clearly, many women seem satisfied with such an arrangement. But for those women who can and would delight in having their femininity blossom in maternal and domestic roles, the arrangement seems constricted and sterile. And the intentionality of the man's sexual ministrations within such an arrangement must be similarly constricted. These ministrations are not designed to embody an individual who delights in developing her feminine role to its fullest dimensions, but to embody one who must narrow that feminine role sufficiently to become fungible with, and thus more closely resemble, her husband. This is why, in so using her, the man can be said to demonstrate despite of femininity. Women have thus harvested what feminism sowed; for some, the fruit has turned to ashes on their lips.

Yet, feminists who ceaselessly inveigh against their own oppression by men (often hardly specifying its exact nature) would ignore how they themselves have oppressed these feminine women. It oppresses a woman who could delight in domesticity to tell her that her domesticity makes her a parasitic inferior of men. It oppresses a woman who yearns to stay home with her children to tell her she is worthy only insofar as she achieves in the workplace. The woman who believes that the differences between herself and her husband enliven the sexual experience would concur in Roger Scruton's statement, cited earlier, that the "energy released when man and woman come together is proportional to the distance which divides them when they are apart."[45] Even Jessie Bernard, an ardent feminist, acknowledged the concern that "emphasizing the similarities rather than the differences between the sexes would jeopardize [sexual] relations, especially the difference which highlights sexual aggression on the part of men and resistance but inevitable submission on the part of women."[46]   Charles Winick argued that "when femaleness and maleness become blurred, the differences between them can hardly help one to enrich the other": "Each sex can best find itself if the other provides a balance." Scandinavians, who pioneered abandonment of polarized sex roles, represent, says Winick, "the most conspicuous western example of an emancipated culture, and there seems little doubt about their comparative sexual inactivity."[47]

Since its revival in the 1960s, feminism has been an implacable enemy to any woman who delights in her femininity and welcomes dependency on her husband. This dependency not only makes possible her devotion to child-nurturing and domesticity, but also it is the prerequisite for the sexual rewards that can flow from a relationship between different, complementary individuals who do not seek to replicate each other. Feminists sought to isolate, demoralize, and put this feminine woman at risk. She will remain at risk until our society repudiates the ideology of feminist advocates such as Justice Ruth Bader Ginsburg—who describes the traditional woman as "reduced to dependency on a man"—Karen DeCrow— who decrees that no man should allow himself to support a woman— and Professor Martha Fineman—who defends our no-fault divorce laws on the grounds that marriage "is not a realistic bedrock for social policy" and no-fault reflects the interests of those women who are "economically self-sufficient and not dependent on a husband."[48]

But if success in the workplace equal to men's is their goal, women must exert themselves—with what, for some, will require extraordinary effort—to compensate for the encumbrances with which they enter that arena: their menstruation and propensity to conceive, gestate, lactate, and cherish children. What can be sources of happiness and contentment to a woman are impediments to career achievement. Femininity is her deficiency in the market. Feminists sought to convince women of femininity's deficiency through (to

employ their usefully descriptive word) "marginalizing" the traditionally feminine woman, just as women are "marginalized" by male
homosexuals. Woman's pathetic demoralization when faced with
such rejection is captured in David Leavitt's short story "Dedicated." After being forbidden to accompany a male homosexual
into a bar, his female friend muses:

> "When all the men you love can only love each other . . . you
> can't help but begin to wonder if there's something wrong
> with being a woman. . . ." That night she stood before those
> closed steel doors and shut her eyes and wished, the way a
> small child wishes, that she could be freed from her loose
> skirts, her make-up and jewels, her interfering breasts and
> buttocks. If she could only be stripped and pared, made sleek
> and svelte like Nathan and Andrew, then she might slip between
> those doors as easily as the men who hurried past her that
> night . . . ; she might be freed of the rank and untrustworthy
> baggage of femininity.[49]

This is the reaction of a woman whose body is rejected by the
male, her femaleness held in contempt.

The woman on Dworkin's pages likewise feels herself held in
contempt. Although her body is used by the male, she has, nonetheless, absorbed the message that her femininity is "rank [strong
and offensive in smell or taste, coarse, indecent] and untrustworthy
baggage." Enough of that baggage—in particular, the daily care
of her children—can be "stripped and pared" to enable her to compete
in the marketplace as a co-worker of men and childless women.
But for the woman who *could* delight in developing the uniquely
feminine dimension of her nature through domestic endeavors, it
is—to borrow Dworkin's powerful articulation—"a tragedy beyond
the power of language to convey" that society encourages her to
become stripped and pared so that she can function as an ersatz
male. That men seek the freedom of having wives who are independent, self-supporting co-workers, who resemble their husbands
as much as possible, is only a confirmation of her femininity's rank-

ness. Androgyny was a goal of contemporary feminism. Have not men traveled far towards that goal when they want their wives to be so stripped and pared of the feminine that they can find themselves replicated in their women, made sleek and svelte like Nathan and Andrew?

Dworkin's concluding chapter, "Dirt/Death," demonstrates how rank indeed can be the baggage of femaleness for a spiritual virgin. There has been no resolution, no redemption for the woman who, as a little girl, looked with shame and fear into the mirror. She knows that there "are so many dirty names for her that one rarely learns them all. . . . There are dirty names for every female part of her body and for every way of touching her." "Her genitals are dirty in the literal meaning: stink and blood and urine and mucous and slime." The woman knows that "Were she loved sufficiently, or even enough, she could not be despised so much. Were she sexually loved, or even liked, she and what is done with or to her, in the dark or in the light, would not, could not, exist rooted in the realm of dirt, the contempt for her apparently absolute and irrevocable; horrible; immovable; help us, Lord; unjust. She is not just less; she and the sex she incarnates are a species of filth."[50] "The filth of women," laments Dworkin, "is a central conceit in culture." To that "smelly, dirty gash" men go "for sex, for love, believing it is a place of filth; finding it dirty and liking it dirty, wanting it dirty and needing it dirty."[51]

Now, Dworkin is not simply expressing, in her very passionate and dramatic fashion, a fastidious woman's reaction to the fact that the nitty gritty of sexual activity is more animal than spiritual, a messy and indecorous enterprise that can resemble the habits of dogs greeting one another on their daily walk. The explanation for her tormented outpouring of despairing rage is not fastidious distaste, but her conviction that men's sexual usage of women expresses men's contempt for them. Again, Dworkin speaks a partial truth: there are a lot of dirty names for us and for every female part of our body; males' undifferentiated lust for females does, as

Midge Decter says, make each woman an undifferentiated member of a species. But as Brünnhilde discovers, the man's acknowledgment of her concrete irreplaceability *can* bring resolution and redemption by dispelling the fear and disaffection which first arose when the little girl, taking up the mirror, devised her silly notions of dirt and shame.

Belief that this can be so seems beyond Dworkin's grasp. Her words reflect anguished acceptance that, to males, femaleness is and will forever be only baggage of rankness. What does she think will make it otherwise? What does she believe can affirm femaleness? Will any of the supposed achievements of contemporary feminism do it? Will working even harder in the marketplace do it; receiving ever higher pay; aborting ever more babies; becoming ever more detached from child-rearing; working uninterruptedly enough to break through the alleged glass ceiling? Will further repressing the demands of femininity and becoming ever more like men really do it? Would her complete fungibility with males finally dissolve the despairing shame and hatred of Dworkin's spiritual virgin?

Near the end of her book, Dworkin does indeed pay homage to that daily domesticity which is a part of what, for some of us, goes far towards affirming femaleness. She quotes from Primo Levi's *Survival in Auschwitz*, where he describes the inmates' preparations for death: "But the mothers stayed up to prepare the food for the journey with tender care, and washed their children and packed the luggage; and at dawn the barbed wire was full of children's washing hung out in the wind to dry. Nor did they forget the diapers, the toys, the cushions and the hundred other small things which mothers remember and which children always need. Would you not do the same? If you and your child were going to be killed tomorrow, would you not give him to eat today?"[52]

Then Dworkin rhetorically asks a collection of male philosophers, doctors, and writers whether they have ever done the same. Of course they had not; they could not. If and when they tried, it still would not *be* the same, for at their best, they would only be acting in the place of mothers in attending to the particularities of their children's daily lives.

I have read Levi's words many times, and each time I am profoundly grateful that I had a Siegfried who kept me safe and made it possible for me to stay at home and do these things for my children. No matter how many "todays" I was to be granted, I wanted to spend each one at home with my children and not in an office writing another brief. Is it possible that she who chides the male for failing to "do the same" does not recognize the barbarity of feminism's attack on those women who would choose to do the same?

OUR DOUBLE-BIND SOCIETY

In explaining her rejection of the spiritual virginity that is a prerequisite for attaining fungibility with her husband, Brünnhilde must address a society in which the received opinion on women and their roles has been molded by the forked tongue of contemporary feminism. By creating a veneer of "pseudo-mutuality" that pays lip-service to the very values their actions consistently undermine, feminists successfully packaged their own version of "the double bind." The words "double bind" were used by Gregory Bateson in his famous description of the contradictory messages that parents of schizophrenics give their children: "In Bateson's theory, it is the mother's fabricated warmth—not the overly solicitous attention conventionally deplored in the myth of the 'Jewish mother'—that drives her son crazy. [Lyman] Wynne has shown that pseudo-mutuality, not mutuality itself, underlies the dynamics of schizophrenic families."[53]

The process which enabled contemporary feminism to create today's double bind society is illustrated by two letters in *Commentary* magazine responding to a Michael Levin article critical of feminism. Iris Mitgang, then chair of the National Women's Political Caucus, attacked Levin's criticism by arguing that feminists simply want each individual to have the opportunity to fulfill "his/her potential": "That means that if a woman is capable of being a scientist or a professor, the barriers of society should not be strung so tightly around her goal that she has little or no chance of success. It means that a man who is compassionate and tuned into the feelings of others should not be criticized because he turns his thoughts into poetry or into dance."

"Goals," Mitgang said, "can include being a homemaker—solely that." Another correspondent supported Levin by relating the experience of reviewing secondary school textbooks written under "anti-gender" instructions which required, for example, that female children be shown playing catch or hockey and that all children be dressed similarly without distinctive male/female attire. When this reviewer had criticized the material as very poor quality propaganda, the textbook editor conceded the criticism's accuracy, but argued that teachers and students must rethink their concepts of human beings; it did not matter if such role-switching was plausible or not, said the editor, because "adults will have to get used to the idea" and "children must be taught correctly from the beginning."[54]

Both representing contemporary feminism, the textbook editor expressed the so-called correct views that the movement was very successfully fighting to impose on society, while Iris Mitgang stated what it has always falsely claimed to stand for.[55] Like the textbook editor, feminists sometimes candidly acknowledge their goals, but often, like Mitgang, they deny their real goals or hide them in a morass of disingenuity. Thus, contrary to Mitgang's assertion, the concern of contemporary feminism—as Betty Friedan made pellucidly clear—was never to assure women the *opportunity* to fulfill their potential within the marketplace. Opportunities, Friedan correctly pointed out in 1963, already abounded. The problem that concerned her was how to convince women that the domesticity they believed fulfilled their potential, did not in fact do so.

Within the memory of no contemporary feminist had the
"barriers of society" been strung so tightly that women could not
achieve Mitgang's alleged goal of becoming scientists and professors.
When I entered college in 1947, I knew that women were represented, albeit sparsely, in all the professions. The doctor who
performed my pre-college physical examination was a woman. The
lawyer who had represented my mother in her divorce in 1936 was
a woman. And the president of The Trenton Trust Company, where
I opened my first bank account in 1942, was a woman, Mary G.
Roebling; she said in a speech in 1965 that American women have
"almost unbelievable economic power" but "do not use the influence
their economic power gives them."[56] Women's failure to take
advantage of the available opportunities and exert their influence
within the public arena has always been much more of a choice on
women's part than feminists want to admit. The most significant
barrier strung around a woman's marketplace goal has always been—
and remains today and will remain—her *own* unwillingness to constrict her maternal and domestic roles sufficiently to achieve that
goal.

Mitgang's second concern—protecting from criticism those men
who turn their thoughts into poetry and dance—is wholly fatuous. The greatest choreographers and impresarios of classical bal-
let have been male. The genius of impresario Diaghilev and choreographers Petipa, George Balanchine, Frederick Ashton, and Antony
Tudor flowered without feminist midwifing. Nor did Nijinsky,
Anton Dolin, Sir Robert Helpmann, Michael Somes, Rudolf Nureyev
and a multitude of other *danseurs nobles* require feminist encouragement before they could dance to world acclaim. As for poetry,
with very few exceptions, the canonical writings are by men. Rather
than encouraging male poets, academic feminism has done the
opposite by attacking the largely male canon and demanding the
inclusion of lesser female writers. That the poetic canon is overwhelmingly the work of males—from Homer, Vergil, Dante, and
Shakespeare to Byron, Shelley, Wordsworth and Keats to Yeats,

Eliot, and Pound—must surely refute any claim that males possibly required feminist encouragement in order to produce poetry.

Exemplifying the double bind, the actions of contemporary feminism wholly belie the sincerity of Mitgang's avowal that it was appropriate for a woman's goal to be homemaking—"solely that." On the contrary, feminists have consistently portrayed the homemaker role as parasitical and without social or individual worth. That feminists speak with a forked tongue when saying that homemaking can be a woman's goal, is evidenced by the underlying premise of the movement that, absent discrimination, women would be represented equally with men at all levels within every workplace. If feminists did in fact accept homemaking as a legitimate goal for women, women's disproportionate representation in workplaces would likewise be viewed as legitimate, rather than as a problem to be deplored and corrected.

The perceived illegitimacy of homemaking as a woman's career is reflected in Judith R. Shapiro's inaugural address as president of Barnard College. It is precisely because the propriety of a woman's full-time devotion to children and domesticity is beyond her ken that she condemns the fact that women "make up less than 30 percent of full-time faculty at four-year colleges and universities." This lag in what she considers women's "progress" can only be criticized because, like Justice Ruth Bader Ginsburg, she cannot believe that any woman would *willingly* choose domesticity. Only a society in which homemaking is *not* a legitimate goal for women can ever produce educational institutions that meet Shapiro's demands: "places where men and women are *equally likely* to study in all fields, to hold positions of responsibility and authority in extracurricular activities and to be found at all ranks of the faculty and administration." Toward this end, she exhorts us, "the roles men and women play in society" must "move progressively forward."[57]

That apologists for a cause exaggerate and misrepresent is certainly not surprising. Feminist disingenuity, however, is especially vicious because feminism's forked tongue speaks to the most important aspects of our happiness and well-being: the relationships between men, women, and their children and our perception of what is owed to these children. The pseudo-mutuality that Bateson described within schizophrenic families now permeates our society. In the depth and pervasiveness of the social ills that were detailed previously, our society can be seen to resemble a dysfunctional, even schizophrenic, family enmeshed in the web of a double bind. Whenever lip service is paid to a value by those who take action to undermine—or deliberately refrain from action to support—that value, the web of pseudo-mutuality is enlarged and strengthened. A woman, for example, who devotes herself to home and children is ordering her life to maximize the value that our society *supposedly* places on familial well-being. She will be caught, nonetheless, in the double bind web spun by feminism's stigmatization of her role as parasitical, a stigmatization that our no-fault divorce laws painfully brand upon her.

Contemporary feminism's deliberate destruction of "the women's pact" epitomized this pseudo-mutuality of the double bind. The very movement that turned against the traditional woman, vilifying and isolating her and compromising her social and economic security, claimed to be—and was accepted by society as—representing the interests of all women. The assailants of the traditional woman masqueraded as her champions. Many of these crusaders against the woman at home have been lesbians. Often frightened of and hostile towards heterosexual men, lesbians may find incomprehensible—as did Virginia Woolf's Lily Briscoe—the needs and feelings of any heterosexual, reproductive woman who would happily trade marketplace rewards for the dependence on a strong, reliable—and yes, even dominant—husband which can make possible both her sexual well-being and her devotion to home and children.

A traditional woman does indeed have very different needs and interests from lesbians and those heterosexual women who are committed to constricting the demands of motherhood and domesticity to the extent required for them to succeed as full-time market producers. Yet, these other kinds of women claim a mutuality of interest with a traditional woman, while at the same time, disdaining her choice and depicting her life as one defined by trivial concerns and misperceived needs. What lesbians and other women of constricted familial commitment represent can frighten a traditional woman (and also a mature heterosexual man who understands what is involved).

When I first began reading feminists' scornful denunciation of my own life and their exhortation that I return to market production—in Friedan's words, that I juggle pregnancies and turn my children and home over to nannies and housekeepers—my stomach would turn, and I would be suffused with a chilling dread. Seeking the source of my fear, I realized it came from my perception that what the women's movement was asking me to become seemed, to me, something like the witch figure described by Margaret Mead. This figure, said Mead, is "a statement of human fear of what can be done to mankind by the woman who denies or is forced to deny child-bearing, child-cherishing. She is seen as able to withhold herself from men's desire, and so to veil the nexus with life itself. 'She may ride away leaving her empty skin by her husband's side.'"[58]

Contemporary feminism created a frightening dilemma for any woman who finds herself attracted to domesticity and child-rearing or who, at any event, rejects surrogate care as inconsistent with her vision of child-cherishing. Our opinion-making cultural elite endorsed feminist ideology; the two-career family lifestyle touted by feminism became fashionable. But a woman like me believes that if she conscientiously fulfills the demands of market production, she will leave a much dessicated, if not wholly empty, skin by her husband's side. Nor did I want my children to grow up without receiving the best I had to give; I did not want to give my best to the market. I saw feminism as a force beckoning me to ride away from husband and children—not on a broomstick, but on a briefcase.

To children, feminism has presented no dilemma. Children rarely have choices, but endure as best they can whatever comes to them. I know no better statement of this fact than Rudyard Kipling's description of his own childhood. According to the custom of his time, he was boarded from the ages of six to twelve at the home of a woman who kept children whose parents, like his, were in India. He called her home the House of Desolation, "smelling of aridity and emptiness." What saved him, he said, was a month of paradise each year, visiting an aunt whose love and affection helped counteract eleven months of brutality. Kipling recalled how: "Often and often afterwards, the beloved Aunt would ask me why I had never told anyone how I was being treated. Children tell little more than animals, for what comes to them they accept as eternally established. Also, badly-treated children have a clear notion of what they are likely to get if they betray the secrets of a prison-house before they are clear of it."[59]

What has come to children from feminism is the pseudo-mutuality of a society that incessantly voices concern for their well-being, while deliberately undertaking to deny them one of the best guarantees of that well-being—an Eden at the beginning. This Eden can be created by a mother who, having been freed from the workplace, permits herself to fall in love with her children and spends those long, tranquil hours of daily child care which will help lay the foundation for their well-being. My own initial joyful response to motherhood was, I believe, grounded in my physical and emotional reactions to the many satisfactions the role provided. This initial response in no way depended upon evidence as to the disutility of surrogate child care, although such evidence may corroborate the social utility of a response like mine.[60] Experience, however, did convince me that surrogate care would have been inferior to my own efforts, and I have always been grateful that I was spared the conflicts and dilemmas which, according to Julia Wrigley, face high-status, high income professional women who rely on nannies to raise their children.[61] Wrigley believes that child care centers are a better alternative. It should give her pause, however, that a recent four-state study of hundreds of child-care centers conducted by child psychologists and economists at four universities concluded that the care in most centers "is so poor that it threatens children's intellectual and emotional development."[62]

Child care centers do at least provide the assurance of having other adults around, so that your child is not fatally dependent on your choice of a caretaker. In the most recent of many nanny horror tales, an eighteen-year-old British girl, who came to the United States to work as a nanny for the children of two doctors, was tried for the death of their nine-month-old child. The nanny said she "had shaken the baby lightly because he was fussy and would not stop crying." She also indicated that "when giving him a bath, she threw him down on the bathroom floor." Autopsy results showed a skull fracture as the cause of death, and x-rays also showed the baby had a four to six week old wrist fracture.[63] The strength of concerns about children's caretakers has caused a boom in the nanny-surveillance industry which supplies hidden-camera set-ups to watch baby-sitters; one manufacturer's sales of "nannycams" has tripled in the past few years.[64] One must wonder whether feminist apologists, who plead economic necessity as the reason mothers work, would defend the claim that a doctor's family "needs" a second income. But perhaps society "needed" the services of both these parent doctors more than their son did.

Yet denial of the worth of an Eden at the beginning or, at least, of a mother's worth as its provider, was crucial to achieving the feminist goal of male-female fungibility. Children were seen as the enemy—and they surely can be—of women's freedom wholeheartedly to pursue the careers that the women's movement believed possessed merits substantially outweighing any rewards that a mother's devotion to home and child-rearing can afford either her or her child. In these attitudes towards children, contemporary feminists are spiritual descendants of Jean-Jacques Rousseau, who immediately placed in a foundling home all five of the babies born to his mistress Thérèse.

Like a feminist who verbalizes some regret that a working woman is unable personally to rear her children, Rousseau expressed his confidence that "no father is more tender than I would have been," but, alas, having children about was inconvenient, could not be afforded: "How could I achieve the tranquillity of mind necessary for my work, my garret filled with domestic cares and the noise of children?" Moreover, he argued, it was a "good and sensible arrangement," such as Plato had advocated. Anticipating both feminism's rejection of the traditional family and its demand that the government assume responsibility for the bulk of child-rearing, Rousseau regretted that he himself had not been nurtured by the State, as his own children were. Transferring his parental responsibilities to the State was seen by Rousseau to be an appropriate "act of a citizen and a father." It might more accurately be described, Paul Johnson observed, as the act of one who, feeling himself a child, was incapable of bringing up children of his own—a description that may not be too wide of the mark for many of the women who spearheaded the women's movement.[65]

Most discussions today—whether academic or journalistic—about men, women, and their children are based on premises reflecting the biases of the feminist descendants of Rousseau. Although the majority of women today reject the label of "feminist,"[66] many of them, nevertheless, conduct their daily lives exactly according to feminist dogma, accepting as a given what should be the highly controversial and debatable tenets of that dogma. Indeed, insofar as issues involving women are concerned, the effort to enforce "political correctness" on our college campuses seeks to make these tenets sacrosanct by discouraging anyone from subjecting them to critical analysis. Efforts to dictate so-called bias-free writing, for example, are explicitly designed to remove from the language expressions that suggest concepts feminists decry. Thus, writers are warned not to use a sentence like "A stallion guards his brood of mares."[67] In the world as falsified by feminism, of course, it would be just as likely—and certainly desirable—for a mare to guard a herd of stallions. But to a traditional woman there can be something very satisfying—even erotic—in the thought of a stallion guarding his mares. Do feminists really think they can extirpate my physical and emotional reactions to thoughts of stallions behaving in stallion fashion by eliminating a phrase from our language? They will only succeed in making themselves, and some other women as well, even more unhappy and confused than they already are.

THE PARTICULARITIES OF DAILY LIFE

If a woman is to reject the spiritual virginity that contemporary feminists urge upon her, she must disentangle herself from the double-bind web that feminist ideology has spun about our society. In that effort, she will find the Chinese writers, who are now affirming femininity, vastly more encouraging than our own "difference feminists," who offer a woman only the opportunity to sublimate her maternal and domestic longings into a "feminist playpen" within the marketplace. The Chinese writers validate both her maternal longings and her worth as a woman who does not choose to sublimate these longings, but seeks to give them full rein to flourish in her role as a wife and mother at home. Such a woman can find encouragement in Li Xiaojiang's insight that a good name must be given to the "'incurably' petty qualities of femininity." Li Xiaojiang has learned what Leo Tolstoy knew—and Western feminists have yet to discover—about the critical importance of the particularities of daily life and how affirmative of her femininity a woman's attention to these particularities can be.

The attitude of Western feminists towards these particularities that are integral to a traditional female role is encapsulated in two recent letters responding to an article by David Gelernter encouraging mothers to stay home with their children.[68] One woman wrote that some women "simply do not want to be home with their children": "Child care is boring, tedious, and lonely. Being financially dependent on a spouse is irksome and humiliating. Professional life offers an outlet for talents and the promise of prestige."[69] Another woman recounted that

> I did stay home with my children for several years and I then clawed my way out of the house and the depression I experienced there. For many of us, full-time mothering was beyond endurance. Have you tried it, Mr. Gelernter: tried having your day limited to wiping Cheerios off the floor and . . . wiping off your children's bottoms and tops, with nary an opportunity to talk in complete sentences? . . . . spend a good half-hour getting the kids into their snowsuits, take the snowsuits off again because they decided they have to go to the bathroom, put the snowsuits back on, get them into their car seats, go to the supermarket; come home and unload kids and groceries from the car; get the kids out of their snowsuits, put the groceries away, feed the kids lunch, start making supper—and give me a call in your spare time, so I can see if you are still able to talk in complete sentences.[70]

These two women fully concur in Friedan's appraisal of the housewife's role, an appraisal diametrically opposed to my own. Caring for my children never seemed remotely boring, tedious, or lonely. Unlike the correspondent who found full-time mothering depressing and "beyond endurance," far from being depressing, I experienced those years as a mother at home as an everyday epiphany of exquisite happiness. When I wiped their tops and bottoms, got them in and out of their snowsuits (often many times in a day because being in a snowsuit did seem to inspire trips to the bathroom), loaded them in and out of the car, fed them lunch, and cooked supper with them, my most common reaction was awe at how delightful they were, how fresh and exciting each of these daily activities seemed in their eyes, and how lucky I was to have the privilege of sharing in this thrilling adventure that we created out of their daily growth.

Years later I read Carl Jung's statement that childhood "sketches a more complete picture of the self, of the whole man in his pure individuality, than adulthood,"[71] and I thought how accurately Jung had described my feelings about those glorious childhood years. I daily witnessed in my children a depth of feeling, a breadth of interest, and a delight in the wonder of life of far greater intensity than I had ever before seen in anyone. To participate in and guide the unfolding of these unique and always fascinating individuals made my days joyful undertakings that were not only incomparably satisfying, but were also the best learning experiences of my life.

Nor did I ever speak in less than complete sentences. The alleged inability to speak in complete sentences when one is caring for young children is one of the mantras feminists recite when denouncing the mother's role. The logic and clarity of my speech and writing always compared favorably, I thought, with what is often the jargon-laden output of many academic feminists, most of whom would not claim extensive acquaintance with the full-time care of young children. Nor have I ever found it "irksome" or "humiliating" to be financially dependent on my husband. To the contrary, when I stopped practicing law and became a housewife, an unexpected benefit was that I felt even better loved than before. I began to experience a glow of contentment and self-satisfaction which derived in part from the realization that my husband cared for me enough to exert himself as mightily as he did to provide so well for me and our children.

At the foundation of my contentment and self-satisfaction was a belief that indicates the vast gulf separating me from contemporary feminists. This belief explains why I find inconsequential a statement from William Henry's *In Defense of Elitism* which feminists find shocking: "The unvarnished truth is this: You could eliminate every woman writer, painter, and composer from the caveman era to the present moment and not significantly deform the course of Western culture."[72] My belief, which makes Henry's statement irrelevant to my life, is that although I did a workmanlike job in the marketplace, many others could have done that job equally well. But no one could have performed my mother's role for me. The course of

Western culture, I thought, could manage well enough without me. Most important to me was what happened in the nursery, in my bedroom, in the kitchen and the living-room, on the swings and in the sandbox. These were the fields I chose to make my own. If I had chosen otherwise, I would have constantly felt torn between the demands of home and work, never able fully to enjoy either. I agree with the insight of Dorothea Tanning, who said that her existence as an artist was dramatically compromised by her existence as the wife of Max Ernst, a far more famous artist than she. In her poem "Stain," Tanning acknowledges the disparate impact the marital relationship can have on the careers of husbands and wives and how painful this disparity can be for the woman who values a career. The poem begins:

> Many years ago today
> I took a husband tenderly
> This simple human gentle act
> Seen as a hard decisive fact
> By all who dote on category
> Did stain my work indelibly
> I don't know why that is
> For it has not stained his.[73]

I avoided the pain of this disparity that Tanning expresses so well, because I valued a career far less than I valued my maternal and domestic roles. What was the alternative I declined? I declined taking advantage of the workplace benefit of having a room and electric breast pump supplied by my employer so that, like a mother who returned to work when her child was three months old, I could pump out breast milk for twenty minutes, twice a day. This benefit is offered "to assist and encourage new mothers who want to return quickly from maternity leave," furthering Rhona Mahony's objective of helping mothers to avoid forming an attachment to their children that would lead them to sacrifice their careers.[74]

Our double-bind society tells us that there is little difference between pumping out breast milk at the office to be bottle-fed to your baby by a surrogate (it is called workplace nursing) and sitting in a rocking chair with your child sucking on your breast. Those of us who loved nursing our babies and thought that our intimate contact with the nursing infant could be even more important than the nutritional content of breast milk simply hadn't had our consciousness adequately raised. We were probably immune to such consciousness-raising because we knew in our bones what Selma Fraiberg tells us of the baby's need "to experience intimacy in a close ventral clasp." "The breast," she says, "was 'intended' to bind the baby and his mother for the first year or two years of life. If we read the biological program correctly, the period of breast feeding insured continuity of mothering as part of the program for the formation of human bonds."[75]

I also declined having to wake up my five-year-old early in the morning to "begin another crowded day" where before her "stretches a six-hour school day followed by a three-hour after-school program."[76] To my very unenlightened consciousness, two-and-a-half hours a day of kindergarten were perfectly adequate for my children's needs; the rest of their day would be in my hands. And finally, I declined having to convince myself that I was doing for my children what I was not. Marriott Hotels runs an advertisement that shows a woman in her hotel room with all the services she will need because she has "a lot to juggle" and "wants to put a deal to bed in Memphis and her daughter to bed in Chicago."[77] It was, unfortunately, only the deal she could put to bed. When your consciousness is adequately raised, however, you can believe that saying goodnight on the telephone is about the same as rocking a child, reading her a story, kissing her, and being there if she wakes up and wants you. And then there is the insurance company advertisement that shows a mother holding an infant who looks little more than newborn—identified as her new son whom she is saying good-bye to for the first time, as she returns to work. But she knows, says the ad, "that he's as safe in his room as he is in my arms."[78] And with adequate social conditioning, we can all believe it is so. Probably the parents of the dead nine-month-old believed it at the time.

It is presumptuous for women to tell other women how they should make these relative valuations of maternal and marital demands versus market demands. But this is precisely what the feminist movement has done by seeking to prevent women from leading a life the satisfactions of which flow largely from the marital and maternal relationships and the accompanying domestic endeavors that comprise the traditional female role. In her indictment of such a woman, Friedan made clear what she found most offensive about her. She quoted a psychiatrist who complained: "We have made woman a sex creature"; "She waits all day for her husband to come home at night to make her feel alive"; "It is terrible for the women, to lie there, night after night, waiting for her husband to make her feel alive."[79] One is tempted to respond that the solution, perhaps, was to find out why she had to wait so long and then try to do something about it. But that, of course, was not what Friedan was getting at. She thought it wrong that the women believed sex was important and were looking forward to it, not that they were waiting in vain.

This antipathy to woman's sexuality has always been a deep current in contemporary feminism; it pervaded the writings of Charlotte Perkins Gilman, who, Carl Degler observed, "did not relish sex for its own sake." In the first year of her marriage, Charlotte became "increasingly and inexplicably despondent" and "her severe fits of depression and prolonged weeping" continued after the birth of her daughter. She convinced her husband to agree to a separation and later a divorce; when he married her closest friend, she let her daughter live with them. Charlotte later remarried, but had no more children. "In several places," says Degler, "she made it clear that she thought sex was intended by nature only for procreation, not for 'recreation.'"[80] The antipathy to woman as a sexual being is consistent with feminism's promotion of the sexual revolution with its meaningless, casual sex—the sex of pornography. It is not this casual sex that Gilman and Friedan feared would keep women away from the marketplace, but rather as Andrea Dworkin saw so clearly, the meaningful sex that overwhelms, that transforms. This sex makes of the woman the sexual being that Gilman and Friedan so despised and can go far toward keeping the housewife content in her domesticity. And so Friedan admonished the domestic sex creatures to hie into the market and find work to bring them to life.

I have always wondered if either Friedan or the psychiatrist she cited had any idea what it was like to read judicial decisions, draft interrogatories, write a prospectus, or draw up articles of incorporation. It's a clean way to make a good living—better than mining coal—but it's overrated as a way to make you "feel alive." For feeling alive, I would always bet on the sexual ministrations of my husband over reading judicial decisions, even of the Supreme Court. But if she distances herself far enough from the demands of children and domesticity, if she reads enough opinions, writes enough briefs, meets enough deadlines, and takes Prozac to help her perform like a man for a long enough time, the woman in the workplace may become far enough removed from being a sex creature to meet even Friedan's approval.[81]

THOSE WHO WOULD DEFEND anti-feminist traditionalism today are like heretics fighting a regnant Inquisition. To become a homemaker, a woman may need the courage of a heretic. This is one reason that the defense of traditional women is often grounded in religious teachings, for the heretic's courage usually rests on faith. The source of courage I offer is the conviction, based on my own experience, that contemporary feminism's stereotypical caricature of the house-wife did not reflect reality when Friedan popularized it, does not reflect reality today, and need not govern reality.

Feminists claimed a woman can find identity and fulfillment only in a career; they are wrong. They claimed a woman can, in that popular expression, "have it all"; they are wrong—she can have only some. The experience of being a mother at home is a different experience from being a full-time market producer who is also a mother. A woman can have one or the other experience, but not both at the same time. Combining a career with motherhood requires a woman to compromise by diminishing her commitment and exertions with respect to one role or the other, or usually, to both. Rarely, if ever, can a woman adequately perform in a full-time career if she diminishes her commitment to it sufficiently to replicate the experience of being a mother at home.

Women were *never* told they could *not* choose to make the compromises required to combine these roles; within the memory of all living today there were always some women who did so choose. But by successfully degrading the housewife's role, contemporary feminism undertook to force this choice upon all women. I declined to make the compromises necessary to combine a career with motherhood because I did not want to become like Andrea Dworkin's spiritual virgin. I did not want to keep my being intact, as Dworkin puts it, so that I could continue to pursue career success. Such pursuit would have required me to hold too much of myself aloof from husband and children: the invisible "wedge-shaped core of darkness" that Virginia Woolf described as being oneself[82] would have to be too large, and not enough of me would have been left over for them.

I feared that if I cultivated that "wedge-shaped core of darkness" within myself enough to maintain a successful career, I would be consumed by that career, and that thus desiccated, too little of me would remain to flesh out my roles as wife and mother. Giving most of myself to the market seemed less appropriate and attractive than reserving myself for my family. Reinforcing this decision was my experience that when a woman lives too much in her mind, she finds it increasingly difficult to live through her body. Her nurturing ties to her children become attenuated; her physical relationship with her husband becomes hollow and perfunctory. Certainly in my case, Dr. James C. Neely spoke the truth in *Gender: The Myth of Equality*: "With too much emphasis on intellect, a woman becomes 'too into her head' to function in a sexual, motherly way, destroying by the process of thought the process of feeling her sexuality."[83]

Virginia Woolf never compromised her market achievements with motherhood; nor did the Brontë sisters,[84] Jane Austen, or George Eliot. Nor did Helen Frankenthaler who, at the time she was acknowledged to be the most prominent living female artist, said in an interview: "We all make different compromises. And, no, I don't regret not having children. Given my painting, children could have suffered. A mother must make her children come first: young children are helpless. Well, paintings are objects but they're also helpless."[85] I agree with her; that is precisely how I felt about the briefs I wrote for clients. Those briefs were, to me, like helpless children; in writing them, I first learned the meaning of complete devotion. I stopped writing them because I believed they would have been masters too jealous of my husband and my children.[86]

Society never rebuked these women for refusing to compromise their literary and artistic achievements. Neither should it rebuke other kinds of women for refusing to compromise their own artistry of motherhood and domesticity. Some women may agree that the reality I depict rings truer to them than the feminist depiction. This conviction may help them find the courage of a heretic. Some others, both men and women, may see enough truth in the reality I depict that they will come to regret society's acquiescence in the status degradation of the housewife. They may then accept the currently unfashionable notion that society should respect and support women who adopt the anti-feminist perspective.

It is in society's interest to begin to pull apart the double-bind web spun by feminism and so order itself as not to inhibit any woman who *could* be an awakened Brünnhilde. Delighted and contented women will certainly do less harm—and probably more good—to society than frenzied and despairing ones. This is not to suggest that society should interfere with a woman's decision to follow the feminist script and adopt any form of spiritual virginity that suits her. But neither should society continue to validate destruction of the women's pact by the contemporary feminists who sought to make us all follow their script. We should now begin to dismantle our regime that discourages and disadvantages the traditional woman who rejects feminist spiritual virginity and seeks instead the very different delight and contentment that she believes best suits her.

Notes

Introduction

1. Charles Murray, *Losing Ground* (New York: Basic Books, 1984).

2. Kate Millett, *Sexual Politics* (Garden City, N.Y.: Doubleday, 1969), p. 127.

3. This is a theme, for example, of Ellen Willis's *No More Nice Girls: Countercultural Essays* (Wesleyan University/University Press of New England, 1993).

4. Philip Wylie, *Generation of Vipers* (New York: Holt, Rinehart, and Winston, 1942, new annotated edition published in 1955), pp. 52-53.

5. *The New York Times*, April 1, 1993, p. A1. This study by the Alan Guttmacher Institute estimates that if "current trends continue, one-half of all women who were 15 in 1970 will have had [pelvic inflammatory disease] by the year 2000."

6. *Time*, Fall 1990, pp. 12, 79.

7. Ibid., p. 12.

8. Judith S. Wallerstein and Joan Berlin Kelly, *Surviving the Breakup: How Children and Parents Cope with Divorce* (New York: Basic Books, 1980), pp. 4-5, 10-11.

9. Judith S. Wallerstein and Sandra Blakeslee, *Second Chances: Men, Women & Children a Decade After Divorce* (New York: Ticknor & Fields, 1989). In *The Divorce Culture* (New York: Knopf, 1996), Barbara Dafoe Whitehead presents a heartrending picture of the blighting of children's lives and the permanent damage they suffer because of their parents' divorce. Rather than calling for a reform of no-fault that would reinstitute strict legal controls over divorce, she would rely on exhorting parents to behave more responsibly towards their children and each other.

10. *Time*, Fall 1990, pp. 12-13.

11. Ibid., p. 32. Christina Hoff Sommers has described the incredulity of American feminists when Russian women writers, alleging that socialism "had denied women their femininity," encouraged women "to pay more attention to their traditional role as 'keepers of the hearth,'" and proclaimed that they "have nothing to do with feminism." *Who Stole Feminism?: How Women Have Betrayed Women* (New York: Simon & Schuster, 1994), pp. 39-40.

12. *Time*, Fall 1990, pp. 35-36.

13. Nicholas D. Kristof, "Japan Is a Woman's World Once the Front Door Is Shut," *The New York Times*, June 19, 1996, pp. A1, A6. The contrast between Japanese women's public powerlessness and private authority is analyzed by Takie Sugiyama Lebra in *Japanese Women: Constraint and Fulfillment* (Honolulu: University of Hawaii Press, 1984).

14. Marcia Cohen, *The Sisterhood* (New York: Simon and Schuster, 1987).

15. Betty Friedan, *The Feminine Mystique* (New York: Dell, 1984, originally published in 1963 by W. W. Norton), pp. 307-08, 381.

16. Ibid., pp. 140-41, 376, 381, 394.

17. *Time*, May 2, 1988, p. 88. Steinem's name was on a list *Ms.* published of prominent women who had had an illegal abortion. Katherine Dalton, "Hard Cases," *The American Enterprise*, May/June 1995, p. 71.

18. Germaine Greer, *The Female Eunuch* (New York: McGraw Hill, 1970), p. 43.

19. Germaine Greer, *Sex and Destiny: The Politics of Human Fertility* (New York: Harper & Row, 1984), pp. 124-43, 149-53, 353-55, 363-64.

20. *Insight*, June 8, 1987, pp. 62-3.

21. De Beauvoir's adopted daughter, Sylvie Le Bon, published de Beauvoir's letters to Sartre which discussed her sexual trysts with young female students. Simone de Beauvoir, *Letters to Sartre*, edited and translated by Quintin Hoare (New York: Arcade Publishing/Little, Brown & Co., 1992). After charges were brought by the parents of one of her female students, de Beauvoir was barred from the university and lost her licence to teach anywhere in France. Paul Johnson, *Intellectuals* (New York: Harper & Row, 1988), pp. 238-39.

22. *Time*, April 28, 1986, p. 77.

23. Simone de Beauvoir, *Memoirs of a Dutiful Daughter* (New York: Harper Colophon Books, 1974) (originally published in 1958), pp. 340-44.

24. Simone de Beauvoir, *The Second Sex* (New York: Knopf, 1978), p. 711. *Le Deuxième Sexe* was originally published in France by Librairie Gallimard, 1949.

25. *The Diary of Beatrice Webb: Two*, edited by Norman and Jeanne MacKenzie (Cambridge, Mass: The Belknap Press of Harvard University Press, 1983), p. 52.

26. Johnson, *Intellectuals*, p. 235.

27. David M. Buss, *The Evolution of Desire: Strategies of Human Mating* (New York: Basic Books, 1994), pp. 19-48.

28. Johnson, *Intellectuals*, pp. 235, 239, 251. Ronald Hayman, a biographer of Sartre, has noted that in a fifty-year friendship, the sexual relationship lasted only about sixteen. Ronald Hayman, "Having Wonderful Sex, Wish You Were Here," *The New York Times Book Review*, July 19, 1992, p. 13.

29. Simone de Beauvoir, *The Coming of Age* (New York: G. P. Putnam's Sons, 1972), pp. 539, 540.

30. William Butler Yeats, *Vacillation* (1932).

31. *The New York Times*, June 15, 1993, pp. A1, A13. Although this lead article on her nomination stated that her first job was as a "legal secretary," a letter from the Columbia Law Women's Association detailing her alleged victimization by sex bias states that when "she could not find a job in a law firm commensurate with her credentials," she served "as law clerk to Judge Edmund L. Palmieri of the United States District Court, Southern District of New York." This is confirmed in *Columbia, The Magazine of Columbia University*, Summer 1980, p. 11, and it was so reported in *The Wall Street Journal*, June 15, 1993, p. A6.

32. The same is true for women graduates of Harvard Law School. Because she transferred to Columbia in her final year at Harvard Law School, Justice Ginsburg is a member of the Harvard Law class of 1959. On the occasion of that class's 25th reunion, an examination of the careers of its female members disclosed that "[m]ost of the women in the class ended up following career paths similar to the men—law firm partners, judges, academics, public-interest lawyers and in-house corporate lawyers. In the late 1970s and 1980s, many found themselves established as the senior women in their field—and enjoying the benefits." Jill Abramson, "Class of Distinction," *The Wall Street Journal*, July 20, 1993, p. A1.

33. "Barbara Aronstein Black: A Conversation," *The Observer* (Columbia Law School Alumni Association, August 1986), p. 4.

34. Ethnicity would sometimes be overlooked in the presence of other factors— for example, the ability to bring business to the firm.

35. Kingsley R. Browne, "Sex and Temperament in Modern Society: A Darwinian View of the Glass Ceiling and the Gender Gap," *Arizona Law Review* 37 (1995), pp. 995, n.112, 1089, n.810.

36. George Gilder, *Sexual Suicide* (New York: Quadrangle, 1973), p. 67.

37. Ted L. Huston, "Path to Parenthood," *Discovery: Research and Scholarship at The University of Texas At Austin* 14 (1996), pp. 59, 63.

38. George Orwell, *Nineteen Eighty-Four* (New York: Harcourt, Brace & World, 1949), pp. 86-87.

39. Letters to the Editor, *The New York Times Magazine*, May 31, 1992, p. 12.

40. Andrea Dworkin, *Intercourse* (New York: The Free Press, 1987), p. 100.

41. Roger Scruton, *Sexual Desire: A Moral Philosophy of the Erotic* (New York: The Free Press, 1986), p. 273.

42. *The New York Times*, June 27, 1993, p. 10.

43. Transcript of Proceedings, United States Commission on Civil Rights, Forum on Early Childhood Education, Dallas, Texas, May 20, 1989, pp. 90, 103.

44. These are the typical reactions of the working mothers and women considering motherhood who were surveyed by anthropologist Katherine S. Newman in her study of a New York suburban community. *Declining Fortunes: The Withering of the American Dream* (New York: Basic Books, 1993). In *Feminism Is Not the Story of My Life* (New York: Nan A. Talese/Doubleday, 1996), p. 194, Elizabeth Fox-Genovese describes how "the pull between family and work can drive working mothers to distraction" and "the feelings of guilt may become almost too much to bear."

1. *Women's Divine Discontent*

1. Margaret Mead, *Male and Female* (New York: Morrow Quill Paperbacks, 1977, originally published 1949), p. 160.

2. Philip Wylie, *Generation of Vipers*, pp. 52-53.

3. Christopher Lasch, *Haven in a Heartless World: The Family Beseiged* (New York: Basic Books, 1977), p. 84.

4. Ibid., pp. 168-71.

5. Ibid., p. 7.

6. Gertrude Himmelfarb, *The De-Moralization of Society: From Victorian Virtues to Modern Values* (New York: Knopf, 1995), p. 55.

7. Brigitte Berger and Peter L. Berger, *The War Over the Family: Capturing the Middle Ground* (Garden City, New York: Anchor Press, 1983), p. 111.

8. De Beauvoir, *The Second Sex*, pp. 526-27.

9. Mark Helprin, "The Arcadian Lyricism of Edward Schmidt," *American Arts Quarterly* (The Newington-Cropsey Foundation, Spring 1993), p. 10.

10. Henry James, *The Portrait of a Lady* (New York: W. W. Norton, 1975, 1908 edition), p. 17.

11. Berger, *The War over the Family*, p. 114.

12. Robert Wright, *The Moral Animal: Evolutionary Psychology and Everyday Life* (New York: Pantheon Books, 1994), p. 123.

13. Sandra M. Gilbert and Susan Gubar, *The Madwoman in the Attic* (New Haven: Yale University Press, 1979), pp. 17, 22-23.

14. Himmelfarb, *The De-Moralization of Society*, p. 63 (quoting Frederic Harrison).

15. George F. Gilder, *Sexual Suicide*, p. 66.

16. Carl N. Degler, *At Odds: Women and the Family in America from the Revolution to the Present* (New York: Oxford University Press, 1980), p. 447.

17. Mead, *Male and Female*, pp. 85, 92.

18. Amaury de Riencourt, *Sex and Power in History* (New York: David McKay, 1974), pp. 161, 329, 422-23.

19. Ibid., p. 393.

20. Stanley Rothman and S. Robert Lichter, *Roots Of Radicalism: Jews, Christians, and the Left* (New Brunswick: Transaction, 1996) (Originally published by Oxford University Press, 1982), pp. 109, 129.

21. Jay P. Lefkowitz, "Jewish Voters and the Democrats," *Commentary*, April 1993, p. 40.

22. *Time*, February 28, 1994, p. 34.

23. Helena Z. Lopata, *Occupation: Housewife* (New York: Oxford University Press, 1971; reprinted, Westport, Conn.: Greenwood Press, 1980), pp. 98, 104, 95.

24. Rothman and Lichter, *Roots Of Radicalism*, p. 129.

25. Bruno Bettelheim, *The Children of the Dream* (London: Macmillan, 1969), p. 24.

26. *The New York Times*, June 15, 1993, p. A1.

27. Betty Smith, *A Tree Grows in Brooklyn* (New York: Harper & Row, 1943), pp. 289, 330.

28. "Gilliganism" refers to Carol Gilligan's claims that there is "a feminine form or method of reasoning" and that this feminine voice "has been drowned out or silenced by traditional (male) reasoning." Charlotte Witt, "Feminist Metaphysics," in *A Mind of One's Own: Feminist Essays on Reason and Objectivity*,

edited by Louise M. Antony and Charlotte Witt (Boulder, Colo.: Westview Press, 1993), pp. 280-81.

29. Christina Hoff Sommers, *Who Stole Feminism?: How Women Have Betrayed Women* (New York: Simon & Schuster, 1994), p. 63.

30. Julius Getman, *In the Company of Scholars: The Struggle for the Soul of Higher Education* (Austin, Texas: University of Texas Press, 1992), p. 170.

31. Lopata, *Occupation: Housewife*, p. 196.

32. Berger, *The War over the Family*, pp. 118-20. See also, Lasch, *Haven in a Heartless World*, pp. 11-12.

33. Lopata, *Occupation: Housewife*, pp. 139-43.

34. Ibid., p. 146.

35. Ibid., pp. 152-55.

36. Lasch, *Haven in a Heartless World*, pp. 99-100, 118, 172. Lasch's last book is a collection of essays that reflect his continuing concern with the intrusion of the elite experts of our helping professions into the private domain to supplant habit and custom and direct our daily lives. Christopher Lasch, *Women And The Common Life: Love, Marriage, And Feminism*, edited by Elisabeth Lasch-Quinn (New York: W. W. Norton, 1996).

37. Lasch, *Haven in a Heartless World*, p. 220, n.8.

38. Ibid., p. 216, n.29. See also Marie Winn, *Children Without Childhood* (New York: Pantheon, 1983), p. 55.

39. Lopata, *Occupation: Housewife*, pp. 182-86.

40. Ibid., pp. 204, 206, 211-12.

41. Berger, *The War over the Family*, pp. 14, 33-35.

42. Rita Kramer, *In Defense of the Family: Raising Children in America Today* (New York: Basic Books, 1983), pp. 20, 202, 254, n.4.

43. Lasch, *Haven in a Heartless World*, pp. 12-15, 120-23, 137. The continuing intimidation and undermining of parents by "child-rearing professionals" is cogently analyzed by Dana Mack in *The Assault on Parenthood: How Our Culture Undermines the Family* (New York: Simon & Schuster, 1997).

44. De Riencourt, *Sex and Power in History*, pp. 369-70.

45. Ernest Hemingway, *A Farewell to Arms* (New York: Charles Scribner's Sons, 1929), p. 27.

46. Berger, *The War over the Family*, p. 102.

47. Michael Novak, "Men Without Women," *The American Spectator*, October 1978, p. 15.

48. Harold Voth, *The Castrated Family* (Kansas City: Sheed Andrews and McMeel, 1977), p. 13.

49. Mead, *Male and Female*, pp. 277-80.

50. George Eliot, *Middlemarch* (New York: W. W. Norton, 1977) (A Norton Critical Edition), pp. 570-71, 574.

51. Lopata, *Occupation: Housewife*, pp. 108, 111.

52. Ibid., pp. 113, 115, 120.

53. Friedan, *The Feminine Mystique*, p. 204.

54. Wang Zheng, "Three Interviews: Wang Anyi, Zhu Lin, Dai Qing," in *Gender Politics in Modern China: Writing and Feminism*, Tani E. Barlow, editor (Durham: Duke University Press, 1993), p. 163.

55. Lopata, *Occupation: Housewife*, p. 121.

56. Lasch, *Haven in a Heartless World*, p. 156.

57. Wylie, *Generation of Vipers*, p. 210.

58. Ibid., p. 209.

59. James Nuechterlein, "The Feminization of the American Left," *Commentary*, November 1987, p. 43.

60. Steven Goldberg, *The Inevitability of Patriarchy* (New York: Morrow, 1973), pp. 227-28.

61. Quoted in James C. Neely, *Gender: The Myth of Equality* (New York: Simon & Schuster, 1981), p. 44.

62. De Riencourt, *Sex and Power in History*, p. 411.

63. Friedan, *The Feminine Mystique*, pp. 391-92.

64. Nuechterlein, "The Feminization of the American Left," *Commentary*, p. 45.

65. Christopher Caldwell, "The Feminization of America," *The Weekly Standard*, December 23, 1996, p. 18. Perhaps the societal quest for androgyny peaked when thirty-nine members of the androgynous Heaven's Gate cult committed suicide in an attempt to rendezvous with a UFO: "[S]hedding any signs of sexuality was integral to the cult, and six of the men, including [the leader], went so far as to get castrated years ago." *Time*, April 7, 1997, pp. 30, 32.

66. Charles Winick, *The New People: Desexualization in American Life* (New York: Pegasus, 1968).

67. Ibid., pp. 17-19, 23.

68. Barbara Ehrenreich, *The Hearts of Men: American Dreams and the Flight From Commitment* (Garden City, N. Y.: Anchor Press/Doubleday, 1983).

69. Ibid., pp. 11-12.

70. David Reisman with Nathan Glazer and Reuel Denney, *The Lonely Crowd* (New Haven: Yale University Press, 1950).

71. Wylie, *Generation of Vipers*, p. 203.

72. Ibid., pp. 49-50, 200, 213, 237.

73. Ibid., p. 216.

74. Diana Trilling, "Please Don't Make Me a Joke," *The New York Times Book Review*, December 21, 1986, pp. 1, 23 [reviewing Gloria Steinem, *Marilyn* (New York: Henry Holt & Co., 1986)].

75. Ehrenreich, *The Hearts of Men*, pp. 42, 49–51.

76. The best known "proponent of masculine irresponsibility," Kerouac had two brief marriages and a daughter whom he refused to acknowledge; he lived with his mother for most of his last two decades. He described his mother—who supported him by working in shoe factories until "On the Road" gave him an income—as "the most important person in this whole story and the best." Ann Douglas, "On the Road Again," *The New York Times Book Review*, April 9, 1995, p. 2 [reviewing *The Portable Jack Kerouac* and *Jack Kerouac: Selected Letters, 1940–1956*, edited by Ann Charters (New York: Viking, 1995)].

77. Ehrenreich, *The Hearts of Men*, pp. 53–54.

78. Ibid., pp. 70–71, 76–77, 84, 86.

79. Ibid., pp. 90–91, 94–95.

80. Charles A. Reich, *The Greening of America* (New York: Random House, 1970).

81. Charles A. Reich, *The Sorcerer of Bolinas Reef* (New York: Random House, 1976), pp. 27, 29, 39, 40, 76–77.

82. Reich, *The Greening of America*, pp. 150, 241, 279.

83. *The New York Times*, July 14, 1993, pp. A1, A9; ibid., August 5, 1993, p. B1.

84. Richard Easterlin, *Birth and Fortune: The Impact of Numbers on Personal Welfare* (New York: Basic Books, 1980), pp. 4, 134–136.

85. *The Wall Street Journal*, September 2, 1986, pp. 1, 22; ibid., August 23, 1993, p. A1.

86. Easterlin, *Birth and Fortune*, pp. 9–13; Kramer, *In Defense of the Family*, p. 190.

87. Lopata, *Occupation: Housewife*, p. 47.

88. Easterlin, *Birth and Fortune*, pp. 37, 39–49, 91–93.

89. Ibid., pp. 58–65, 75.

90. Ibid., pp. 76, 148–50.

91. Louis S. Richman, "Are You Better Off Than in 1980?," *Fortune*, October 10, 1988, p. 44.

92. Jennifer Roback Morse, "Beyond 'Having It all,'" 18 *Harvard Journal of Law & Public Policy*, Spring 1995, p. 573.

93. In 1988, for example, almost two-thirds of college-educated women with infants under one year old were employed, but only 38 percent of high school-educated women. *The Wall Street Journal*, July 21, 1988, p. 17. By

1990, the former's employment exceeded two-thirds. Myron Magnet, "The American Family, 1992," *Fortune*, August 10, 1992, p. 52.

94. *The New York Times*, January 22, 1993, pp. A1, A10; *Time*, February 1, 1993, p. 29; *Austin* (Texas) *American-Statesman*, February 8, 1993, pp. A1, A9.

95. *The New York Times*, February 10, 1993, p. A15.

96. Ibid., January 24, 1993, pp. 1, 13; ibid., February 15, 1993, p. A7; *Austin* (Texas) *American-Statesman*, January 29, 1993, p. A19.

97. Zoë Baird recently resigned as general counsel for Aetna, Inc. to join her husband on the faculty of Yale Law School. Her severance package on leaving Aetna is $2.5 million, which follows an earlier one time "retention" payment of $900,000 that was made when she had threatened to leave the company after a restructuring. *The Wall Street Journal*, December 9, 1996, p.B8.

98. Bettelheim, *The Children of the Dream*, pp. 34-35.

99. William R. Allen, *Midnight Economist*, July, 1988, December, 1988 (Institute for Contemporary Studies, San Francisco, California).

100. Louis S. Richman, "Are You better Off Than in 1980?," p. 40.

101. *The Wall Street Journal*, May 23, 1989, p. A1.

102. Louis S. Richman, "Are You better Off Than in 1980?", p. 41.

103. Ibid.

104. *Time*, Fall 1990, p. 13.

105. Ibid., p. 73.

106. *The Wall Street Journal*, September 22, 1986, pp. 1, 16.

107. Diana Furchtgott-Roth, "Working Wives Widen 'Income Gap,'" *The Wall Street Journal*, June 20, 1995, p. A22.

108. Richard J. Herrnstein and Charles Murray, "The Aristocracy of Intelligence," *The Wall Street Journal*, October 10, 1994, p. A14, an essay based on their book, *The Bell Curve: Intelligence and Class Structure in American Life* (New York: The Free Press, 1994).

109. As a woman who earned $500 a week observed, "at the end of the day I have gone absolutely nuts and am exhausted and all I have is $20 to show for it?" Charles A. Jaffe, "2nd Income May Not Be So Indispensable," *Austin* (Texas) *American-Statesman*, March 8, 1994, pp. E1, 2. U. S. Labor Department data show that work-related costs such as child care, household help, clothing, food away from home, and transportation take 46 percent of the second income in low-income families, 56 percent in middle-income families, and 68 percent in upper-income families. Sue Shellenbarger, "Work & Family," *The Wall Street Journal*, April 22, 1992, p. B1.

110. Tamar Lewin, "Men Whose Wives Work Earn Less, Studies Show," *The New York Times*, October 12, 1994, p. A1. A 1993 study of male managers

showed that those with nonworking wives earned 32 percent more than those whose wives worked either part- or full-time. Betsy Morris, "Is Your Family Wrecking Your Career? (and vice versa)," *Fortune*, March 17, 1997, p. 72.

111. Pepper Schwartz, "Some People With Multiple Roles Are Blessedly Stressed," *The New York Times*, November 17, 1994, p. B1. She also noted her study of couples that showed "the man had more respect for the woman when she was working full time rather than part time." Ibid., p. B4. In *The Time Bind: When Work Becomes Home and Home Becomes Work* (New York: Metropolitan Books, 1997), Arlie Russell Hochschild analyzes her findings that working mothers decline opportunities to decrease their working hours because work has become like a friendly "home" where they "get relief from the 'work' of being at home," a place of "unresolved quarrels and unwashed laundry." Arlie Russell Hochschild, "There's No Place Like Work," *The New York Times Magazine*, April 20, 1997, pp. 53, 55.

112. *Time*, Fall, 1990, p. 74.

113. Ibid., pp. 73-4.

114. Richard T. Gill & T. Grandon Gill, "A New Plan for the Family," *The Public Interest*, Spring, 1993, p. 88.

115. David Gelernter, "Why Mothers Should Stay Home," *Commentary*, February 1996, p. 26.

116. Easterlin, *Birth and Fortune*, p. 145.

117. Berger, *The War over the Family*, pp. 100-04, 126, 135-36.

118. Norbert Elias, *The Civilizing Process, Vol. I* (New York: Urizen Books, 1978), pp. 104-08.

119. Gary Saul Morson, "What is the Intelligentsia? Once More, an Old Russian Question," *Academic Questions*, Summer 1993, p. 23.

120. Gary Saul Morson, "Opinion and the World of Possibilities," *Academic Questions*, Winter 1994-95, p. 53.

121. Himmelfarb, *The De-Moralization of Society*, p. 244.

122. Jane J. Mansbridge, *Why We Lost the ERA* (Chicago: University of Chicago Press, 1986), pp. 105-07.

123. *The Wall Street Journal*, July 23, 1993, p. A1.

124. S. Robert Lichter, Stanley Rothman, Linda S. Lichter, *The Media Elite* (Bethesda, Md.: Adler & Adler, 1986), pp. 28-31, 295.

125. With the growth of newspaper chains, national news magazines, and national TV networks, regional differences have dissolved as what the public knows depends "increasingly upon the beliefs of the small elite which determines what they should know." Ibid., p. 8.

126. The uniformity of mainly liberal views is analyzed in S. Robert Lichter, Linda S. Lichter, Stanley Rothman, *Watching America: What Television*

Tells Us About Our Lives (New York: Prentice Hall, 1992); S. Robert Lichter, Linda S. Lichter, Stanley Rothman, *Prime Time: How T V Portrays American Culture* (Wash., D. C.: Regnery, 1994); and Stanley Rothman, Stephen Powers, David Rothman, "Feminism in Films," *Society*, March/April 1993. This monolithic opinion-making has now been challenged by conservative talk radio and television. R. Emmett Tyrrell, Jr., "Limbaugh Tips Scale of Discontent," *Insight*, March 28, 1994, p. 34; Michael Rust, "TV Cameras Turn Right," *Insight*, May 22, 1995, p. 6. The recent advent of the interactive computer network has, of course, created virtually limitless opportunities for the dissemination of a vast spectrum of views.

127. Walker Percy, *The Thanatos Syndrome* (New York: Farrar Straus Giroux, 1987), p. 254.

128. Allan Bloom, *The Closing of the American Mind* (New York: Simon & Schuster, 1987), p. 107.

129. Ibid.

130. Theodore Roosevelt, "The Parasite Woman: The Only Indispensable Citizen," in *The Works of Theodore Roosevelt*, Volume 19, Hermann Hagedorn, editor (New York: Scribner's Sons, 1926), p. 144.

131. *The Americanism of Theodore Roosevelt*, compiled by Hermann Hagedorn (Cambridge, Mass.: Houghton Mifflin, 1923), pp. 65–66.

2. Status Degradation Achieved

1. Jane J. Mansbridge, *Why We Lost the ERA*, p. 100.

2. Bloom, *The Closing of the American Mind*, p. 102.

3. It has been noted that "whether through the direct effects of participation in child care or the indirect impact of the overload on an employed wife, a dual-earning household is not optimal for men of ambition." Browne, "Sex and Temperament in Modern Society," p. 1097, n.862.

4. James M. Barrie, *What Every Woman Knows*, Act iv.

5. Katherine Kersten, "What Do Women Want?: A Conservative Feminist Manifesto," *Policy Review*, Spring 1991, p. 6.

6. Louise Iscoe and Diane Welch, *Mother Care: A Career Option For Now* (Hogg Foundation for Mental Health 1992, The University of Texas at Austin), pp. 7, 10. In *The Myths of Motherhood: How Culture Reinvents the Good Mother* (New York: Houghton Mifflin, 1994), p. xix, Shari L. Thurer notes that while "1950s' culture accorded its full-time mothers unconditional positive regard," today's "stay-at-home mothers I know dread the question 'And what do *you* do?'"

7. Elizabeth Fox-Genovese, *Feminism Without Illusions: A Critique of Individualism* (Chapel Hill: University of North Carolina Press, 1991), p. 255.

8. Browne, "Sex and Temperament in Modern Society," p. 1076.

9. Friedan, *The Feminine Mystique*, p. 209.

10. *Time*, July 25, 1988, p. 22.

11. *Austin* (Texas) *American-Statesman*, October 4, 1980, p. D5.

12. *The New York Times*, May 4, 1990, p. AI.

13. *The New York Times*, June 7, 1993, p. A2; David E. Sanger, "The Career and the Kimono," *The New York Times Magazine*, May 30, 1993, p. 18.

14. Jean-Paul Sartre, *The Family Idiot: Gustave Flaubert 1821-1857, Volume II* (Chicago: University of Chicago Press, 1987), p. 359.

15. Letter from Andrea Dworkin, *The New York Times Book Review*, May 3, 1992, p. 15; Ronald Dworkin, "Liberty and Pornography," *The New York Review of Books*, August 15, 1991, p. 12.

16. Steven Marcus, *The Other Victorians: A Study of Sexuality and Pornography in Mid-Nineteenth Century England* (New York: Basic Books, 1964), p. 279.

17. Dworkin, *Intercourse*, pp. 193-94.

18. Marcus, *The Other Victorians*, p. 280.

19. Ibid., p. 123.

20. Ibid., p. 233.

21. Dworkin, *Intercourse*, pp. 188, 186-87.

22. Scruton, *Sexual Desire*, pp. 150-51.

23. Marcus, *The Other Victorians*, pp. 180, 188, 195.

24. Ibid., p. 278.

25. Ibid., p. 281.

26. Dworkin, *Intercourse*, p. 113.

27. Marcus, *The Other Victorians*, p. 194.

28. Ibid., pp. 133, 139.

29. Carolyn G. Heilbrun, *Writing a Woman's Life* (New York: W. W. Norton, 1988), pp. 21, 130.

30. Allan C. Carlson, "Treason of the Professions: The Case of Home Economics," *The Family in America* (August 1987, The Rockford Institute), pp. 2-3; Allan C. Carlson, *Family Questions: Reflections on the American Social Crisis* (New Brunswick: Transaction Books, 1988), pp. 172-73, 246.

31. Charlotte Perkins Gilman, *Women And Economics: A Study of the Economic Relation Between Men and Women as a Factor in Social Evolution*, edited by Carl N. Degler (New York: Harper & Row, 1966) (originally published in 1898), pp. 5, 11, 62, 118.

32. Ibid., pp. 118, 141, 168.

33. Ibid., pp. 227-230, 241-47.

34. As described by Samuel Gompers of the American Federation of Labor, this was "a living wage—which when expended in an economic manner shall be

sufficient to maintain an average-sized family in a manner consistent with whatever the contemporary local civilization recognizes as indispensable to physical and mental health." This "average-sized family" came to be accepted as a standard family of five. Allan C. Carlson, "American Business and the New Politics of the Family," *Family in America* (June 1987, The Rockford Institute), pp. 2-3.

35. Ibid., pp. 3-4.

36. William Tucker, "A Return to the 'Family Wage'," *The Weekly Standard* , May 13, 1996, p. 27. Commenting on Tucker's article, Phyllis Schlafly noted that she made a similar suggestion in her 1977 book, *The Power of the Positive Woman*, recommending that each married couple could designate which spouse would be the "principal wage earner" for the purpose of job preferences and protections. "Correspondence," *The Weekly Standard*, June 10, 1996, p. 7.

37. De Beauvoir, *The Second Sex*, p. 508.

38. Ibid., p. 510, quoting from "At the Bay," in *The Short Stories of Katherine Mansfield.*

39. De Beauvoir, *The Second Sex*, pp. 511, 513.

40. Ibid., pp. 454, 456.

41. Ibid., pp. 481-82.

42. Ibid., pp. 526, 525.

43. Ibid., pp. 698-99.

44. Ibid., pp. 699, 724.

45. Jessie Bernard, *The Future of Marriage* (New Haven: Yale University Press, 1982 edition), p. 173.

46. Simone de Beauvoir, "Sex, Society, and the Female Dilemma: A Dialogue Between Simone de Beauvoir and Betty Friedan," *Saturday Review*, June 14, 1975, p. 16.

47. P. J. Kavanagh, *A G. K. Chesterton Anthology* (San Francisco: Ignatius Press, 1985), p. 113.

48. *The Wall Street Journal*, February 28, 1994, p. A1.

49. Friedan, *The Feminine Mystique*, p. 150.

50. Jessie Bernard, *Academic Women* (University Park, Pa.: The Pennsylvania State University Press, 1964), p. 67.

51. Gilman, *Women And Economics*, pp. 167-68.

52. Friedan, *The Feminine Mystique*, pp. 67, 68, 206.

53. Ibid., pp. 101, 128, 133, 135.

54. Ibid., pp. 162, 166, 179.

55. Ibid., pp. 190, 202-04.

56. Ibid., pp. 226, 230-32, 243-45.

57. Ibid., pp. 253-55, 271, 274, 281.

58. Ibid., pp. 290, 304.

59. Ibid., pp. 305-06.

60. Ibid., p. 307.

61. Hannah Arendt, *Eichmann in Jerusalem* (Harmondsworth, England: Penguin Books, 1964), p. 283. See also, pp. 11-12, 117-25, 155-56, 230-33.

62. Friedan, *The Feminine Mystique*, pp. 312, 316.

63. Adolf Hitler, *Mein Kampf* (Boston: Houghton Mifflin, 1971) (originally published 1925-27), pp. 150, 302, 303-05.

64. Michael Levin, *Feminism and Freedom* (New Brunswick: Transaction Books, 1987), p. 277.

65. Gloria Steinem, "What It Would Be Like if Women Win," *Time*, August 31, 1970, p. 22.

66. Helen Gurley Brown, *Sex and the Single Girl* (New York: Pocket Books, 1965), quoted in Jessie Bernard, *The Future of Marriage*, p. 226.

67. Nena O'Neill and George O'Neill, *Open Marriage: A New Life Style For Couples* (New York: M. Evans and Company, 1972), pp. 27, 41, 143-45.

68. Ibid., pp. 194-96.

69. Virginia Woolf, *A Room of One's Own* (New York: Harcourt Brace Jovanovich, 1929) (Harvest/HBJ edition 1989), p. 65.

70. Louise Kapp Howe, ed., *The Future of the Family: Mothers, Fathers and Children—Sex Roles and Work—Communities and Child Care—Redefining Marriage and Parenthood* (New York: Simon & Schuster, 1972), pp. 21, 175, 253.

71. *U. S. News & World Report*, June 7, 1976, p. 46.

72. Ibid., pp. 46, 48.

73. Ibid., p. 47.

74. Urie Bronfenbrenner, "Who Cares for America's Children?" in Louise Kapp Howe, ed., *The Future of the Family*, pp. 139, 142; Urie Bronfenbrenner, "The Origins of Alienation," *Scientific American* 231 (August 1974), pp. 53-61.

75. *U. S. News & World Report*, June 7, 1976, p. 49.

76. Raju Narisetti and Rochelle Sharpe, "Take It Or Leave It," *The Wall Street Journal*, August 29, 1995, p. A1.

77. Berger, *The War over the Family*, p. 102.

78. Bernard, *The Future of Marriage*, pp. 16-18, 28-32.

79. Ibid., pp. 38, 42-44, 48, 51.

80. Ibid., pp. 142, 106-07, 165, 287.

81. Mary Jo Bane, *Here To Stay: American Families in the Twentieth Century* (New York: Basic Books, 1976), p. 141.

82. Ibid., pp. 29, 28, 164, n.19.

83. Ibid., pp. 79, 82-84.

84. Bernard, *The Future of Marriage*, pp. 43, 33.

85. Bane, *Here to Stay*, p. 76.

86. Gilder, *Sexual Suicide*, pp. 94, 194.

87. Carla Rivera, "Violence Against Children at Crisis Level," *Austin* (Texas) *American-Statesman*, April 26, 1995, p. A1.

88. Bane, *Here to Stay.*, pp. 80, 164, n.21.

89. Arlie Hochschild with Anne Machung, *The Second Shift: Working Parents and the Revolution at Home* (New York: Viking Press, 1989); Mary Ann Mason, *The Equality Trap* (New York: Simon & Schuster, 1988); Carol M. Rose, "Bargaining and Gender," 18 *Harvard Journal of Law & Public Policy*, Spring 1995, p. 552, n.12, citing Paula England and George Farkas, *Households, Employment, and Gender* (1986), pp. 94-99 (stating that working women do most of the housework); *The Christian Science Monitor*, April 6, 1988, p. 23 (85 percent of working wives do almost all the cooking). 46 percent of men and 33 percent of women surveyed in 1946 thought women had "the easier time in present-day America," but only 22 percent of the men and 13% of the women thought so in 1993. *The Wall Street Journal*, September 9, 1994, p. B1.

90. Richard Vigilante, "Workingman's Blues?," *National Review*, April 27, 1992, p. 47. Surveys show that, despite their desire for more help with domestic chores, "most mothers do not want greater involvement of their husbands in child care." Browne, "Sex and Temperament in Modern Society," p. 1097, n.861.

91. *Austin* (Texas) *American-Statesman*, October 29, 1987, p. E8.

92. Bane, *Here to Stay*, p. 85.

93. Buss, *The Evolution of Desire*, pp. 23-25.

94. Betty Friedan, *The Second Stage* (New York: Summit Books, 1981), p. 46.

95. Ibid., pp. 41, 47, 287.

96. Ibid., pp. 286-87, 290-91.

97. Gilman, *Women And Economics*, pp. 242-44.

98. George Gilder, *Men and Marriage* (Gretna, La.: Pelican, 1986), p. viii.

99. Brigitte Berger, "Academic Feminism and the 'Left,'" *Academic Questions*, Spring 1988, p. 10.

100. Friedan, *The Second Stage*, p. 48.

101. Ayn Rand, *Atlas Shrugged* (New York: Random House, 1957), p. 1054.

102. The terms "social or religious" are used to distinguish two groups which may reason from different premises but reach similar conclusions with respect to family interests.

103. Karen De Witt, "New Cause Helps Feminists Appeal to Younger Women," *The New York Times*, February 5, 1996, p. A6; *The Christian Science Monitor*, May 11, 1988, p. 3.

104. Cynthia Harrison, *On Account of Sex* (Berkeley: University of California Press, 1988), p. 200.

105. Jane O'Reilly, "Talking About Women, Not to Them," *The New York Times Magazine*, September 11, 1988, pp. 32, 34.

106. *The Wall Street Journal*, January 19, 1994, p. A1. Effective in the 1997 tax year, this bias against one-income families will begin to change, when families with a stay-at-home spouse will be permitted to invest the same amount in IRAS as two-income families, *Austin* (Texas) *American-Statesman*, January 19, 1997, p. J1.

107. Elizabeth Janeway, "Child Care Inc.," *World Monitor, The Christian Science Monitor Monthly* (October 1988), pp. 68, 70, 72.

108. Ibid., p. 68.

109. Vigilante, "Workingman's Blues?," p. 49. The relationship between falling wages and entry of women into the work force is sometimes adverted to, e.g., John B. Judis, "Why Your Wages Keep Falling," *The New Republic*, February 14, 1994, p. 26. Costs of race and sex quotas in 1991 were estimated to be about 4 percent of GNP, as much as the entire public school system. Peter Brimelow and Leslie Spencer, "When Quotas Replace Merit, Everybody Suffers," *Forbes*, February 15, 1993, p. 80. The economic costs of our antidiscrimination laws are thoroughly documented in Walter K. Olson, *The Excuse Factory: How Today's Employment Laws Promote Mediocrity in the Workplace* (New York: The Free Press, 1997) and Richard A. Epstein, *Forbidden Grounds: The Case Against Employment Discrimination Laws* (Cambridge, Mass.: Harvard University Press, 1995).

110. Levin, *Feminism and Freedom*, pp. 43-44 (quoting the United States Equal Employment Opportunity Commission statement that "[a]bsent discrimination, it is to be expected that work forces will be more or less representative of the population in the community from which employees are hired"), 98-104; Browne, "Sex and Temperament in Modern Society," pp. 1099-1100 (discussing how rules of proof in affirmative action law have incorporated the feminist assumption that "a lack of proportional representation in a class of jobs—at least attractive jobs—presumptively demonstrates discrimination").

111. Lenore J. Weitzman, *The Divorce Revolution: The Unexpected Social and Economic Consequences for Women and Children in America* (New York: The Free Press, 1985), pp. 32-36, 43, 147-183.

112. Ibid., p. 143.

113. Mary Ann Glendon, *Abortion and Divorce in Western Law* (Cambridge, Mass.: Harvard University Press, 1987), p. 111.

114. *The Wall Street Journal*, October 31, 1988, p. B1.

115. Mansbridge, *Why We Lost the ERA*, pp. 87, 140.

116. Ibid., pp. 108-09.

117. Ehrenreich, *The Hearts of Men: American Dreams and the Flight from Commitment*, pp. 146, 147.

118. Bane, *Here to Stay*, p. 91.

119. Lopata, *Occupation: Housewife*, pp. 362, 373.

120. Bloom, *The Closing of the American Mind*, p. 128.

121. Ibid., pp. 127, 128.

122. Winn, *Children Without Childhood*, pp. 114, 115, 117, 120.

123. De Riencourt, *Sex and Power in History*, p. 411.

124. David Popenoe, "Parental Androgyny," *Society*, September/October 1993, pp. 6-7. In *The Lost City* (New York: Basic Books, 1995), Alan Ehrenhalt defends the much-maligned 1950s which were, for some, the best years of their lives.

125. Himmelfarb, *The De-Moralization of Society*, pp. 252-53.

126. Ibid., pp. 78, 81, 85, 104, discussing Elizabeth Roberts, *A Woman's Place: An Oral History of Working-Class Women 1890-1940* (Oxford: Blackwell, 1984), pp. 1-3, 117, 203.

127. These goals are vigorously promoted, for example, by Beverly LaHaye's Concerned Women for America, Phyllis Schlafly's Eagle Forum, The Rockford Institute's Center on The Family in America, and James C. Dobson's Focus on the Family. The Independent Women's Forum, with its publications, *The Women's Quarterly* and *Ex Femina*, has undertaken to rebut feminist misrepresentations and present a more conservative view on women's issues.

128. In *Who Stole Feminism?*, Christina Hoff Sommers ably documents the misrepresentations and exaggerations of the feminist-oriented media and the travesties involved in the machinations of those feminists who have sought to restructure academic disciplines to reflect so-called lateral female thought processes that are supposedly very different from what they call men's vertical thinking. The degeneration of "women's studies" into forms of female consciousness-raising indoctrination is also masterfully analyzed by Daphne Patai and Noretta Koertge in *Professing Feminism: Cautionary Tales from the Strange World of Women's Studies* (New York: New Republic/Basic, 1994).

129. Sommers, *Who Stole Feminism?*, pp. 17, 22-24.

130. The difficulties encountered by Gilder, Davidson, and Levin are discussed in Gilder, *Men and Marriage*, p. viii, and "Books in Review," *Commentary* (May 1988), p. 70. Steven Goldberg's *The Inevitability of Patriarchy* (republished in a revised version as *Why Men Rule: A Theory of Male Dominance* (Open Court, 1994)) was once in *The Guinness Book of World Records* for having been rejected more times (69) than any book eventually published. Daniel Seligman, "Testosterone Power," *National Review*, April 4, 1994, p. 65.

131. For example, Joan K. Peters, *When Mothers Work: Loving Our Children without Sacrificing Our Selves* (Reading, Mass.: Addison-Wesley, 1997); Rosalind C. Barnett and Caryl Rivers, *She Works, He Works: How Two-Income Families Are Happier, Healthier, and Better-Off* (San Francisco: HarperSan Francisco, 1996);

Sharon Hays, *The Cultural Contradictions of Motherhood* (New Haven: Yale University Press, 1996); Daniel J. Levinson with Judy D. Levinson, *The Seasons of a Woman's Life* (New York: Knopf, 1996); Thurer, *The Myths of Motherhood*.

132. *Insight*, June 6, 1994, p. 16. The membership of NOW is estimated to be up to forty percent lesbian (Dalton, *The American Enterprise*, May/June, 1995, p.74), and the organization has certainly never had the best interests of traditional women at heart .

133. James Atlas, "The Counter Counterculture," *The New York Times Magazine*, February 12, 1995, pp. 34, 37-38.

134. The pressures from so-called radical feminists against Professor Fox-Genovese are discussed in Carol Iannone, "How Politicized Studies Enforce Conformity: Interviews with Julius Lester and Elizabeth Fox-Genovese," *Academic Questions*, Summer 1992, p. 56.

135. Fox-Genovese, *Feminism Without Illusions*, pp. 3, 5, 27, 251.

136. Fox-Genovese, *Feminism Is Not The Story Of My Life*, pp. 195, 250. Her own interviews disclosed the concerns of working mothers that "teenagers come home after school to empty houses and cars," some saying that "you worry less about infants than about teenagers." Ibid., p. 113. Their concerns are well-founded. The high school senior who was charged with murdering her newborn son after giving birth in the bathroom at her prom was described as finishing her classes at 1:00 p.m. and then spending the rest of the day at her boyfriend's home. Abby Goodnough and Bruce Weber, "Before Prom, Ordinary Life for Suspect in a Murder," *The New York Times*, July 3, 1997, p. A10. When Brenda Barnes recently resigned as president of Pepsi-Cola North America to spend more time with her husband and three children (ages seven, eight, and ten), she cited years of "hectic travel, dinner meetings, missing children's birthdays, and even living in separate cities from her husband as they both pursued their careers." Nikhil Deogun, "Top PepsiCo Executive Picks Family Over Job," *The Wall Street Journal*, September 24, 1997, p. B1.

137. Ibid., pp. 111-12.

138. Ibid., pp. 111, 149, 152, 228-29.

139. Ibid., pp. 157, 256.

140. Fox-Genovese, *Feminism Without Illusions*, pp. 255-56.

141. Fox-Genovese, *Feminism Is Not The Story Of My Life*, p. 256.

142. The papers from this Symposium at the University of Virginia Law School, "Feminism, Sexual Distinctions, and the Law," are published in 18 *Harvard Journal of Law & Public Policy*, Spring 1995.

143. Fox-Genovese, *Feminism Is Not The Story Of My Life*, pp. 115-16.

144. Gwen J. Broude, "The Realities of Day Care," *The Public Interest*, Fall 1996, p. 104.

145. Carolyn G. Heilbrun, *Writing A Woman's Life* (New York: W. W. Norton, 1988), pp. 17, 130.

3. *The Groined Archway*

1. Letter to George Sand, *Correspondence*, Volume V, quoted in André Maurois, *Lelia: The Life of George Sand* (New York: Harper, 1953), p. 429.

2. Lawrence Sterne, *The Life and Opinions of Tristram Shandy*, *Great Books of the Western World*, Vol. 36 (Robert Maynard Hutchins, ed.), p. 346.

3. Jean-Paul Sartre, *The Family Idiot: Gustave Flaubert 1821-1857*, Volume II (Chicago: University of Chicago Press, 1987), pp. 344, 379-90, 396-97, 403, 418-28.

4. *The Wall Street Journal*, September 11, 1986, p. 32.

5. Quoted in Robert Blake, *Disraeli* (New York: St. Martin's Press, 1967), p. 149.

6. Yeats, *Vacillation* (1932).

7. Eliot, *Middlemarch*, p. 249.

8. Midge Decter, *The New Chastity and Other Arguments Against Women's Liberation* (New York: Coward, McCann & Geoghegan, 1972), p. 125.

9. Euripides, *Medea and Other Plays*, Tr. Philip Vellacott (Harmondsworth: Penguin Books, 1963), p. 24 (243-48).

10. Fox-Genovese, *Feminism Without Illusions*, p. 2.

11. Ibid., p. 3.

12. In *Who Stole Feminism*, pp. 19-33, Sommers describes the concern of academic feminism, in particular the National Women's Studies Association, with anti-rational "victim studies" that often resemble mass therapy and New Age healing rituals more than scholarly endeavors. Michael Weiss presented a similar analysis in "Feminist Pedagogy in the Law Schools," *Academic Questions*, Summer 1992, p. 75.

13. Eliot, *Middlemarch*, p. 269.

14. Virginia Woolf, *To the Lighthouse* (San Diego: Harvest/HBJ, 1927), p. 182.

15. Herb Goldberg, *The Hazards of Being a Male: Surviving the Myth of Masculine Privilege* (New York: Signet, 1976), p. 162, as quoted in Ehrenreich, *The Hearts of Men*, p. 119.

16. Mead, *Male and Female*, p. 217.

17. Mary R. Lefkowitz, *Women in Greek Myth* (Baltimore: The Johns Hopkins University Press, 1986), p. 10.

18. Lasch, *Haven in a Heartless World*, p. 102. Although Richard A. Posner describes the sexual revolution as "well-advanced in the 1950s" (*Sex*

and Reason, p. 239), the explosive increase in female premarital sexual activity did not occur until feminist sexual revolutionaries joined in promoting an ideal of female sexual promiscuity in the 1960s.

19. Decter, *The New Chastity and Other Arguments Against Women's Liberation*, p. 93.

20. Scruton, *Sexual Desire*, pp. 87, 289.

21. Gertrude Himmelfarb has documented the Marxist roots of this feminist charge that "bourgeois marriage is a form of legalized prostitution." *The De-Moralization of Society*, p. 53.

22. Kenneth Lasson, "Feminism Awry: Excesses in the Pursuit of Rights and Trifles," *Journal of Legal Education*, March 1992, pp. 12-19. Women's difference is the theme of Carol Gilligan's *In a Different Voice: Psychological Theory and Women's Development* (Cambridge, Mass.: Harvard University Press, 1982).

23. For example, Sylvia Ann Hewlett, *A Lesser Life: The Myth of Women's Liberation in America* (New York: Morrow, 1986); Felice A. Schwartz, "Management Women and the New Facts of Life," *Harvard Business Review* (Jan.-Feb. 1989). Schwartz's recommendation of what others dubbed "the Mommy Track" aroused significant controversy among feminists. *The New York Times*, March 28, 1993, p. F29; *The Wall Street Journal*, September 11, 1989, p. A7A; ibid., March 13, 1989, p. B1; *The Christian Science Monitor*, March 21, 1989, p. 14; *Time*, March 27, 1989, p. 72.

24. Decter, *The New Chastity and Other Arguments Against Women's Liberation*, p. 84.

25. Robert Wright, *The Moral Animal: Evolutionary Psychology and Everyday Life* (New York: Pantheon, 1994), pp. 122, 146.

26. Kersten, "What Do Women Want?: A Conservative Feminist Manifesto," p. 13.

27. "Even physical tests of female virginity are unreliable, whether from variations in the structure of the hymen, rupture due to nonsexual causes, or deliberate alteration." Buss, *The Evolution of Desire*, p. 68.

28. Despite these practices, some premarital intercourse still occurs, and then the brides' vulvas are re-sutured before marriage. Hanny Lightfoot-Klein, *Prisoners of Ritual: An Odyssey into Female Genital Circumcision in Africa* (Binghamton, New York: The Haworth Press, 1989), pp. 100, 152, 158, 280.

29. Posner, *Sex and Reason*, pp. 85, 330.

30. Ibid., pp. 181, 240, 204.

31. Ibid., p. 169, quoting Bertrand Russell, *Marriage and Morals* (1929), p. 27.

32. Johnson, *Intellectuals*, pp. 217-218.

33. Ibid., pp. 213, 214, 216, 217-18.

34. Dworkin, *Intercourse*, p. 94.

35. Ibid., p. 190.

36. Leo Tolstoy, *The Kreutzer Sonata*, in *Great Short Works of Leo Tolstoy*, translated by Louise and Aylmer Maude (New York: Harper & Row, 1967) (Perennial paperback), p. 365.

37. Wright, *The Moral Animal*, pp. 36-40.

38. Seymour Fisher, *Understanding the Female Orgasm* (New York: Basic Books, 1973), p. 210. This is a condensed version of Fisher's *The Female Orgasm: Psychology, Physiology, Fantasy* (New York: Basic Books, 1973), based on studies of the sexual feelings and fantasies of approximately three hundred middle-class married women. *Understanding the Female Orgasm*, pp. vii, xi.

39. Neil Gilbert, "Realities and Mythologies of Rape," *Society*, May/June 1992, p. 10.

40. Katie Roiphe, *The Morning After: Sex, Fear, and Feminism on Campus* (Boston: Little, Brown & Co., 1993).

41. Katie Roiphe, "Date Rape's Other Victim," *The New York Times Magazine*, June 13, 1993, pp. 30, 40.

42. *The New York Times*, September 25, 1993, pp. 1, 7.

43. Dworkin, *Intercourse*, pp. 63, 122.

44. Ibid., p. 64.

45. Gilder, *Sexual Suicide*, p. 37.

46. Ibid., pp. 39, 22, 38, 39.

47. Scruton, *Sexual Desire*, pp. 87-88.

48. Barbara Ehrenreich, Elizabeth Hess, Gloria Jacobs, *Remaking Love: The Feminization of Sex* (Garden City, New York: Anchor Books, 1987), pp. 71, 196.

49. This last suggestion comes from Shere Hite, quoted in Dworkin, *Intercourse*, pp. 128-29.

50. Gilder, *Sexual Suicide*, pp. 58, 33.

51. In *Enemies of Eros* (Chicago: Bonus Books, 1989), p. 240, Maggie Gallagher very acutely observes that it places a great burden on a child to be "chosen to live when others die." The deleterious effects of abortion on surviving children is discussed in David C. Reardon, *Aborted Women: Silent No More* (Chicago: Loyola University Press, 1987), pp. 225-30.

52. Ehrenreich et al., *Remaking Love*, pp. 194-95.

53. Ibid., pp. 192, 196.

54. Maggie Gallagher, "The New Pro-Life Rebels," *National Review*, February 27, 1987, pp. 37, 38.

55. Ehrenreich et al., *Re-Making Love*, pp. 24-25.

56. Helen Hazen, *Endless Rapture: Rape, Romance, and the Female Imagination* (New York: Charles Scribner's Sons, 1983), p. 63.

57. Lefkowitz, *Women in Greek Myth*, p. 53.

58. Elizabeth Hardwick, *Seduction and Betrayal: Women and Literature* (New York: Random House, 1974), p. 185.

59. Lefkowitz, *Women in Greek Myth*, p. 52.

60. Buss, *The Evolution of Desire*, p. 73; David M. Buss, "Evolution and Human Mating, 18 *Harvard Journal of Law & Public Policy*, Spring 1995, pp. 544-45.

61. Romance novels account for almost half of all paperback sales in the United States. *The Wall Street Journal*, September 6, 1994, p. B1.

62. Buss, *The Evolution of Desire*, pp. 82-3.

63. Pediatrician T. Berry Brazelton has speculated that parents who know they will be returning to work shortly after a child's birth defend "themselves against too intense an attachment to the new son or daughter in anticipation of the pain of being separated prematurely from their child." *The Christian Science World Monitor*, March 1989, p. 14.

64. Philippe Ariès, *Centuries of Childhood* (New York: Knopf, 1962), pp. 373-75; Lloyd deMause, Editor, *The History of Childhood* (New York: The Psychohistory Press, 1974), pp. 184-86, 263-67, 308-11, 410-11.

65. Kramer, *In Defense of the Family*, pp. 12-13, 23, 201.

66. John Bowlby, *Attachment and Loss, Volume I: Attachment* (New York: Basic Books, 1969), pp. 241-42.

67. Rhona Mahony, *Kidding Ourselves: Breadwinning, Babies, and Bargaining Power* (New York: Basic Books, 1995).

68. Morse, "Beyond 'Having It All,'" p. 574.

69. Harry F. Harlow performed experiments which substituted cloth and wire monkey surrogates for the mother monkeys. The experiments demonstrated both the devastating effects of separation from the mother and the fact that holding and cuddling of the infant are as important as feeding. Gene Bylinsky, "New Clues to the Causes of Violence," *Fortune*, January 1973, pp. 138-42.

70. Lionel Tiger and Robin Fox, *The Imperial Animal* (New York: Holt, Rinehart, and Winston, 1971), p. 65.

71. A related kind of blanking out of experiences of casual sex with a series of sexual partners is described in Megan Marshall's *The Cost of Loving: Women and the New Fear of Intimacy* (New York: G. P. Putnam's Sons, 1984), p. 103.

72. Bloom, *The Closing of the American Mind*, p. 99.

73. De Beauvoir, *The Second Sex*, p. 491.

74. Robert D. Goldstein, *Mother-Love and Abortion, A Legal Interpretation* (Berkeley: Univ. of Calif. Press, 1988), p. 88.

75. Mead, *Male and Female*, pp. 364-65.

76. Gertrude Himmelfarb, *Marriage and Morals Among the Victorians* (New York: Knopf, 1986), p. 21.

77. Mansbridge, *Why We Lost the ERA*, pp. 71-77.

78. Goldberg, *The Inevitability of Patriarchy*, p. 149.

79. *Austin* (Texas) *American-Statesman*, June 30, 1992, p. A1; ibid., June 11, 1992, p. A27. Resolutions of the National Organization for Women favor removing restrictions on women's military service in combat because these restrictions interfere with women's career opportunities.

80. Gilbert, "Realities and Mythologies of Rape," p. 4; Posner, *Sex and Reason*, pp. 32-33; Neil Gilbert, "The Phantom Epidemic of Sexual Assault," *Public Interest*, Spring 1991, p. 54; Hazen, *Endless Rapture*, pp. 75-79.

81. Posner, *Sex and Reason*, p. 276. The United States "substantially leads all Western countries in the rate of legal abortions per thousand women of child-bearing age." Glendon, *Abortion and Divorce in Western Law*, p. 59.

82. David Horowitz, "The Feminist Assault on the Military," *National Review*, October 5, 1992, p. 48.

83. *The Washington Times National Weekly Edition*, February 20-26, 1995, p. 9.

84. K. L. Billingsley, "Dancing with the Elephant," *Heterodoxy* March/April 1995 (Los Angeles: Center for the Study of Popular Culture), p. 12.

85. Rowan Scarborough, "Pilot Error Acknowledged in Death of Woman Flier," *The Washington Times National Weekly Edition*, April 17-23, 1995, p. 11.

86. John Corry, "The Death of Kara Hultgreen," *The American Spectator*, June 1995, p. 41.

87. Ibid.

88. Billingsley, "Dancing with the Elephant," pp. 13-14.

89. Ehrenreich et al., *Re-Making Love*, pp. 6, 11, 20.

90. Ibid., p. 168.

91. Ibid., pp. 4, 72, 188, 193.

92. A religious-feminist alliance fighting pornography and supporting the Pornography Victims' Compensation Act is opposed by other feminists who reject these initiatives as destructive of women's rights. Chi Chi Sileo, "Pornographobia: Feminists Go to War," *Insight*, February 27, 1995, p. 6.

93. Hazen, *Endless Rapture*, pp. 101-05, 115.

94. Ibid., pp. 116-17.

95. Ehrenreich et al., *Re-Making Love*, pp. 162-63, 172.

96. Ibid., pp. 174-75.

97. Ibid., pp. 177–80.

98. Warren E. Leary, "U.S.'s Rate of Sexual Diseases Is Highest in Developed World," *The New York Times*, November 20, 1996, p. c21 (noting that "these diseases cost the nation at least $10 billion a year, not including the cost of sexually transmitted H.I.V., the virus that causes AIDS").

99. *The Wall Street Journal*, May 18, 1988, p. 29.

100. "Ectopic Pregnancies Reported on the Rise," *The New York Times*, January 27, 1995, p. A10.

101. Kenneth Prager, "Infant Mortality, Mother's Morality," *The Wall Street Journal*, February 1, 1995, p. A12.

102. Robin Marantz Henig, "Is the Pap Test Valid," *The New York Times Magazine*, May 28, 1989, p. 38. A recent study concludes that "women are 5 to 11 times as likely to develop cervical cancer if their male partners frequent prostitutes or have many sexual partners" because "the cancer risk for a woman increases with the number of direct or indirect sexual exposures." *The New York Times*, August 7, 1996, p. A11.

103. Lawrence K. Altman, "Women Who Have Abortions Increase Their Risk of Breast Cancer," *The New York Times*, October 27, 1994, p. A12.; Christine Gorman, "Do Abortions Raise the Risk of Breast Cancer?," *Time*, November 7, 1994, p. 61.

104. Jane E. Brody, "Big Study Fails to Link Abotion and Cancer," *The New York Times*, January 9, 1997, p. A1.

105. Lucette Lagnado, "Abortion Study Fuels Debate On Cancer Link," *The Wall Street Journal*, January 9, 1997, p. B1. See also, Joel Brind, "Abortion, Breast Cancer, and Ideology," *First Things*, May 1997, p. 12; John McGinnis, "The Politics of Cancer Research," *The Wall Street Journal*, February 28, 1997, p. A14.

106. Anne Taylor Fleming, *Motherhood Deferred: A Woman's Journey* (New York: G. P. Putnam's Sons, 1994), pp. 13, 17, 25, 26, 87.

107. Ibid., pp. 115, 187, 195.

108. Ibid., pp. 115, 105, 108, 226.

109. Gina Kolata, "Study Finds 2-Decade Decline in Sperm Counts of Fertile Men," *The New York Times*, February 2, 1995, p. A12. Two later studies show sperm counts to be steady. *The New York Times*, April 29, 1996, p. A8.

110. Gilder, *Sexual Suicide*, pp. 39–40.

111. Posner, *Sex and Reason*, pp. 340–41.

112. Marshall, *The Cost of Loving*, pp. 22–25, 67, 217–21.

113. Ehrenreich et al., *Remaking Love*, pp. 195–96.

114. Decter, *The New Chastity and Other Arguments against Women's Liberation*, p. 84.

115. Robert J. Collins, M.D., "A Physician's View of College Sex," *Journal of the American Medical Association*, Vol. 232, April 28, 1975, p. 392.

116. Gilder, *Sexual Suicide*, pp. 23-4.

117. Barbara Dafoe Whitehead, "The Failure of Sex Education," *The Atlantic Monthly*, October 1994, p. 68.

118. Alex Witchel, "Now It's Sex and the Senior Woman," *The New York Times*, April 1, 1993, p. B1.

119. Fleming, *Motherhood Deferred*, pp. 102-03.

120. Ibid., pp. 17, 207.

121. *Time*, October 12, 1987, p. 72.

122. Shere Hite, *Women and Love: A Cultural Revolution in Progress* (New York: Knopf, 1987).

123. Collins, *Journal of the American Medical Association*, Vol. 232, p. 392.

124. Hazen, *Endless Rapture*, p. 117.

125. Scruton, *Sexual Desire*, p. 32.

126. Neely, *Gender, The Myth of Equality*, pp. 60-62.

127. *The New York Times*, May 18, 1994, p. A10. 81 percent of the sexually active boys surveyed found sex "a pleasurable experience" versus 59 percent of the girls; 71 percent of the girls said they were in love with their last sexual partner versus 45 percent of the boys.

128. Marcus, *The Other Victorians*, p. 281.

129. *De l'Influence des Passions* (1796).

4. *The Mocking of Conjugal Sexuality*

1. Isaac Bashevis Singer, *The Penitent* (New York: Farrar Straus Giroux, 1983), p. 162.

2. From a letter to his wife quoted in Julian Hawthorne, *Nathaniel Hawthorne and His Wife: A Biography* (Boston: James R. Osgood and Co., 1885)(republished, Grosse Pointe, Mich.: Scholarly Press, 1968), Vol. I, p. 294. The biographer said of his parents' marriage: "if true love and married happiness should ever be in need of vindication, ample material for that purpose may be found in these volumes." Preface, pp. v-vi.

3. Ehrenreich et al., *Re-Making Love*, pp. 5, 169.

4. Dworkin, *Intercourse*, p. 136.

5. Gilder, *Sexual Suicide*, pp. 22, 39.

6. One feminist author's survey revealed Réage's book to be a "top turn-on" for women. Hazen, *Endless Rapture*, p. 106.

7. Posner, *Sex and Reason*, p. 367.

8. Marcus, *The Other Victorians*, p. 159.

9. Mead, *Male and Female*, pp. 209-10.

10. Hanny Lightfoot-Klein, *Prisoners of Ritual: An Odyssey into Female Genital Circumcision in Africa* (Binghamton, New York: Harrington Park Press, 1989), pp. 33-35, 98-99.

11. Ibid., p. 69.

12. Ibid., pp. 40, 72.

13. Ibid., pp. 23, 39, 66. One doctor defended excising one-half of the clitoris because a large clitoris causes trouble: girls are subject to "sexual overstimulation" and in the cities fall from their bicycles "in a sexual swoon." Ibid., p. 12.

14. Ibid., p. 8.

15. Ibid., pp. 87-89. Husbands who ignore the invitation are sometimes awakened by "dropping dishes [plastic] or banging pots around."

16. Scruton, *Sexual Desire*, p. 178.

17. This linkage was "plainly admitted by some" but "evasively denied by most" of Lightfoot-Klein's informants. Lightfoot-Klein, *Prisoners of Ritual*, p. 101.

18. Informants disclosed periods of one and two days (brutal events caused by impatience or village custom requiring penetration on the first night) (ibid., pp. 249, 255), ten days (p. 260), two weeks (p. 253), three weeks (pp. 7, 252), two months (p. 259), four to five months (p. 247), and two years (p. 256).

19. Ibid., pp. 103-05, 282.

20. Ibid., pp. 21, 70.

21. Ibid., pp. 149, 152.

22. Ehrenreich et al., *Re-Making Love*, pp. 45, 76.

23. Marshall, *The Cost of Loving*, p. 103.

24. Woolf, *To the Lighthouse*, p. 93.

25. Giles St. Aubyn, *Queen Victoria: A Portrait* (New York: Atheneum, 1992), pp. 259-60.

26. Marcus, *The Other Victorians*, p. 194.

27. *Selected Letters of Fyodor Dostoyevsky* (Rutgers, The State University, 1987), excerpted in *The World & I*, October, 1987, pp. 340, 357.

28. Posner, *Sex and Reason*, p. 28. That there may be some link between orgasm and conception is indicated by the fact that orgasmic women do retain more sperm. Buss, *The Evolution of Desire*, p. 76.

29. Degler, *At Odds*, p. 262.

30. Posner, *Sex and Reason*, pp. 52-3.

31. Marcus, *The Other Victorians*, p. 22.

32. Ibid., pp. 26-7, 29. These Victorian views may find support in research on fruit flies and roundworms showing that making sperm hastens

death; male soil nematode worms that copulate a lot and therefore produce a lot of sperm live only two-thirds as long as those that copulate but do not make sperm. *The New York Times*, June 21, 1994, p. B12; *Time*, December 14, 1992, p. 25.

33. Marcus, *The Other Victorians*, pp. 146, 148.

34. Himmelfarb, *Marriage and Morals Among the Victorians*, p. xiii.

35. Marcus, *The Other Victorians*, pp. 148-49.

36. In *When Passion Reigned: Sex and the Victorians* (New York: Basic Books, 1995), Patricia Anderson has marshalled the facts which rebut this myth of Victorian sexual repression.

37. Himmelfarb, *The De-Moralization of Society*, pp. 75-76.

38. Degler, *At Odds*, pp. 253, 258, 271-2.

39. Ibid., p. 225.

40. Ibid., p. 257.

41. Ibid., p. 269.

42. Ibid., pp. 259, 260.

43. Ibid., pp. 260, 261.

44. Ibid., pp. 262-63.

45. Quoted in Alfred Kazin, "The Opera of 'The Scarlet Letter,'" *The New York Review of Books*, October 8, 1992, p. 54. I did not find this statement in Julian's two volume biography of his parents. Possibly it was withheld as "a matter of taste" or "too intimate and lovable to be published." Vol. I, Preface, p. v, Vol. II, p. 295.

46. Degler, *At Odds*, pp. 263-64.

47. Ibid., pp. 264-65.

48. Ibid., pp. 265-66.

49. Kersten, "What Do Women Want?: A Conservative Feminist Manifesto," p. 5.

50. Woolf, *A Room of One's Own*. Girton and Newnham opened in 1869 and 1870; Somerville and Lady Margaret Hall opened for women ten years later at Oxford; women were admitted to London University in 1878. Himmelfarb, *The De-Moralization of Society*, p. 109.

51. Vera Brittan, *Testament of Youth* (New York: Seaview Books, 1980) (originally published in 1933).

52. Peter Ackroyd, *Dickens* (New York: Harper Collins, 1990), pp. 64-68, 74-75.

53. Virginia Woolf, *Three Guineas* (New York: Harvest/HBJ, 1938), pp. 5, 86.

54. Norbert Elias, *Power & Civility, The Civilizing Process: Volume II* (New York: Pantheon Books, 1982), p. 81.

55. Susan Mann, "Learned Women in the Eighteenth Century," in *Engendering China: Women, Culture, and the State*, edited by Christina K. Gilmartin, Gail Hershatter, Lisa Rofel, Tyrene White (Cambridge, Mass.: Harvard University Press, 1994), pp. 27, 29, 45.

56. Himmelfarb, *The De-Moralization of Society*, pp. 106-07.

57. Degler, *At Odds*, pp. 250-51.

58. *The Letters of Abelard and Héloise*, translated by Betty Radice (Harmondsworth: Penguin, 1974), pp. 113, 115, 133.

59. Ibid., p. 133.

60. *The Holy Bible: Authorized King James Version* (Cleveland & New York: The World Publishing Co.).

61. Posner, *Sex and Reason*, pp. 146-47.

62. W. K. Lacey, *The Family in Classical Greece* (Ithaca, New York: Cornell University Press, 1968), pp. 31-33, 247, n.1.

63. *Homer: The Iliad*, translated by Robert Fagles (New York: Viking, 1990), Book 9, pp. 262-63, 265.

64. Ibid., Book 6, pp. 210-12.

65. Ibid., Book 24, pp. 612-13.

66. Jasper Griffin, "The Love that Dared to Speak its Name," *The New York Review of Books*, October 22, 1992, p. 30.

67. Upon attending the gymnasium and wrestling-school, boys of about sixteen might become catamites and themselves become the lovers during military training and for a short time thereafter. Lacey, *The Family in Classical Greece*, pp. 157-58.

68. Ibid., pp. 9, 100-03.

69. Ibid., pp. 112-13.

70. Ibid., pp. 33, 175, 218, 173.

71. Ibid., pp. 82, 158, 304, n.44, 172.

72. Ibid., p. 114.

73. Ibid., pp. 158, 303, n.42.

74. Ibid., pp. 173, 163, 171.

75. Ibid., pp. 216, 169-70.

76. Ibid., pp. 309, n.110, 198-99.

77. I saw these sculptures in the exhibit, "The Greek Miracle," at the Metropolitan Museum of Art in April, 1993. The Grave Stele of a Little Girl is from the Metropolitan's collection; the Grave Stele of Ktesilaos and Theano is from the National Archeological Museum of Athens.

78. Lacey, *The Family in Classical Greece*, pp. 100-03, 174. Camille Paglia has criticized the scholarship that portrays Greek women as oppressed, while failing "to acknowledge the historical fact that male law and order also provided

protection, security, and physical sustenance to women and children." *Sex, Art, and American Culture* (New York: Vintage, 1992), p. 205.

79. Griffin, *The New York Review of Books*, October 22, 1992, p. 32.

80. Lefkowitz, *Women in Greek Myth*, pp. 28, 134-35.

81. Ibid., pp. 28, 35-36, 69. This analysis is supported in Bruce S. Thornton, *Eros: The Myth of Ancient Greek Sexuality* (Boulder, Colo.: Westview, 1996). Susan Treggiari's *Roman Marriage* (New York: Oxford Univ. Press, 1991) presents a similar picture of marriage in the Roman world.

82. John M. Riddle, *Contraception and Abortion from the Ancient World to the Renaissance* (Cambridge: Harvard University Press, 1993).

83. This much of my description appears in the catalogue entry for the bowl. Ann C. Gunter and Paul Jett, *Ancient Iranian Metalwork in the Arthur M. Sackler Gallery and the Freer Gallery of Art*, pp. 161-63. The bowl is exhibited in the Gallery of Luxury Arts of the Silk Route Empires.

84. St. Aubyn, *Queen Victoria*, p. 330. Victoria was only forty-two when Albert died, but she strongly opposed the remarriage of widows.

85. Lasch, *Haven in a Heartless World*, p. 58.

86. Ehrenreich et al., *Re-Making Love*, pp. 76, 172, 184, 166.

87. Midge Decter, "Whatever Happened to America?," *The American Spectator*, December, 1982, p. 8.

88. Winick, *The New People: Desexualization in American Life*, pp. 313-17.

89. Buss, *The Evolution of Desire*, p. 69.

90. Ibid., pp. 126, 129-30.

91. Zora Neale Hurston, *Jonah's Gourd Vine* (New York: Harper Perennial, 1990) (originally published, 1934), pp. 110-111.

92. In "A Farewell to Feminism," *Commentary*, January 1997, pp. 23, 30, Elizabeth Powers details many of these regrets and asks the crucial question, "is a woman's experience of sex part of a larger moral, indeed spiritual, equation?" While Katie Roiphe has movingly described the doubt and confusion of young sexual revolutionaries about the rewards of loveless sex, she seeks no answers in any moral equation. Katie Roiphe, *Last Night in Paradise* (New York: Little, Brown, 1996). The need for such an attempt is recognized in Naomi Wolf's critique of the sexual revolution, *Promiscuities: The Secret Struggle for Womanhood* (New York: Random House, 1997).

93. Decter, *The New Chastity and Other Arguments Against Women's Liberation*, pp. 95, 80, 98.

94. Ibid., pp. 101-02.

95. Marshall, *The Cost of Loving*, pp. 152-53. In *The New Victorians: A Young Woman's Challenge to the Old Feminist Order* (New York: Warner Books,

1995), p. 45, Rene Denfeld describes lesbianism as "far more than a sexual orientation or even a preference," for it "has always been political."

96. Ehrenreich et al., *Re-Making Love*, pp. 202-03.

97. Ibid., pp. 70, 77, 182.

98. Posner, *Sex and Reason*, pp. 440, 132.

99. Francine du Plessix Gray, "Splendor and Miseries," *The New York Review of Books*, July 16, 1992, p. 35.

100. "Norplant Joins War on Teen Pregnancy," *Insight*, March 8, 1993, p. 6.

101. Thomas Sowell, *Inside American Education* (New York: The Free Press, 1993), p. 187.

102. Ehrenreich at al., *Re-Making Love*, p. 93.

103. *Time*, October 12, 1987, p. 72.

104. Her biographer depicted somewhat different dynamics in her own marriage to Leonard Woolf, who cared for her with unflagging dedication through illnesses, bouts of madness, and suicide attempts. She gave him neither sexual responsiveness nor children, but he had the satisfaction of nurturing a talent that would probably have been far less fruitful without his attentive devotion. Quentin Bell, *Virginia Woolf: A Biography* (New York: Harcourt Brace Jovanovich, 1972).

105. Woolf, *To the Lighthouse*, pp. 223-25.

106. Daniel Albright, *Personality and Impersonality: Lawrence, Woolf, and Mann* (Chicago: University of Chicago Press, 1978), pp. 152-3.

107. Bell, *Virginia Woolf*, Vol. II, pp. 5-8. Sexual activity forced upon her by her older stepbrother is implicated in Virginia's problems. Ibid., Vol I, pp. 42-44, Vol. II, p. 6.

108. Woolf, *To the Lighthouse*, pp. 240-41.

109. Ibid., pp. 267, 266, 239-41.

110. Ehrenreich et al., *Re-Making Love*, pp. 70-71, 81.

111. Ibid., pp. 35, 193, 196.

112. There is apparently no evidence that sex education programs have so far been successful in substituting noncoital sex for coitus. Whitehead, "The Failure of Sex Education," pp. 64, 68. Such success would seem unlikely absent an effort to promote abstention from pre-marital coitus as the cultural norm.

113. Ellen Fein and Sherrie Schneider, *The Rules: Time Tested Secrets for Capturing the Heart of Mr. Right* (New York: Warner Books, 1996).

114. Wright, *The Moral Animal*, pp. 139-40. *The Rules* has provoked a response: Nate Penn and Lawrence LaRosa, *The Code: Time-tested Secrets for Getting What You Want from Women Without Marrying Them!* (Fireside, 1997).

115. Paglia, *Sex, Art, and American Culture*, p. 182.

116. Ehrenreich et al., *Re-Making Love*, p. 52.

117. Ibid., p. 199.

118. Lightfoot-Klein, *Prisoners of Ritual*, pp. 13, 247-77.

119. Ibid., pp. 81, 84-86.

120. Ehrenreich et al., *Re-Making Love.*, p. 98.

121. Gordon S. Haight, *George Eliot: A Biography* (New York: Oxford University Press, 1968), p. 137. Ludwig Feuerbach developed this concept in *The Essence of Christianity*, which Marian Evans translated from the German.

122. Erik Erikson, *Identity, Youth, and Crisis* (New York: W.W. Norton, 1968), pp. 277-78.

123. D. H. Lawrence, *Lady Chatterley's Lover* (New York: Grove Press, 1957), p. 164.

124. *The Wall Street Journal*, September 11, 1986, p. 32.

125. Brigitte Berger, "Academic Feminism and the 'Left,'" *Academic Questions* (Spring 1988), pp. 6, 10.

126. Peter D. Kramer, *Listening to Prozac* (New York: Viking Press, 1993), pp. xv, 270-71.

127. David J. Rothman, "Shiny Happy People," *The New Republic*, February 14, 1994, pp. 34, 36.

128. Ehrenreich et al., *Re-Making Love*, p. 81.

129. Winick, *The New People*, pp. 319, 321.

130. Ibid., p. 319.

131. Ehrenreich et al., *Re-Making Love*, p. 204.

132. Ibid., p. 130.

133. Ibid., p. 119.

134. Scruton, *Sexual Desire*, pp. 177-78, 298.

135. Ibid., pp. 177, 303.

136. Fisher, *Understanding the Female Orgasm*, pp. 72-4, 78-9, 203.

137. Ibid., pp. 207, 209.

138. Ehrenreich et al., *Re-Making Love.*, p. 159.

139. *Time*, October 17, 1994, p. 68.

140. "Along with the family," said Hillary Rodham, "marriage, slavery, and the Indian reservation system" are examples of arrangements which deprive "people of rights in a dependency relationship" on the theory that they "are incapable or undeserving of the right to take care of themselves." "Children Under the Law," 43 *Harvard Educational Review* (November 1973), p. 493.

141. Ehrenreich, et al. *Re-Making Love.*, p. 152.

142. Buss, 18 *Harvard Journal of Law & Public Policy*, Spring 1995, p. 537; Buss, *The Evolution of Desire*, pp. 97-98, 112-13, 119-20.

5. *Feminism's Totalitarian Impulse*

1. F.A. Hayek, *Law, Legislation and Liberty, Vol. 1* (Chicago: Univ. of Chicago Press, 1973), pp. 50-51.

2. Edmund Burke, *Reflections on the Revolution in France*, reprinted in *Edmund Burke on Government, Politics and Society*, edited by B. W. Hill (International Publications Service, 1976), p. 327.

3. Whittaker Chambers, *Witness* (New York: Random House, 1952), p. 9.

4. Nicholas Davidson's *The Failure of Feminism* (Buffalo, New York: Prometheus Books, 1988) acutely criticizes many aspects of feminism, although Davidson also defends abortion and the sexual revolution, while decrying feminists' ideological and confrontational approach to sexual transactions.

5. Juliet B. Schor, *The Overworked American: The Unexpected Decline of Leisure* (New York: Basic Books, 1991); Susan Faludi, *Backlash: The Undeclared War Against American Women* (New York: Crown, 1991); "The War Against Feminism," *Time*, March 9, 1992, p. 50.

6. *What Is to Be Done?* trans. Joe Fineberg and George Hanna, ed. Victor J. Jerome (New York: International Publishers, New World Paperbacks Edition, 1969), p. 11 (quoted in John Attarian, "Chips off the Old Bloc," *Academic Questions*, Spring 1993, p. 76).

7. Michael Levin's *Feminism and Freedom* is a detailed analysis of feminist success in restructuring our society. Frederick R. Lynch's *Invisible Victims: White Males and the Crisis of Affirmative Action* (New York: Greenwood Press, 1989) examines the use of race and sex preferences to reconstitute the work force, pointing up the impact on the homemaker wives of the men these preferences discriminate against.

8. Weitzman, *The Divorce Revolution*, p. 360.

9. Michael Kelly, "Saint Hillary," *The New York Times Magazine*, May 23, 1993, pp. 22, 25.

10. Simon Schama, *Citizens: A Chronicle of the French Revolution* (New York: Knopf, 1989), p. 577.

11. Kelly, "Saint Hillary," p. 65.

12. Leon Wieseltier, "Total Quality Meaning," *The New Republic*, July 19 & 26, 1993, p. 17.

13. Ibid. These statements appear in a speech given by Hillary Rodham Clinton at the University of Texas in Austin.

14. Mark Helprin, *Winter's Tale* (New York: Simon & Schuster, 1983) (Pocket Books edition), p. 656.

15. Norman Cohn, *The Pursuit of the Millennium* (New York: Oxford University Press paperback, 1970), p. 120.

16. Wieseltier, "Total Quality Meaning," p. 17.

17. Cohn, *The Pursuit of the Millennium*, pp. 281, 286.

18. Quoted in Blake, *Disraeli*, p. 510.

19. Norbert Elias, *The Civilizing Process Power & Civility, The Civilizing Process: Vol. II*; (both volumes translated by Edmund Jephcott).

20. Elias, *The Civilizing Process: Vol. II*, p. 160.

21. Ibid., pp. 354-55, n.129.

22. Ibid., p. 230.

23. Ernest Gellner, *Conditions of Liberty: Civil Society and its Rivals* (New York: Allen Lane, Penguin Press, 1994).

24. Kenneth Minogue, "Necessary Imperfections," *The National Interest*, Winter 1994/1995, pp. 83, 85.

25. John Saar, "The Great Wall Comes Down," *Life*, April 30, 1971, p. 33.

26. *Austin* (Texas) *American-Statesman*, October 4, 1971, p. 23.

27. Millett, *Sexual Politics*, pp. 126-27, 225.

28. While often identified as a lesbian, Millet was married to a man who left her, an event that one commentator suggests may have aggravated her problems with mental illness. Katherine Dalton, "Hard Cases," *The American Enterprise*, May/June 1995, p. 72.

29. Mansbridge, *Why We Lost The ERA*, pp. 98, 100.

30. Simone de Beauvoir, "Sex, Society, and the Female Dilemma: A Dialogue Between Simone de Beauvoir and Betty Friedan," *Saturday Review*, June 14, 1975, p. 18. Friedan replied to de Beauvoir that "there is such a tradition of individual freedom in America that I would never say that every woman must put her child in a child-care center." This sentiment did not, however, prevent her from supporting measures designed to pressure women into making that choice.

31. Ibid., p. 20.

32. Ibid., p. 16.

33. De Beauvoir, *The Second Sex*, pp. 724-25 (footnote omitted).

34. Gertrude Himmelfarb, *On Liberty and Liberalism: The Case of John Stuart Mill* (New York: Knopf, 1974), p. 324.

35. De Riencourt, *Sex and Power in History*, pp. 115-16, 126-27, 207.

36. Ibid., pp. 370-76.

37. Lasch, *Haven in a Heartless World*, pp. 85-86, 91.

38. Mead, *Male and Female*, pp. 193-94.

39. Crane Brinton, *The Anatomy of Revolution* (New York: Vintage, 1965), p. 224.

40. Ibid.; de Riencourt, *Sex and Power in History*, pp. 374-78; Urie Bronfenbrenner, *Two Worlds of Childhood: U.S. and U.S.S.R.* (New York: Russell Sage Foundation, 1970), pp. 81-84.

41. Francine du Plessix Gray, *Soviet Women: Walking the Tightrope* (New York: Doubleday, 1990); *Balancing Acts: Contemporary Stories by Russian Women*, edited by Helena Goscilo (Bloomington, In.: Indiana University Press, 1989); *The New Soviet Fiction: Sixteen Short Stories*, compiled by Sergei Zalygin (New York: Abbeville Press, 1989).

42. Patricia Cayo Sexton, *The Feminized Male: Classrooms, White Collars, and the Decline of Manliness* (New York: Vintage, 1969). The most common diagnosis for "childhood misbehavior" is ADD, attention-deficit disorder; boys make up 80 to 90 percent of all ADD cases, which have nearly doubled in the last five years. What "used to be considered ordinary boyhood traits are now thought of as abnormal or deviant." Pressure by gender-equity advocates "to make schools 'fairer' for girls" has led to "a crackdown on 'boyish' behavior" with the result, psychologists note, that schools "have pathologized what is simply normal for boys" and often now operate as if "boyhood is defective." G. Pascal Zachary, "Male Order," *The Wall Street Journal*, May 2, 1997, p. AI.

43. Gilder, *Sexual Suicide*, pp. 195-203.

44. Wieseltier, "Total Quality Meaning," pp. 20, 24-26.

45. Walter Kiechel III, "The Workaholic Generation," *Fortune*, April 10, 1989, pp. 50, 54.

46. Berger, *The War over the Family*, pp. 87-91, 98-101.

47. Ibid., pp.116-17,134,177-78; Kramer, *In Defense of the Family*, pp.32-33.

48. Berger, *The War over the Family*, pp. 157-58. Lasch, *Haven in a Heartless World*, pp. 174-75, n.11; Bettelheim, *The Children of the Dream*, pp. 97, 128-30, 169-73.

49. *Austin* (Texas) *American-Statesman*, August 14, 1993, p. C3.

50. Erikson, *Identity, Youth, and Crisis*; John Bowlby, *Attachment and Loss, Volume I, Attachment; Volume II, Separation, Anxiety, and Anger* (New York: Basic Books, 1969, 1973).

51. *Austin* (Texas) *American-Statesman*, August 23, 1988, p. A9.

52. *The New York Times*, July 14, 1993, pp. AI, A9.

53. David Popenoe, "Family Decline in the Swedish Welfare State," *The Public Interest*, Winter 1991, pp. 66, 71; Allan C. Carlson, *Family Questions* (New Brunswick: Transaction Books, 1988), pp. 20-25, 71, 117-18.

54. Don Belt, "Sweden: In Search of a New Model," *National Geographic*, August 1993, p. 22.

55. Wang Zheng, "Three Interviews," in Barlow, *Gender Politics in Modern China*, pp. 165-67.

56. Zhu Hong, "Women, Illness, and Hospitalization: Images of Women in Contemporary Chinese Fiction," in Gilmartin, et al., *Engendering China*, pp. 324-25, 329-31.

57. Wang Zheng, "Three Interviews," in Barlow, *Gender Politics in Modern China*, pp. 193-94, 203.

58. Gao Xiaoxian, "China's Modernization and Changes in the Social Status of Rural Women," in Gilmartin et al., *Engendering China*, p. 92.

59. Chen Yiyun, "Out of the Traditional Halls of Academe," ibid., p. 77.

60. Li Xiaojiang, "Economic Reform and the Awakening of Chinese Women's Consciousness," ibid., pp. 364-65, 374, 376, 378-79.

61. Tani E. Barlow, "Politics and Protocols of Funü: (Un)Making National Woman," ibid., pp. 349-50.

62. Lisa Rofel, "Liberation Nostalgia and a Yearning for Modernity," ibid., pp. 243-44.

63. Ibid., pp. 229, 231.

64. Li Ziyun, "Women's Consciousness and Women's Writing," ibid., pp. 308, 317.

65. Barlow, "Politics and Protocols of Funü," ibid., p. 347.

66. Jonathan Mirsky, "The Bottom of the Well," *The New York Review of Books*, October 6, 1994, p. 28.

67. Rudolf Flesch, *The New Book of Unusual Quotations* (New York: Harper & Row, 1966), p. 37.

6. *A Tangle of Pathology*

1. Daniel P. Moynihan, *The Negro Family: The Case for National Action* (Washington, D.C.: Department of Labor, March 1965, reprinted, Westport, Conn.: Greenwood Press, 1981), pp. 5, 6-9, 29.

2. Ibid., pp. 30-34.

3. Ibid., pp. 35-37.

4. Daniel P. Moynihan, *Family and Nation: The Godkin Lectures, Harvard University* (San Diego: Harcourt Brace Jovanovich, 1986), p. 52.

5. Ibid., p. 112.

6. Ibid., pp. 111, 146.

7. *Austin* (Texas) *American-Statesman*, November 5, 1986, p. A2; ibid., July 17, 1992, p. A1; William J. Bennett, *The Index of Leading Cultural Indicators* (The Heritage Foundation, March 1993), p. 15.

8. These criticisms of Moynihan's 1965 report are discussed in Allan C. Carlson, "Sex According to Social Science," *Policy Review* (Spring 1982), pp. 115, 125, and in Lasch, *Haven in a Heartless World*, pp. 159-63.

9. Carlson, "Sex Acccording to Social Science," p. 126.

10. Moynihan, *The Negro Family*, p. 6 (of the 22.9 percent of Black women, 5.6 percent were divorced and 17.3 percent had absent husbands, and of the 7.9 percent of white women, 4 percent were divorced and 3.9 percent had absent husbands).

11. *Insight*, October 13, 1986, pp. 10, 11; Weitzman, *The Divorce Revolution*, p. 187 (in the past twenty-five years, divorces of couples married more than fifteen years increased from 4 percent to 20 percent of all divorces).

12. *The Wall Street Journal*, September 25, 1986, pp. 1, 26.

13. *The Wall Street Journal*, September 1, 1988, p. 20.

14. Marital Status and Living Arrangements: March 1981 (Wash., D.C.: Bureau of the Census, July 1982).

15. *Insight*, October 13, 1986, pp. 8, 14-15; *Austin* (Texas)*American-Statesman*, January 21, 1988, p. A10.

16. *The Wall Street Journal*, September 25, 1986, p. 1; Moynihan, *Family and Nation*, pp. 48, 147.

17. Moynihan, *Family and Nation*, p. 147.

18. Ibid, pp. 51-52, 101, 111.

19. *The New York Times*, June 15, 1993, pp. A1, A12.

20. Weitzman, *The Divorce Revolution*, pp. 49, 243.

21. Glendon, *Abortion and Divorce in Western Law*, p. 111.

22. Weitzman, *The Divorce Revolution*, p. 338; *The Wall Street Journal*, December 8, 1988, p. B1.

23. *The Wall Street Journal*, October 29, 1986, p. 28; Weitzman, pp. 283-84; *Austin* (Texas) *American-Statesman*, November 14, 1986, p. A5.

24. Weitzman, *The Divorce Revolution*, p. 343.

25. Moynihan, *The Negro Family*, p. 8.

26. *Austin* (Texas) *American-Statesman*, November 5, 1986, p. A2.

27. Peter Uhlenberg & David Eggebeen, "The Declining Well-Being of American Adolescents," *The Public Interest* (Winter 1986), p. 32.

28. Murray, *Losing Ground*, pp. 127-28.

29. Moynihan, *Family and Nation*, pp. 167-68; *Austin* (Texas) *American-Statesman*, December 18, 1986, p. A21.

30. *The Wall Street Journal*, September 25, 1986, p. 26.

31. Moynihan, *Family and Nation*, pp. 166-68.

32. *The Wall Street Journal*, September 22, 1986, pp. 1, 16.

33. Ibid.; Moynihan, *Family and Nation*, pp. 111-12.

34. *The Wall Street Journal*, October 2, 1986, p. 26.

35. Moynihan, *Family and Nation*, p. 112.

36. Murray, *Losing Ground*, pp. 114-15.

37. Easterlin, *Birth and Fortune*, p. 105.

38. Uhlenberg & Eggebeen, "The Declining Well-Being of American Adolescents," p. 32.

39. These statistics are compiled in William J. Bennett, *The Index of Leading Cultural Indicators* (The Heritage Foundation, March 1993).

40. Robert H. Bork, *Slouching Towards Gomorrah* (New York: Regan Books, 1996), p. 343.

41. Leon R. Kass, "The End of Courtship," *The Public Interest*, Winter 1997, p. 63.

42. *The Wall Street Journal*, May 28, 1986, p. 34; *Austin* (Texas) *American-Statesman*, October 21, 1984, pp. E1, E26; Easterlin, pp. 103-04.

43. *The Wall Street Journal*, May 28, 1986, p. 34.

44. *Time*, March 23, 1987, p. 12; *Austin* (Texas) *American-Statesman*, October 29, 1983, p. D1; K. D. Breault, "Suicide in America: A Test of Durkheim's Theory of Religious and Family Integration, 1933-1980," *American Journal of Sociology* 92 (November 1986), pp. 651-52.

45. *Austin* (Texas) *American-Statesman*, August 26, 1988, p. A6.

46. Elizabeth Gleick, "Suicide's Shadow," *Time*, July 22, 1996, pp. 40-41.

47. *Austin* (Texas) *American-Statesman*, September 15, 1986, p. A4; Bennett, *The Index of Leading Cultural Indicators*, p. 12.

48. Easterlin, *Birth and Fortune*, p. 100.

49. Uhlenberg & Eggebeen, "The Declining Well-Being of American Adolescents," p. 32.

50. Bennett, *The Index of Leading Cultural Indicators*, p. 19; Cait Murphy, "High Times in America," *Policy Review* (Winter 1987), p. 46.

51. *The New York Times*, December 13, 1994, p. A1.

52. Moynihan, *Family and Nation*, pp. 182-83.

53. *Austin* (Texas) *American-Statesman*, August 30, 1988, p. A1; ibid., September 6, 1988, p. A1; *Time*, September 19, 1988, p. 85.

54. *The Wall Street Journal*, November 19, 1986, p. 29; *Austin* (Texas) *American-Statesman*, March 2, 1989, p. A1.

55. *Insight*, November 17, 1986, p. 68.

56. Marie Winn, *Children Without Childhood* (New York: Pantheon, 1983), p. 83; *Austin* (Texas) *American-Statesman*, November 10, 1984, p. F4; ibid., December 12, 1986, p. E1; *The New York Times*, January 11, 1994, p. B7. The teenage suicide rate now equals that of adults. It is estimated that "four millon American children—or 5 percent—suffer depression," and in 1996 nearly 600,000 children and adolescents were prescribed an antidepressant. Between 1995 and 1996 the number of children, ages six to twelve, who took Prozac increased 298 percent to 203,000. Barbara Strauch, "Use of

Antidepression Medicine for Young Patients Has Soared," *The New York Times*, August 10, 1997, p. 1.

57. *Austin* (Texas) *American-Statesman*, September 12, 1985, p. D30.

58. Ibid., March 2, 1989, pp. A1, A10; ibid., April 17, 1989, p. A2.

59. Uhlenberg & Eggebeen, "The Declining Well-Being of American Adolescents," p. 31. Because the College Board, sponsor of the test, "recentered the scores" in 1994, what was supposed to be the test's "unchanging standard" has been lowered so that the recent seemingly higher scores "are the result of statistical legerdemain." Diane Ravitch, "Defining Literacy Downward," *The New York Times*, August 28, 1996, p. A15.

60. *Austin* (Texas) *American-Statesman*, September 24, 1986, p. A5.

61. Ibid., December 18, 1986, p. A21; Ibid., September 15, 1986, p. A4.

62. Uhlenberg & Eggebeen, "The Declining Well-Being of American Adolescents," pp. 32–33.

63. *The Wall Street Journal*, October 14, 1986, p. 32.

64. Moynihan, *Family and Nation*, p. 171.

65. Winn, *Children Without Childhood*, p. 121; *The Wall Street Journal*, October 29, 1986, p. 28.

66. *Time*, October 3, 1988, p. 47.

67. *Austin* (Texas) *American-Statesman*, February 29, 1984, p. C1; *The Wall Street Journal*, January 24, 1989, p. B1; ibid., July 16, 1992, p. B1.

68. Allan C. Carlson, "What happened to the 'family wage'?," *The Public Interest* (Spring 1986), p. 3; Fern Schumer Chapman, "Where Have All the Babies Gone?," *Fortune*, July 6, 1987, p. 113; *The Wall Street Journal*, October 13, 1986, p. 1; ibid., May 5, 1987, p. 39; ibid., June 18, 1987, p. 1.

69. *Austin* (Texas)*American-Statesman*, July 9, 1985, Onward, p. 28; *The Wall Street Journal*, March 24, 1987, p. 29; *Austin American-Statesman*, September 10, 1987, p. A11; *The Christian Science Monitor*, September 20, 1988, p.4.

70. Ben J. Wattenberg, *The Birth Dearth* (New York: Pharos Books, 1987).

71. *The Wall Street Journal*, December 30, 1985, p. 12; Chapman, "Where Have All the Babies Gone?," p. 113; *Austin* (Texas)*American-Statesman*, January 1, 1989, pp. A1, A12.

72. Chapman, "Where Have All the Babies Gone?," p. 113; Richard Tomlinson, "The French Population Debate," *The Public Interest* (Summer 1984), pp. 111, 118; *The Wall Street Journal*, June 20, 1984, p. 29.

73. *The Wall Street Journal*, May 24, 1988, p. 23.

74. Ibid., June 24, 1987, p. 25.

75. *Austin* (Texas) *American-Statesman*, October 28, 1986, p. A6.

76. David Andrew Price, "A Good Man is Hard to Find," *The Wall Street Journal*, February 21, 1995, p. A24.

77. *Austin* (Texas) *American-Statesman*, June 28, 1988, p. A4; ibid., January 17, 1989, p. A2; ibid., February 29, 1988, p. B9.

78. Ibid., February 21, 1989, p. A8. Claude Brown depicted a similar picture of Harlem youth in "Manchild in Harlem," *The New York Times Magazine*, September 16, 1984, p. 36.

79. Price, *The Wall Street Journal*, February 21, 1995, p. A24.

80. *Time*, May 21, 1990, pp. 83-4.

81. Jewelle Taylor Gibbs, "Young Black Males in America: Endangered, Embittered, and Embattled," in *Young, Black, and Male in America: An Endangered Species*, edited by Jewelle Taylor Gibbs et al. (Dover, Mass.: Auburn House, 1988), p. 5.

82. Ibid., p. 27. Studies indicate that the rising rate of female participation in the work force has hurt job opportunities for young blacks, but that the rise in the Hispanic population, where immigrants are concentrated, has not significantly worsened job prospects of black youth. Richard B. Freeman & Harry J. Holzer, "Young Blacks and Jobs: What We Now Know," *The Public Interest*, Winter 1985, p. 25.

83. Dorothy J. Gaiter, "The Gender Divide," *The Wall Street Journal*, March 8, 1994, p. A1.

84. Quoted in Andrew Delbanco, "The Mark of Zora," *The New Republic*, July 3, 1995, p. 35 [reviewing *Novels & Stories by Zora Neale Hurston* and *Folklore, Memoirs & Other Writings by Zora Neale Hurston*, edited by Cheryl A. Wall (The Library of America, 1995)].

85. William Tucker, "Black Family Agonistes," *The American Spectator*, July 1984, pp. 15-16.

86. *Insight*, May 30, 1994, p. 14.

87. George Gilder, *Visible Man: A True Story of Post-Racist America* (New York: Basic Books, 1978); Gilder, *Sexual Suicide*, pp. 110-21, 167; Murray, *Losing Ground*.

88. Marvin Olasky, *The Tragedy of American Compassion* (Washington, D.C.: Regnery Gateway, 1992).

89. Myron Magnet, "America's Underclass: What To Do?," *Fortune*, May 11, 1987, p. 130.

90. Daniel Goleman, "75 Years Later, Study Is Still Tracking Geniuses," *The New York Times*, March 7, 1995, p. B9.

91. Wright, *The Moral Animal*, p. 100.

92. *Austin* (Texas) *American-Statesman*, July 17, 1992, pp. A1, A15.

93. David Blankenhorn, *Fatherless America: Confronting Our Most Urgent Social Problem* (New York: Basic Books, 1995).

94. Myron Magnet, *The Dream and the Nightmare:The Sixties' Legacy to the Underclass* (New York: Morrow, 1993).

95. D. Keith Mano, "The Black Sex War," *National Review*, September 26, 1986, p. 57.

96. *Austin* (Texas) *American-Statesman*, November 30, 1994, p. F6.

97. Sam Roberts, "Black Women Graduates Outpace Male Counterparts," *The New York Times*, October 31, 1994, p. A8.

98. Lopata, *Occupation: Housewife*, pp. 125-26, 128, 274-75.

99. Alice Walker, *The Color Purple* (New York: Harcourt Brace Jovanovich, 1982), pp. 38, 187, 203, 253.

100. Darryl Pinckney, "Black Victims, Black Villains," *The New York Review of Books*, January 29, 1987, p. 17.

101. Reid Buckley, *The American Spectator*, November 1983, p. 39.

102. Posner, *Sex and Reason*, pp. 401, 398.

103. Wright, *The Moral Animal*, p. 103.

104. Walker, *The Color Purple*, pp. 1, 108-09, 171-72.

105. The fact is that in an ethnic breakdown, the rate of child sexual abuse by black men is relatively low. Posner, *Sex and Reason.*, p. 402. Awareness of this fact may be implicit in Shug's reaction to Celie's account of her stepfather's abuse: "Wellsah, and I thought it was only whitefolks do freakish things like that." Walker, *The Color Purple*, p. 109.

106. *The American Spectator*, July 1984, pp. 10-11.

107. David L. Kirp, Mark G. Yudof, and Marlene Strong Franks, *Gender Justice* (Chicago: The University of Chicago Press, 1986), p. 142; *Austin* (Texas) *American-Statesman*, June 27, 1984, p. F1.

108. *Austin* (Texas) *American-Statesman*, August 28, 1994, p. B1; *Fortune*, August 22, 1994, p. 24. In 1993 women received 54 percent of Bachelor's and Master's degrees, and men received 46 percent. *Time* January 30, 1995, p. 67. In 1994 eighteen medical schools had a majority of women in their entering class (56 percent at Yale and 53 at Harvard and Johns Hopkins). *The Washington Times National Weekly Edition*, June 5-11, 1995, p. 4. Women were in the first medical school class at Johns Hopkins 104 years ago. Martha Irvine, "Briefs," *The Wall Street Journal*, August 25, 1994, p. A1. To reduce the surplus of doctors, the federal government will pay forty-one teaching hospitals in New York state, which trains the greatest number of the nation's doctors, $400 million not to train physicians. Elizabeth Rosenthal, "U.S. to Pay New York Hospitals Not to Train Doctors, Easing Glut," *The New York Times*, February 18, 1997, p. A1.

109. Diane Crispell, "People Patterns," *The Wall Street Journal*, March 10, 1995, p. B1.

110. Sylvia Nasar, "More Men in Prime of Life Spend Less Time Working," *The New York Times*, December 1, 1994, p. A1.

111. Christopher Jencks, *The Homeless* (Cambridge: Harvard University Press, 1994); Magnet, *The Dream and the Nightmare*, pp. 76-114; Rick White, Jr., *Rude Awakenings: What the Homeless Crisis Tells Us* (San Francisco: Institute for Contemporary Studies, 1992); *Insight*, May 16, 1988, pp. 8-18; *Time*, February 2, 1987, pp. 26-29.

112. Wright, *The Moral Animal*, pp. 101-02.

113. David T. Courtwright, *Violent Land: Single Men and Social Disorder from the Frontier to the Inner City* (Cambridge, Mass.: Harvard University Press, 1996), pp. 12, 5, 279, 280.

114. *The New York Times*, April 15, 1993, p. A1.

115. Posner, *Sex and Reason*, pp. 117, 147, 298.

116. *The New York Times*, September 4, 1994, p. 30.

117. Philip Elmer-Dewitt, "Now for the Truth About Americans and Sex," *Time*, October 17, 1994, p. 68.

118. Julie Connelly, "The Trophy Wife Is Back—With Brains," *Fortune*, April 3, 1995, p. 102.

119. Brian O'Reilly, "Agee in Exile," *Fortune*, May 29, 1995, pp. 52, 56.

120. Gilder, *Men and Marriage*, pp. 76-7.

121. Mead, *Male and Female*, p. 318. Mead's Samoan researches have been proved to be seriously flawed. Derek Freeman, *Margaret Mead and Samoa: The Making and Unmaking of an Anthropological Myth* (Cambridge: Harvard University Press, 1983). This fact does not, however, vitiate her many insights into the differences between male and female which are daily confirmed by our own experiences.

122. *The Wall Street Journal*, June 12, 1996, p. A1.

123. Maggie Gallagher, *The Abolition of Marriage: How We Destroy Lasting Love* (Washington, D.C.: Regnery, 1996); William A. Galston, "Divorce American Style," *The Public Interest*, Summer 1996, pp. 12, 25 (discussing the injury no-fault does to long-married housewives whose husbands can obtain non-consensual divorces without making "financial rectification" and recommending restoration of the all but vanished long-term alimony); William A. Galston, "Braking Divorce for the Sake of Children," *The American Enterprise*, May/June 1996, p. 36 (noting accumulating evidence that no-fault laws have accelerated the pace of divorce); William W. Van Alstyne, "Notes on the Marginalization of Marriage in America: Altered States in Constitutional Law," in *Problems and Conflicts Between Law and Morality in a Free Society*, James E. Wood Jr. & Derek Davis, eds. (Waco, Texas: Baylor University, J.M. Dawson Institute of Church-State Studies, 1994); Margaret F. Brinig

and Steven M. Crafton, "Marriage and Opportunism," *The Journal of Legal Studies*, June 1994, p. 869. Movements to reform no-fault divorce laws have begun in a number of states. Glenn T. Stanton, "The Counter-Revolution Against Easy Divorce," *The American Enterprise*, May/June 1996, p. 37; Elizabeth Schoenfeld, "Drumbeats for Divorce Reform," *Policy Review*, May/June 1996, p. 8. In June 1997, Louisiana became the first state to permit a more binding form of marriage contract called "covenant marriage." Kevin Sack, "Louisiana Approves Measure to Tighten Marriage Bonds," *The New York Times*, June 24, 1997, p. A1.

7. The Awakened Brünnhilde

1. Ernest Newman, *The Wagner Operas* (New York: Knopf, 1981), pp. 534-35; *Siegfried* , Opera Guide 28, English National Opera (London: John Calder, 1984), pp. 120-24.

2. Among the cracks recently appearing in the monolith is Anne Roiphe's *Fruitful: A Real Mother in the Modern World* (New York: Houghton Mifflin, 1996). While writing passionately of the joys of motherhood and taking feminism to task for downgrading it, Roiphe does not consider herself antifeminist, and, like Elizabeth Fox-Genovese, she is not concerned with validating full-time domesticity. In *Surrendering to Motherhood: Losing Your Mind, Finding Your Soul* (New York: Hyperion, 1997), Iris Krasnow movingly describes her odyssey from journalism to a satisfying full-time motherhood.

3. Eliot, *Middlemarch*, p. 339.

4. Virginia Woolf, *Mrs. Dalloway* (New York: Harvest/HBJ, originally published 1925), p. 46.

5. Mead, *Male and Female*, pp. 92, 191-2.

6. Erikson, *Identity, Youth, and Crisis*, p. 82.

7. Dworkin, *Intercourse*, pp. 47, 50-51, 58-61, 40.

8. Ibid., pp. 42-43. Dworkin has Blanche say that one night she found the boy kissing an older man, but I do not find this in the text of the play. Her husband killed himself after Blanche told him that "I saw! I know! You disgust me." Stella told Stanley that this "beautiful and talented young man was a degenerate." Tennessee Williams, *A Streetcar Named Desire* in *Twenty-Five Modern Plays*, edited by S. Marion Tucker and Alan S. Downer (New York: Harper & Row, 1953), pp. 935-36, 938.

9. Tucker and Downer, *Twenty-Five Modern Plays*, p. 924.

10. Dworkin, *Intercourse*, p. 41.

11. Ibid., pp. 40-41.

12. Tucker and Downer, *Twenty-Five Modern Plays*, pp. 924-25.

13. Gabriel García Márquez, *One Hundred Years of Solitude* (New York: Avon Books, 1971), pp. 94-95.

14. Dworkin, *Intercourse*, p. 67.

15. Henrik Ibsen, *A Doll's House* in *Ghosts and Three Other Plays by Henrik Ibsen*, translated by Michael Meyer (Garden City, New York: Anchor Books, 1966), p. 99.

16. Dworkin, *Intercourse*, p. 67.

17. Ibid., p. 72.

18. Ibid., pp. 85, 94, 99-100.

19. Ibid., pp. 106-07, 110-11.

20. Ibid., p. 113.

21. Scruton, *Sexual Desire*, pp. 90-91, 89.

22. Gabriel García Márquez, *Love in the Time of Cholera* (New York: Penguin Books, 1989), p. 246.

23. Dworkin, *Intercourse*, pp. 122-23.

24. *The Wall Street Journal*, March 27, 1992, p. A13.

25. St. Aubyn, *Queen Victoria*, p. 159.

26. Mina Loy, "Parturition," *Lunar Baedeker* (1923), as quoted in Helen Vendler, "The Truth Teller," *The New York Review of Books*, September 19, 1996, p. 59.

27. Fisher, *Understanding the Female Orgasm*, pp. 170-71.

28. *The New York Times*, May 22, 1994, p. 30.

29. St. Aubyn, *Queen Victoria*, p. 258.

30. Ibid., pp. 259-60.

31. Variants on the theme of inevitable submission to inevitable pain can be readily seen underlying some of women's sexual fantasies discussed in Fisher, *Understanding the Female Orgasm*, pp. 142-45.

32. Dworkin, *Intercourse*, p. 123.

33. One such demonstration at Vassar College is described in Richard Miniter, "Married Women Need Not Apply," *Heterodoxy*, May/June 1994 (Center for the Study of Popular Culture, Los Angeles, Calif.), p. 4.

34. Dworkin, *Intercourse*, p. 132.

35. Scruton, *Sexual Desire*, pp. 73, 82.

36. Ibid., pp. 92, 120-21.

37. Hurston, *Jonah's Gourd Vine*, p. 143.

38. Decter, *The New Chastity and Other Arguments Against Women's Liberation*, p. 81.

39. Dworkin, *Intercourse*, p. 132.

40. Woolf, *Mrs. Dalloway*, p. 43.

41. Dworkin, *Intercourse*, pp. 137-38, 139.

42. Ibid., p. 143.

43. Barbara Herman, "Could It Be Worth Thinking About Kant on Sex and Marriage?," in *A Mind of One's Own: Feminist Essays on Reason and Objectivity*, edited by Louise M. Antony and Charlotte Witt (Boulder, Colo.: Westview Press, 1993), pp. 55, 57, 60.

44. Dworkin, *Intercourse.*, pp. 154-55, quoting Norman Mailer, *The Prisoner of Sex* (Boston: Little, Brown, 1971), pp. 172, 173.

45. Scruton, *Sexual Desire*, p. 273.

46. Bernard, *The Future of Marriage*, p. 141.

47. Winick, *The New People: Desexualization in American Life*, pp. 354-55, 304.

48. Martha Albertson Fineman, "Icon of Marriage Has Had its Day," *Insight*, June 27, 1994, pp. 20, 22.

49. David Leavitt, *Family Dancing* (New York: Knopf, 1984), pp. 182-83. The message of Leavitt's writing is analyzed in Carol Iannone, "Post-Counterculture Tristesse," *Commentary*, February, 1987, p. 59.

50. Dworkin, *Intercourse*, p. 170.

51. Ibid., p. 184.

52. Ibid., p. 191, quoting Primo Levi, *Survival in Auschwitz* in *Survival in Auschwitz and The Reawakening: Two Memoirs*, trans. Stuart Woolf (New York: Summit Books, 1985), p. 15.

53. Lasch, *Haven in a Heartless World*, pp. 153, 155-56.

54. "Letters from Readers," *Commentary*, March 1981, pp. 4, 6.

55. In his extensive examination of elementary-school readers and social studies texts and high-school history texts, psychology professor Paul C. Vitz demonstrated how successful has been this effort to teach children "correctly," according to feminist ideology: "Nowhere is it suggested that being a mother or homemaker was a worthy and important role for a woman." Never is it noted that many people, such as homemakers, do not work for money, but do volunteer work. Throughout the readers, feminism is "the most noticeable ideological position" so that no story "clearly supports motherhood for today's woman," nor "shows any woman or girl with a positive relationship to a baby or young child," nor presents "any positive portrayal of traditional womanhood." Paul C. Vitz, *Censorship: Evidence of Bias in Our Children's Textbooks* (Ann Arbor, Mich.: Servant Books, 1986), pp. 2, 43, 73.

56. Mary G. Roebling's obituary notes that in 1937 she became the first woman to head a major American bank. *The New York Times*, October 27, 1994, p. C19.

57. Judith R. Shapiro, "What Women Can Teach Men," *The New York Times*, November 23, 1994, p. A15.

58. Mead, *Male and Female*, p. 233.

59. Rudyard Kipling, *Something of Myself: For My Friends Known And Unknown* (Garden City, New York: Doubleday, Doran & Co., 1937), pp. 6-7, 11, 13, 17.

60. In *Children First: What Our Society Must Do—And Is Not Doing—For Our Children Today* (New York: Knopf, 1994), Penelope Leach sets forth one of the best descriptions of the crucially important role a mother plays in securing the well-being and healthy emotional development of her child.

61. Julia Wrigley, *Other People's Children* (New York: Basic Books, 1995).

62. Susan Chira, "Care at Child Day Centers is Rated as Poor," *The New York Times*, February 7, 1995, p. A6. In her famous critique of day care, Selma Fraiberg stated that typically day care is not "substitute mother care," but "child storage houses, staffed by caregivers who are mostly indifferent and often outrageously neglectful." Selma Fraiberg, *Every Child's Birthright: In Defense of Mothering* (New York: Basic Books, 1977), p. 131.

63. "Nanny Pleads Not Guilty in Death of Infant," *The New York Times*, February 14, 1997, p. A15; Christopher Daly, "Trial of Nanny Accused of Murder Begins," *Austin* (Texas) *American-Statesman*, October 13, 1997, p. A18.

64. "Eye Spy . . . the Baby-Sitter," *Time*, July 22, 1996, p. 65; Kirk Johnson, "The Nanny Track," *The New York Times*, September 29, 1996, p. F9; Omar Gallaga, "Parents Can Watch Kids over Internet," *Austin* (Texas) *American-Statesman*, July 12, 1997, p. D1.

65. Johnson, *Intellectuals*, pp. 22-23. The incongruity between Rousseau's treatment of his own children and his denunciation of sending infants off to wet nurses in the country confirms Johnson's description of him as often "inconsistent and contradictory."

66. A 1992 *Time*/CNN poll reported that 63 percent of the women responding did not consider themselves feminists, and another poll reported only 16 percent of college women "definitely" considered themselves feminists. Sommers, *Who Stole Feminism*, p. 18.

67. P. J. O'Rourke, *The American Spectator*, August 1995, p. 63 (reviewing Marilyn Schwartz and the Task Force on Bias-Free Language of the Association of American University Presses, *Guidelines For Bias-Free Writing* (Indiana University Press, 1995).

68. David Gelernter, "Why Mothers Should Stay Home," *Commentary*, February 1996, p. 25.

69. "Letters from Readers," *Commentary*, June 1996, p. 3.

70. Ibid., p. 4.

71. C. G. Jung, *Memories, Dreams, Reflections*, recorded and edited by Aniela Jaffé (New York: Vintage Books edition, 1989), p. 244.

72. William A. Henry III, *In Defense of Elitism* (New York: Anchor Books, Doubleday, 1994), p. 119.

73. Michael Kimmelman, "Interwoven Destinies As Artist and Wife," *The New York Times*, August 24, 1995, p. CII.

74. Andrea Gerlin, "Workplace Nursing Becoming a Benefit," *The Wall Street Journal*, December 29, 1994, p. B1; Glenn Burkins, "Breastfeeding Moms," *The Wall Street Journal*, May 20, 1997, p. A1.

75. Fraiberg, *Every Child's Birthright*, pp. 27-28.

76. Jonathan Kaufman, "At Age 5, Reading, Writing and Rushing," *The Wall Street Journal*, February 4, 1997, p. B1.

77. *Fortune*, April 15, 1996, p. 17.

78. Ibid., September 30, 1996, pp. 42-3.

79. Friedan, *The Feminine Mystique*, p. 29.

80. Carl N. Degler, "Introduction," in Gilman, *Women And Economics*, pp. x-xii, xv.

81. One of the side effects of this Prozac that lets a woman be like a man is sexual dysfunction, particularly, failure to experience orgasm. "Prozac can cause difficulties in achieving orgasm, more noticeably in men but in women as well. Probably because it is underreported, this side effect is not listed in standard references as being frequent, but clinicians see it fairly often." Kramer, *Listening to Prozac*, p. 366, n.265. "For the Prozac-style drugs, one of the commonest downsides is loss of libido and orgasmic capacity." Natalie Angier, "Drugs for Depression Multiply, and So Do the Hard Questions," *The New York Times*, June 22, 1997, "A Special Section on Women's Health", p. 11. See also Marilyn Chase, "Drugs for Depression, Hypertension Can Take Toll on Sex Lives," *The Wall Street Journal*, July 7, 1997, p. B1.

82. Woolf, *To the Lighthouse*, p. 95.

83. Neely, *Gender: The Myth of Equality*, p. 228.

84. As one biographer states, however, "the ambitious Currer Bell emerged as compliant Mrs. Nicholls" when Charlotte Brontë chose to marry and "relinquish without a murmur what had been the prime activity of her life." It was "at the pinnacle of her career" that she made this choice—"a genius who resigned art in favor of life"—but then died nine months later, apparently pregnant. Lyndall Gordon, *Charlotte Brontë: A Passionate Life* (New York: W. W. Norton, 1994), pp. 292, 306, 316-17.

85. Deborah Solomon, "Artful Survivor," *The New York Times Magazine*, May 14, 1989, p. 66.

86. Joseph Story, "The Value and Importance of Legal Studies," August 5, 1829 ("The Law . . . is a jealous mistress"); Ralph Waldo Emerson, *Conduct of Life: Wealth*, 1860 ("Art is a jealous mistress").

Select Bibliography

Ackroyd, Peter, *Dickens*. New York: Harper Collins, 1990.

Albright, Daniel, *Personality and Impersonality: Lawrence, Woolf, and Mann*. Chicago: University of Chicago Press, 1978.

Anderson, Patricia, *When Passion Reigned: Sex and the Victorians*. New York: Basic Books, 1995.

Arendt, Hannah, *Eichmann in Jerusalem*. Harmondsworth, England: Penguin Books, 1964.

Ariès, Philippe, *Centuries of Childhood*. New York: Alfred A. Knopf, 1962.

Atlas, James, "The Counter Counterculture," *The New York Times Magazine*, February 12, 1995.

Bane, Mary Jo, *Here To Stay: American Families in the Twentieth Century*. New York: Basic Books, 1976.

Barlow, Tani E., editor, *Gender Politics in Modern China: Writing and Feminism*. Durham: Duke University Press, 1993.

_____, "Politics and Protocols of Funü: (Un)Making National Woman," in Gilmartin et al., *Engendering China: Women, Culture, and the State*. Cambridge, Mass.: Harvard University Press, 1994.

Barnett, Rosalind C., and Caryl Rivers, *She Works, He Works: How Two-Income Families Are Happier, Healthier, and Better-Off.* SanFrancisco: HarperSan Francisco, 1996.

Bell, Quentin, *Virginia Woolf: A Biography.* New York: Harcourt Brace Jovanovich, 1972.

Berger, Brigitte, "Academic Feminism and the 'Left,'"*Academic Questions,* Spring 1988.

Berger, Brigitte, and Peter L., *The War Over the Family: Capturing the Middle Ground.* Garden City, New York: Anchor Press, 1983.

Bernard, Jessie, *Academic Women.* University Park, Pa.: The Pennsylvania State University Press, 1964.

_____, *The Future of Marriage.* New Haven: Yale University Press, 1982 edition.

Bettelheim, Bruno, *The Children of the Dream.* London: Macmillan, 1969.

Billingsley, K. L., "Dancing with the Elephant," *Heterodoxy* March/April 1995.

Blake, Robert, *Disraeli.* New York: St, Martin's Press, 1967.

Blankenhorn, David, *Fatherless America: Confronting Our Most Urgent Social Problem.* New York: Basic Books, 1995.

Bloom, Allan, *The Closing of the American Mind.* New York: Simon & Schuster, 1987.

Bork, Robert H., *Slouching Towards Gomorrah.* New York:Regan Books, 1996.

Bowlby, John, *Attachment and Loss, Volume I: Attachment; Volume II: Separation, Anxiety, and Anger.* New York: Basic Books, 1969, 1973.

Brimelow, Peter, and Leslie Spencer, "When Quotas Replace Merit, Everybody Suffers," *Forbes,* February 15, 1993.

Brind, Joel, "Abortion, Breast Cancer, and Ideology", *First Things,* May 1997.

Brinig, Margaret F., and Steven M. Crafton, "Marriage and Opportunism," *The Journal of Legal Studies,* June 1994.

Brinton, Crane, *The Anatomy of Revolution.* New York: Vintage, 1965.

Brittan, Vera, *Testament of Youth.* New York: Seaview Books, 1980.

Bronfenbrenner, Urie, "The Origins of Alienation," *Scientific American* 231, August 1974.

_____, *Two Worlds of Childhood: U.S. and U.S.S.R.* New York: Russell Sage Foundation, 1970.

Broude, Gwen J., "The Realities of Day Care," *The Public Interest,* Fall 1996.

Brown, Claude, "Manchild in Harlem," *The New York Times Magazine,* September 16, 1984.

Browne, Kingsley R., "Sex and Temperament in Modern Society: A Darwinian View of the Glass Ceiling and the Gender Gap," *Arizona Law Review* 37, 1995.

Burke, Edmund, *Reflections on the Revolution in France*, reprinted in *Edmund Burke on Government, Politics and Society*, edited by B. W. Hill. International Publications Service, 1976.

Buss, David M., "Evolution and Human Mating", 18 *Harvard Journal of Law & Public Policy*, Spring 1995.

_____, *The Evolution of Desire: Strategies of Human Mating*. New York: Basic Books, 1994.

Bylinsky, Gene, "New Clues to the Causes of Violence," *Fortune*, January 1973.

Caldwell, Christopher, "The Feminization of America," *The Weekly Standard*, December 23, 1996.

Carlson, Allan C., "American Business and the New Politics of the Family," *The Family in America* (The Rockford Institute) June 1987.

_____, *Family Questions: Reflections on the American Social Crisis*. New Brunswick: Transaction Books, 1988.

_____, "Sex According to Social Science," *Policy Review*, Spring 1982.

_____, "Treason of the Professions: The Case of Home Economics," *The Family in America* (The Rockford Institute) August 1987.

_____, "What Happened to the 'Family Wage'?," *The Public Interest*, Spring 1986.

Chambers, Whittaker, *Witness*. New York: Random House, 1952.

Chapman, Fern Schumer, "Where Have All the Babies Gone?," *Fortune*, July 6, 1987.

Chen Yiyun, "Out of the Traditional Halls of Academe," in Gilmartin et al., *Engendering China*.

Cohen, Marcia, *The Sisterhood*. New York: Simon & Schuster, 1987.

Cohn, Norman, *The Pursuit of the Millennium*. New York: Oxford University Press paperback, 1970.

Collins, Robert J., M.D., "A Physician's View of College Sex," *Journal of the American Medical Association*, Vol. 232, April 28, 1975.

Connelly, Julie, "The Trophy Wife Is Back—With Brains," *Fortune*, April 3, 1995.

Corry, John, "The Death of Kara Hultgreen," *The American Spectator*, June 1995.

Courtwright, David T., *Violent Land: Single Men and Social Disorder from the Frontier to the Inner City*. Cambridge: Harvard University Press, 1996.

Dalton, Katherine, "Hard Cases," *The American Enterprise*, May/June 1995.

Davidson, Nicholas, *The Failure of Feminism*. Buffalo, New York: Prometheus Books, 1988.

De Beauvoir, Simone, *Letters to Sartre*, edited and translated by Quintin Hoare. New York: Arcade Publishing/Little, Brown & Co. 1992.

_____, *Memoirs of a Dutiful Daughter*. New York: Harper Colophon Books, 1974.

_____, "Sex, Society, and the Female Dilemma: A Dialogue Between Simone de Beauvoir and Betty Friedan," *Saturday Review*, June 14, 1975.

_____, *The Coming of Age*. New York: G. P. Putnam's Sons, 1972.

_____, *The Second Sex*. New York: Knopf, 1978.

DeMause, Lloyd, editor, *The History of Childhood*. New York: The Psychohistory Press, 1974.

De Riencourt, Amaury, *Sex and Power in History*. New York: David McKay, 1974.

Decter, Midge, *The New Chastity and Other Arguments Against Women's Liberation*. New York: Coward, McCann & Geoghegan, 1972.

_____, "Whatever Happened to America?," *The American Spectator*, December, 1982.

Degler, Carl N., *At Odds: Women and the Family in America from the Revolution to the Present*. New York: Oxford University Press, 1980.

Denfield, Rene, *The New Victorians: A Young Woman's Challenge to the Old Feminist Order*. New York: Warner Books, 1995.

Douglas, Ann, "On the Road Again," *The New York Times Book Review*, April 9, 1995.

Dworkin, Andrea, *Intercourse*. New York: The Free Press, 1987.

Dworkin, Ronald, "Liberty and Pornography," *The New York Review of Books*, August 15, 1991.

Easterlin, Richard, *Birth and Fortune: The Impact of Numbers on Personal Welfare*. New York: Basic Books, 1980.

Ehrenhalt, Alan, *The Lost City*. New York: Basic Books, 1995.

Ehrenreich, Barbara, *The Hearts of Men: American Dreams and the Flight From Commitment*. Garden City, N. Y.: Anchor Press/Doubleday, 1983.

Ehrenreich, Barbara, Elizabeth Hess, Gloria Jacobs, *Remaking Love: The Feminization of Sex*. Garden City, New York: Anchor Books, 1987.

Elias, Norbert, *The Civilizing Process, Vol. I*. New York: Urizen Books, 1978; *Power & Civility, The Civilizing Process: Vol. II*. New York: Pantheon, 1982.

Eliot, George, *Middlemarch*. New York: W. W. Norton, 1977.

Epstein, Richard A., *Forbidden Grounds: The Case Against Employment Discrimination Laws*. Cambridge, Mass.: Harvard University Press, 1995.

Erikson, Erik, *Identity, Youth, and Crisis*. New York: W.W. Norton, 1968.

Fagles, Robert, translator, *Homer: The Iliad*. New York: Viking, 1990.

Faludi, Susan, *Backlash: The Undeclared War Against American Women*. New York: Crown, 1991.

Fein, Ellen, and Sherrie Schneider, *The Rules: Time Tested Secrets for Capturing the Heart of Mr. Right*. New York: Warner Books, 1996.

Fineman, Martha Albertson, "Icon of Marriage Has Had its Day," *Insight*, June 27, 1994.

Fisher, Seymour, *Understanding the Female Orgasm*. New York:Basic Books, 1973.

Fleming, Anne Taylor, *Motherhood Deferred: A Woman's Journey*. New York: G. P. Putnam's Sons, 1994.

Fox-Genovese, Elizabeth, *Feminism Is Not the Story of My Life*. New York: Nan A. Talese/Doubleday, 1996.

_____, *Feminism Without Illusions: A Critique of Individualism*. Chapel Hill: University of North Carolina Press, 1991.

Fraiberg, Selma, *Every Child's Birthright: In Defense of Mothering*. New York: Basic Books, 1977.

Freeman, Richard B., and Harry J. Holzer, "Young Blacks and Jobs: What We Now Know," *The Public Interest*, Winter 1985.

Friedan, Betty, *The Feminine Mystique*. New York: Dell, 1984.

_____, *The Second Stage*. New York: Summit Books, 1981.

Gallagher, Maggie, *Enemies of Eros*. Chicago: Bonus Books, 1989.

_____, *The Abolition of Marriage: How We Destroy Lasting Love*. Washington, D.C.: Regnery, 1996.

_____, "The New Pro-Life Rebels," *National Review*, February 27, 1987.

Galston, William A., "Braking Divorce for the Sake of Children," *The American Enterprise*, May/June 1996.

_____, "Divorce American Style," *The Public Interest*, Summer 1996.

Gao Xiaoxian, "China's Modernization and Changes in the Social Status of Rural Women," in Gilmartin et al., *Engendering China*.

Gelernter, David, "Why Mothers Should Stay Home," *Commentary*, February 1996.

Gellner, Ernest, *Conditions of Liberty: Civil Society and its Rivals*. New York: Allen Lane, Penguin Press, 1994.

Getman, Julius, *In the Company of Scholars: The Struggle for the Soul of Higher Education*. Austin, Texas: University of Texas Press, 1992.

Gibbs, Jewelle Taylor, "Young Black Males in America: Endangered, Embittered, and Embattled" in *Young, Black, and Male in America: An Endangered Species*, edited by Jewelle Taylor Gibbs et al. , Dover, Mass.: Auburn House, 1988.

Gilbert, Neil, "Realities and Mythologies of Rape," *Society*, May/June 1992.

_____, "The Phantom Epidemic of Sexual Assault," *The Public Interest*, Spring 1991.

Gilbert, Sandra M., and Susan Gubar, *The Madwoman in the Attic*. New Haven: Yale University Press, 1979.

Gilder, George, *Men and Marriage*. Gretna, La.: Pelican, 1986.

_____, *Sexual Suicide*. New York: Quadrangle, 1973.

_____, *Visible Man: A True Story of Post-Racist America*. New York: Basic Books, 1978.

Gill, Richard T., & T. Grandon Gill, "A New Plan for the Family," *The Public Interest*, Spring, 1993.

Gilligan, Carol, *In a Different Voice: Psychological Theory and Women's Development*. Cambridge, Mass.: Harvard University Press, 1982.

Gilman, Charlotte Perkins, *Women And Economics: A Study of the Economic Relation Between Men and Women as a Factor in Social Evolution*, edited by Carl N. Degler. New York: Harper & Row, 1966.

Gilmartin, Christina K., Gail Hershatter, Lisa Rofel, Tyrene White, editors, *Engendering China: Women, Culture, and the State*. Cambridge, Mass.: Harvard University Press, 1994.

Glendon, Mary Ann, *Abortion and Divorce in Western Law*. Cambridge, Mass.: Harvard University Press, 1987.

Goldberg, Herb, *The Hazards of Being a Male: Surviving the Myth of Masculine Privilege*. New York: Signet, 1976.

Goldberg, Steven, *The Inevitability of Patriarchy*. New York: Morrow, 1973.

_____, *Why Men Rule: A Theory of Male Dominance*. Chicago: Open Court, 1994.

Goldstein, Robert D., *Mother-Love and Abortion, A Legal Interpretation*. Berkeley: Univ. of Calif. Press, 1988.

Gordon, Lyndall, *Charlotte Brontë: A Passionate Life*. New York: W. W. Norton, 1994.

Goscilo, Helena, editor, *Balancing Acts: Contemporary Stories by Russian Women*. Bloomington, In.: Indiana University Press, 1989.

Gray, Francine du Plessix, *Soviet Women: Walking the Tightrope*. New York: Doubleday, 1990.

_____, "Splendor and Miseries," *The New York Review of Books*, July 16, 1992.

Greer, Germaine, *Sex and Destiny: The Politics of Human Fertility*. New York: Harper & Row, 1984.

_____, *The Female Eunuch*. New York: McGraw Hill, 1970.

Griffin, Jasper, "The Love that Dared to Speak its Name," *The New York Review of Books*, October 22, 1992.

Haight, Gordon S., *George Eliot: A Biography*. New York: Oxford University Press, 1968.

Hardwick, Elizabeth, *Seduction and Betrayal: Women and Literature*. New York: Random House, 1974.

Harrison, Cynthia, *On Account of Sex*. Berkeley: University of California Press, 1988.

Hawthorne, Julian, *Nathaniel Hawthorne and His Wife: A Biography*. Boston: James R. Osgood and Co., 1885 (republished, Grosse Pointe, Mich.: Scholarly Press, 1968).

Hayek, F. A., *Law, Legislation and Liberty*, Vol. 1. Chicago: Univ. Of Chicago Press, 1973.

Hayman, Ronald, "Having Wonderful Sex, Wish You Were Here," *The New York Times Book Review*, July 19, 1992.

Hays, Sharon, *The Cultural Contradictions of Motherhood*. New Haven: Yale University Press, 1996.

Hazen, Helen, *Endless Rapture: Rape, Romance, and the Female Imagination*. New York: Charles Scribner's Sons, 1983.

Heilbrun, Carolyn G., *Writing a Woman's Life*. New York: W. W. Norton, 1988.

Henry III, William A., *In Defense of Elitism*. New York: Anchor Books/ Doubleday, 1994.

Herman, Barbara, "Could It Be Worth Thinking About Kant on Sex and Marriage?," in *A Mind of One's Own: Feminist Essays on Reason and Objectivity*, edited by Louise M. Antony and Charlotte Witt. Boulder, Colo.: Westview Press, 1993.

Hewlett, Sylvia Ann, *A Lesser Life: The Myth of Women's Liberation in America*. New York: Morrow, 1986.

Himmelfarb, Gertrude, *Marriage and Morals Among the Victorians*. New York: Knopf, 1986.

_____, *On Liberty and Liberalism: The Case of John Stuart Mill*. New York: Knopf, 1974.

_____, *The De-Moralization of Society: From Victorian Virtues to Modern Values*. New York: Knopf, 1995.

Hite, Shere, *Women and Love: A Cultural Revolution in Progress.* New York: Knopf, 1987.

Hochschild, Arlie Russell, *The Time Bind: When Work Becomes Home and Home Becomes Work,* New York: Metropolitan Books, 1997.

_____, "There's No Place Like Work," *The New York Times Magazine,* April 20, 1997.

Hochschild, Arlie Russell, with Anne Machung, *The Second Shift: Working Parents and the Revolution at Home.* New York: Viking Press, 1989.

Horowitz, David, "The Feminist Assault on the Military," *National Review,* October 5, 1992.

Howe, Louise Kapp, editor, *The Future of the Family: Mothers, Fathers and Children—Sex Roles and Work—Communities and Child Care—Redefining Marriage and Parenthood.* New York: Simon & Schuster, 1972.

Hurston, Zora Neale, *Jonah's Gourd Vine.* New York: Harper Perennial, 1990.

Huston, Ted L., "Path to Parenthood," *Discovery: Research and Scholarship at The University of Texas at Austin* 14, 1996.

Iannone, Carol, "How Politicized Studies Enforce Conformity: Interviews with Julius Lester and Elizabeth Fox-Genovese," *Academic Questions,* Summer 1992.

_____, "Post-Counterculture Tristesse," *Commentary,* February, 1987.

Ibsen, Henrik, *A Doll's House,* in *Ghosts and Three Other Plays by Henrik Ibsen,* translated by Michael Meyer. Garden City, New York: Anchor Books, 1966.

Iscoe, Louise, and Diane Welch, *Mother Care: A Career Option For Now.* The University of Texas at Austin: Hogg Foundation for Mental Health, 1992.

James, Henry, *The Portrait of a Lady.* New York: W. W. Norton, 1975, (1908 edition).

Janeway, Elizabeth, "Child Care Inc.," *World Monitor, The Christian Science Monitor Monthly,* October 1988.

Jencks, Christopher, *The Homeless.* Cambridge; Mass.: Harvard University Press, 1994.

Johnson, Paul, *Intellectuals.* New York: Harper & Row, 1988.

Judis, John B., "Why Your Wages Keep Falling," *The New Republic,* February 14, 1994.

Kass, Leon R., "The End of Courtship," *The Public Interest* Winter 1997.

Kavanagh, P. J., *A G. K. Chesterton Anthology.* San Francisco: Ignatius Press, 1985.

Kelly, Michael, "Saint Hillary," *The New York Times Magazine*, May 23, 1993.

Kersten, Katherine, "What Do Women Want?: A Conservative Feminist Manifesto," *Policy Review*, Spring 1991.

Kiechel III, Walter, "The Workaholic Generation," *Fortune*, April 10, 1989.

Kipling, Rudyard, *Something of Myself: For My Friends Known And Unknown*. Garden City, New York: Doubleday, Doran & Co., 1937.

Kirp, David L., Mark G. Yudof, and Marlene Strong Franks, *Gender Justice*. Chicago: The University of Chicago Press, 1986.

Kramer, Peter D., *Listening to Prozac*. New York: Viking Press, 1993.

Kramer, Rita, *In Defense of the Family: Raising Children in America Today*. New York: Basic Books, 1983.

Krasnow, Iris, *Surrendering to Motherhood: Losing Your Mind, Finding Your Soul*. New York: Hyperion, 1997.

Lacey, W. K., *The Family in Classical Greece*. Ithaca, New York: Cornell University Press, 1968.

Lasch, Christopher, *Haven in a Heartless World: The Family Beseiged*. New York: Basic Books, 1977.

_____, Christopher, *Women And The Common Life: Love, Marriage, and Feminism*, edited by Elisabeth Lasch-Quinn. New York: W. W. Norton, 1996.

Lasson, Kenneth, "Feminism Awry: Excesses in the Pursuit of Rights and Trifles," *Journal of Legal Education*, March 1992.

Lawrence, D. H., *Lady Chatterley's Lover*. New York: Grove Press, 1957.

Leach, Penelope, *Children First: What Our Society Must Do—And Is Not Doing—For Our Children Today*. New York: Knopf, 1994.

Leavitt, David, *Family Dancing*. New York: Knopf, 1984.

Lebra, Takie Sugiyama, *Japanese Women: Constraint and Fulfillment*. Honolulu: University of Hawaii Press, 1984.

Lefkowitz, Jay P., "Jewish Voters and the Democrats," *Commentary*, April 1993.

Lefkowitz, Mary R., *Women in Greek Myth*. Baltimore: The Johns Hopkins University Press, 1986.

Levi, Primo, *Survival in Auschwitz and The Reawakening: Two Memoirs*, translator by Stuart Woolf. New York: Summit Books, 1985.

Levin, Michael, *Feminism and Freedom*. New Brunswick: Transaction Books, 1987.

Levinson, Daniel J., with Judy D. Levinson, *The Seasons of a Woman's Life*. New York: Knopf, 1996.

Li Xiaojiang, "Economic Reform and the Awakening of Chinese Women's Consciousness," in Gilmartin et al., *Engendering China*.

Li Ziyun, "Women's Consciousness and Women's Writing," in Gilmartin et al., *Engendering China*.

Lichter, S. Robert, Linda S. Lichter, Stanley Rothman, *Prime Time: How TV Portrays American Culture*. Washington, D. C.: Regnery, 1994.

———, *The Media Elite*. Bethesda, Md.: Adler & Adler, 1986.

———, *Watching America: What Television Tells Us About Our Lives*. New York: Prentice Hall, 1992.

Lightfoot-Klein, Hanny, *Prisoners of Ritual: An Odyssey into Female Genital Circumcision in Africa*. Binghamton, New York: The Haworth Press, 1989.

Lopata, Helena Z., *Occupation: Housewife*. New York: Oxford University Press, 1971 (reprinted, Westport, Conn.: Greenwood Press, 1980).

Lynch, Frederick R., *Invisible Victims: White Males and the Crisis of Affirmative Action*. New York: Greenwood Press, 1989.

Mack, Dana, *The Assault on Parenthood: How Our Culture Undermines the Family*. New York: Simon & Schuster, 1997.

Magnet, Myron, "America's Underclass: What To Do?," *Fortune*, May 11, 1987.

———, "The American Family, 1992," *Fortune*, August 10, 1992.

———, *The Dream and the Nightmare: The Sixties' Legacy to the Underclass*. New York: Morrow, 1993.

Mahony, Rhona, *Kidding Ourselves: Breadwinning, Babies, and Bargaining Power*. New York: Basic Books, 1995.

Mann, Susan, "Learned Women in the Eighteenth Century," in Gilmartin et al., *Engendering China*.

Mano, D. Keith, "The Black Sex War," *National Review*, September 26, 1986.

Mansbridge, Jane J., *Why We Lost the ERA*. Chicago: University of Chicago Press, 1986.

Marcus, Steven, *The Other Victorians: A Study of Sexuality and Pornography in Mid-Nineteenth Century England*. New York: Basic Books, 1964.

Márquez, Gabriel García, *Love in the Time of Cholera*. New York: Penguin Books, 1989.

———, *One Hundred Years of Solitude*. New York: Avon Books, 1971.

Marshall, Megan, *The Cost of Loving: Women and the New Fear of Intimacy*. New York: G. P. Putnam's Sons, 1984.

Mason, Mary Ann, *The Equality Trap*. New York: Simon & Schuster, 1988.

Mead, Margaret, *Male and Female*. New York: Morrow Quill Paperbacks, 1977.

Millett, Kate, *Sexual Politics*. Garden City, New York: Doubleday, 1969.

Miniter, Richard, "Married Women Need Not Apply," *Heterodoxy*, May/June 1994.

Minogue, Kenneth, "Necessary Imperfections," *The National Interest*, Winter 1994/1995.

Mirsky, Jonathan, "The Bottom of the Well," *The New York Review of Books*, October 6, 1994.

Morris, Betsy, "Is Your Family Wrecking Your Career? (and Vice Versa)," *Fortune*, March 17, 1997.

Morse, Jennifer Roback, "Beyond 'Having It All,'" 18 *Harvard Journal of Law & Public Policy*, Spring 1995.

Morson, Gary Saul, "Opinion and the World of Possibilities," *Academic Questions*, Winter 1994.

Morson, Gary Saul, "What is the Intelligentsia? Once More, an Old Russian Question," *Academic Questions*, Summer 1993.

Moynihan, Daniel P., *Family and Nation: The Godkin Lectures, Harvard University*. San Diego: Harcourt Brace Jovanovich, 1986.

_____, *The Negro Family: The Case for National Action*. Washington, D.C.: Department of Labor, March 1965 (reprinted, Westport, Conn.: Greenwood Press, 1981).

Murray, Charles, *Losing Ground*. New York: Basic Books, 1984.

Neely, James C., *Gender: The Myth of Equality*. New York: Simon & Schuster, 1981.

Newman, Katherine S., *Declining Fortunes: The Withering of the American Dream*. New York: Basic Books, 1993.

Novak, Michael, "Men Without Women," *The American Spectator*, October 1978.

Nuechterlein, James, "The Feminization of the American Left," *Commentary*, November 1987.

Olasky, Marvin, *The Tragedy of American Compassion*. Washington, D.C.: Regnery, 1992.

Olson, Walter K., *The Excuse Factory: How Today's Employment Laws Promote Mediocrity in the Workplace*. New York: The Free Press, 1997.

O'Neill, Nena, and George O'Neill, *Open Marriage: A New Life Style For Couples*. New York: M. Evans and Company, 1972.

O'Reilly, Brian, "Agee in Exile," *Fortune*, May 29, 1995.

O'Reilly, Jane, "Talking About Women, Not to Them," *The New York Times Magazine*, September 11, 1988.

Orwell, George, *Nineteen Eighty-Four*. New York: Harcourt, Brace & World, 1949.

Paglia, Camille, *Sex, Art, and American Culture*. New York: Vintage, 1992.

Patai, Daphne, and Noretta Koertge, *Professing Feminism: Cautionary Tales from the Strange World of Women's Studies*. New York: New Republic/Basic, 1994.

Percy, Walker, *The Thanatos Syndrome*. New York: Farrar Straus Giroux, 1987.

Peters, Joan K., *When Mothers Work: Loving Our Children Without Sacrificing Our Selves*. Reading, Mass.: Addison-Wesley, 1997.

Pinckney, Darryl, "Black Victims, Black Villains," *The New York Review of Books*, January 29, 1987.

Popenoe, David, "Family Decline in the Swedish Welfare State," *The Public Interest*, Winter 1991.

Popenoe, David, "Parental Androgyny," *Society*, September/October 1993.

Posner, Richard A., *Sex and Reason*. Cambridge, Mass.: Harvard University Press, 1992.

Powers, Elizabeth, "A Farewell to Feminism," *Commentary*, January 1997.

Radice, Betty, translator, *The Letters of Abelard and Héloise*. Harmondsworth, England: Penguin, 1974.

Reardon, David C., *Aborted Women: Silent No More*. Chicago: Loyola University Press, 1987.

Reich, Charles A., *The Greening of America*. New York: Random House, 1970.

_____, *The Sorcerer of Bolinas Reef*. New York: Random House, 1976.

Reisman, David, with Nathan Glazer and Reuel Denney, *The Lonely Crowd*. New Haven: Yale University Press, 1950.

Richman, Louis S., "Are You Better Off Than in 1980?," *Fortune*, October 10, 1988.

Riddle, John M., *Contraception and Abortion from the Ancient World to the Renaissance*. Cambridge, Mass.: Harvard University Press, 1993.

Roberts, Elizabeth, *A Woman's Place: An Oral History of Working-Class Women 1890-1940*. Oxford: Blackwell, 1984.

Rofel, Lisa, "Liberation Nostalgia and a Yearning for Modernity," in Gilmartin et al., *Engendering China*.

Roiphe, Anne, *Fruitful: A Real Mother in the Modern World*. New York: Houghton Mifflin, 1996.

Roiphe, Katie, "Date Rape's Other Victim," *The New York Times Magazine*, June 13, 1993.

_____, *Last Night in Paradise*. New York: Little, Brown, 1996.

_____, *The Morning After: Sex, Fear, and Feminism on Campus*. Boston: Little, Brown & Co., 1993.

Roosevelt, Theodore, *The Americanism of Theodore Roosevelt*, compiled by Hermann Hagedorn. Cambridge, Mass.: Houghton Mifflin, 1923.

_____, "The Parasite Woman: The Only Indispensable Citizen," in *The Works of Theodore Roosevelt*, Vol. 19, Hermann Hagedorn, editor, New York: Scribner's Sons, 1926.

Rose, Carol M., "Bargaining and Gender," 18 *Harvard Journal of Law & Public Policy*, Spring 1995.

Rothman, David J., "Shiny Happy People," *The New Republic*, February 14, 1994.

Rothman, Stanley, Stephen Powers, David Rothman, "Feminism in Films," *Society*, March/April 1993.

Rothman, Stanley, and S. Robert Lichter, *Roots Of Radicalism: Jews, Christians, and The Left*. New Brunswick: Transaction, 1996.

Sanger, David E., "The Career and the Kimono," *The New York Times Magazine*, May 30, 1993.

Sartre, Jean-Paul, *The Family Idiot: Gustave Flaubert 1821-1857*, Vol. II. Chicago: University of Chicago Press, 1987.

Schama, Simon, *Citizens: A Chronicle of the French Revolution*. New York: Knopf, 1989.

Schoenfeld, Elizabeth, "Drumbeats for Divorce Reform," *Policy Review*, May/June 1996.

Schor, Juliet B., *The Overworked American: The Unexpected Decline of Leisure*. New York: Basic Books, 1991.

Schwartz, Felice A., "Management Women and the New Facts of Life," *Harvard Business Review*, January/February, 1989.

Scruton, Roger, *Sexual Desire: A Moral Philosophy of the Erotic*. New York: The Free Press, 1986.

Sexton, Patricia Cayo, *The Feminized Male: Classrooms, White Collars, and the Decline of Manliness*. New York: Vintage, 1969.

Singer, Issac Bashevis, *The Penitent*. New York: Farrar Straus Giroux, 1983.

Smith, Betty, *A Tree Grows in Brooklyn*. New York: Harper & Row, 1943.

Solomon, Deborah, "Artful Survivor," *The New York Times Magazine*, May 14, 1989.

Sommers, Christina Hoff, *Who Stole Feminism?: How Women Have Betrayed Women*. New York: Simon & Schuster, 1994.

Sowell, Thomas, *Inside American Education*. New York: The Free Press, 1993.

St. Aubyn, Giles, *Queen Victoria: A Portrait*. New York: Atheneum, 1992.

Stanton, Glenn T., "The Counter-Revolution Against Easy Divorce," *The American Enterprise*, May/June 1996.

Steinem, Gloria, "What It Would Be Like if Women Win,"*Time*, August 31, 1970.

Thornton, Bruce S., *Eros: The Myth of Ancient Greek Sexuality*. Boulder, Colo.: Westview Press, 1996.

Thurer, Shari L., *The Myths of Motherhood: How Culture Reinvents the Good Mother*. New York: Houghton Mifflin, 1994.

Tiger, Lionel, and Robin Fox, *The Imperial Animal*. New York: Holt, Rinehart and Winston, 1971.

Tolstoy, Leo, *The Kreutzer Sonata*, in *Great Short Works of Leo Tolstoy*, translated by Louise and Aylmer Maude. New York: Harper & Row, 1967 (Perennial paperback).

Tomlinson, Richard, "The French Population Debate," *The Public Interest*, Summer 1984.

Treggiari, Susan, *Roman Marriage*. New York: Oxford University Press, 1991.

Trilling, Diana, "Please Don't Make Me a Joke," *The New York Times Book Review*, December 21, 1986.

Tucker, William, "A Return to the 'Family Wage,'" *The Weekly Standard*, May 13, 1996.

Tucker, William, "Black Family Agonistes," *The American Spectator*, July 1984.

Uhlenberg, Peter, & David Eggebeen, "The Declining Well-Being of American Adolescents," *The Public Interest*, Winter 1986.

Van Alstyne, William W., "Notes on the Marginalization of Marriage in America: Altered States in Constitutional Law," in *Problems and Conflicts Between Law and Morality in a Free Society*, James E. Wood, Jr. and Derek Davis, editors, Waco, Texas: Baylor Univ., J. M. Dawson Institute of Church-State Studies, 1994.

Vigilante, Richard, "Workingman's Blues?," *National Review*, April 27, 1992.

Vitz, Paul C., *Censorship: Evidence of Bias in Our Children's Textbooks*. Ann Arbor, Mich.: Servant Books, 1986.

Voth, Harold, *The Castrated Family*. Kansas City: Sheed Andrews and McMeel, 1977.

Walker, Alice, *The Color Purple*. New York: Harcourt Brace Jovanovich, 1982.

Wallerstein, Judith S., and Sandra Blakeslee, *Second Chances: Men, Women & Children a Decade After Divorce.* New York: Ticknor & Fields, 1989.

Wallerstein, Judith S., and Joan Berlin Kelly, *Surviving the Breakup: How Children and Parents Cope with Divorce.* New York: Basic Books, 1980.

Wang Zheng, "Three Interviews: Wang Anyi, Zhu Lin, Dai Qing," in Barlow, *Gender Politics in Modern China.*

Wattenberg, Ben J., *The Birth Dearth.* New York: Pharos Books, 1987.

Webb, Beatrice, *The Diary of Beatrice Webb: Two*, edited by Norman and Jeanne MacKenzie. Cambridge, Mass: The Belknap Press of Harvard University Press, 1983.

Weiss, Michael, "Feminist Pedagogy in the Law Schools," *Academic Questions*, Summer 1992.

Weitzman, Lenore J., *The Divorce Revolution: The Unexpected Social and Economic Consequences for Women and Children in America.* New York: The Free Press, 1985.

White, Jr., Rick, *Rude Awakenings: What the Homeless Crisis Tells Us.* San Francisco: Institute for Contemporary Studies, 1992.

Whitehead, Barbara Dafoe, *The Divorce Culture.* New York: Knopf, 1996.

_____, "The Failure of Sex Education," *The Atlantic Monthly*, October 1994.

Wieseltier, Leon, "Total Quality Meaning," *The New Republic*, July 19 & 26, 1993.

Williams, Tennessee, *A Streetcar Named Desire*, in *Twenty-Five Modern Plays*, edited by S. Marion Tucker and Alan S. Downer. New York: Harper & Row, 1953.

Willis, Ellen, *No More Nice Girls: Countercultural Essays.* Wesleyan University/University Press of New England, 1993.

Winick, Charles, *The New People: Desexualization in American Life.* New York: Pegasus, 1968.

Winn, Marie, *Children Without Childhood.* New York: Pantheon, 1983.

Witt, Charlotte, "Feminist Metaphysics," in *A Mind of One's Own: Feminist Essays on Reason and Objectivity*, edited by Louise M. Antony and Charlotte Witt. Boulder, Colo.: Westview Press, 1993.

Wolf, Naomi, *Promiscuities: The Secret Struggle for Womanhood.* New York: Random House, 1997.

Woolf, Virginia, *A Room of One's Own.* New York: Harcourt Brace Jovanovich, 1929 (Harvest/HBJ edition 1989).

_____, *Mrs. Dalloway.* New York: Harvest/HBJ, 1925.

_____, *Three Guineas.* New York: Harvest/HBJ, 1938.

_____, *To the Lighthouse*. San Diego: Harvest/HBJ, 1927.

Wright, Robert, *The Moral Animal: Evolutionary Psychology and Everyday Life*. New York: Pantheon, 1994.

Wrigley, Julia, *Other People's Children*. New York: Basic Books, 1995.

Wylie, Philip, *Generation of Vipers*. New York: Holt, Rinehart, and Winston, 1942 (annotated edition published in 1955).

Zalygin, Sergei, editor, *The New Soviet Fiction: Sixteen Short Stories*. New York: Abbeville Press, 1989.

Zhu Hong, "Women, Illness, and Hospitalization: Images of Women in Contemporary Chinese Fiction," in Gilmartin et al., *Engendering China*.

Index

view of femaleness, 286, 335-337, 339, 342, 347, 352-53

Easterlin, Richard, 67-71, 78-79
economic necessity of two incomes, 12, 69, 114, 276, 361
  myth of, 71-78, 94, 145-46, 153
ecstasy, 268, 270, 277
Ehrenreich, Barbara, 62, 65-66, 138, 177
Ehrenreich et al., 179, 193-96, 205, 212, 237-38, 241-45, 248-251, 258-260
ejaculation, as debilitating men, 217, 238
Elias, Norbert, 79, 225, 270-71
Eliot, George, 55, 150, 154, 163, 180, 189, 255, 323, 371
Eliot, T. S., 37, 357
emotional intimacy, 245
Engels, Friedrich, 3, 272-73
entrepreneur, 280-82
equal protection clause, 27
Equal Rights amendment (ERA), 27, 39, 104-05, 137-39, 189
Erikson, Erik, 255, 284, 326
Ernst, Max, 366
Euphiletus, 234
Euripides, 152
European Common Market, 306
evolutionary psychology, 169, 240

family (families). *See also* bourgeois
  as barrier against government, 278, 280
  as object of scientific quantification, 47
  as peripheral to marketplace, 38, 122-23, 179
  as tangle of pathology, 290-93
  Bolshevism and, 279-80
  destruction of, 2, 3, 5, 30, 263, 293, 306, 310, 317
  deterioration in relationships in, 25, 57, 280, 320
  feminist attack on, 1, 5, 13, 17, 27, 79, 97, 123, 179, 263-64, 272
  matriarchal, 292-93, 309
  one-income, 19, 28, 66, 72, 74, 78, 134
  power structure in, 25, 55

  sacrifices in f life, 38, 45, 79, 193
  single-parent, 291-92
  traditional, 1, 5, 25, 35, 38, 79, 140-42, 181, 317
  two-income, 72-78, 134, 142, 146, 359
  two-parent, 72, 172, 276
  well-being of, 25, 88, 248, 311, 358
family allowances, 28, 127, 134, 307
Family in Classical Greece, The (Lacy), 229, 231-34
family wage, 105
Farewell to Arms, A (Hemingway), 33
father
  diminished status of, 54
  living with children, 278, 306, 308, 311
  woman's childhood relationship with, 260
Fatherless America (Blankenhorn), 311
female. *See also* woman
  awakening through union, 338-39
  dependence upon men, 255, 260, 347-48
  impersonator, 146
  inhibiting sexual assertiveness, 207
  masculinization, 59
  pain and messiness, 341
  preciousness, 163, 165, 177-78, 182-83, 187, 191-93
  prisoners of war, 190-92
  sexual anesthesia, 215-16, 223, 225, 227-28
  sexual responsiveness, 213, 260
  sexual strategy, 169-70, 195, 198-201
  submission, 259
Female Eunuch, The (Greer), 14
female orgasm
  and conception, 215-16
  as casual, 237
  as counting, 212-14, 226
  clitoral, 243-45, 248, 249, 252-55
female orgasm (cont.)
  focus on as frightening, 238
  potential for, 170, 221, 237-38, 260, 338
female role. *See* domesticity
femaleness. *See* femininity
feminine
  narcissism, 58
  nature, 6, 33, 351

A Note on the Author

F. Carolyn Graglia received her undergraduate degree from Cornell University in 1951 and her law degree from Columbia University in 1954, where she was an editor of the law review.

She served as an attorney in the general litigation section of the civil division of the Justice Department before working as a law clerk for Judge Warren E. Burger of the U. S. Court of Appeals, District of Columbia Circuit. She later returned to the Justice Department as Special Counsel for Federal Housing Administration Litigation.

After practicing with the firm of Covington & Burling in Washington, D.C., she retired from legal practice and became a housewife and mother of three daughters. Now a writer, lecturer, and legal consultant in constitutional law and antitrust litigation, she lives in Austin, Texas, with her husband, Lino A. Graglia, a law professor at the University of Texas.

This book was designed and set into type
by Mitchell S. Muncy
and printed and bound
by Thomson-Shore, Inc., Dexter, Michigan.

❧

Head of a Woman by Sebastiano Luciani
is reproduced with the gracious permission
of the Kimbell Art Museum,
Fort Worth, Texas,
on a jacket designed by Matthew Smith.

❧

The text face is Adobe Caslon,
designed by Carol Twombly,
based on faces cut by William Caslon, London, in the 1730s,
and issued in digital form by Adobe Systems,
Mountain View, California, in 1989.

❧

The paper is acid-free and is of archival quality.